The American Academy of Political and Social Science

A message from the President

The Board of Directors has elected to enter into a contractual relationship with SAGE Publications to promote, print, and distribute THE ANNALS, beginning with the September 1981 issue.

The headquarters of The Academy and the editorial offices of THE ANNALS remain in Philadelphia. Editorial decisions about topics, special editors, and all other matters concerned with The Academy and THE ANNALS remain unchanged.

Invitations for membership in the Academy, requests for membership dues, and mailing and sales of THE ANNALS will be made from the offices of SAGE Publications, Inc., 275 South Beverly Drive, Beverly Hills, California, 90212. (From the United Kingdom, Europe, the Middle East, and Africa, write SAGE Publications, Ltd., 28 Banner Street, London EC1Y 8QE, England.)

The Board and I are pleased with this cooperative relationship, for we believe that the promotion, marketing, and publishing capacity of SAGE will not only be economical for The Academy, but will help to increase the distribution of our publications. SAGE is a leading publisher of behavioral and social science books and articles. Sara and George McCune, directors and owners of SAGE, have a distinguished record of quality publications.

The format of THE ANNALS will be the same, even the famous orange cover. Perhaps we may use more readable type and may improve the quality of the paper. Whatever is done will be under the authority of The Academy and for the benefit of our members and subscribers.

The Editor, Richard D. Lambert, in consultation with the Board, has some exciting issues of THE ANNALS planned for the remainder of this year and for 1982. Every reader of this announcement will want to renew or begin membership in The Academy and encourage friends and colleagues to join in the spirited discussion and dissemination of the most important political, economic, and social issues of our times.

Marvin E. Wolfgang
President

VOLUME 455

MAY 1981

THE ANNALS

of The American Academy *of* Political
and Social Science

(ISSN 0002-7162)

RICHARD D. LAMBERT, *Editor*

ALAN W. HESTON, *Assistant Editor*

GUN CONTROL

Special Editor of This Volume

PHILIP J. COOK
Associate Professor of
Public Policy Studies and Economics
Duke University
Durham, North Carolina

PHILADELPHIA

Copy Editor

PRISCILLA A. ESTES

The articles appearing in THE ANNALS are indexed in
the *Book Review Index*, the *Public Affairs Information
Service Bulletin, Social Sciences Index, Monthly Peri-
odical Index*, and *Current Contents: Behavioral, Social,
Management Sciences* and *Combined Retrospective
Index Sets.* They are also abstracted and indexed in *ABC
Pol Sci, Historical Abstracts, United States Political
Science Documents, Social Work Research & Abstracts,
International Political Science Abstracts* and/or *Amer-
ica: History and Life.*

International Standard Book Numbers (ISBN)

ISBN 0-87761-263-3, vol. 455, 1981; paper—$6.00 (Institutions—$7.00)
ISBN 0-87761-262-5, vol. 455, 1981; cloth—$7.50 (Institutions—$9.00)

*Issued bimonthly by The American Academy of Political and Social Science at 3937 Chestnut
St., Philadelphia, Pennsylvania 19104. Cost per year: Individual Membership— $20.00 paper-
bound, $26.00 clothbound; Institutional Membership—$35.00 paperbound, $41.00 clothbound.
Add $2.00 to above rates for membership outside U.S.A. Second-class postage paid at Philadelphia
and at additional mailing offices.*

*Claims for undelivered copies must be made within the month following the regular month
of publication. The publisher will supply missing copies when losses have been sustained in
transit and when the reserve stock will permit.*

Editorial and Business Offices, 3937 Chestnut Street, Philadelphia, Pennsylvania 19104.

CONTENTS

iii

CONTENTS

PAGE

UNITED STATES HISTORY AND POLITICS

SOCIOLOGY

CONTENTS

ECONOMICS

PREFACE

The study of gun control has never lacked for polemicists, but there was little in the way of respectable analytical research in this area before George Newton, Jr., and Franklin E. Zimring's work for the National Commission on the Causes and Prevention of Violence.[1] Their monograph initiated a trickle that only in the last year or two has become a steady stream of dispassionate, scholarly research. The articles in this issue are intended to provide a cross section of the best of this new and important work.

We begin in the future, with Zimring's interesting effort to project the evolution of firearms regulation into the twenty-first century. National prohibition is not one of his likely scenarios, but John Kaplan's article is a useful reminder of the foreseeable consequences if we should try another "Great Experiment"—the lessons from marijuana and alcohol are clear.

The next section, dealing generally with the politics and history of gun control, includes two articles that present a collection of startlingly definitive findings from national public opinion surveys. James D. Wright is able to resolve the apparent contradictions in two polls taken in 1978—sponsored by rival camps—and leaves us with a satisfying sense that the American public has well-defined beliefs about guns and gun control and that these beliefs are subject to measurement. Howard Schuman and Stanley Presser use results from a series of public opinion survey experiments to shine new light on why the large majority of the American public who favor stricter federal regulations have not had their way with Congress. Another perspective on this same conundrum emerges from the history of federal legislative efforts during the 1920s and 1930s, reviewed in the article by Carol Skalnik Leff and Mark H. Leff.

There remain the questions of policy design and evaluation: which of the alternative gun control strategies appear most promising? My article on the role of weapons in violent crime leads off this section, serving as deep background for assessing alternative approaches. My second article, with James Blose, describes the current structure of state and federal regulations intended to prevent certain groups of people from obtaining firearms. Mark H. Moore's article is a natural sequel; he assesses the relative importance of alternative sources of guns used in crime and suggests some interesting conclusions about the appropriate role for each level of government in the effort to regulate firearms commerce. James Lindgren concludes this section with a policy analysis of a different sort of gun control problem—discouraging inappropriate use of firearms by the police.

The final section presents three case studies, assessing the effects of the Bartley-Fox Amendment in Massachusetts (Glenn L. Pierce and William J. Bowers); the District of Columbia's ban on handgun transfers (Edward D. Jones, III); and Michigan's mandatory sentencing provisions for criminals

1. *Firearms & Violence in American Life* (Washington, DC: U.S. Government Printing Office).

vii

who use guns (Colin Loftin and David McDowell). The three articles document the provisions of these legal interventions and the implementation strategies adopted by law enforcement officials. Each of them also attempts to measure their effects on violent crime rates, although this proves to be a difficult task indeed.

Much of the work presented here is relevant to policy, without being strongly prescriptive. The state of the art in gun control research simply does not permit powerful conclusions concerning the potential efficacy or net social value of alternative schemes for regulating firearms. This collection does serve to narrow the range of justifiable assertions with respect to gun control while providing a rather complete description of the current context and helping to define the major issues more clearly.

PHILIP J. COOK

Handguns in the Twenty-First Century: Alternative Policy Futures

By FRANKLIN E. ZIMRING

ABSTRACT: This article speculates about public policy toward handguns in the United States a generation in the future. Two mutually exclusive national policies are described. The first policy, federal support for state and local variation in handgun control, represents a logical extension of historical trends in federal firearms control since the 1930s. The second policy, federal commitment to reduce substantially the availability of handguns nationwide, would represent a significant departure from previous federal regulatory approaches. This more stringent regulatory approach might evolve from increasing interdependence, continuing high rates of handgun violence, and public perception that handgun control based on state and local variation is fundamentally unworkable. Public attitudes toward handguns as instruments of household self-defense are one key leading indicator of future federal policy directions. If the handgun in the house remains a respectable means of self-defense, restrictive proposals at the national level are probably doomed. A future decline in the social status of the loaded handgun in the home would create a policy climate more favorable to sharp reduction of the civilian handgun inventory.

Franklin E. Zimring is a professor of law and director of The Center for Studies in Criminal Justice at the University of Chicago. In 1968–69, he served as director of research for the Task Force on Firearms of the National Commission on the Causes and Prevention of Violence. His recent writings include Confronting Youth Crime *(1978);* The Criminal Justice System, *with Richard Frase (1980); and* The Changing Legal World of Adolescence *(forthcoming).*

WHAT types of public policy toward handgun ownership and use are likely in the United States of 2010? What are some of the probable consequences of these policies in the United States on our children's adulthood, and what kinds of changes can we anticipate during the transition from present circumstances to particular policy futures? No one of my acquaintance possesses a crystal ball sufficiently unclouded to provide clear answers to such questions, yet using the long-range future as a frame of reference can impose a useful discipline on current debates about firearms control. In the first place, thinking about the future requires more sustained analysis of historical trends than one usually encounters in contemporary discussion of firearms control in America. Quite simply, addressing the issue of where we are going over the course of the next few decades suggests an examination of where we have come from of at least equal length.

The second advantage of "futuristic" examination of handgun policy is that it requires the analyst to coordinate projections of public policy toward handguns with other social, technical, structural, and governmental trends that will shape the United States 30 years from now. A projected handgun policy must either fit with other anticipated future developments or create a form of intellectual friction in which handgun policy elements or other anticipated future conditions must be reexamined.

This article sketches two alternative national handgun futures. The first, "historically" derived, is a complex amalgam of federal, state, and local regulations characterized by federal minimum standards of accountability and eligibility for purchase and by wide variation among states and localities in imposing supplemental restrictions on possession and sale of handguns. The second, designed to "fit" with other anticipated future developments, projects much more restrictive federal control on eligibility for handgun ownership. The first section discusses the major elements of the historically derived national handgun policy. The second section sketches a more restrictive federal handgun policy that would be implemented to fit more closely with anticipated social conditions 30 years from now. The third section discusses a few of the more important midterm trends that will determine which of these alternative futures will emerge.

CONTINUING PRESENT TRENDS

If history is an appropriate guide, the next 30 years will bring a national handgun strategy composed of three parts: (1) federally mandated or administered restrictions on handgun transfers that amount to permissive licensing and registration;[1] (2) wide variation in state and municipal handgun possession and transfer regulation, with an increasing number of municipal governments adopting restrictive licensing schemes or "bans" on handgun ownership; and (3) increasing federal law enforcement assistance to states, and more particularly, to cities attempting to enforce more restrictive regimes than the federal minimum. Under such a scheme, federal law will

1. As used in this article, the terms "permissive licensing," "restrictive licensing," and "registration" are defined following George D. Newton and Franklin E. Zimring, *Firearms and Violence in American Life*, Staff Report to the National Commission on the Causes and Prevention of Violence, 7: 83–84 (1969) (hereafter cited as Newtown and Zimring). See also Franklin E. Zimring, "Getting Serious About Guns," *The Nation*, 214: 457, 459–60 (1972).

neither set quotas on the number of handguns introduced into civilian markets nor dictate ownership policy to the states. Rather, designated high-risk groups, such as minors, convicted felons, and former mental patients, will be excluded from ownership, as is presently the case.

The two major changes in federal law I anticipate are, first, a registration scheme that will link individual handguns to first owners in a central data bank and will require prior notification before handguns are transferred[2] and second, a federal law prohibiting firearms transfers where the possession of a handgun by the transferee would violate the laws of the municipality in which he resides—current federal protection of this kind is only available if a state law would be violated.[3] Centrally stored ownership data would permit federal law to extend to transfers made by nondealers, and regulations requiring timely prior notice of private transfers through dealers or local officials would be added to existing regulations.[4]

The changes in federal law outlined in the preceding paragraphs would facilitate minimal municipal standards for residents acquiring handguns that could not be frustrated by more lenient state government standards. This new power, and a climate favorable to handgun regulation in the big cities, would produce a much larger list of metropolitan or city governments attempting to impose restrictive licensing or bans on civilian ownership among their populations. Presently existing systems in cities such as New York, Boston, Philadelphia, and Washington, D.C. would be emulated in cities such as San Francisco, Los Angeles, Chicago, and Detroit and in most nonsouthern metropolitan areas. Within the South, municipal or metropolitan governments in areas like Miami and Atlanta might follow suit.

All of this would in turn increase the demand, particularly on the part of cities, for federal law enforcement support to protect city boundaries from in-state guns. Within five years after extension of federal protection to municipal handgun control, the intrastate, rather than interstate, migration of handguns will emerge as a top priority in federal firearms law enforcement.

It is, of course, one thing to make up a scheme of handgun regulation and quite another to argue that it is historically derived. Why is it that federal regulation will expand? What is the basis for suggesting that municipal handgun controls will increase? The answers to such questions are neither easy nor obvious.

National handgun registration is only peculiar in that it has not yet been accomplished. Since 1938, federal law has required most of the essential data for registration, but the records have been decentralized in a way that has effectively guaranteed they cannot be used.[5] Two trends suggest momentum in the coming decades toward effectively

2. Prior notification of transfer could be instituted without comprehensive handgun registration, as discussed by Newton and Zimring in their description of "transfer notice." See Newton and Zimring, p. 84.

3. See Franklin E. Zimring, "Firearms and Federal Law: The Gun Control Act of 1968," *J. Legal Studies*, 4:133, 149 (1975) (hereafter cited as "Firearms and Federal Law").

4. Central storage of ownership data is possible even if records of purchase continue to be maintained by individual dealers. Duplicate forms could be forwarded to automatic data-processing systems probably without any changes in the provisions of the Gun Control Act of 1968. See Franklin E. Zimring, "Firearms and Federal Law," supra note 3, pp. 151–54.

5. See Zimring, "Firearms and Federal Law," supra note 3, pp. 139–40.

centralized weapon ownership information. First, the development of efficient and cheap information processing removes any technical barrier to a national handgun data bank. Whatever the circumstances of 1938, we now face a situation where the marginal cost of creating an accountability system for handguns is minimal and central data files are neither technically nor economically difficult.

The ease and cheapness with which weapons can be first-owner registered suggest a shift in the debate about registration from cost factors to more basic principles. Public opinion seems solidly behind handgun-owner accountability if registration is viewed solely as an accountability system and not as a first step toward confiscation of all the guns linked to registered owners. Registration thus seems inevitable, if its proponents can make a creditable case that a registration scheme will not be used to facilitate a shift from permissive to restrictive licensing policies. This could be achieved by "grandfathering" all guns registered to eligible owners so that any subsequent shift in federal regulatory policy would exempt validly registered guns.

The momentum toward tighter municipal licensing is easier to demonstrate. In the cities, pressure for handgun restriction has increased dramatically in the past 15 years, and those cities that have adopted controls almost never repeal them. The momentum toward further handgun restriction in major metropolitan areas appears substantial in all regions except the South and the Southwest.

However, federal handgun registration and more restrictive municipal handgun control are by no means inevitable. Each initiative carries with it seeds of its own defeat. In the case of registration, the principal

potential villain is public and gun-owner perception that accountability measures are merely one further step toward prohibition. The effort to secure prohibition in the name of registration has an old federal pedigree, dating from the National Firearms Act of 1934 and its successful attempt to deal with machine guns, if not sawed-off shotguns.[6] Gun-owner perception that registration means confiscation is widespread. Whether such perceptions can ward off a general trend toward centralization of automatic data processing is questionable.

The momentum toward further municipal handgun control seems unstoppable, but this, too, may be misleading. The key issue here is whether sustained attempts at municipal restriction are viewed as successful. In large part, municipal efforts to create handgun scarcity have failed. Very few cities have experienced either the costs or benefits of tight controls. All this may end as we accumulate a decade of experience with the new Washington, D.C., statute and with those cities that will follow in D.C.'s wake.

Substantial changes in municipal and state regulation of handgun ownership have become the rule rather than the exception in those American jurisdictions that have reconsidered handgun regulation in the last 20 years.[7] This has occurred despite complaints about the power of the gun control lobby.

The trend, viewed historically, is toward a patchwork quilt of federal, state, and local regulation. This is

6. See Zimring, "Firearms and Federal Law," supra note 3, pp. 138–39.
7. See Edward D. Jones, III, "The District of Columbia's 'Firearms Control Regulations Act of 1975': The Toughest Handgun Control Law in the United States—Or Is It?" in *The Annals* of the American Academy of Political and Social Science, 455:138–49 (May 1981).

not surprising. Significant variations exist in attitudes toward handguns, and it should only be expected that these attitudinal differences would more quickly lead to a wider spectrum of state and local variation than to a unified national strategy. But will such incremental and differential policies produce adequate public protection three decades hence?

HANDGUN SCARCITY AS FEDERAL POLICY

The principal difficulty associated with evolution of a national handgun policy based on state and local variation is that it might not work. Federal attempts to protect tight-control cities and states would continue to be frustrated by interstate and intrastate movement of handguns; the large civilian inventory of handguns would make efforts at accountability based on registration data both expensive and easy to frustrate at the point of first purchase.

Under such circumstances, growing dependence on public transportation, and increased residential desegregation that spreads the risk of violent crime more evenly across metropolitan areas, may produce a climate where more stringent handgun controls may be demanded. Unless the increased fear associated with interdependence is offset by lower rates of violence, it is unlikely that increased public police expenditure or further increases in imprisonment rates will alone lead to tolerable levels of citizen risk. Progress toward a "cashless society" may reduce the incentive for personal robbery and may redistribute the risk of commercial robbery from cashless to cash-holding institutions. But the coincidence of interdependant urban life and freely available handguns will put pressure on "evolutionary" federal handgun policy.

An alternative federal handgun policy would stress reducing, substantially, the population of handguns and thus reducing general handgun availability. Federal standards would require the states to administer handgun licensing systems that would deny most citizens the opportunity to possess handguns and handgun ammunition. The central features of this scheme are the commitment of federal policy to nationwide handgun scarcity, a policy that would be imposed on states and cities where more permissive approaches were preferred, and a policy shift making continuing possession of handguns by millions of households unlawful. Further, whatever the division of responsibility among federal, state, and local law enforcement, this approach would, unlike others, put the federal government in the standard-setting—and most likely, production-control—business.

What one calls such regulation is a secondary matter. Federal "restrictive licensing" is the equivalent of a "national handgun ban!" Indeed, many "ban" bills would leave more guns in circulation than would restrictive licensing because the exceptions—for example, security guards—are broad. The thrust of such a policy is the transition from a 30-million-handgun society to a 3-million-handgun society. This is no small step.

Even if a national policy of handgun scarcity were wholeheartedly adopted, there are limits on the capacity of federal authorities to implement policy without state and local cooperation. Handgun production quotas and regulations governing the distribution of new weapons could be administered at the federal level. Individual determination of whether citizens who apply for licenses meet "need" criteria is best left to local officials, however, and removing unlawfully possessed handguns is a by-product of local police activity.[8] The only way to shift this burden to the federal level is to create a national street police force, a radical departure from current practice that should not be expected or desired. Thus even federal policies that attempt to centralize authority to reduce existing handgun ownership will operate at the mercy of state and local law enforcement.

Still, any such national standard setting would represent two major departures from present federal law. First, the federal government would attempt to limit the supply of handguns nationwide. Second, in order to substantially reduce the handgun population, citizens would be denied the opportunity to own weapons even if they were not part of special high-risk groups and in spite of less restrictive policy preferences at the state and local level where they reside.

This type of plenary federal policy has never been seriously considered in the United States. Early in the New Deal, Attorney General Homer Cummings proposed tight federal handgun controls that received scant congressional attention.[9] In the 1970s, a series of proposals to create federal restrictive licensing were introduced and soundly defeated. The urban experiments with restrictive licensing in New York City and Washington,

D.C. both involved jurisdictions with small inventories of lawfully possessed handguns and cooperative local law enforcement.

If present trends continue, 30 years from now the majority of American citizens will still live in states with less restrictive handgun policies than the proposed federal standard. Under what conditions, then, would this majority's congressional representatives vote for more stringent regulation than state legislatures would support? A restrictive national handgun policy would represent a turning point in public opinion and legislative climate, a relatively sharp departure from the previous twentieth-century politics of handgun control.

MIDTERM POLICIES AND LONG-RANGE GOALS

The road to patchwork federalism in handgun policy requires different midterm regulatory approaches than if the long-term goal were civilian scarcity. Patchwork federalism can, of course, be achieved through the gradual accretion of actions by cities, states, and the federal government. To the extent that we follow this path, however, it will become increasingly difficult to make a later shift to a national scarcity policy, for three reasons. First, city regulations will have the effect of legitimizing handgun possession for those who obtain their guns legally in the city. Second, the inventory of handguns in circulation is likely to grow rapidly under patchwork federalism. Third, people who registered their guns under a federal registration plan would almost certainly be "grandfathered" when the shift to a national scarcity policy occurs. Each of these problems is discussed in more detail in the following pages.

8. See Franklin E. Zimring, "Street Crime and New Guns, Some Implications for Firearms Control," *J. Criminal Justice*, 4:95, 101–2 (1976).

9. See Zimring, "Firearms and Federal Law," supra note 3, pp. 138. See also "The Politics of Ineffectiveness: Federal Firearms Legislation, 1919–38," *The Annals* of the American Academy of Political and Social Science, 455:48–62 (May 1981).

The impact of local registration

Those states and cities that institute programs of owner registration create a population of handguns registered in good faith. One important consequence of registration is that it confers an explicit legal legitimacy on the continued ownership of the weapon by its owner. If a city adopts a registration scheme and later decides to create further restrictions on handguns, the more restrictive policy will usually exempt those owners with prior registration from additional eligibility requirements as long as they continue to possess their registered weapons.

The impact of this type of "grandfather clause" on the inventory of firearms or the availability of guns for misuse will vary from city to city. In a city with a small number of registered guns, such as New York or Washington, D.C., the effect of a grandfather clause on handgun availability would be small. In Chicago, where the population of registered handguns is several hundreds of thousands, the inevitable result of the grandfather clause is a large pool of guns at risk of theft or illegal transfer for many years after a shift to more restrictive ownership criteria.[10] Most major cities have very large handgun inventories. Registration systems, if effective, would legitimate millions of handguns. And the handgun owner wishing to immunize himself from restrictions on continued ownership is well advised to enter the system.

Grandfathering a large number of registered handguns may put pressure on the principles as well as on the practicality of municipal restrictive licensing. With so many prior registrants legally able to own weapons, it will be more difficult to argue that latecomers should be required to prove a special need for a gun before being eligible to acquire one. Further, the period during which a shift to more restrictive strategies is debated might create a large volume of handgun sales to new purchasers anticipating further restriction.

Inventory consequences of continued federalism

In the 12 years following the Gun Control Act of 1968, more than 20 million handguns were added to the civilian handgun inventory in the United States.[11] This total probably represents more than half the stock of operable handguns in the United States and a larger proportion of the handguns involved in violent crime.[12] Each year of federal indifference to handgun supply adds about two million pistols and revolvers to an inventory of weapons that a restrictive policy would seek to shrink. How much of an additional burden this imposes on future restrictive efforts cannot be estimated because we do not know how long new handguns remain operable and because it is not possible to estimate the impact of government repurchase efforts. But each year of unrestricted aggregate handgun supply makes the transition to national handgun scarcity more difficult and more expensive.

Federal registration as a national grandfather clause

Federal handgun registration would replicate the problems that state and

10. Richard Greenberg, "Pistols Pour Through Sieve of Unenforceable Handgun Laws," *Chicago Reporter*, 10(2):7(Feb. 1981).

11. Mark Moore, "Keeping Handguns From Criminal Offenders," *The Annals* of the American Academy of Political and Social Science, 455:92–109 (May 1981).

12. Zimring, "Firearms and Federal Law," supra note 3, pp. 169–70.

local systems present for restrictive policies on a grand scale. At minimum, gun registration records could not be used as the basis for a recall of handguns once more restrictive policies were put in place. This stricture would almost certainly be inserted into the legislation that would initially enable central storage of handgun ownership information. It is also likely that considerable pressure would be exerted to exempt registered handguns from whatever new ownership restrictions might subsequently be imposed as long as the guns remain in possession of the registrant. This would make the move toward tight eligibility prospective in its effect and gradual in its impact on handgun inventory. How much delay this type of provision would produce is not known because there are no good data on how long handguns are retained in particular households.

"Specter effects" of restrictive control proposals

Public discussion of handgun restrictions or bans has an important influence on all aspects of the debate over firearms control. As previously mentioned, permissive licensing and registration are frequently opposed because they are regarded as "first steps" toward more restrictive policies. Restrictive proposals for handguns are feared as a step toward restrictions on longgun ownership. And fear about future restriction may play a role in the high level of demand for weapons available now and possibly not available in the future. Further, there is evidence that opposition to restrictive control has increased as the issue has received public attention.[13] From

13. See Tom Smith, "The 75% Solution," *J. Criminal Law and Criminology*, 71(3):314.

the standpoint of an advocate firmly committed to permissive licensing and registration as ultimate federal law, the policy climate would probably have been better if proposals for restrictive handgun policies had not surfaced in the late 1960s.

What are the prospects now for shelving the debate about handgun restriction in favor of a permanent compromise at the federal level? Any such proposal would probably be regarded as inauthentic at this late date. And doubts about the effectiveness of federal neutrality on handgun ownership policy suggest that any "permanent compromise" of that sort would fail to satisfy those who regard handgun violence as a serious national problem. The issue of national handgun policy is thus unlikely to be resolved with a long-standing compromise despite the manifold impact of restrictive federal handgun proposals.

A turning point?

Many factors can influence the direction of future handgun policy. A sharp decline in public fear of crime would decrease demand for handguns; at the same time, if this resulted in reduced violent crime, it would reduce the need for handgun control. An increase in burglary rates or, more significantly, in rates of home-invasion robbery would work the other way.

However, the most important element of future policy is not the crime rate, but social notions of appropriate crime countermeasures. In my view, the "social status" of the household self-defense handgun in our cities and suburbs will emerge as a critical leading indicator of future federal handgun control. Public opinion research has indicated that self-defense in the home is the most important "good reason" given for handgun ownership.[14] If citizens continue to believe that possessing a loaded handgun is a respectable method of defending urban households, handgun demand and opposition to restrictive policy will continue. If owning loaded handguns in the home comes to be viewed more as part of the gun problem than as a respectable practice, the prospects for restrictive control will improve over time. The residual uses of handguns—informal target shooting, collection, and hunting sidearms—are peripheral to the handgun contol controversy. Household self-defense is a central issue.

Public attitudes toward handguns for self-defense are related to fear of crime, but there are other factors that bear on the respectability of the urban housegun. One is alternative self-defense measures, such as burglar alarms, silent alarms that trigger police or private security responses, and the urban house dog. Most of these systems are more effective against burglary than handguns, but are less effective against home invaders.

A second influence on attitudes toward handguns in the home is public perceptions about the costs of weapon ownership within the household and in the wider community. Household accidents and guns recycled from homes to street crime are two kinds of loss that may influence public opinion about loaded guns in the home. Gun homicide involving family members may also influence the attitude of nongun owners, but I suspect that most gun-owning families would believe this kind of loss "can never happen to them."

An increase in the social stigma associated with household defense guns will influence the demand for handguns long before it affects national policy toward handgun supply. In the midterm, increasing stigma should reduce the proportion of households purchasing guns and increase the households that report considering and rejecting a handgun purchase. These indications should first appear in younger age segments of the population, rather than households with older heads and established patterns of handgun ownership. Upper-middle-class families "resettling" in older city neighborhoods might be a particularly interesting group to watch. These families have the economic resources to pursue alternative methods of household security. This segment of the population is well known for its trend-setting influence in other issues of style and consumption.

The early indications of a turning point in attitudes toward handguns will be more a function of attitude than hard data trends in crime rates or aggregate gun ownership. This is, in one sense, appropriate because the distinctive feature of the growth in handguns for self-defense has been more a question of perceived need than statistical risk.[15] Whatever happens will probably happen

14. Newton and Zimring, supra note 2, pp. 62.

15. Handgun ownership reported in public opinion polls is higher among high-income groups than among low-income groups and as great in small cities as in big cities (Newton and Zimring, supra note 2, ch. 2). Crime risks are greater for low-income groups and in larger cities. While the polls show white household ownership in excess of black household ownership, the risk of violent crime victimization is greater among black city residents. See also "Estimated Rates of Victimization," in *Sourcebook of Criminal Justice Statistics* (National Criminal Justice Information and Statistical Service, various years), tables and figures.

gradually. Thus the precondition for what might be viewed as a revolutionary shift in public policy is an evolutionary change in public attitude. As is so often the case, any discussion of this kind of shift as a future development must acknowledge that this type of attitude change may already be in progress.

CONCLUSIONS

Speculation about future trends is a high-risk enterprise. The values of discussion of long-range futures are the discipline it can impose on assertions about historical trends and the perspective one gains on present trends by examining the likely impact of their continuation. I hope the preceding pages will stimulate others to undertake similar efforts at constructing handgun policy "futures" consistent with the lessons of our recent history, yet suited to the needs of the social order our children will inherit.

The Wisdom of Gun Prohibition

By JOHN KAPLAN

ABSTRACT: The fact that not everyone will obey a law is a very important determinant of the wisdom of its enactment. As applied to gun prohibition legislation, widespread violation of the law may place upon us unacceptable societal costs of enforcement, which would cast doubt upon the wisdom of enacting what might be thought to be a reasonable policy.

John Kaplan is the Jackson Eli Reynolds Professor of Law at Stanford Law School. He is the author of the Court Martial of the Kaoshiung Defendants *(1981);* Criminal Justice *(1973); and* Marijuana, The New Prohibition *(1970).*

NOTE: This article was prepared as part of an ongoing project supported by the Law Enforcement Assistance Administration, Grant No. 76-NI-99-0113. An earlier draft of portions of this article appeared in the Cleveland State Law Review, 28(1):1-28, (1979).

MANY discussions of what is called gun control proceed by demonstrating the advantages, in terms of the homicide, assault, and robbery rate, of our disarming all or part of the civilian population of the United States.[1] Rarely does anyone embark on a serious attempt to compute either the cost or the likely success of the policies designed to achieve these ends—and social realities are brought into the area only in denunciations of the political groups and attitudes that prevent the adoption of gun control policies that will "work."

In this respect, one must be struck by the similarity between the arguments for gun control and those concerning the prohibition of drugs.[2] With respect to the latter, the discussion typically focuses on the dangerousness of the drug in question and the kinds and amounts of harm it can be expected to do if available to the population. Little time and energy are spent in computing the costs of attempting to enforce such laws and the degree of effectiveness that can be expected from any particular policy, considering the abilities and other demands upon our criminal justice system.

Indeed, both with respect to drugs and various gun policies, it is often assumed that the mere passage of a law, with very little more, will guarantee that people obey it. Unfortunately, in both cases we are dealing with large numbers of people who think that they have strong reasons and justifications for engaging in a kind of conduct—possession

1. See, for example, "The Case to Control Handguns" (Washington, DC: National Council to Control Handguns, 1978).
2. See John Kaplan, "Controlling Firearms," Cleveland State Law Review, 28(1) (1979) (hereafter cited as "Controlling Firearms").

or even sale—and can do so in private, so that it is difficult to catch them. In both cases, therefore, it is difficult for the law to raise the risk of apprehension of law violators high enough to outweigh their desires.

THE LIKELY EXTENT OF VOLUNTARY COMPLIANCE

Gun owners have a variety of reasons for owning guns. Often owners enjoy the use of their guns in hunting or other sports, the feeling of power that comes from hefting such a lethal device, the feeling of security, whether or not warranted, that comes from knowledge that one has such a weapon at hand, and the symbolic association of guns with the frontier and with a large portion of the history of America. In addition, those who like guns often find a certain fascination in the precision with which they are built. The gun, after all, is a remarkable piece of engineering that can send a small piece of metal at extremely high speeds with an accuracy that one would regard as phenomenal if he did not know in advance about the properties of such weapons. Indeed, the gun is comparable only to the camera in its precision and in the intricacies of its mechanical engineering. Though there are no data on the issue, one might hypothesize that the same aspects of personality that may cause one person to be interested in cameras would cause another to be equally fascinated with guns.

Gun owners may also be prepared to offer rationalizations and justifications for their behavior in terms of contributing to a better world. Even if these reasons are not very persuasive to the rest of us, they bolster the desires of the users with the kind of ideology that makes such behavior more tenacious than if defended solely in hedonistic terms. Thus a gun owner defends his gun ownership with reference to the Second Amendment. He may assert that an armed citizenry is important in a democracy to protect the freedoms of all from Communist coups; to be ready to engage in guerrilla warfare should the country's armed forces be overwhelmed by those of a foreign power; or in the words of one well-known civil libertarian, simply to make sure that we do not have to "trust the military and the police with a monopoly on arms and with the power to determine which civilians have them."[3]

It is not necessary to agree with these justifications; of course, a large fraction of the society does not. The problem, however, is that in a criminal justice system that needs a sizable degree of consensus in order to operate, what may be a large enough percentage of the population does agree.

Moreover, entirely apart from the strengths of the justifications used to defend an illegal behavior, there may well be a distinction between making criminal a behavior before it is widespread and doing so after it is engaged in by large numbers of people.

Where the formerly legal behavior was popular—as was the case in Prohibition and as would be the case if guns were prohibited—one would expect the law to meet more resistance. Those who engage in the behavior may not only have the force of habit to push them toward continuing, but they also are more likely to see the law as a direct attack upon them. And having joined others openly engaging in the behavior while it was legal, they may be able to count on the support of more or less organized groups in disobeying the law.

If this is so, it may be very important that gun ownership holds a unique place in American history. The continent was settled after the invention of firearms, and firearms were necessary not only to the body politic and for the militia, but also necessary for protection from hostile natives. Perhaps even more important, guns were used to provide a food supply. In large areas of the United States, gun ownership still forms part of a rite of passage where boys learn to use weapons from their fathers and pass this along to their sons. Interestingly, the situation was quite different in Europe, which was well settled before the invention of practical firearms; there were no hostile natives, gun possession by the ordinary citizen was repressed as a threat to the classes in power, and hunting, for the most part, was a monopoly of the rich.[4] It is not surprising that they do not have the kind of gun problem that we do today.

It is possible, of course, that the gun owner's respect for law would outweigh his desire to continue his behavior—should the law so provide. After all, the gun user, so far as we can tell, is more likely to be conservative and devoted to law and order than is the average person.

Nonetheless, one cannot make too much of this factor. Many groups in society denounce the lack of respect for law and order in others, but have rationalizations for their own misbehavior. The same police who deplored the law violations of

---

3. D. Cates, "Why a Civil Libertarian Opposes Gun Control," *Civil Liberties*, 3:24 (1976).

4. See Lee B. Kennett, *The Gun in America* (Westport, CT: Greenwood Press, 1975), pp. 13–18.

draft evaders and antiwar demonstrators have joined in illegal strikes, and the very men who orchestrated the American presidential campaign most devoted to law and order felt little compunction about obstructing justice themselves.

It is an empirical question in each case whether the desire of an individual to engage in illegal behavior is outweighed by his adherence to law. Moreover, the issue is more precisely whether the desire to engage in the illegal behavior is outweighed by some kind of sum of his adherence to law and his fear of apprehension. So far as the first term of the sum is concerned, probably the best guess is that a sizable portion of the gun-owning population would simply ignore any law interfering with their possession of weapons, unless the likelihood of apprehension could threaten them into obedience. So far as the second term is concerned, it is likely that any given gun owner would run an extremely small risk of apprehension. First of all, the great majority of gun owners do nothing to attract police attention. Even if the authorities suspected someone, they would probably not have the probable cause necessary for a search warrant. Moreover, if the number of illegal handgun possessors were very large, it would be impractical to obtain and execute search warrants for any sizable percentage of their homes.

In fact, it is hard to think of any way we could coerce those gun owners determined to ignore any prohibition into giving up their weapons, short of instituting a massive program of house-to-house searches. These are, in fact, practiced occasionally in other countries—often in the wake of a revolution—to remove weapons from private hands. Typically, they are buttressed with summary and extremely high penalties, usually death, for those caught in violation. On constitutional, practical, political, and moral grounds, this would be inconceivable in America today.

In any event, if the rate of violation of a gun prohibition approached what we are presently experiencing with respect to marijuana or what we experienced with respect to alcohol during Prohibition, we would be faced with a whole series of problems. I will discuss later the rallying cry, "When guns are outlawed, only outlaws will have guns." For the purpose here, it is more relevant to state, "When guns are outlawed, all those who have guns will be outlaws." Laws that turn a high percentage of the citizenry into criminals impose serious costs on society over and above those incurred in attempted enforcement.

A variety of sociological studies have shown that an important social norm may very commonly be broken without serious consequences to the individual or society. For instance, studies of college cheating have revealed that a very high—indeed, an amazingly high—percentage of college students have cheated on at least one occasion.[5] Significantly, however, even those who have cheated tend to regard the rules against cheating as morally justified and, though they typically have some rationalization to justify their conduct to themselves, they consider themselves supporters of the rules against cheating and are fully prepared to censure those who are caught in violations. The same is almost certainly true of tax evasion and a whole series of other misbehaviors.

5. See William J. Bowers, "Student Dishonesty and its Control in College" (Bureau of Applied Social Research, Columbia University Press, 1964).

Where the laws are not only widely violated, but violated on the basis of widely accepted rationalizations, such laws are often not even considered morally binding by those who have violated them.[6]

COSTS OF PROHIBITION

Presumably gun owners—unlike cheaters—would not rationalize their use of the gun as an aberrant event unrelated to their total personality, and as a result it would become especially unhealthy for their society to declare them criminals. It is obvious that when any society criminalizes a large percentage of its people, it raises very serious social problems. We do not know whether those who violate such serious criminal laws will thereby become more likely to violate others. It may or may not be true that the second crime comes easier. It is hard to see, however, how a realization that one has committed what is officially a serious crime can fail to engender at least a somewhat more generalized lack of respect for both the law and the society that has so defined his action.

This alienation from both the rule of law and our democratic society would then be a serious cost of many gun control laws.

Moreover, it is likely that if the violation rate is high, attempting to enforce any law against gun possession will be extremely expensive. Prohibition and the marijuana laws resulted in a paradox in which the threat of laws sanctioned was not sufficient to deter huge numbers of violators. As a result, violations are so common that they frequently come to police attention without great police effort. Even though those

apprehended constitute a very small number compared with the total number of violators, they are numerous enough to constitute a major burden on the criminal justice system.[7] If a similar situation is created with respect to gun owners, their numbers would presumably raise similar problems, further overtaxing a criminal justice system already unable to cope with the kinds of violent and predatory crimes that upset us much more than does the private possession of guns.

Few people who are not directly involved in it can appreciate the degree to which our criminal system is already overcrowded. A recent editorial in a local newspaper gives details on a typical situation—in this case in one of California's most affluent counties:

One day recently, Judge Stone's calendar listed a record 269 cases. A courthouse holding cell designed to accommodate 20 defendants was jammed with 100. The judge says they were unguarded because the sheriff didn't have enough deputies to assign one to the holding cell. . . .

Judge Stone estimates it could cost up to $1 million a year to provide Santa Clara County with enough prosecutors, public defenders and adult probation officers to keep the courts operating efficiently, which is to say justly. He doesn't know where the money will come from and, at this point, neither does the board of supervisors, which is facing the prospect of a budget deficit. . . .

A million dollars isn't going to build a new jail, but $1 million would go a long way toward clearing the Superior Court's criminal trial calendar, thus reassuring the public that the criminal justice system isn't about to collapse.[8]

---

6. See John Kaplan, *Marijuana, The New Prohibition* (NY: World Publishers, 1970), p. 34 (hereafter cited as *Marijuana*).

7. Ibid.

8. "Overloaded Justice," *San Jose Mercury News*, 20 Jan. 1981, p. 6B.

This and worse is the case throughout the nation. The police are unable to investigate all but the most serious crimes; in court-processing institutions the prosecutors, the public defenders, and the judiciary are all so crowded that some 85 percent of cases are disposed of by plea bargains, which leave neither side nor the public satisfied;[9] and our jails and prisons are grossly overcrowded—with offenders that almost all of us would regard as considerably more serious than simple, otherwise law-abiding gun possessors.

As a result of this, we would be forced to adopt one of three courses if voluntary compliance did not produce an adequate level of obedience to the gun control laws. First, we would have to transfer a very sizable amount of resources into the criminal system, in all probability a political and perhaps even economic impossibility today. Second, we would have to make room for the gun possessors by treating more leniently the rapist, armed robber, drug peddler, and others who make up the grist of our present criminal system. Third, we would simply have to treat gun possession very much like marijuana possession or a number of other very trivial crimes that are on the books, but are so sporadically enforced that the criminal law is not regarded as a serious molder of behavior.

Obviously, none of these choices is an attractive one, but it is quite clear that one of these choices—in all probability, the second and third, with emphasis on the third—will in fact be the course we adopt.

Another serious consequence of asking the police to enforce a law that results in violations so numerous that the police cannot possibly pursue them is that this invites selective enforcement, a problem all too common in American law with respect to drug and various other "nonvictim" offenses.[10] Allowing the police to pick and choose among a group and to decide whom they will and whom they will not investigate or arrest for a crime leads to a feeling of unfairness among those selected for prosecution, to the bribery and corruption of the police, and to the covert use of all kinds of discriminations—including race, class, and "appropriate" attitude toward the arresting officer—which we would not condone if they were overt. Since political deviants of the Right or the Left are among the most paranoid of Americans, and perhaps the least likely to obey a gun prohibition, we would soon find the police bearing down most heavily upon them. This should be a matter of considerable concern to those worried about restrictions on First Amendment freedoms.

To be sure, gun owners presumably would not come to the attention of the police as often as marijuana users, since marijuana use gives off a discernible odor. Nonetheless, we are familiar with the cast of characters that adds to the number of arrests in marijuana—the inquisitive baby-sitter, the former lover working off a grudge, and the fireman on the premises fighting a blaze. All of these would presumably cause gun arrests as well.

It is likely that in the case of guns, a death or injury resulting from the use of the illegal weapon would bring the violation to public attention. In

9. See J. Casper, American Criminal Justice: The Defendant's Perspective (Englewood Cliffs, NJ: Prentice-Hall, 1972), pp. 77–81.

10. See Norval Morris and Gordon Hawkins, The Honest Politician's Guide to Crime Control (Chicago, IL: University of Chicago Press, 1970), pp. 4–6.

many cases, the event would demonstrate the wisdom of the gun prohibition. Where the gun owner commits a murder with his weapon, prosecution on a gun possession charge might be a superarrogation, but the event itself would serve to reinforce the educational purposes of the criminalization. Similarly, the lessons of the law would be taught where the illegal gun goes off accidentally, though perhaps where a family member is killed, some would be offended by the additional prosecution of the bereaved on a gun possession charge.

Enough of the cases coming to the public attention, however, would involve a householder who fought off a burglar or rapist with an illegal gun. We may speculate that these cases would cause law enforcement serious problems. Since the prosecutorial authorities presumably would not regard the subsequent use of the weapon as negating its initial illegality, they would probably feel forced to prosecute the householder. In such cases, however, one would expect it to be extremely difficult to keep the jury's attention focused upon the violation of the gun possession law and away from the fact that the case before them was one where, to put it bluntly, the defendant was right and the law was wrong about his or her need for the protection of a firearm. The result of this, then, would be jury nullification and a refusal to convict.

Not only would convincing a unanimous jury to convict be a difficult and time-consuming task, thus adding to the expense of enforcing gun prohibition, but such cases would probably achieve political significance. Groups working to repeal the prohibition would have every incentive to make the case a cause célèbre in their campaign against the gun

laws. Since the case might drag on long after the burglar or rapist had been disposed of, its facts would be given greatly increased publicity, leaving the public with the impression that instances of successful self-defense with firearms are far more common than they actually are. This, in turn, would help convince more people of the need to possess guns for self-defense and would encourage resistance to the gun law.

In short, the basic problem here is that while the benefits of even a successful prohibition are due to its effect on the relatively small numbers of those who would cause social harm by their activity, the costs of the prohibition are proportional to the number of people who nonetheless continue to engage in the activity.

The fact is that the solid majority of gun owners do not cause any social problem at all. The great majority of gun owners are noncriminal, and their guns create no social problems. It is true that the gun that created no problem at all this year may, next year, kill in an accident or in a crime of passion, or be sold or stolen and thereafter used in a robbery. Even so, when one considers that there are over 100 million guns in private possession, it seems clear that on a per-gun basis, the great majority of guns in private hands will impose no costs at all upon society.[11]

Moreover, prohibitions are differentially effective with respect to different kinds of users. Often, they are most effective with respect to the users about whom we are least worried. For instance, the laws against marijuana are most effective in deny-

11. Philip J. Cook, "Guns and Crime—The Perils and Power of Long Division," unpublished manuscript (Duke University, Dec. 1980).

ing access to the drug to middle-class citizens of middle age or above. They are far less successful, indeed almost completely unsuccessful, with respect to the high school students, the unstable, and the marginally adjusted—those who are far more likely to harm themselves through their use of the drug.

With respect to guns, it is likely that the reduction in gun possession would not produce a proportionate decrease in the social harm caused by guns. It is, of course, a considerable exaggeration to say that "when guns are outlawed, only outlaws will have guns" if by this one means that all those criminals now involved in gun crimes would continue to have access to guns. A prohibition, even imperfectly enforced, would lower somewhat the number of guns in private hands and even in the hands of some outlaws. Nonetheless, we would expect that individuals who already risk more serious criminal sanctions for committing crimes with their guns would be among those least affected by a gun prohibition.

The more interesting question involves the basically law-abiding individuals who would otherwise use their guns in crimes of passion. To the extent that they give up their guns because of the law, their homicide rate presumably would be lowered. However, not only are we unable to predict the overall rate of noncompliance with a gun prohibition law by otherwise law-abiding citizens, we are also unable to tell whether those who would use their guns in a crime of passion would be less likely to obey a prohibition than the average noncriminal gun owner. It is hard to think of any reason why those individuals who would commit crimes of passion with their guns would be more likely to obey a

prohibition. And if, as seems likely, those who commit the crimes of passion are less law-abiding than the rest of noncriminal gun owners, they might be less likely to obey the gun prohibition law as well.

Since the crucial determinant of the balance of costs and benefits in any prohibition law is the extent of violation, a matter very difficult to predict, one can only speculate upon the result of a gun prohibition. We do not now have any such prohibition, and it is impossible to prove any hypothetical statement to be true or false. Nonetheless, my own guess is that the magnitude of violations would be such that the costs of attempting to enforce general prohibition of gun ownership would far outweigh the benefits we might achieve from the somewhat lowered availability of firearms that such a law would produce.

Such a conclusion, of course, does not resolve the issue of gun control. The great majority of Americans already live under laws that prohibit the carrying in public places of concealed weapons. Similarly, different kinds of guns have already been subjected to differing regulations. Machine guns and sawed-off shotguns are prohibited; sales of handguns are legally restricted, though in a somewhat halfhearted way; and longguns are subject in some areas to regulation.[12] As a result, it may be argued that even if the criminalization of all firearms imposed costs that outweighed its benefits, the balance might tilt the other way with respect to a more specific category of guns. Of course, the type that first comes to mind is the handgun. After

12. Philip J. Cook and James Blose, "State Programs for Screening Handgun Buyers," *The Annals* of the American Academy of Political and Social Science, 455:80–91 (May 1981).

all, there are far fewer handguns than longguns in private hands, and on a per-gun basis, handguns are far more dangerous, accounting for about 80 percent of the gun homicides.[13]

LIMITING THE PROHIBITION FOR HANDGUNS

Though a prohibition of handguns would have many aspects in common with the more general prohibition of all guns, the fewer weapons involved and the greater social cost per weapon would lead us to expect that, all other things being equal, prohibition would achieve a better balance of costs and benefits. Despite this, there are still a great many handgun owners whose resistance to complying with the prohibition would impose on us many of the costs I have previously discussed. We cannot tell, of course, whether handgun owners as a class will be more or less resistant to a prohibition than other gun owners. There are reasons, however, to expect some differences.

While the owners of longguns primarily give hunting and sport as their reasons for gun ownership, the most common reason given by handgun owners is self-protection.[14] One would think that this kind of elemental justification, whether valid or not, would be the hardest to override through the threat of legal punishment. Nonetheless, it may be that the much greater danger to the owner and his family inherent in handguns makes the owners more

ambivalent about their possession. It is interesting, as well, that whereas the longgun has deep cultural roots in America, the widespread possession of handguns is a relatively recent phenomenon. In fact, in 1964, less than 750,000 new handguns were purchased in this country. The number had doubled by 1967 and increased more than threefold in 1968.[15]

It can be argued that if the handgun prohibition is partially effective, the law might lower the perceived need to own firearms for self-defense. This, in turn, might increase obedience to the prohibition and become part of a circular process that feeds upon itself to make the prohibition more and more effective. The problem is that most handgun owners do not see their weapons as necessary to protect them from others with handguns. Rather, they see their weapons as protection from unarmed but younger or stronger intruders. It is, of course, possible that if handgun owners really do keep their guns for protection, they can perhaps be talked out of the idea. So far as we can tell, handguns are not much good for defense, since they are much more likely to injure the owner and his family than to protect them.[16]

Again, the major unknown in computing the likely costs and benefits of a handgun prohibition is the extent of cooperation by the citizenry. An experimental buy-back program in Baltimore offered $50 per operable handgun, which was considerably above the average cost of those weapons. The program managed to recover only 8400 handguns in a period of almost a year.[17] This figure

13. See George D. Newton and Franklin E. Zimring, *Firearms and Violence in American Life* (Washington, DC: U.S. Government Printing Office, 1970), p. 49.

14. James D. Wright, "Public Opinion and Gun Control: A Comparison of Results From Two Recent National Surveys," *The Annals* of the American Academy of Political and Social Science, 455:24–39 (May 1981).

15. Newton and Zimring, p. 174.

16. See "The Case to Control Handguns," p. 14.

17. *Baltimore News American*, 19 Oct. 1974, p. 5, col. 1.

was estimated to represent about one fourth of the handguns in the city. The relatively high price offered for the weapons, as compared to the cost of replacing them, may well have induced people simply to replace their old guns with better weapons at government expense. Moreover, there is no reason to believe that the second quarter of the handguns would be as easy to remove from circulation as the first—or the third as the second. Again, the most we can say is though the issue is not so clear with respect to a blanket prohibition of all gun ownership by civilians, a prohibition of handgun ownership would also produce costs far in excess of its benefits.

THE "VICE MODEL"

Instead of attempting to deal with the huge reservoir of guns or even only of handguns, a more cost-effective means of gun control might be the application of what is called the vice model, which forbids the sale of firearms, but not their ownership. The major advantage of such a law would be the avoidance of the large social costs inherent in turning millions of otherwise law-abiding citizens into criminals. At the same time, an effective prohibition on sale would, over time, gradually reduce the number of guns in private possession.

At first glance, criminalizing the selling of guns might appear logically inconsistent with our failing to punish the buying as well. In fact, this is not the case. In drafting laws, we often draw the line between legal and illegal conduct so that maximum reduction in the proscribed behavior can be gained at minimum social cost. Frequently it turns out that

laws aimed solely at suppressing sales are more cost-effective in reducing the possession and use of a substance than are laws that attempt to suppress possession directly.[18]

There are several reasons for this. First, there are fewer sellers than buyers; this permits a concentration of law enforcement efforts where they do the most good. Second, juries are likely to be more sympathetic to a "mere" user, who may be ill-advised, than to a businessman who makes a profit from the weaknesses of others. States that have decriminalized small-scale marijuana possession and other "non-victim" crimes have relied on this technique. Offenses treated under the vice model range from gambling, where the person who takes illegal bets is guilty of a crime, while the person who places them is not, to the offense of selling new automobiles not equipped with seat belts, where the seller, rather than the buyer, is guilty of an offense.

Although it is true that a simple prohibition on sales or transfers of guns would probably be more efficient than a broader prohibition that also forbade their use or possession, even prohibitions on sales would be ineffective if the demand for the product and the resistance to the law were too great. We must remember that Prohibition itself never criminalized the possession or use of alcohol. As a result, we will examine a prohibition upon the sale of guns as if it encompassed only handguns, on the theory that the same factors that would make a complete prohibition on handguns more cost-effective than one on all guns would also apply to application of the vice model.

18. See Kaplan, *Marijuana*, p. 315 ff.

There is, however, a very important difference between guns and alcohol. In theory, alcohol can be handled to the complete satisfaction of the prohibitionist simply—or not so simply—by cutting off the sources of supply. After all, the average drinker rarely has on hand more than enough to tide him over a few weeks. Guns, however, are not perishable, consumable items. A gun in private possession is presumably dangerous for its entire useful life, a period not only of years, but of decades—though, as recent research has shown, guns used in crimes are disproportionately newer weapons.[19] As a result, the enormous reservoir of firearms in private possession will greatly lower the effect of even an enforceable prohibition on handgun sales in reducing the social cost of the use of such weapons.

In this respect, the best analogy to alcohol would be prohibiting the sale of ammunition, which is moderately perishable, rather than the sale of guns. The problem here, however, is technical. First, handgun ammunition is basically the same as longgun ammunition, so any attempt to control handguns by this method would involve the more difficult, costly, and stubborn problem of longgun regulation as well. Second, serviceable ammunition is simpler to make than any of the illegal drugs being manufactured in the laboratories all over the United States. The difficulty of manufacturing ammunition lies somewhat closer to distilling liquor than to making phenyl-cyclohexyl-piperidine (PCP)

or amphetamines.[20] In other words, the likelihood is that by forbidding the sale or manufacture of handgun ammunition, we would be adding yet another major substance-abuse problem to our already crowded inventory.

On the other hand, the very permanence of the gun works to lower the social costs of attempting to suppress sales of the weapon. In the case of guns, the illegal seller will have a much smaller market for repeat business than is the case with alcohol or drugs. It is difficult to speculate on what an illegal handgun supply industry would look like if sales were forbidden. It is by no means clear that it would look like the alcohol industry under Prohibition or our present illegal drug industry, since both the total demand and the economies of scale would seem to be far greater in the former cases than with respect to guns. Even if the robber had to dispose of his weapon more often, illegal sellers would probably lack the repeat business that characterizes a drug connection.

That is not to say that an illegal market would not spring up to serve those who wish to buy illegal handguns. Even without the economies of scale or the repeat business of the illegal drug industry, enough people living on the fringes of legality might accommodate acquaintances and provide large numbers of guns to noncriminal users. The analogy here might be to the procuring of prostitutes. According to the folklore, sizable numbers of taxi drivers, bellhops, and bartenders make some extra cash at this illegal activity, even though it generally does not constitute a large fraction

19. Franklin E. Zimring, "Street Crime and New Guns: Some Implications for Firearms Control," *J. Criminal Justice*, 4:95–107 (1976); and Steven Brill, *Firearms Abuse* (Washington, DC: The Police Foundation, 1977).

20. Kaplan, "Controlling Firearms," p. 20.

of their total income. Of course, we can predict that a prohibition on gun sales will raise the price of guns, since the seller will demand additional profit to compensate him for his risk of detection.

To examine further the effect of a sales prohibition on the social cost of handgun ownership, we must look more carefully at two kinds of handgun owners: the basically law-abiding owner and the criminal who acquires his gun with the intention of using it in illegal activity. The law-abiding owner, even though he may not be willing to give up or register his handgun, may draw the line at acquiring one illegally. Moreover, it is quite possible that he will not know an illegal seller and will be unwilling to go to the trouble of finding one. The criminal gun owner, on the other hand, presumably will have a greater incentive to obtain a handgun and will be more likely to know an illegal seller.

We cannot tell at this point how common handgun purchases would be under such conditions. This depends on two factors: (1) whether large numbers of potential purchasers see their need for handgun protection as great enough to justify purchasing from illegal sellers and (2) whether an illegal market can operate under the constraints of whatever law enforcement can be brought to bear on the situation.

So far as the latter is concerned, our experience with alcohol and other drugs indicates that if the demand exists, there will be many who, despite the efforts of law enforcement, will step in to supply the need. Al Capone could rationalize his bootlegging empire by saying the following:

I'm a businessman. I've made my money by supplying a popular demand.
If I break the law my customers are as guilty as I am. When I sell liquor it's bootlegging. When my patrons serve it on silver trays on Lake Shore Drive it's hospitality. The country wanted booze and I've organized it. Why should I be called a public enemy?[21]

There will be many who can justify selling guns to respectable people even if such sale is illegal. Moreover, if they cannot justify it satisfactorily, experience indicates that they will do it anyway.

Nor is it clear that salesmen would be unable to find the guns to sell. Even if the illegal gun market would not in itself support many full-time sellers, illegal wholesaling and smuggling might still be quite profitable activities. We must remember that marijuana, which at least on a per-volume basis is less valuable than handguns, is quite profitably smuggled into the United States in enormous quantities.

There are several serious costs to any partially successful effort to stop the sale of handguns. On a smaller scale, though, many of these drawbacks parallel the costs of attempting to prevent handgun ownership directly. The chances are that there will be a considerable number of illegal handgun sales, including sales by those who are in the business of handgun supply and sales by handgun owners who wish to sell their guns rather than give them away or destroy them. It is very likely that an attempt to interdict what may be a considerable demand for guns will consume a good deal of investigatory time and prosecutorial and judicial resources, although this would not be as expensive as attempting to administer sanctions directed at the user himself.

21. A. Sinclair, *Prohibition, Era of Excess* (NY: Harper & Row, 1964), p. 220.

If the citizenry is sympathetic to such prosecutions, enforcement expenses might be worthwhile. Unfortunately, however, it is possible that once we have made the sale of all handguns illegal, those who sell them will appear to some otherwise law-abiding citizens as Robin Hoods, violating the unpopular laws for the greater good. It does not take a very significant minority of the population to deadlock juries and cause the legal system a considerable amount of difficulty and expense.

The means that the police would have to use to enforce such laws are already familiar to us because of their use in the drug area. Preventing a sale between a willing buyer and a willing seller requires intrusive techniques. Indeed, even to inadequately enforce such laws, the police must use informants, undercover agents, methods that border on entrapment, searches and seizures, wiretapping, and a whole panoply of enforcement techniques that not only often transcend the borders of constitutionality, but that, even where they are legally permissible, tend to bring the police into disrepute. Use of such means against relatively small numbers of serious criminals may be worth this kind of cost. However, where the police are asked to enforce laws by such methods against large numbers of people who have public support, the consequences can be more serious.

Other contributors in this volume discuss a variety of measures that fall short of prohibition, including licensing and registration. If these are to be considered seriously, the social costs of the measure, including the problems of enforcement, must also be weighed against the benefits of possible reductions in violent crime.

Public Opinion and Gun Control: A Comparison of Results From Two Recent National Surveys

By James D. Wright

ABSTRACT: This article compares results from two recent national surveys of public opinion on gun control and related weapons–policy issues. One survey was commissioned by the National Rifle Association, the other by the Center for the Study and Prevention of Handgun Violence. Despite the vastly different outlooks of the two sponsoring organizations, the results from both surveys are nearly identical everywhere a direct comparison is possible. Together, the two surveys thus provide a very detailed empirical portrait of the state of popular thinking on the regulation of private arms in the United States.

James Wright is a professor of sociology and is associate director of the Social and Demographic Research Institute, University of Massachusetts–Amherst. He is author of The Dissent of the Governed: Alienation and Democracy in America *(1976);* After the Cleanup: Long Range Effects of Natural Disasters *(1979); and* Social Science and Natural Hazards *(1981), as well as numerous articles and papers appearing in journals, from* Dissent *and* The Nation *to the* American Sociological Review. *He has recently completed a study of weapons and violent crime in the United States, from which this article is derived.*

NOTE: This article was prepared under Grant Number 78NI-AX-0120 from the Law Enforcement Assistance Administration, U.S. Department of Justice. Opinions and points of view stated here are mine and do not necessarily reflect the official positions or policies of the sponsoring agency.

ABUSE, use, and availability of privately owned firearms in the United States is a hotly contested political issue.

Majorities of American voters believe that we do *not* need more laws governing the possession and use of firearms and that more firearms laws would *not* result in a decrease in the crime rate.[1]

It is clear that the vast majority of the public (both those who live with handguns and those who do not) want handgun licensing and registration. . . . [T]he American public wants some form of handgun control legislation.[2]

As is evident from these two quotations, both pro- and anticontrol factions can and do claim the weight of public thinking for their side. In itself, this is scarcely surprising: political organizations routinely use phrases such as "public opinion," "most Americans," or "the vast majority" as rhetorical devices. What makes these quotations of special interest, however, is that they are not taken from political speeches or organizational press releases, but from the executive summaries of two recent national surveys conducted specifically to explore the state of public thinking on gun control issues.

The first quotation is from a report entitled "Attitudes of the American Electorate Toward Gun Control 1978." The report was prepared by Decision Making Information, Inc. (DMI), of Santa Ana, California, a private, for-profit research and polling firm. The report is based on a national survey conducted during 1978, and it was commissioned by the National Rifle Association.

The second quotation is from a report entitled "An Analysis of Public

1. From the report of a survey sponsored by the National Rifle Association.
2. From the report of a survey sponsored by the Center for the Study and Prevention of Handgun Violence.

Attitudes Toward Handgun Control," prepared by Cambridge Reports, Inc., better known as Patrick Caddell's political polling firm. The Caddell report is also based on a large national survey conducted in 1978, and was commissioned by the Philadelphia-based Center for the Study and Prevention of Handgun Violence.

A detailed comparison of the results of these two surveys is instructive for several reasons. Of these, the most important involves the substance of the issue, namely, whether "most Americans" do or do not favor stricter weapons controls. Together the two reports are nearly encyclopedic in their coverage of contemporary public opinion on weapons-related issues. As I show next, the comparison of results across surveys demonstrates that the majority opinion depends critically on the specific kinds of "stricter controls" envisioned, the likely costs, and the end purposes that additional controls are meant to serve.

A second aim of the comparison is to evaluate what I will call the "anti-survey hypothesis," which at the most general level, states that surveys in essence create the "reality" they purport to measure. The general idea behind this hypothesis is that there is really no such thing as "public opinion," except as it is called into being by public opinion polls; respondents, it is said, simply "manufacture" the answers that they think the investigators want to hear. The kinds of answers one gets are thus —or perhaps, can be—predetermined by the advance hypotheses or political purposes of the investigators: one needs only to design the study in such a way as to generate whatever response one or one's client wishes to hear. The alternative possibility, of course, is that there is an underlying reality to public opinion, a reality that will tend to surface despite the a priori expectations, aims, or purposes of the researchers or their sponsors. A comparison between these two surveys thus provides a unique opportunity to consider whether poll findings are biased by the outlooks and ideologies of the organizations who conduct the research or by the clients who pay for it and how these findings are biased.[3]

TECHNICAL COMPARISONS

Neither report was prepared for an academic audience; as such, the amount of technical information provided about the two surveys is meager. So far as can be told, however, both surveys were competently done and both appear to have been conducted well within the current standards and practices of survey research.

The Caddell survey is based on a national probability sample of adults 18 years old and over. The data consist of 1500 personal interviews conducted between 20 April and 15 May 1978 by Caddell's professional interviewing staff. The DMI report is based on two surveys, both involving nationally representative samples of registered voters, rather than of all adults. The first consists of 1500 personal interviews conducted between

19 May and 9 June 1978 by DMI's professional interviewing staff.[4] Note that DMI's surveying began just four days after Caddell's ended. The sample of registered voters was achieved by an initial filter question; persons not registered to vote, or with no intention of registering before the November 1978 elections, were terminated from the interview. The second survey, also of registered voters, consisted of 1010 telephone interviews conducted during 9–12 December.[5]

There is an important difference in the substantive foci of the two reports: the Caddell report focuses exclusively on handguns, whereas the DMI report deals with handguns and longguns, which are then kept separate in the analysis.

A comparison of the sample demographics obtained in the two surveys with the March 1978 Current Population Survey shows that both surveys achieve demographic distributions that are respectably close to the "true" values.[6] The major differences between surveys are as one would expect, given the initial difference in sampling frames; that is, the DMI registered voters sample is somewhat older, contains more whites, and is more "middle class"

---

3. Indeed, the situation here is most fortunate. DMI and Cambridge Reports, Inc., are both reasonably well known and respected private research and polling firms. DMI works primarily for "conservative" candidates and causes; Caddell, primarily for "liberals." Both organizations were in the field with their studies at about the same time; both studies are ostensibly concerned with the same subject matter. With the exceptions of their own organizational proclivities and those of the study sponsors, "all else is equal," or at least equal enough for the purposes at hand.

4. Thus both DMI's and Caddell's face-to-face surveys are said to be based on a final N of 1500 respondents. It seems unlikely that both would achieve identical N's of exactly 1500 respondents, so I assume that both organizations have reported only their approximate sample sizes.

5. Unless otherwise noted in the text, I treat the two DMI surveys as a single survey throughout this article.

6. Because of space limitations, it is not possible to include the actual tabulations of results from the surveys. Full tabular presentations of all findings discussed in this article appear in James Wright, Peter Rossi, et al., *Weapons, Crime and Violence in America*, mimeographed (Amherst, MA: Social and Demographic Research Institute, 1981).

than is Caddell's sample of U.S. adults.

Social status is correlated with the tendency to own a weapon and with attitudes toward gun control; in general, both weapons ownership and opposition to stricter weapons controls increase with social status.[7] For this reason alone, we would thus expect the DMI sample to be somewhat less supportive of gun control measures than the Caddell sample. However, the magnitude of the difference introduced by this factor should not be large, first, because the socioeconomic status (SES) differences between the surveys are themselves modest and second, because the correlation of gun control attitudes with SES is itself weak—in the range of .1 to .2.

WEAPONS OWNERSHIP

The Caddell and DMI surveys both obtained information on gun ownership. Despite differences in question wording, the overall results are broadly consistent across the two surveys: 47 percent of the DMI respondents and 42 percent of the Caddell respondents report that they have one or more weapons in the home, and the proportion reporting that they own a handgun is virtually identical in both surveys—23 percent and 24 percent.

A weapons ownership question has been included periodically in Gallup polls since 1959 and in the National Opinion Research Center (NORC) General Social Surveys since 1973; in all available surveys, the proportion of families owning a weapon of any type has hovered right around 50 percent.[8] In the most recent NORC survey concerning this question (1977), the proportion owning any weapon was 51.1 percent, and the proportion owning a handgun was 20.5 percent. The convergence of results among all surveys is thus most impressive: roughly one American family in two possesses a gun and roughly one in four or five owns a handgun.[9]

There is no firm consensus anywhere on the number of firearms in private hands; estimates range from 90 million to 200 million and up. DMI's poll asks gun owners how many guns they own, and the results can thus be used to generate an estimate of the total number. Given about 75 million U.S. households in 1978, their data and a few simple calculations suggest about 30.85 million handguns and about 75.26 million longguns, or about 106 million guns total, currently in private hands. This should probably be taken as a conservative, or lower-bound, estimate, since it seems certain to under-

7. This finding is reported in the Caddell survey and is also reported in the academic literature. See James O'Connor and Alan Lizotte, "The 'Southern Subculture of Violence' and Patterns of Gun Ownership," *Social Problems*, 25(4): 420–29 (April 1978); or James Wright and Linda Marston, "The Ownership of the Means of Destruction: Weapons in the United States," *Social Problems*, 23(1): 93–107 (Oct. 1975).

8. See James Wright and Linda Marston or Hazel Erskine, "The Polls: Gun Control," *Public Opinion Quarterly*, 36(3): 455–69 1972). Marginal results for the NORC General Social Surveys are shown in *General Social Surveys, 1972–1978: Cumulative Codebook*, available through the Roper Public Opinion Research Center, Yale University, P.O. Box 1732, Yale Station, New Haven, CT.

9. DMI also asks, "Thinking about the country as a whole, about how many families would you say own at least one gun?" Fifteen percent thought that "almost every family" would have a weapon, 34 percent said "most families," 31 percent said "about half of the families" (the correct response), and the remainder felt that less than half of all families would have a gun.

estimate illegally owned weapons or weapons kept for criminal purposes.[10]

Why do people own their weapons? Both surveys explore this question for the case of handguns. The DMI survey asks a parallel question about longguns. The results for handguns are again remarkably similar: protection and self-defense is the modal response in both surveys, mentioned by 40 to 43 percent, and the proportions giving other reasons are also very close. For longguns, the pattern is reversed: hunting, other sporting uses, and collecting account for more than two thirds—71 percent—of all reasons mentioned, with protection and self-defense a distant second, receiving about 20 percent of the mentions.[11]

USES OF AND EXPERIENCES WITH WEAPONS

Both surveys are concerned with the kinds of experiences respondents have had with their guns, although each tends to emphasize a different aspect of that experience. Most of Caddell's questions along these lines focus on handgun accidents and on respondents' experiences with handgun threats or attacks. DMI's questions, in contrast, focus heavily on the uses of weapons by respondents for their own self-defense.

10. On the other hand, to the extent that registered voters are more likely to possess a weapon than are citizens not registered to vote, the DMI figures would tend to overestimate the true value by some proportional amount.

11. Along these same lines, DMI asks, "What would you say is the main reason people own guns?" "For protection" was the response to this item much more frequently than it was to the item, "Why do *you* own a gun?" The ownership of weapons for protection or self-defense, in other words, is seen to be rather more widespread than it actually is.

Altogether, 24 percent of Caddell's respondents say they possess a handgun, 17 percent of the total—or 71 percent of the handgun owners only—say they own a handgun "for protection or self-defense," and 7 percent of the total—or 29 percent of the handgun owners only—say that they carry their handgun with them for protection outside the home. Likewise, 3 percent of the total sample—or 13 percent of the handguns owners only—have "had to use" their weapon in self-defense; two thirds of those who have "had to use" their weapon in this manner actually fired it. It thus appears that 2 percent of the total adult population of the country has at some time in their lives actually fired a hangun in self-defense.[12]

The text of Caddell's report tends to downplay these self-defensive uses of weapons: "Since defense is a primary reason behind the ownership of many guns, it is interesting to see whether owners have actually used their handguns for protection. As the table shows, most have not." The theme here seems to be that while many people buy their guns for self-protection, they are seldom used for that purpose.

The data on accidents, threats, and attacks are featured more prominently. According to Caddell's data, about 4 percent of the respondents have been involved in a handgun accident, with half of the incidents resulting in personal injury. Likewise, 10 percent report that a family member has been involved in such an

12. It is impossible to determine from Caddell's report just how much of this two percent is comprised, say, of veterans who have used sidearms in combat situations or of policemen or other security personnel using handguns in the context of their jobs. Presumably, these kinds of experiences would contribute a sizable fraction of the total.

accident, and 15 percent report a similar experience for a "close personal friend." Caddell's data suggest that 5 percent of the adults in the United States have had a family member killed in a handgun accident, and 7 percent have had a close friend killed in the same manner. The evidence on handgun threats and attacks is similar: 11 percent of the respondents say they have personally experienced such an attack, 13 percent report such an attack for a member of the family other than themselves, and 19 percent report such an attack on a close personal friend.[13] Roughly half of all these attacks are said to have resulted in personal injury or death. Additional analysis reveals that both handgun accidents and handgun threats and attacks are more common among households possessing a handgun than among households that do not. The Caddell report comments: "What these numbers say is this: handgun violence touches a lot of people in this country." Certainly, the data show that a handgun is more apt to be involved in an accident than to be fired in self-defense, which might be construed as another argument against owning a handgun for protection.

None of the DMI questions are precisely comparable to any of Caddell's, so direct comparisons between results are hazardous. Also, all of Caddell's questions ask about handguns, whereas the DMI items

deal with all guns, irrespective of type. A further important difference is that Caddell's questions on self-defensive weapons uses ask for information only about the respondent, whereas the corresponding DMI questions ask about both the respondent and the respondent's family members. These differences in question format are of some interest in themselves. Restricting the questions to handguns only and to respondents only will necessarily show less defensive weapons use than will expanding the questions to include all guns and all family members.

According to the DMI data, 15 percent of all registered voters—or their family members—have "used a gun" for self-defense or other protective reasons at some point in their lives. In the DMI telephone poll, the corresponding percentage for an identical question was 12 percent. The telephone survey shows that roughly half of these defensive weapons uses are to protect against a person, and the rest, to protect against animals. Of the 15 percent reporting a defensive weapons use in the face-to-face survey, 31 percent say the incident was important enough to report to the police. The weapon was actually fired, it appears, in 40 percent of the incidents; 9 percent of the incidents apparently resulted in injury or death—presumably to the "other guy." A parallel series of questions about personal friends produces similar, but uniformly higher, numbers on all items.

The DMI face-to-face survey thus suggests that six percent[14] of all registered voters or their families have, at some point in their lives, fired a weapon of some sort in self-defense. This finding is thus not inconsistent with Caddell's finding

---

13. The NORC General Social Surveys have periodically asked, "Have you ever been threatened with a gun, or shot at?" The percentage responding "yes" varies between 16 and 20 percent, or somewhat higher than Caddell's 11 percent (for respondents only). Caddell's question, however, stipulates a handgun threat or attack, whereas the NORC item says nothing about the kind of gun, which would account for the difference in observed results.

14. $.40 \times .15 = .06$.

that two percent of all U.S. adults have themselves fired a handgun in self-defense. There is, in short, no serious disparity between the two surveys about the facts of self-defensive weapons use.

DMI's telephone poll reveals another finding that figures prominently in their report: 10 percent of the DMI respondents say they can recall a situation where they "needed a gun but no gun was available." Most of these incidents, it appears, involved a person rather than an animal. Caddell has no comparable item with which this result might be compared.

The results just discussed exhaust the DMI information on uses of and experiences with weapons; their two surveys do not contain even a single item on firearms accidents or on respondents' experiences on the receiving end of handgun threats or attacks.[15]

In contrast to Caddell, the conclusions DMI draws from these data strongly emphasize the uses of guns in self-defense:

> It is sometimes asserted that firearms in general, and handguns in particular, have limited use for defensive purposes. . . . The surveys found that almost 14% of the American electorate, or about 13 million Americans, could recall a time when they or another member of their household had used a gun for protection. . . . Of those who remember such an experience, 40% indicated that the gun was fired, . . . 31% said that the incident was important enough to report to the police, and 9% responded that someone was killed or injured in the incident. It is clear that guns are frequently used for protection. In a substantial minority of those remembered instances of gun use, it was necessary to fire the weapon, although few such incidents resulted in injury or death.

Thus while the actual data from the two surveys are notably consistent everywhere direct comparison is possible, the contrast in emphasis is rather pronounced.

Despite the differences in emphasis, however, both surveys touch enough common ground to sustain at least a few conclusions. First, some 20 to 25 percent of all U.S. households possess a handgun, and about twice that percentage possess a weapon of some sort. Second, many —although certainly not all—handguns are owned for protection or self-defense; approximately 40 percent of the handgun owners in both surveys cite self-defense or protection as the primary reason they possess the weapon, and an additional percentage cite this as a secondary reason. Third, at least some of the weapons that are owned for self-defense are actually used for this purpose at some point: perhaps as many as 15 percent of all registered voters or their families have "used" a gun for self-defense; a rather lower percentage—7 percent in the Caddell survey—carry their weapons with them for defense outside the home; a lower percentage still say that they, personally, have "had to use" their handguns for self-defense, which is clearly a more restrictive phrasing than simply "used"; and the pro-

15. DMI does ask respondents to agree or disagree that "occasional domestic shootings are tragic, but do not justify taking away the right of everyone to own a handgun." This seems to be DMI's way of addressing the pro-control argument that stricter weapons controls would cut down on "junk crimes"—the domestic shootings that typically occur just because there is a weapon at hand. Unfortunately, this is not a very compelling survey question; in order to disagree with it, respondents have to risk suggesting that they think "occasional domestic shootings" are somehow not tragic. In any case, 72 percent of the DMI respondents "agree" with the statement.

portion of U.S. adults that have actually fired a weapon in self-defense is somewhere in the range of 2 to 6 percent. Fourth, the incidence of firearms accidents and handgun threats and attacks is at least as prevalent as, and probably somewhat more prevalent than, the incidence of weapons use for self-defense; in other words, people are fired at at least as often as they fire.

OPINIONS ON WEAPONS CONTROLS AND RELATED TOPICS

Pollsters have been measuring gun control opinions in the United States since at least 1938; in the Gallup poll of that year, 79 percent of the public favored "gun control," and most surveys and polls conducted since then have reported more or less similar results. Erskine reviewed the poll data on the topic from 1938 through 1972 and reported that "the vast majority of Americans have favored some kind of action for the control of civilian firearms at least as long as modern polling has been in existence." The best-known "gun control" question was instituted by Gallup in 1959; it reads, "Would you favor or oppose a law which would require a person to obtain a police permit before he or she could buy a gun?" The proportion favoring such a law stood at 75 percent in 1959 and has varied from 68 to 78 percent in all Gallup polls since. NORC has included the identical item in its annual General Social Surveys; from 1972 through 1977, the proportion in favor of such a law varied between 70 and 75 percent.[16]

16. The material in this paragraph is from the sources cited in fn. 8, and from Howard Schuman and Stanley Presser, "Attitude Measurement and the Gun Control Paradox," *Public Opinion Quarterly*, 41(4): 427–38 (winter 1977–78).

The other poll materials reviewed by Erskine, however, do not all suggest the same uniformly high pro-control percentages that are revealed in the police permit question. One item from an Opinion Research Center poll for 1968, for example, asked, "Do you think that people like yourself have to be prepared to defend their homes against crime and violence, or can the police take care of that?" Somewhat more than half the sample—52 percent—felt that people should "be prepared," and only 40 percent thought that such matters could be left to the police. In 1971, Harris asked a similar question: "Do you tend to agree or disagree that the way things are today, people should own guns for their own protection?" Forty-nine percent of the sample agreed with this viewpoint, 43 percent disagreed, and the remainder had no opinion. And in March 1968, Harris also found that 51 percent of the U.S. population would "use your gun to shoot other people in case of a riot." The same Harris poll also found 93 percent of the population agreeing that "individual shootings can happen any time because it only takes one madman to shoot another man" and found a 50-50 split on the statement "Control of guns might not cut down on violence at all."

The lesson to be learned here, rather an obvious one, is that public opinion is divided on the gun control issue; as in all other areas of public opinion measurement, different questions, posed in different ways and dealing with different aspects of the issue, generate somewhat different results. A second lesson, also obvious, is that with some selective picking and choosing among topics, questions, and phrasings, one can elicit a very wide range of results. This wide range, of course, does not imply that public opinion is ephemeral or ill-formed, but rather that the issue itself is complex and multifaceted.

Specific control measures

Caddell has the more extensive question sequence on opinions about specific handgun control measures; DMI's questionnaires, surprisingly, contain rather little along these lines. The Caddell sequence is prefaced with a lead-in stipulating that the measures in question are to the end of "controlling handgun violence" and does not mention the control of crime. As in most prior polls on the topic, Caddell finds large majorities favoring most, but not all, of the control measures asked about.

Some of the larger of Caddell's majorities are registered for relatively innocuous, easy-to-agree-with items. We should not be surprised to learn, for example, that some 85 percent would favor a "crackdown on illegal sales," since cracking down on anything illegal is bound to enjoy sizable majority support. Strengthening existing regulations or making them stricter is also something that most people would presumably find easy to support, for instance, "the rules for becoming a commercial handgun dealer"—81 percent favor making them stronger —or the rules for owning or carrying a handgun—72 and 76 percent, respectively, favor making them more strict. Making existing regulations and laws tougher is what one might call a "Why Not?" item: the surprising finding from such items is not that so many people say they favor them, but rather that anybody says they do not.

All the measures offered in the Caddell sequence that deal with permits to own handguns or registration of handguns also receive sizable majority support. For example, 82 percent favor requiring a permit or license in order to buy a handgun, and 84 percent would favor the registration of such handguns at the time of purchase; as for the handguns now in private hands, 74 percent would favor requiring a license for them and the same percentage would also favor their registration. Seventy-nine percent favor requiring a permit to carry a handgun outside the home, and 88 percent also like the idea of some "waiting period" as a part of the permit/registration process, "to allow for a criminal records check." These findings are all very similar to the findings from the Gallup police permit item.

One should be wary, however, of reading more into these results than is warranted. The specific measures being supported are all similar to measures taken to control other potentially lethal items whose use by irresponsible or incompetent persons might lead to injury or harm. Perhaps there is a metaphorical parallel here to the private automobile: all legally owned automobiles are registered with state governments, and all states require a license or a permit before one is allowed to drive. Likewise, or so the substantial majority seem to be saying, all privately owned handguns should also be registered, and one should be required to get a permit or a license to own or use them. What these data suggest, in short, is that most people feel that the ownership and use of handguns should be taken at least as seriously by governments as the ownership and use of automobiles is.

Measures more extreme than those

currently used to regulate automobile ownership and use, in general, do not enjoy much public support. Substantial majorities, for example, oppose a "buy back" law, such as was tried once in Baltimore and a few other places, either on a voluntary or mandatory basis. The idea of an outright ban on the manufacture, sale, or ownership of handguns is likewise rejected by sizable majorities, with the exception of a ban on the manufacture and sale of "cheap, low quality handguns," which is favored by 70 percent.

There is very little in either DMI survey to compare with these results from Caddell. One item shows that 13 percent feel there are already too many laws governing the possession and use of firearms; these, one presumes, are the same people who fall among the 10 to 20 percent opposing each of the Caddell registration and permit items already discussed. Some 41 percent say that "the present laws are about right," and 44 percent believe we need even more laws along these lines. Since the DMI question does not say anything about just what additional laws they have in mind, one hardly knows what to make of the result. Many of the Caddell items suggest measures similar to ones already in force or a strengthening of those already in force, so the 41 percent who believe that the present laws are about right is by no means inconsistent with the large majorities who favor many of the measures from the Caddell sequence.

DMI also shows a substantial 69 percent majority opposing "a law giving police the power to decide who may or may not own a firearm." This is DMI's version of the standard Gallup police permit item. But again, there is no fundamental inconsistency: requiring a police permit in order to purchase a weapon —which a sizable majority favors —is obviously not the same thing as giving police the power to decide who may or may not own a gun— which a sizable majority opposes. As is the case for most other permit mechanisms, for example, a permit to use explosives or have a parade, legislatures or other democratically elected bodies set the criteria by which the decision is made, and the function of the police is to determine whether the criteria are satisfied and to issue the permit if they are.

The only other DMI item that relates directly to any of the Caddell items so far discussed is one showing that 61 percent of the electorate would oppose "the Federal government's spending $4 billion to enact a gun registration program." But there is again no inconsistency in wanting some sort of registration or permit system and not wanting it to cost $4 billion. The DMI item serves the useful purpose of convincing us that the public does not want a registration system at any price, but that they do—or rather, some three-fourths of them do, according to the relevant Caddell items—want it at some price less than $4 billion.

Banning the manufacture, sale, or ownership of weapons

Of the many available options for stricter gun controls, the only one asked about directly in both surveys deals with an outright ban on the private ownership of handguns. Again, Caddell has the more extensive question series. There are three Caddell items dealing with bans on the manufacture and sale of handguns and one dealing with a ban on private ownership of same. DMI asked a question about banning handgun ownership in both the face-to-face and the telephone surveys.

As noted previously, some 70 percent of the adult population would apparently favor a ban on the manufacture and sale of "Saturday Night Specials." A much lower percentage, but interestingly still a plurality, would "ban the future manufacture and sale of non-sporting type handguns": 48 percent favor this ban, 41 percent oppose it, and the remainder have no opinion. As for banning "the future manufacture and sale of *all* handguns," however, the majority is opposed: 32 percent favor such a ban, 58 percent oppose it, and the remainder have no opinion.

Only a small minority would favor an outright ban on the private ownership of all handguns. In the Caddell survey, 31 percent of the population favor such a ban, 18 percent are "neutral," and 51 percent are opposed. Recalculating the results with the "neutrals" omitted, we get a 62 to 38 percent split against an outright ban on private ownership of handguns. The comparable DMI item is rather different: it offers no "neutral" category and is framed as an "agree–disagree" item. The Caddell item, in contrast, is a seven-point "self-rating" item. In the DMI surveys, 83 percent and 84 percent—in the telephone and personal interview surveys, respectively—disagree with the statement that "no private individual should be allowed to own a handgun." It is thus plain that a sizable majority of the U.S. population disapproves of the notion of an outright ban on the ownership of handguns. The size of the majority on this issue, however, does vary, apparently depending on the specific wording of the question and the context in which it is asked.

Weapons, weapons controls, and the crime rate

Both surveys have a sizable number of items probing people's opinions about what effects, if any, stricter weapons controls would have on the incidence of crime, particularly violent crime, in the country. Given the number of questions devoted to this topic, one must assume that both organizations feel something of importance turns on this issue, so one point must be established in advance: whether the public thinks that stricter gun controls would reduce the crime rate and whether stricter gun controls actually would reduce the crime rate are entirely separate questions, and only the former is at issue here.

Both surveys find immense majority support for the concept of mandatory and severe prison sentences for persons who use a gun to commit a crime. The Caddell majority on the relevant item is 83 percent; the DMI majority is 93 percent in both administrations of a comparable item. Caddell also finds a 55 percent majority favoring mandatory sentences for persons carrying handguns without a license.

DMI asks, "If there were to be more firearms laws, would you expect the crime rate to decrease or increase?" One can only wish that the question would have said something about what kinds of laws or about the strictness of the enforcement. Still, the plurality, in this case 43 percent, say they expect that this would cause the crime rate to decrease, most only by a "small" amount. Another large minority—41 percent—believes that this measure would leave the crime rate unaffected, and the remaining 16 percent think the crime rate would actually increase. Caddell's version of the item is an agree–disagree version with no neutral or middle category; he finds 49 percent agreeing that "requiring all handgun owners to be licensed would reduce crime," 42 percent disagreeing, and 10 percent with no opinion. A later item asking specifically about violent crime produces nearly identical results.

Obviously, persons disagreeing with the Caddell item could believe either that this licensing provision would have no effect on crime or that it would actually increase crime. One may also assume that most of the people who reply "don't know" to Caddell's item would, if pressed, respond "stay the same" to the DMI item. With these allowances for differences in question format and the response options provided, it is clear that the two surveys get very similar results: roughly 40 to 50 percent of the public think that crime would go down with stricter weapons controls, and the remainder think the crime rate would either not be affected or might even increase.[17]

It should also be noted that the proportion saying they think the crime rate would go down under stricter gun controls is lower everywhere than the proportion who say they favor licensing or registration of handguns. It must therefore follow that many people support such measures for reasons other than their assumed effects on the crime rate.

17. It is uncertain what people have in mind when they say they think the crime rate would increase with stricter weapons controls. One possibility is that they believe private weaponry is a crime deterrent and that the rate would thus increase as the deterrent was removed or restricted. Another possibility is that these people anticipate substantial noncompliance with stricter weapons controls, which would, by definition, increase the amount of "crime" being committed.

Both surveys also find very large majorities who believe that criminals will always be able to get their hands on weapons, no matter what laws are passed. Caddell finds 78 percent agreeing that "gun control laws affect only law abiding citizens, criminals will always be able to find guns." Likewise, 85 percent of the telephone respondents and 91 percent of the face-to-face respondents in the DMI surveys agreed that "registration of handguns will not prevent criminals from acquiring or using them for illegal purposes." In the same vein, 81 percent of DMI's phone respondents disagree that "assassination attempts on public officials could be avoided by banning private ownership of handguns."

Weapons control as a mechanism of crime control is the object of a long series of DMI questions. Respondents were given a list of 17 measures that "have been proposed [to] fight crime" and were asked to rate how effective they thought each measure would be. The measures asked about ranged from "increasing punishment for using a gun or other deadly weapon while committing a crime," which was seen as the most effective of the 17 options—86 percent thought this would be effective—down through "outlawing private possession of all handguns," which was rated as least effective—27 percent thought this would be effective.

The general theme that surfaces in this question sequence is that most "get tough" measures—mandatory sentences for gun crimes, "making criminals pay damages to their victims," "increasing punishment for serious crimes," and so on—are perceived as being more effective crime-fighting devices than are most measures involving stricter controls on gun ownership or use among the general population. This, of course, is consistent with the previous finding that fewer than half the population believes that stricter controls would have any effect on lowering the crime rate at all and that most who do anticipate such an effect expect that it would only be "small." The one item from the DMI series that comes closest to an analogous Caddell item asks about "requiring detailed record-keeping of gun purchases and sales by federally licensed gun dealers." Just over half —54 percent—believed this would be "very effective"—rated six or seven on a seven-point scale. In the Caddell item, the comparable proportion is 49 percent.

In this same vein, DMI also has a question series that asks respondents how many people they think would comply with various weapons control measures, if passed. Again, how many people the public thinks would comply and how many people actually would comply are different questions. Still, the public anticipates a substantial degree of noncompliance, not only with new gun laws, but also with laws outlawing smoking in public places or outlawing the sale and manufacture of hard liquor. On the item involving federal registration of guns, for example, only 4 percent think that all gun owners would comply, 25 percent respond "most," and 28 percent say half; the remaining 43 percent think less than half of all gun owners would comply with this measure. Anticipated compliance with measures more strict than federal registration is even lower.

Personal protection and safety

According to DMI, 83 percent of the electorate believes that "people who have guns in their home feel safer because of it." At the same time, a majority in Caddell's survey —52 percent of the total, 57 percent of those with an opinion—rejects the argument that "requiring all handgun owners to be licensed would prevent law-abiding citizens from protecting themselves." In short, most people do not think that licensing handgun ownership would deprive anyone of the security they derive from weapons ownership, so there is again no basic inconsistency in these results.

DMI has a seven-item sequence that asks people what kinds of crime they fear most. Murder in the course of another crime is apparently most feared, followed by burglary, robbery, and rape; murder by a friend or relative and various white-collar crimes are apparently feared least. "How do these findings relate to the issue of gun control?" the DMI report asks.

First, note that the anti-gun argument of reducing "murder by a friend or relative" is not a crime which many fear. Note [too] that robbery/mugging, rape, and, to some extent, "murder in the course of another crime" are crimes which possession of guns by intended victims tends to discourage or prevent —and these are crimes about which the public is *very* concerned. . . . Finally, note that precisely those crimes most likely to be reduced by gun ownership are those *less* feared by gunowners.

This is a creative, but possibly misleading, reading of the DMI results. Obviously, not many people would sit around in a high state of anxiety over the prospect of being murdered by a relative or close friend. That people do not fear this crime does not in any sense deny the well-known reality that most murders are in fact committed by relatives and friends, and, of course, neither the lack of fear nor the reality of this crime says anything about whether its incidence would be reduced by stricter gun controls. Also, that DMI's gun owners are less fearful of certain kinds of crimes than the nonowners cannot be interpreted in the absence of additional analysis of region and city size, since weapons ownership is disproportionately a rural, small-town phenomenon, whereas the kinds of crimes being asked about in the sequence are disproportionately urban. On the average, that is, gun owners may very well be less fearful of a mugging or a rape, as DMI reports, but that may only reflect that the average gun owner lives in a place where muggings and rapes are infrequent.

The right to keep and bear arms

Eighty-nine percent of the respondents in DMI's personal survey and 87 percent in the telephone survey believe that they "as a citizen have a right to own a gun." In the personal survey, 87 percent also said that the Constitution gives them that right. But at the same time, a substantial majority of Caddell's respondents—53 percent of the total, 60 percent of those with an opinion —disagree with the statement that "requiring all handgun owners to be licensed would violate people's constitutional rights." Thus most Americans believe they have a right to own a gun and most also believe that requiring a license for handgun ownership would not be a violation of that right. Again, there is no inconsistency: most people, it appears, understand that all rights and freedoms in a democratic society are subject to at least some constraints, the right to keep and bear arms apparently included.

"One thing leads to another"

The more dramatic anticontrol polemicists have in the past argued that registration or permit mechanisms for handgun ownership or use are "just the first step" toward first, regulation of all guns; then, confiscation of all guns; and last, once the population has been disarmed and lacks the means to resist, the decimation of all our freedoms. To emphasize a recurring theme, whether any of these things would actually come to pass and whether the public thinks they would come to pass are different questions; in either case, both polls contain a fair number of items addressing public thinking on such matters.

A plurality of Caddell's respondents—47 percent of the total, or 55 percent of those with an opinion— disagree with the statement that "requiring all handgun owners to be licensed is just the first step in confiscating all guns, including shotguns." The comparable DMI item is somewhat different. In their personal survey, 51 percent agreed that "a national gun registration program might well eventually lead to the confiscation of all registered firearms by the government." Obviously, the split in public thinking on this issue is so close to 50-50 that no certain statement about majority sentiment can be made; roughly half the population thinks such measures might lead to confiscation of all weapons, and the other half does not. Reflecting the same ambivalence, 37 percent of Caddell's respondents think "it is possible to have effective controls on handguns without having controls on long guns," 40 percent think not, and the remainder are "not sure." On the other hand, DMI finds a fairly sizable majority —62 percent—who agree that "prohibiting private possession of handguns will *not* lead to prohibiting all types of guns."

On the "larger issues," Caddell finds a clear majority—53 percent of the total, 59 percent of those with an opinion—disagreeing that "requiring all handgun owners to be licensed is just another step by government to interfere in people's lives and limit their freedoms." DMI has no comparably direct item; the closest they come is an item that asks people how they feel about the "loss of privacy" that might result if persons' "credit ratings, income, gun ownership, or medical reports" were "kept in government computers." Most people, some 71 percent, would be "concerned" about all this. The quadruple-barreled nature of the question, however, renders it uninformative for our purposes, since we cannot tell from the item just what kinds of information keeping people find objectionable.

The only remaining item that relates, even indirectly, to the topic at hand is Caddell's agree–disagree question: "The only way to control handguns is by Federal law; state laws which allow them to be purchased in some states but not others are ineffective." A large majority, 70 percent, agree with this statement, but since the question is double-barreled, it is impossible to say just what the majority is agreeing to. One could, for example, readily agree with the second clause in the statement, but disagree with the first; that is, one could believe that the "solution" to this problem is a set of state-level laws that are, nonetheless, uniform across states.

CONCLUSIONS: WEAPONS AND THEIR CONTROL

Despite the occasionally sharp differences in emphasis and interpretation between the DMI and Caddell reports, the actual empirical findings from these two surveys are remarkably similar. Results from comparable—even roughly comparable—

items rarely differ between the two surveys by more than 10 percentage points, well within "allowable" limits, given the initial differences in sampling frame and the usual margin of survey error. The major difference between the two reports is not in the findings, but in what is said about or concluded from the findings: what aspects of the evidence are emphasized or de-emphasized, what interpretation is given to a finding, and what implications are drawn from the findings about the need, or lack thereof, for stricter weapons controls. I thus conclude that the "anti-survey" hypothesis is not confirmed in this comparison; the two surveys differ in the aspects of public opinion they examine and in the conclusions they try to draw, but on virtually all points where a direct comparison is possible, the evidence from each survey says essentially the same thing.

What does the evidence say? To begin with, large majorities favor any measure involving the registration or licensing of handguns, both for new purchases and for handguns presently owned.[18] The public would not favor such measures if their costs were astronomical; likewise, there is substantial agreement that such measures would only be effective if they were uniform across states. There is very little popular support for an outright ban on private ownership of handguns, although the majority would favor a ban on the manufacture and sale of Saturday Night Specials. Large majorities believe they have a right to own guns and that the Constitution guarantees that right; most people also think that a licensing requirement for handgun ownership would

18. Neither survey deals with the registration or licensing of longguns in any direct way; the standard police permit item suggests that most people would favor this as well.

not be a violation of that right. No more than about half the population thinks that stricter controls would decrease the crime rate; many measures other than stricter weapons controls are thought to be more effective to this end. Virtually everyone agrees that criminals will always be able to acquire guns, no matter what laws are passed; likewise, nearly everyone favors strict and mandatory sentences for persons using guns to commit crimes. Opinion is divided on the issue of whether handgun controls will eventually lead to control—or even confiscation—of all weapons; this notwithstanding, the large majority favors such controls. There is little popular support for the idea that gun controls are somehow violations of Americans' basic freedoms.

So far as public opinion on such a complex issue can be summarized at all, the thrust of majority thinking on gun control seems to be that the government should be just as careful about who is allowed to own and use a firearm as it is about who is allowed to own and use automobiles or other potentially hazardous commodities.

And just as licensing and registration of automobiles seem to have very little effect on reducing automobile accidents, so too do most people anticipate that stricter weapons controls would have little or no effect on crime. This, however, does not prevent them from favoring at least some stricter gun control measures. The underlying concept here seems to be that weapons, as automobiles, are intrinsically dangerous objects that governments ought to keep track of for that reason alone. Whether doing so would reduce the level of crime or violence in the society seems to be taken as a separate issue entirely.

These few conclusions are, I believe, fully consistent with all evidence reported in both the Caddell and DMI surveys; they are also consistent with the evidence from NORC, Gallup, Roper, and indeed, all other polls and surveys of which I am aware. I thus suggest that the conclusions summarized here are as close to an adequate statement of popular thinking on gun control issues as the present state of public opinion research allows.

The Attitude–Action Connection and the Issue of Gun Control

By HOWARD SCHUMAN and STANLEY PRESSER

ABSTRACT: This article examines the claim that opponents of gun permit laws feel much more intensely about the matter than do proponents and that this helps explain the political success of the opponents, despite their smaller number. Surprisingly, results from a national sample survey provide no support for the claim at the purely subjective level. In fact, when respondents were asked how strongly they felt about the issue of gun permits, supporters of a permit law responded with slightly more intensity. However, when asked whether they had ever acted on the issue—written letters, contributed money, or both—opponents were markedly more likely to respond in the affirmative. The apparent inconsistency between these findings seems to be due to the fact that strength of feeling and taking action are highly related for permit opponents, but not for proponents. Thus among respondents who believe the issue to be most important, opponents are quite likely to act on their beliefs, whereas this is not so for proponents—a difference that may well reflect the superiority in organizational effectiveness of the forces opposed to gun control. The concept of single issue politics is therefore more complex than is often realized and requires investigation of both the individual and the organizational levels, as well as of the connection between them.

Howard Schuman is a professor of sociology and program director in the Institute for Social Research, University of Michigan.

Stanley Presser is a research associate, Institute for Research in Social Science, and visiting assistant professor, Department of Sociology, University of North Carolina.

This article is drawn from research reported in *Questions and Answers in Attitude Surveys: Experiments on Question Form, Wording, and Context* (Academic Press, fall 1981).

A STANDARD question on requiring police permits for the purchase of guns has been asked regularly in national polls since 1959:

> Would you favor or oppose a law which would require a person to obtain a police permit before he or she could buy a gun?

In response to this question, a clear and nearly constant majority of about three fourths of the population has favored a permit requirement over the past two decades.[1] Yet Congress has thus far failed to enact legislation that would require or at least strongly encourage a nationwide police permit system. One explanation for the discrepancy is that the poll results are misleading because the standard question is defective in some way. However, analyses of other versions of the question, as well as of questions about such closely related issues as "gun registration," indicate that results do not vary greatly with a variety of changes in phrasing, even though they do vary substantially when entirely different issues—such as banning all guns—are introduced.[2]

Because the standard question does not specify a national law, it might be further argued that the discrepancy is more apparent than real, since almost two thirds of the population live in states that already have police permit laws.[3] Yet the available evidence indicates that asking specifically about a federal law yields levels of support that are just as high, at least for the related issue of gun registration. In Harris surveys conducted in 1968 and 1975, over 70 percent of national samples responded "favor" to the question, "Do you favor or oppose federal laws which would control the sale of guns, such as making all persons register all gun purchases no matter where they buy them?"[4] Thus there clearly are forces that have thwarted the public's support for gun control at the national level, forces that, interestingly, have not prevailed in many states.

Still another explanation for the discrepancy between public opinion and congressional action is that the polls fail to capture the true meaning of public opinion, since the relative strengths with which attitudes are held and applied may be even more important than the numbers on each side of the issue. According to this hypothesis, the antipermit minority includes a disproportionately large number of individuals who feel very strongly about the issue and who therefore take actions that give their side extra weight in the political arena. Such people overwhelm majority sentiment when it comes to influence on Congress: representatives and senators are hesitant to risk alienating those whose efforts and votes may be determined entirely by this single issue. As John Jackson points out, in a situation in which preferences and the propensity to act on them are correlated, an electoral strategy that accommodates each of

1. Tom Smith, "The 75% Solution: An Analysis of the Structure of Attitudes on Gun Control, 1959–1977," *J. Criminal Law & Criminology*, 71:300–316 (1980).

2. For experimental changes in the wording of the standard question, see Howard Schuman and Stanley Presser, "Attitude Measurement and the Gun Control Paradox," *Public Opinion Quarterly*, 41:427–38 (winter 1977–78) (hereafter cited as "Attitude Measurement"). For questions on related aspects of gun control, see Smith; and James Wright, this issue.

3. Philip Cook and James Blose, this issue.

4. Harris Study Nos. 1813 and 7586. In 7586, the last phrase read: "where the purchases are made."

the more intense preferences will defeat an electoral strategy based on majority preferences.[5]

It is this third hypothesis that we examine closely in this article. We show that the hypothesis does not hold in the simple sense often assumed, but that it does hold once we take into account the difference between attitudes and actions, as well as the reasons why behavior can vary independently of attitudes.

ATTITUDE STRENGTH

Our test of the hypothesis that opponents of gun permits have greater personal involvement in the issue than proponents employed two measures of attitude strength called "intensity" and "centrality." A cross-sectional sample of American adults in August 1978 was first asked a variant of the standard question on gun permits:[6]

Would you favor a law which would require a person to obtain a police permit before he could buy a gun, or do you think such a law would interfere too much with the right of citizens to own guns?

Previous research had shown that this question yields somewhat more antipermit responses than the standard question quoted earlier, but it continues to show a clear majority of over 60 percent favoring gun permits.[7]

After answering the gun permit question, half the sample was asked the intensity item shown on the left in Table 1 and half was asked the centrality item shown on the right in the same table. The two halves were created by dividing the total sample randomly so that each half represented the national population equally well.[8] It will be noted that the intensity question is phrased entirely in terms of subjective strength of feelings, while the centrality question is cast in terms of the importance of the issue and is oriented toward possible action in the form of voting. Although both items can be regarded as ways of measuring subjective involvement in the gun permit issue, they are not interchangeable. The centrality item isolates a smaller—6 percent—and presumably more extreme part of the population at the high

5. John Jackson, "Intensities, Preferences, and Electoral Politics," *Social Science Research*, 2 June 1973, pp. 231–46.

6. The question was asked as part of a regular University of Michigan Survey Research Center telephone survey, using a partly new Random Digit Dial (RDD) sample (response rate = 65 percent) and partly recontacts from an earlier RDD sample (August response rate = 48 percent). Replication data from September 1979 (drawn on on p. 45) are based on a similar design with response rates of 72 percent and 57 percent. No significant difference in results appears between RDD and recontact samples in either survey. Both samples represent the coterminous United States.

7. The question was actually asked in two forms as part of a question-wording experiment. A randomly designated half of the sample was asked the version quoted in the text; the other half, a form that read, "Some people favor a law which would require a person to obtain a police permit before he could buy a gun. Others oppose such a law on the grounds that it would interfere too much with the right of citizens to own guns. Do you favor or oppose a law that would require a police permit to buy a gun?" Since the two forms produced nearly identical results in terms of the major points of interest here, the data are pooled in this presentation. For further details, see Howard Schuman and Stanley Presser, *Questions and Answers in Attitude Surveys: Experiments on Question Form, Wording, and Context* (New York: Academic Press, forthcoming fall 1981), ch. 7 (hereafter cited as *Questions and Answers*).

8. This division of the sample crosscut the one described in fn. 7. Thus the total design was a 2 by 2 factorial.

TABLE 1

INTENSITY AND CENTRALITY RESULTS FOR GUN PERMITS: AUGUST 1978

INTENSITY				CENTRALITY		
Compared with how you feel on other public issues, are your feelings about permits for guns: extremely strong, very strong, fairly strong, or not strong at all?				How important is a candidate's position on permits for guns when you decide how to vote in a congressional election? Is it one of the most important factors you would consider, a very important factor, somewhat important, or not too important?		

	Marginal Total (in percentages)	Gun permit question			Marginal Total (in percentages)	Gun permit question	
		Pro (in percentages)	Anti (in percentages)			Pro (in percentages)	Anti (in percentages)
1. Extremely strong	17.5	18.2	16.6	1. One of the most important	6.3	5.4	7.7
2. Very strong	23.6	23.4	23.9	2. Very important	23.6	22.4	25.5
3. Fairly strong	39.1	41.2	35.6	3. Somewhat important	34.5	38.7	28.4
4. Not strong at all	19.8	17.2	23.9	4. Not too important	35.5	33.5	38.5
	100	100	100		100	100	100
		(N = 325)	(N = 205)			(N = 313)	(N = 208)

$$\chi^2 = 4.0$$
$$df = 3$$
$$P > .25$$

$$\chi^2 = 6.3$$
$$df = 3$$
$$P < .10$$

involvement end than does the intensity item—18 percent. Moreover, the fact that the centrality item is worded in terms of one's voting decision suggests that this more extreme percent may correspond essentially to "single-issue people."

Whatever the similarity or difference of the two items, neither measure of subjective involvement provides clear-cut evidence that there are more high involvement opponents of gun permits in the American population than there are highly involved proponents. This is especially true for the intensity item, where in fact proponents of permits actually report slightly stronger feelings than do opponents. Although this latter trend is not statistically significant in the 1978 survey, it ap-

pears more clearly in other surveys and probably represents a real difference directly counter to the original hypothesis.[9]

The results for the centrality item are more complex, since opponents of gun permits are represented disproportionately at both ends of the scale of issue importance. Again, these slight trends in August 1978 reappear more strongly in other samples, and in particular it does seem to be true that a higher proportion of opponents rate the gun permit issue as "one of the most important" factors to consider in a congressional election.[10] However, since there are fewer opponents than proponents in

9. Schuman and Presser, "Attitude Measurement."
10. Ibid.

TABLE 2

SELF-REPORTED BEHAVIOR ON THE GUN PERMIT ISSUE: AUGUST 1978

BEHAVIOR REPORTED	POSITION ON GUN PERMITS	
	PROPERMIT	ANTIPERMIT
Written a letter	3.7 ⎫	6.5 ⎫
Given money	1.7 ⎬ 7.1	7.7 ⎬ 20.4
Written letter and given money	1.7 ⎭	6.2 ⎭
Neither	92.9	79.6
	100	100
	(N = 653)	(N = 417)

$$\chi^2 = 46.4, df = 3, p < .001$$

the total population, the proportions must be corrected in order to allow estimates of the actual numbers at the extreme end. When this is done, our best estimate is that among those persons considering the permit issue to be "one of the most important," proponents and opponents of permits are roughly equal in actual numbers in the United States.[11] This result begins to indicate why the propermit side lacks the political strength that its overall majority suggests, since among those most likely to be active there is something of a stalemate. Yet the result falls short of explaining the full power of opponents of gun permits in blocking national legislation so decisively and, indeed, in occasionally—so it is claimed—contributing to the defeat of a procontrol legislator.

BEHAVIOR

That only the centrality item detects signs of the high involvement

11. The correction involves simply multiplying each proportion by the base N on which it was originally calculated. For Table 1 data, this results in 17 cases (representing approximately 4.4 million people) on the pro side and 16 cases (representing about 4.1 million people) on the anti side. A similar 50-50 division appears in our other surveys.

of opponents of gun permits had earlier suggested to us the possible value of a more fully behavioral measure of involvement. Therefore after the intensity and centrality items were asked in August 1978, the entire sample was asked a direct question about overt actions with respect to the gun permit issue:

Have you ever written a letter to a public official expressing your views on gun permits or given money to an organization concerned with this issue?

The results shown in Table 2 are striking. About 12 percent of the total sample reports having written a letter, contributed money, or done both with regard to the gun permit issue. But the percentage of permit opponents who have done any of these things is nearly three times as large as the percentage of proponents active in these ways. Even when one allows for the fact that the number of "pros" considerably exceeds the number of "antis," almost two thirds of all letter writers and financial contributors on this issue come from the anti side. If we trust these self-reports as approximately accurate, then politicians, editors, and others who take stands on the gun permit issue will hear from permit opponents noticeably more often than from permit proponents, even though it is the latter who clearly predominate in the country.[12] Moreover, beyond their willingness to write letters, permit opponents are even more conspicuous in donating money to their cause. This no doubt multiplies the effectiveness of their communication system, and it also doubtless plays an important role in election campaigns when financial support is given to one candidate rather than another. Even these results may underestimate the activity of antis, since we did not obtain frequency of letter writing or amounts of contributions.

SOCIAL ACTION AND SOCIAL ORGANIZATION

The difference between gun permit opponents and proponents in action is much more impressive than was the case for subjective strength. The difference in behavior is clearcut and decisive, whereas the variation at the subjective level was slighter, more uncertain, and insufficient to account for the political potency of antipermit partisans. How is it that those opposing permits are a great deal more active than those favoring permits in terms of writing letters and giving money, yet show up as only about equally likely to regard the issue as more important when subjective measures are employed? The answer may lie in the remarkable interaction presented in Figure 1, where

the association between the centrality and behavior measures is examined separately for proponents and opponents of gun permits.

Among opponents of permit legislation, there is a strong monotonic relation (gamma = .61, p < .001), which can be interpreted to mean that opponents who consider the issue important are quite likely to translate their convictions into political actions, such as letter writing and contributions. Among proponents, on the other hand, there is little if any relation between centrality of opinion and behavior (gamma = .12, not statistically significant), so that subjective conviction about the importance of the issue apparently does not lead to instrumental political behavior.[13] Because of the fundamental importance of this finding, we replicated it in a September 1979 survey. The spread between the centrality–behavior correlations for opponents and proponents is not quite so extreme—the gammas are .70 and .30, respectively —but with more cases (N = 867) the difference between them attains higher statistical significance.[14]

What these findings seem to us to point to, albeit without direct evi-

---

12. While we do not assume that the self-reports in Table 2 are without error, we can see little reason to think that there is differential bias in reporting between opponents and proponents. If opponents were more likely to exaggerate their actions, why should they not similarly have exaggerated their intensity of feeling on the issue?

13. This difference between proponents and opponents, as measured by the linear component of the three-way interaction of behavior, centrality, and pro/anti position, is statistically significant: X^2 = 4.18, df = 1, p < .05. The corresponding interaction for behavior, intensity, and pro/anti position shows the same general pattern, but the gammas are not as far apart, and they vary systematically by the form of the original question (see fn. 7). We believe the latter variation is due to the more labile nature of the intensity measure, as discussed in Schuman and Presser (Questions and Answers, ch. 9).

14. Linear X^2 = 5.59, df = 1, p < .02. The differences shown earlier in tables 1 and 2 for centrality and behavior also replicate well in September 1979. Intensity was not included in that survey.

FIGURE 1

THE RELATION OF BEHAVIOR TO CENTRALITY FOR GUN PERMIT
PROPONENTS AND OPPONENTS: AUGUST 1978

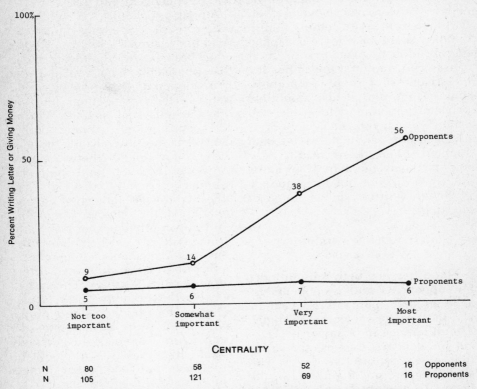

| N | 80 | 58 | 52 | 16 | Opponents |
| N | 105 | 121 | 69 | 16 | Proponents |

NOTE: The behavioral measure is dichotomized into those showing any behavior (letters, money, or both) and those showing none. For opponents, gamma = .61, s.e. = .09; for proponents, gamma = .12, s.e. = .19.

dence, is an efficient lobby against gun control legislation, which is able to activate adherents whenever necessary, while those on the other side remain unable to come together for effective action. Such a picture of the antigun control lobby is entirely consistent with information about the efficiency of the National Rifle Association in mobilizing supporters rapidly whenever an issue arises where letters, funds, or votes are needed.[15] The activation is not in-dependent of the attitude strength of permit opponents, however, since it is just those with strong positions who appear to respond to such mobilizing efforts. The interaction of pro/anti position, centrality, and behavior, therefore, suggests a way in which individual dispositions can be related to social organization and social mobilization to produce politically important effects.[16] Additional studies will be needed, however, to test these interpretations by

15. Lee Kennett and James LaVerne Andersen, *The Gun in America* (Westport, CT: Greenwood Press, 1975), p. 238.

16. Cf., John McCarthy and Mayer Zald, "Resource Mobilization and Social Movements," *Am. J. Soc.* 82:1212–41 (May 1977).

means of direct questions on organizational memberships, solicitations, and other mobilizing activities.

THE DIVERSE MEANINGS OF SINGLE-ISSUE POLITICS

There is increasing discussion of the importance of single-issue politics in the United States. Our findings about the gun permit issue point to the need for some essential distinctions between the ways in which single-issue commitment can come about and be manifested. On some issues there is probably a greater degree of subjective involvement by one side than the other, and this rather naturally leads to parallel differences in political activity. Such seems to be the case for the issue of legalized abortion, where we have found that those on the negative side tend to be more involved than those on the positive side, regardless of what measure of involvement is used—intensity, centrality, or behavior.[17]

But on the issue of gun permits, and perhaps also of other facets of gun control, it is necessary to distinguish subjective from objective indicators of single-issue involvement. At the purely subjective level,

17. Schuman and Presser, *Questions and Answers.*

there is evidence that those favoring gun permits tend overall to feel a little more strongly about the issue than do opponents of permits— quite the opposite of what is usually assumed. When we move to a question that isolates a more extreme group in terms of hypothetical willingness to vote on this single issue alone, we begin to see the source of influence of opponents, though not to the decisive degree that has actually occurred in the political arena. Finally, when we focus directly on overt behavior, the real power of opponents becomes apparent in actions such as letter writing and fund raising. Since subjective feelings alone cannot explain this last difference, we hypothesize that organizational effort plays a crucial role, though it apparently does so by identifying and drawing on the emotional commitments of a relatively small set of opponents in the total population. Our full understanding of the nature and political implications of support for and opposition to gun permits, therefore, requires that we obtain information at both the individual and the organizational levels of society and that we be prepared to see the connection between the two as more subtle and more reciprocal than is often recognized.

The Politics of Ineffectiveness: Federal Firearms Legislation, 1919–38

By CAROL SKALNIK LEFF and MARK H. LEFF

ABSTRACT: The federal firearms legislation proposed and enacted between the two world wars, although a breakthrough in federal activism on the issue, left a neutral legacy for future regulatory efforts. The 1927 statute barred handguns from the U.S. postal system without closing off alternative shipping routes. The National Firearms Act of 1934 ultimately limited its registration provisions to "gangster" weapons, like machine guns. The more inclusive Federal Firearms Act of 1938 proved impossible to effectively enforce. In view of the New Deal Justice Department's ambitious regulatory proposals, which would be considered far-reaching even by later standards, this lackluster record proved decidedly anticlimactic. The minimal impact of federal law was partially rooted in the low enforcement priorities of the Treasury Department and was in part attributable to the influence of a traditional individualist ethos hostile to the "civilizing" pretensions of federal intervention. But just as important as the administrative and cultural barriers to gun control effectiveness was the character of the policymaking process. Antiregulation forces out-organized Justice Department regulators, with their vaguer public anticrime constituency, and parlayed their intensive commitment into a formidable influence on the legislative outcome. This capacity to circumscribe federal initiatives helped to neutralize the impact of the first federal gun control legislation.

Carol Skalnik Leff, Ph.D., Harvard, teaches American and comparative politics at Washington University. Mark H. Leff, Ph.D., University of Chicago, an assistant professor of history at Washington University, teaches modern American political and economic history.

NOTE: This article grew out of a set of unpublished studies for the Center for Studies in Criminal Justice at the University of Chicago.

THE RESORT to federal legislation is often a sign of failure, an indicator of a problem not effectively resolved at lower levels. The resulting federal action, however, is not always tantamount to a federal solution. Firearms regulation is a case in point. This article traces the emergence of gun control as a subject of marked federal concern, focusing on the first substantive federal firearms laws, which achieved passage between World War I and World War II. The ensuing examination of the policymaking process uncovers cultural and organizational responses to the issue that help to explain why the flurry of federal activity between the wars amounted to little more than postponement of substantial federal action.

FEDERAL GUN CONTROL MEASURES BETWEEN THE TWO WORLD WARS: ENACTMENT AND IMPLEMENTATION

As the United States emerged from World War I, the gun control issue was poised on the threshold of serious federal attention. Since the 1880s, states and municipalities had declared legislative war on the carrying of concealed weapons. This campaign was fueled by the stresses of an urbanizing and industrializing nation, with the attendant problems of juvenile delinquency, race tensions, and immigration. Although such problems were national in scope, suspicion of central authority slowed resort to federal action.

The first federal intervention in the sale and manufacture of firearms, the 1919 excise tax on weapons, achieved passage as a belated war revenue measure, though it has persisted with bureaucratic hardihood despite concerted attempts in the 1920s to reduce it. But the interwar period also marked a more significant precedent, the first federal legislative initiatives to directly confront the question of firearms control as more than a revenue expedient. From 1927 through 1938, Congress enacted into law three efforts to regulate the spread and abuse of guns: the exclusion of handguns from the mails in 1927, the National Firearms Act of 1934, and the Federal Firearms Act of 1938.

This upsurge of federal activism was in large part a response to problems encountered in the enforcement of state legislation. From the outset of the 1920s, a central concern was the manner in which laxity in one state could undercut the efforts of another: in 1921, it was pointed out that "the action of an individual State is utterly valueless if a neighboring State fails to take corresponding action."[1] In a decade in which handgun control legislation received a renewed surge of interest in most state legislatures, the inefficiencies of a 48-piece legal patchwork became all the more pressing.

The alternative of central government action, however, ran up against a broad—almost religious—American commitment to the federal ideal. Forced to choose between conflicting state laws on the one hand and central coercion on the other, one typical American solution in the early twentieth century was "uniform state legislation" in which "experts" would draw up model bills to provide guidelines for harmonious state action.[2] The need for a coordinated offensive against the 1920s

1. U.S., Congress, Senate, *Congressional Record*, 67th Cong., 1st sess., 1921, vol. 61: 7161.
2. See William Graebner, "Federalism in the Progressive Era," *J. Am. History*, 64: 331–57 (Sept. 1977).

crime wave assured that a Uniform Firearms Act would join the panoply of model laws approved and disseminated by the National Conference of Commissioners on Uniform State Laws.

The shortcomings of this solution were evident at the outset. No one could force every state to adopt the uniform code. Thus even though a number of states would draw on model firearms bills for legislative inspiration, these laws were undermined by weaker ones in adjacent states.

Thus by process of elimination, a more sympathetic climate for federal action was slowly emerging. The receptivity of this new climate should not, of course, be exaggerated. Though the handful of bills in the U.S. Congress before 1920 to regulate interstate handgun traffic or to bar pistol ownership by minors or aliens had expanded to over a dozen such proposals by the early 1920s, these efforts to federalize gun control were too far ahead of their time. Any federal initiatives would still have to labor under an extraordinary burden of proof in the face of widespread sensitivity about states' rights.

Understandably, then, the earliest federal firearms legislation did not confront the question of federal responsibility head-on. Suspicion of federal activism was particularly well entrenched in an area like law enforcement, traditionally an unquestioned state and local preserve. It is within this limited context that the 1927 act banning the delivery of concealable firearms through the U.S. mails must be seen.

The ritual banishment of handguns from the mails, 1927

At first glance, the mail-order ban of 1927 appears more activist in its purposes and more direct in its application of federal power to meet a national purpose in defiance of tradition than warnings about suspicion of federal power would predict. A closer look, however, suggests that the issue of mail-order firearms succeeded where other federal gun control measures of the 1920s failed, in large part because it could be construed in a way that blunted the edge of the states' rights perspective.

It is quite true that the proposed mail-order ban was ceremonially reviled on Capitol hill as "the child of bureaucratic government at Washington" and that some southern representatives purported to see in the bill a harbinger of the day when "the people of the States will have nothing under the sun to do except dodge the Federal officials."[3] However, proponents of the ban were in a powerful position to rebut the charge of federal encroachment. Undeniably, the most powerful incentive for removing post offices from the firearms business was to avoid having a federal agency be party to the shipment of pistols into states and localities that possessed their own stringent firearms legislation. As Congressman John Miller of Washington, the bill's sponsor, urged, federal legislation in this case would only serve to prevent the Post Office from unwittingly undermining existing state regulation. His supporters queried, "What is the use of enforcing the local laws and regulations with regard to carrying pistols if it is perfectly easy to get them through the mails?"[4]

Throughout the debate on the federal mail-order ban, the bill's

3. U.S., Congress, House of Representatives, Congressional Record, 68th Cong., 2d sess., 1924, vol. 66:733 and 735.

4. Ibid., 731.

advocates presented the federal initiative as protective of state and local law, as a response to urban criticism of the federal role in firearms transmittal. It was contended that the ban would "materially strengthen the several States and increase their power to enforce their police regulations without being crippled by the action of citizens of other States in shipping revolvers into such States."[5]

Despite President Coolidge's publicly expressed doubts that a federal ban on interstate firearms shipments could reduce crime,[6] it was clear from the outset that the Post Office itself was enthusiastic in its cooperation in the mail ban campaign. The postmaster general's 1925 and 1926 annual reports embraced the proposed legislation, its solicitor helped to draft the final bill, and the 1924 convention of Post Office clerks passed a resolution urging the barring of concealable firearms from the mails.[7] While this defense of the mail-order ban can be read as federal activism in the disguise of help to the states, the concerns of the Post Office throughout the bill's consideration suggest that there was more than rationalization involved.

That the agency's motivation in adopting a promail ban stance was hardly imperialistic emerges from the record. Rather than searching for new responsibility, the Post Office seemed intent on divesting itself of unwelcome old obligations.

Thus the postmaster general argued that the requirement that the Post Office handle all properly packaged firearms had resulted in "many complaints against the facility furnished by the Department."[8] Likewise, during the hearings on the bill, committee member C. William Ramseyer noted that the "Post Office Department has received so much criticism because of the manner in which the pistols were distributed easily through the mail to everybody that the Post Office Department itself wants to get out of the business."[9] Above all, the agency revealed its reluctance to become further embroiled in the issue when it recoiled from one proposed solution that would have entailed postal administration of selective mail-order bans only to localities that prohibited firearms sales. Such a selective action would have significantly increased the very involvement that the agency wished to avoid.

In retrospect, it would appear that government thinking paralleled that of Sears Roebuck, which in 1924 had voluntarily withdrawn from the business of mail-order sales on the grounds that to do so would "protect our good name and maintain the public goodwill."[10] Caught in the cross-fire of public concern over guns and crime, the Post Office seemed anxious to purify its own reputation by quitting the field of arms dissemination entirely. This, despite opposition portraits of meddling bureaucrats, seems the fairest reading of federal intent.

5. Ibid., 734.

6. *New York Herald Tribune*, 14 Oct. 1925, p. 6.

7. House, Committee on the Post Office and Post Roads, *Carrying of Pistols . . . in the Mails, Hearings* on H.R. 4502, 69th Cong., 1st sess.,. 1926, pp. 2PV and 10PV, in Record Group 234, Records of the U.S. House of Representatives, 68th and 69th Congress, Committee on Post Office and Post Roads bill file, H.R. 4502 folder, National Archives, Washington, DC.

8. U.S., Post Office Department, *Annual Report of the Postmaster-General 1926* (Washington, D.C.: Government Printing Office, 1926), p. 65.

9. Committee on Post Office, *Hearings* on H.R. 4502, p. 10PV, in Record Group 234, National Archives, Washington, DC.

10. "A Spike for the 'One-hand Gun,'" *Literary Digest*, 83 (13 Dec. 1924).

Though others may have seen the mail-order ban as an encouraging first step, the lack of administration support outside the Post Office reduced the mail-order bill to little more than an isolated symbolic gesture, more expedient than productive of further advance. A House Judiciary Committee bill regulating interstate commerce in handguns never reached the floor, and numerous later attempts to extricate such legislation from the Interstate and Foreign Commerce Committee proved abortive. Efforts to intensify the impact of the mail-order statute by interdicting pistol shipments by common carriers also failed, as did the proposal to extend the mail ban to include firearms advertisements. As for the 1927 act itself, even its advocates conceded to opposition arguments that it "denies him [the criminal] the use of the mails and turns him over to the tender mercies of the express companies."[11] This, coupled with the continued ease with which an individual could cross state lines to make a gun purchase, left the mail ban supporters with a sort of moral argument that focused on making sure that the federal government had clean hands on the gun issue. Congressman Bill Lowrey of Mississippi made this point most clearly when he argued as follows:

It seems to me that admitting this would simply drive this business into the hands of the express companies; that none the less the Government ought to get out of the business, and the agency of the Government, the postal department, ought to refuse to assist in the violation of law and ought to respond to these appeals from the cities that the gentleman has spoken of.[12]

11. House, *Congressional Record*, 68th Cong., 2d sess., 1924, vol. 66:727.
12. House, *Congressional Record*, 69th Cong., 1st sess., 1926, vol. 67:9695.

If, therefore, the ineffectiveness of the 1927 law was envisaged by its own advocates, we are left with a very limited accomplishment indeed. In a decade that saw mounting press and public debate over the evils of pistol-toting, the only congressional action to be taken on the range of proposed bills was the withdrawal of a federal agency from complicity in handgun dissemination.

Gangster weapons under siege: the National Firearms Act of 1934

Only in the early 1930s were the ingredients for further action on gun control established. Clearly, the United States was developing a serious gangster problem. The recognition of this problem was symbolized by the activities of the Wickersham Commission in 1931, but that body's basic reliance on uniform state laws reflected a federal passivity that was increasingly coming under fire as the nation grappled with the crisis of the Great Depression. There was ample foundation in contemporary experience for this intensified concern with crime. The homicide rate maintained its towering 1920s level until the middle of the 1930s—a rate that was not approached again until the late 1960s. In addition, the rudimentary federal crime control apparatus faced a series of challenges all the more disrupting in that the depression-weary public tended to feel a sneaking sympathy for the era's outlaws. The manhunt for John Dillinger, whose 1933–34 string of midwestern bank robberies and murders captivated the nation, dominated the front pages during the consideration of the 1934 firearms legislation and embarrassed impotent local law enforcement officials. A rash of kidnappings, particularly the Lindbergh baby killing, also attracted attention. The recent gangster practice of using machine guns on policemen rather than on each other posed an additional threat, while the bad press that resulted from several less than heroic FBI encounters with the underworld was further incentive to shift the focus from the colorful personalities of crime to the ruthless weapons of the criminal culture.[13]

Accordingly, the first years of the New Deal registered an increase in the number of firearms bills introduced in Congress. Franklin Roosevelt's attitude seemed likely to further facilitate gun regulation efforts. As New York's governor, he came to the support of that state's restrictive handgun licensing law, championed a state machine-gun ban, and supported federal regulation of interstate traffic in handguns. In October of 1933, as president, he injected himself into the National Recovery Act's code-making process in order to ensure that firearms manufacturers would only sell machine guns to legitimate buyers. Roosevelt also expressed approval in late 1933 for registration of all machine guns, thereby bolstering a campaign that his attorney general, Homer Cummings, had already embarked upon.[14]

Indeed, the main advocate of firearms legislation in the 1930s was the Justice Department itself. Attorney General Cummings, who in this instance seemed to transcend his reputation as a mere politico, became perhaps the most vehement public advocate of federal gun registration in U.S. history. In 1937, he would proclaim, "Show me the man who does not want his gun registered and I will show you a man who should not have a gun."[15] Under his leadership, firearms registration became the Justice Department's major repeating legislative proposal of the New Deal years. Cummings embraced an ambitious scheme that involved registration of all handguns, machine guns, and "gangster weapons"—silencers, cane guns, sawed-off shotguns, and so forth. In 1934, that bill received serious consideration as part of the anticrime package that President Roosevelt presented to Congress in January.

The only real law and order year of the New Deal was 1934, but this crusade played a more significant role than most historical accounts would suggest. The nation's obsession with gangsters served as a springboard for another of the New Deal's extensions of jurisdiction into a previously local province. This campaign culminated in legislation strengthening the federal kidnapping law and rendering it a federal crime to rob an FDIC bank, assault a federal agent, or flee across state lines in certain felony cases. Though states' rights arguments contributed to the discarding of four of the original twelve proposals, this popular show of New Deal concern carved out a significant federal role in crime control.[16]

The firearms control bill received less newspaper coverage than many

13. See Robert Sherrill, *The Saturday Night Special* (New York: Charterhouse, 1973), pp. 37–55.

14. *New York Times*, 29 March 1932, p. 4; idem, 3 Sept. 1931, p. 1; idem, 7 Oct. 1933, p. 4; idem, 20 Oct. 1933, p. 1; idem, 26 Oct. 1933, p. 7.

15. Homer Cummings, "Firearms and the Crime Problem," 5 Oct. 1937, in *Selected Papers of Homer Cummings*, ed. Carl B. Swisher (New York: Charles Scribner's Sons, 1939), p. 89.

16. *New York Times*, 19 May 1934, pp. 1 and 3. For an overview of this legislative package, see *Public Papers and Addresses of Franklin D. Roosevelt*, ed. Samuel Rosenman, 3:242–45 (New York: Random House, 1938).

of the other crime-control measures in this package. Interestingly, it was termed the "Anti-Machine Gun Bill," despite the realization that it also contained a handgun registration provision which would, of course, have affected a far greater portion of the populace.[17] Nevertheless, the bill was judged by the company it kept, which meant that it was an anti-gangster measure. Every era distills its conception of crime into an emotional symbol. In the 1920s, when the popular image was a robber escaping from a store or bank while brandishing a handgun, the pistol —or "mankiller," as it was branded —served as that symbol. But starting in the late 1920s, when the first anti-machine-gun laws were passed at the state level, the stereotyped "thug" was being transformed into a "roving gangster," and the pistol became a submachine gun. It was this sensationalist base—not, as certain scholars have implied, the year-old attempted assassination of Franklin Roosevelt by Giuseppe Zangara in February 1933—that was the essential backdrop for early New Deal gun control efforts.[18]

17. New York Times, 25 April 1934, p. 3.
18. The seemingly natural linkage between assassination and gun control, however catalytic it may have been in the 1960s, was in fact surprisingly limited in its effectiveness in stimulating earlier federal initiatives. Rather than propel gun control to the forefront, assassination attempts have seemed to take on the political coloration of the existing landscape of fears that existed at the time. They have historically been a political morality play focused more on public interpretation of the crucial characteristics of the assassin —the anarchist, the disappointed office seeker —than on the weapon itself. Though the $8 pawnshop pistol used in the attempt on Roosevelt's life generated some calls for tighter handgun controls, such comments were few and far between; more concern centered on the fact that the President-elect's assailant was a naturalized citizen, prompting anti-anarchist and anti-alien sentiment.

The firearms bill considered in 1934 used the Harrison Narcotics Act as its model, for New Deal initiatives often ran into trouble in the courts, and the Harrison statute had been declared constitutional as a regulatory measure.[19] It relied on the taxing power rather than the interstate commerce clause. This finessed Second Amendment issues that only achieved resolution in U.S. v. Miller in 1939—the Justice Department particularly feared that an absolute ban on machine guns would be unconstitutional—and permitted control of intrastate firearms transfers. The intent was to regulate firearms with a registration and transfer tax program under which guns could be identified and traced to their owners, as well as to regulate gun dealers through licensing fees. As originally formulated, then, the firearms act proposed in 1934 was a far-reaching, ambitious measure. By the time this bill emerged from the law-making process, however, it had been gutted—stripped of its handgun clauses and revised in line with the objections of the National Rifle Association (NRA) and other interested parties. This revised bill breezed through the House and the Senate on unrecorded votes near the end of the session, arousing neither controversy nor fervor.

After the initial great expectations, the Justice Department was understandably disappointed at the narrow scope of this statute, but it must be observed that the Roosevelt administration partially victimized itself by its own rhetoric. President Roosevelt, with his characteristic flair for spotlighting the most sensational and villainous aspects of an issue, couched his support for crime

19. House, Committee on Ways and Means, Hearings on H.R. 9066, 73d Cong., 2d sess., 1934, p. 6.

control legislation in terms of the machine-gun problem: "Federal men are constantly facing machine-gun fire in the pursuit of gangsters."[20] This emphasis on gangsters and their most deplorable criminal weaponry proved all too riveting a selling point for the 1934 National Firearms Act, inasmuch as it helped validate congressional deletion of all but exotic "gangster weapons" from the category of regulated firearms. Still, the New Deal, by taxing and registering these deadly weapons, had constructed the foundation of a national firearms registration structure. The fact that this structure was never built has resulted in an historical undervaluation of the 1934 law.

Though the president apparently withdrew from his already limited involvement in the gun control debate after 1934, the failure to broaden registration provisions was not the result of government indifference. Throughout the rest of the decade, the Justice Department did not relent in its desire to expand the base of the 1934 act to include other firearms. By the early months of 1935, Attorney General Cummings had already resumed his crusade for registration of revolvers and pistols, but to no avail.[21] Balked in part by interest groups' opposition, the Justice Department evidently decided to practice the art of the possible and to engage in a limited experiment in cooperative compromise. In 1935, a committee, which included representatives from the Senate staff of gun control advocate Royal Copeland, from the Department of Justice, and from the NRA, produced a legislative draft, S.3, which with later amendments would become the Federal Firearms Act of 1938.[22]

A mile wide and an inch deep: the Federal Firearms Act of 1938

Despite the cooperation of both parties to the gun-control controversy in the drafting of S.3, the 1938 act as passed suffered a fate similar to that of the National Firearms Act of 1934. The law did establish a mandatory licensing system for manufacturers, importers, and dealers, under Treasury Department auspices. However, a keystone of the draft bill had been the power to prosecute shippers and manufacturers who put guns into the hands of fugitives or criminals convicted of crimes of violence. The antiregulation forces, however, protested that this stricture would place an unfair burden on the commercial enterprises engaged in gun sales and transport. They offered modifying phrases that assured the act's debilitation; businesses would be liable to penalty only if they could be convicted of "knowing or having reasonable cause to believe" that the purchaser had a criminal background.[23] Despite Assistant Attorney General Joseph Keenan's accurate prediction that the government would be unable to obtain a conviction under that provision, the Commerce Committee nevertheless incorporated the clauses into the final statute.

20. New York Times, 19 May 1934, p. 1.

21. This campaign for a Small Arms Act —to say nothing of the allied recommendation for rifle and shotgun registration—was stillborn in Congress, though it generated endorsements from the American Bar Association, the International Association of Chiefs of Police, and some newspapers. See Homer Cummings to Robert L. Doughton, with attached editorials, 11 April 1938, folder 708, Robert L. Doughton papers in the Southern Historical Collection at the University of North Carolina Library, Chapel Hill, NC.

22. Senate, Committee on Commerce, Hearings on S. 3, 74th Cong., 1st sess., 1935, p. 1; Senate, Congressional Record, 74th Cong., 1st sess., 1935, p. 11973.

23. Senate, Hearings on S.3, 1935, pp. 5 and 15.

The Justice Department, after heading off an NRA proviso in S.3 that would have nullified the federal gun legislation of 1927 and 1934, did halfheartedly acknowledge that it represented an improvement on the status quo.[24] But the department showed open dissatisfaction with the ineffectuality of the proposed law, and held back from active involvement in its passage, fearing that the enactment of S.3 "would militate against the passage" of its own registration bill.[25] S.3, originally formulated by all parties to the controversy, had by a process of revision and deletion effectively become the child of the antiregulators. It passed by unanimous consent in the Senate in 1936 and 1937; the House followed suit on the final day of the 1938 session, and the Federal Firearms Act of 1938 received the president's signature at the end of June. Once again, no fervor greeted this enactment; in fact, it went almost unnoticed by the press. The legislative process had divested the bill of controversial or consequential provisions. Senator Copeland was already claiming in 1936 that "there is no informed person in the United States of America who is not in favor of this bill."[26] This statement was unfortunately a tribute to the bill's negligible impact.

Assessment of federal gun control measures

The trio of federal legislative enactments for firearms regulation in the 1920s and 1930s appears to have established a record of federal intent to address the issue of gun control. Yet it is debatable how much more than this the legislation did. As had been widely predicted, the 1927 closing of the mails to handguns was easily circumvented by using private express companies for mail-order deliveries. The 1934 National Firearms Act, stripped as it was to gangster weapons, seems to have been more effective within its diminutive sphere. Though, by its very nature, the sawed-off shotgun was practically unregulatable, the public market in submachine guns appears to have largely dried up soon after the act's passage.[27] In addition, the fact that this law was made to be broken—gangsters were hardly likely either to pay the intentionally prohibitive tax of $200 on each weapon transfer or to relish the prospect of having their photos and fingerprints taken in order to obtain covered weapons—made it a backhanded law enforcement tool. Thus, for example, possession of a sawed-off shotgun could be grounds for a prison term even if evidence was lacking for the crime in which that weapon was used.

The Federal Firearms Act of 1938, though it nominally covered all firearms, lacked even this tenuous claim of effectiveness. As expected, the "knowing or having reasonable cause to believe" loophole added by firearms interests rendered much of the law unenforceable. The enforcement mechanism itself was crippled by the enforcement agency, the Internal Revenue Service of the Treasury Department. That department could summon up little interest for such a manifestly nonfinancial program. Firearms control thus became a neglected stepchild. The considerable regulatory discretion granted in the act was so sparingly applied that

24. Ibid., pp. 20–21.
25. Ibid., p. 22.
26. Senate, *Congressional Record*, 74th Cong., 2d sess, 1936, p. 2426.

27. Whether this should be attributed to other factors, such as the changing nature of organized crime or the concurrent state anti–machine-gun laws, is, of course, an open question.

gun dealers were not even required to obtain any form of identification from buyers. Clearly this undercut the ban on sending guns to certain out-of-state criminals and other non-residents who had not obtained a required purchase license in their home state. Overall, those who decried the government penchant for throwing money at problems could take comfort from a federal commitment to gun control that as late as 1963 had devoted only 35 person-years to the enforcement of federal firearms laws across the nation.[28] Gun control did not even warrant a title on the office door, as the relevant Treasury Division continued to be known as the Alcohol and Tobacco Tax Division until 1968.

It would hardly be justifiable to condemn this modest record as a perversion of the original legislative intent, as any careful reading of the record of the interwar period would indicate. The passage of legislation without determined enforcement intent is a paradox not without precedent in legislative annals. The 1927 act, as has been shown, was devised more to purge the Post Office of responsibility than to shut down mail-order sales. The key to the paradox in the case of the 1930s legislation lies in the alignment of political forces that produced those

bills, as will become apparent in the next section.

GUN CONTROL AS A CLASH OF CULTURES: THE TRIUMPH OF ORGANIZED INDIVIDUALISM

The gun control debate encompasses a repertoire of arguments with a pedigree dating back at least to the turn of the century. Many of these familiar controversies center on instrumental questions of effectiveness. Almost inevitably, however, the dispute over firearms regulation has not been so much a measured discussion of the means for controlling crime, but a more fundamental clash of world views.[29] From the earliest concealed weapons laws, firearms regulation has been a cultural weapon; at varying times it has been a way of asserting control over "threatening" or low-status groups, such as blacks in the South, youth gangs, or aliens.

More broadly, however, the tone and substance of the gun control debate has been a reflection of divergent responses to what modern America was becoming. On one side could be heard some of the voices of America's ascendant forces: big businessmen and others who predominated on state and national crime commissions and whose interest in economic stability readily carried over into the search for law and order; certain progressive reformers who saw firearms regulation as only part of a general social mobilization against urban problems; and perhaps most prominently, the "expert" professionalizers who saw keeping the peace as the province of organized law enforcement agencies adapting

28. In consequence of the law's defects and of this low allocation of time, arrests under all clauses of the Federal Firearms Act averaged fewer than 100 annually, even in the gun-conscious 1960s. It is further estimated that tens of thousands of fraudulent gun dealers received federal licenses under the Federal Firearms Act, while the act's ban on gun shipments to violent criminals or to nonresidents unqualified for their own state's purchase licenses resulted in almost no convictions. For a useful discussion of the efficacy of both 1930s firearms laws, to which parts of this treatment are indebted, see Franklin E. Zimring, "Firearms and Federal Law: the Gun Control Act of 1968," *J. Legal Studies*, 4:139–42 (Jan. 1975).

29. A similar argument, though a more general one, can be found in Lee Kennett and James L. Anderson, *The Gun in America* (Westport, CT: Greenwood Press, 1975), pp. 254–55.

to a perilous new urban terrain. In their view, modern law enforcement required a legal restructuring that gave more emphasis to their own professional function; police spokesmen were likely, for example, to deprecate the notion that a gun served a valid self-defense function under modern conditions.

On the other side were the spokesmen who cherished the self-reliant citizen of older rural America, where hunting rifles were part of the accession to manhood and where law enforcement was still in part a private responsibility. Thus the emotional fulcrum of the gun control debate was nothing less than a conflicting set of cultural perspectives that, in this instance, wrestled over the proper boundaries between private and public obligations in crime control.

The modern state under the gun

From the defenders of the private sphere of self-protection came appeals against firearms regulation couched in a frontier and even colonial spirit. The evocation of the Second Amendment strictures on preserving a base for citizen militias, loosely construed to extend to the personal protection of the home, linked the modern American with his pistol to his Minuteman forebears facing down the British. It was contended that widespread citizen gun ownership offered insurance against "all the bloody revolutions" and that the "dictatorships of the world have been built upon the disarmament of the common people."[30] Debates over gun control

also elicited the homespun argument that an armed populace was necessary to form a reservoir of volunteer law officers for posse duty.[31] Although this image of explicitly rural self-reliance was rapidly fading from demographic relevance in the face of the largely city-based fears of crime, it constituted an additional link between the citizen's role in earlier times and the desired code of conduct on the mean streets of urban America. By marshaling figures for scattered cities or compilations of newspaper articles reporting specific cases of gun use for self-defense, antiregulation forces pressed the continued value of the firearm as an instrument of self-protection.[32]

The emphasis thus far has been on the importation of older rural values into an urban environment. But although the rural–urban split was an acknowledged factor in the gun control controversy by the interwar period, it would be misleading to let that distinction dominate the clash of cultures. More encompassing than geographic locale was the sense in which the battleground extended to include an assertion of the traditional masculine cultural role, a phenomenon parallel to contemporary conflicts over such male bastions as saloons, red-light districts, or boxing arenas. Hunting and other gun use thus can be seen as one more male preserve threatened by the rising tide of moralism. This outlook is clearly reflected in the editorial position on gun regulation regularly presented in *Field and*

30. Senate, *Hearings* on S.3, 1935, p. 54; NRA press release, in Senate, Committee on Commerce, *To Regulate Commerce in Firearms, Hearings* on S. 885 and S. 2258, 73d Cong. 2d sess., 1934, p. 67.

31. House, *Congressional Record*, 68th Cong., 2d sess., 1924, vol. 66:728.

32. Committee on Ways and Means, *Hearings* on H.R. 9066, 1934, pp. 59 and 113; and Karl T. Frederick, "Pistol Regulation: Its Principles and History," *J. Am. Institute Criminal Law and Criminology*, 23:539 (Aug.–Sept. 1932).

Stream, which frames the issue as a confrontation between real men and less hardy specimens:

Truly we are in a dangerously Puritanical age when a few mollycoddles, with good intentions, can try out their theories for the prevention of crime at the expense of every honest red-blooded man in the land.[33]

The cleavage presented here is further emphasized in the interest group alignment on the gun control issue. Sportsmen's organizations, which touted rifles as a "character builder" while occasionally chastising women for fomenting the firearms controversy out of their instinctive "fear and mistrust" of guns, were pitted against proregulation women's groups, which averred that "the women of the country" hoped that firearms would be treated like "other deadly and antisocial things."[34] Broader even than masculine assertion and rural mores, however, was the essential ideological premise underpinning both, that the true America was and should remain a society of individuals as free as possible from moral meddling on the part of government. Throughout the interwar period, congressional gun control opponents took up these individualist themes in defense of both personal freedom and states' rights.

Less protective of rugged individualism, proponents of gun control tended to emphasize making full use of the capabilities of the modern state to achieve desirable policy consequences. While the opposition might jeer at their "pet theories," the regulators tended to imply in rebuttal that their opponents were not keeping pace with the world, with the clear subtext that citizen self-reliance had become an impossible dream in interwar America. Rejoinders to the social and constitutional arguments against gun control consistently and somewhat condescendingly averted to "the vast change from the conditions to which this part of the Bill of Rights originally applied."[35] Registration schemes were a prime example of the coordinating function of the modern bureaucracy that would inevitably have to displace sporadic and dangerous personal defense. Even the frequent references to the poor comparison between foreign and domestic crime and homicide rates operated to reinforce the central message that the United States was lagging behind other civilized nations in tackling crime effectively. To say that our homicide tally outpaced that of the entire international community combined was to attempt to shame backward America into more serious firearms regulation efforts.

The mobilization of the individualist perspective

In one fundamental sense, the perspective on gun control as a cultural issue can be distorting if it at all implies that the individualist ethos extends to the methods utilized to wage antiregulation campaigns. If anything, the champions of individual rights were decidedly more organized than the regulators. In fact,

33. Cited in "The Necessity of Pistol-Toting," *Literary Digest*, 70:33 (6 Aug. 1921).
34. Bob Nichols, quoted in Kennett and Anderson, p. 215; and Mrs. Geline Bowman, in Attorney General's Conference on Crime, *Proceedings* (Washington, D.C.: n.p., 1934), p. 300. The two million member General Federation of Women's Clubs provided the main organized support outside the Justice Department for pistol regulation in the 1930s.

35. *New York Evening-World,* in "The Battle to Disarm the Gunman," *Literary Digest*, 92:9 (19 Feb. 1927).

the interwar period is notable less for the pervasive impact of its legislation than for the coalescence of the interest group matrix that has resisted firearms legislation ever since.

Although the Justice Department preferred to put the onus for opposition to gun regulation onto the munitions manufacturers, whose unpopularity as "merchants of death" peaked between the wars, the most rigorous and effectual resistance came from sportmen's and wildlife organizations, such as the American Game Association, the National Wildlife Association, the Izaak Walton League, and rifle, pistol, and revolver associations.

Jointly, these groups were to play a decisive role in determining the scope of gun control efforts in the 1920s and 1930s. To understand how this assertion could be valid, one need not resort to conspiracy theories, for the essence of their power was the power of the organized to reshape the aims of government in the face of relative disorganization on the opposing side. The crux of the balance of power between regulators and antiregulators in the interwar period was that the Justice Department fought its gun control crusade with less intense and less mobilized allies, while facing a committed and organized resistance. The consequence was that the nascent national gun lobby was in a strong position, not only to fight gun control, but to co-opt or redefine those initiatives that seemed likely to gain a following.

The history of interwar firearms control outlined here illustrates this point clearly. In the 1920s, opponents of gun regulation faced two challenges: the multiplication of proposed federal initiatives and the unwelcome example of New York's rigorous Sullivan gun law. Although total opposition to all such gun legislation might have been the response to these challenges, canny gun organizations seeking a more profitable approach zeroed in on the vogue for uniform state laws as the essential counterweight. Indeed, the model gun legislation accepted as the Uniform Firearms Act by the National Conference of Commissioners on Uniform State Laws was merely a reworking of the model law championed by the United States Revolver Association.[36]

It was in the 1930s, however, that gun control opponents faced their decisive test. To trace their response to the mounting interest in federal action, it is most useful to focus on the organization that had moved to the forefront of the antiregulation cause, the NRA. The timing of the NRA's emergence as a national force testifies to the galvanizing impact of the federal movement toward firearms regulation. From a roster of 3500 in the early 1920s, the NRA membership rolls expanded to 10 times that many by the time of the legislative debates of 1934, when it had become the "largest association of firearms users in the country and the best organized."[37] Most tellingly, an emerging NRA legislative apparatus crystalized in that same year into an NRA Legislative Division; the organization was thus primed for battle.

Judging by the results, the NRA was more than equal to the task. Its central approach during the New Deal years was never wholly negativist, but the full fruits of its co-optational strategy would become apparent only late in the decade. Miffed by a lack of consultation on

36. John Brabner-Smith, "Firearm Regulation," *Law and Contemporary Problems*, 1:403 (Oct. 1934).

37. Kennett and Anderson, pp. 205–6.

the Justice Department's original draft of the National Firearms Act, the NRA launched a full-fledged campaign of resistance against the 1934 bill. The argument that it was "objectionable in almost every respect and should be killed" was circulated in a stream of letters, press releases, and editorials urging "sportsmen" to telegram or to write congressmen and to lecture local clubs.[38] Congressmen noted the "bitter opposition" expressed in the resultant influx of mail, and the campaign was undoubtedly instrumental in the deletion of reference to all weaponry, save machine guns and sawed-off shotguns, from the law.[39] Thus although a recent NRA source claims that the organization "enthusiastically" supported the act, this manifestly was not the case.[40] Their position at the time was generally pictured as one of "withdrawn" opposition rather than outright advocacy. Nevertheless, the NRA had reason for satisfaction, for their proposed revisions were largely adopted.

In the wake of the 1934 act, the NRA responded to the persistent threat of handgun registration by continuing to lambaste Justice Department proposals editorially, while softening and eventually transforming their position on more circumscribed firearms regulation. Its stance seemed carefully calibrated for just enough flexibility to bleed momentum from the gun control crusade. Evidencing this approach is the path the NRA traveled from coauthor to chief architect of the 1938 act. The NRA's initial collaboration with the Justice Department and congressional representatives in drafting that bill soon gave way to a posture of strategic distance that prompted an exasperated Senator Copeland to snap that the NRA ought to be more forthcoming in support of the bill: "You had a lot to do with writing it. . . . If it isn't a good bill, it is your fault."[41]

Yet the NRA advocated a number of revisions to its legislative offspring, many of which were incorporated into the final statute. Chief among them were the previously mentioned clauses relieving shippers and manufacturers from blame for unknowingly delivering firearms to those the act defined as criminals. In 1937, by the time S.3 finally underwent hearings in the House Interstate and Foreign Commerce Committee, the NRA had unmistakably adopted the bill as its own in a ringing endorsement. In a brief one-day hearing, it was the NRA's Executive Vice-President Milton Reckord who introduced each witness to the committee, marshaling support from the American Legion, the American Wild Life Institute, and major arms manufacturers.[42] The Federal Firearms Act had become the gun lobby's protégé.

It is impossible to fully determine the motivations of the NRA and allied gun organizations in fostering the passage of the Federal Firearms Act. However, the best assessment

38. C. B. Lister to Members and Friends of the National Rifle Association, in Record Group 60, Department of Justice Subject Files—Correspondence, File 80-0, Box 13920, National Archives, Washington, DC. A valuable compendium of these NRA publications is printed in Senate, Committee on Commerce, Hearings on S.885 and S.2258, 1934, pp. 65–83.

39. Senate, Congressional Record, 74th Cong., 1st sess., 1935, p. 11973.

40. James B. Trefether, comp., Americans and Their Guns (Harrisburg, PA: Stackpole Books, 1967), p. 293.

41. Senate, Committee on Commerce, Hearings on S.885 and S.2258, 1934, p. 43.

42. House, Committee on Interstate and Foreign Commerce, Hearings on S.3, 75th Cong., 1st sess., 1937, pp. 6, 17, 18, 22, 23.

on the available evidence is that this legislation constituted an intelligent strategy for deflecting energy and attention from less acceptable approaches to gun control, just as the Justice Department had feared. In fact, the NRA forecasted in May of 1938 that "the passage of this measure would mean the death of the Attorney General's bills" to extend federal registration to handguns.[43] While the impetus for registration may well have been spent by 1938 in any case, it may still have seemed politic for the NRA to make assurance doubly sure by continuing to pursue a defensible anticrime measure.

CONCLUSION

The record of organized antiregulation efforts in the two interwar decades analyzed here emerges as a sustained and a successful campaign to circumscribe the impact of federal activism on behalf of firearms regulation. The persistent and even strident rhetoric of individual self-reliance therefore turned out to overlay the activity of prototypical modern interest groups. Using negotiations and communications skills to mobilize the attentive public on gun issues and to press their case with Congress, the gun lobby helped set the agenda for gun control. It was thus possible to neutralize both an activist Justice Department and the less intense and disorganized majority of the public who favored gun registration.[44] Contemporary historians, perceiving a pattern of susceptibility in New Deal policymaking to groups with defined interests and objectives, would not find this outcome surprising or atypical.

Yet there is an irony in the dynamics of the interwar policy process. The crystalization of firearms regulation as a national concern in a decade of New Deal activism had at last created an environment in which substantive federal legislation could be seriously considered. Yet the threat of such legislation helped launch a national gun lobby. Ultimately, this counterorganization neutralized and outweighed the initial regulatory impulse to the point that the eventual legislative product was a standoff between the regulators and the opposition. Significant federal firearms regulation would have to await the 1960s.

43. Cited in Carl Bakal, *The Right to Bear Arms* (New York: McGraw-Hill Book Co., 1966), p. 177.

44. A 1938 Gallup poll registered 79 percent approval for handgun registration. See Hazel Erskine, "The Polls: Gun Control," *Public Opinion Quarterly*, 37:460(fall 1972).

The Effect of Gun Availability on Violent Crime Patterns

By PHILIP J. COOK

ABSTRACT: Social scientists have started to find answers to some of the questions raised in the ongoing debate over gun control. The basic factual issue in this debate concerns the effect of gun availability on the distribution, seriousness, and number of violent crimes. Some evidence is available on each of these dimensions of the violent crime problem. The distribution of violent crimes among different types of victims is governed in part by the "vulnerability pattern" in weapon choice. The seriousness of robbery and assault incidents is influenced by weapon type, as indicated by the objective dangerousness and instrumental violence pattern. A reduction in gun availability would cause some weapon substitution and probably little change in overall robbery and assault rates—but the homicide rate would be reduced.

Philip J. Cook is an associate professor of public policy studies and economics, Duke University. His research has focused primarily on the criminal justice system and other aspects of social regulation. He has collaborated with Mark H. Moore on a series of studies relating to gun control.

THE DEBATE over the appropriate degree of governmental regulation of firearms has been a prominent feature of the political landscape for the last two decades. The claims and counterclaims for various gun control strategies have been bruited in congressional and state legislative hearings, political campaigns, editorials, and bumper strips. The issues are by this time familiar to even disinterested bystanders: the proper interpretation of the Second Amendment; the value of guns as a means of defense against burglars, or foreign invaders, or local tyrants; the difficulty of depriving criminals of guns without depriving the rest of us of basic rights; and so forth. This "great American gun war"[1] clearly involves both value questions and questions of fact, and the latter have been the subject of numerous statistical skirmishes. Strangely, however, the relevant factual questions have not attracted much attention from scholars until very recently. The role of guns—and other types of weapons—in violent crime is a fit and important subject for scientific inquiry. No etiological theory of violent crime is complete without due consideration of the technology of violent crime. This would be true even in the absence of political interest in gun control.

Each of the major categories of violent crime—criminal homicide, aggravated assault, robbery, and rape—is committed with a variety of weapons. Guns are used in a minority of violent crimes, but are of special concern because they are used in almost two thirds of the most serious events, criminal homicides,

and because, unlike most other commonly used weapons (hands, kitchen knives, and baseball bats), it is conceivable that we might reduce the availability of guns without imposing unacceptable costs on the public. The principal factual question in the gun control debate is whether reducing gun availability would reduce the amount and/or seriousness of violent crime. Can potential violent criminals be deterred from obtaining guns, carrying guns, and using guns in crime? If so, will this reduction in gun use make any difference, or will criminals simply substitute other weapons to equal effect? The answers to these questions are crucial to policy evaluation. Our ability to answer these questions—to make accurate predictions about the effects of legal interventions in this area—is one measure of our scientific understanding of the role of weapons in violent crime.

At the sacrifice of some dramatic tension, I provide a preview of my results here. The type of weapon used in a violent crime is in part determined by the nature of the victim; guns are most likely to be used against the least vulnerable victims in robbery and homicide. The type of weapon used in a violent crime influences the outcome of the crime: gun robberies, when compared with other types of robbery, are more likely to be successful, less likely to result in injury to the victim, and more likely to result in the victim's death; gun assaults are more likely to result in the victim's death than knife assaults, *ceteris paribus*. A general increase in gun availability would probably have little effect on the overall robbery rate, but would increase the homicide rate, including the rate of robbery murder, and possibly reduce

1. A phrase coined by B. Bruce-Briggs, "The Great American Gun War," *The Public Interest*, 45:1–26 (fall 1976).

the number of aggravated assaults. These and other predictions emerge from the empirical results presented here. My overall conclusion is that the technology of violent crime matters a great deal in a number of dimensions, with important implications for the gun control debate.

THE BASIC ISSUES

Gun control measures come in a variety of forms, but most share the objective of reducing the availability of guns for use in violent crime. Most federal and state gun regulations in the United States are moderate interventions intended to reduce criminal use while preserving the majority's access to guns for legitimate uses.[2] Washington, D.C., and New York City have adopted a much broader attack on the handgun problem, with a ban on sales to all but a few people. Whether the regulations are moderate or extreme, some opponents of gun control insist that a regulatory approach will be ineffective in reducing criminal violence. Their position is summarized in two bumper strips: "When guns are outlawed, only outlaws will have guns," and "Guns don't kill people—people kill people." The former suggests that "outlaws" will acquire guns, despite whatever steps are taken to stop them, that is, that criminals will continue to do what is necessary to obtain guns, even if the price, hassle, and legal threats associated with obtaining a gun are increased substantially. The latter bumper strip apparently is meant to suggest that people who decide to kill will find a way even if they do not have access to guns. This is one aspect of a more general issue, the degree of "sub-

stitutibility" between guns and other weapons in homicide and other violent crimes. In short, does the type of weapon matter?

Supposing that we were somehow successful in discouraging some violent people from obtaining guns and using them in crime, how might violent crime patterns change? Three dimensions of the violent crime problem are important: (1) the *distribution* of robberies, aggravated assaults, rapes, and homicides across different types of victims, for example, commercial versus noncommercial robbery; (2) the *seriousness* of robberies, rapes, and aggravated assaults; and (3) the overall *rates* of each of these crimes. These three dimensions are considered in turn in the next three sections.[3]

DISTRIBUTION: THE VULNERABILITY PATTERN

People who attempt robbery or homicide are more likely to succeed with a gun than with other commonly used weapons. A gun is particularly valuable against victims who are physically strong, armed, or otherwise relatively invulnerable—the gun is "the great equalizer." The patterns of weapon use in criminal homicide and robbery demonstrate that perpetrators are most likely to use guns against victims who would have the best chance of defending themselves against other weapons; that is, the likelihood of a gun being chosen by a robber or killer increases with the value of a gun in effecting a successful completion of the crime. These observations suggest that a program that is successful in re-

2. For a summary of federal and state gun control measures, see my article, with James Blose, in this issue.

3. I am indebted to Mark Moore for this approach to carving up the violent crime problem. In the review that follows I omit any discussion of rape, since relevant empirical studies are lacking for this crime.

ducing the rate of gun ownership by potential robbers or killers will change the relative distribution of these crimes among different types of victims. The evidence and implications of the vulnerability pattern are presented in the following sections, beginning with criminal homicide.

Criminal homicide

A decision to kill is easier and safer to implement with a gun than with other commonly available weapons—there is less danger of effective victim resistance during the attack, and the killing can be accomplished more quickly and impersonally, with less sustained effort than is usually required with a knife or blunt object. A gun has greatest value against relatively invulnerable victims, and the vulnerability of the victim appears to be an important factor in determining the probability that a gun will be used as the murder weapon.

The least vulnerable victims are those who are guarded or armed. All presidential assassinations in U.S. history were committed with a handgun or rifle. Almost all law enforcement officers who have been murdered in recent years were shot: in 1978, 91 of 93 murdered officers were killed by guns.[4]

Physical size and strength are also components of vulnerability. In 1977, 68.5 percent of male homicide victims were shot, compared with only 51.0 percent of female homicide victims.[5] The victims' age pattern of

gun use also reflects the vulnerability pattern: about 70 percent of victims aged 20–44 are shot, but this fraction drops off rapidly for younger and older—that is, more vulnerable—victims.[6]

Vulnerability is of course a relative matter. We would expect that the lethality of the murder weapons would be directly related to the difference in physical strength between the victim and killer, other things being equal. To investigate this hypothesis, I used FBI data coded from the supplemental homicide reports submitted for 1976 and 1977 by police departments in 50 large cities. These data include the demographic characteristics of the victim and, where known, the offender, as well as the murder weapon, immediate circumstances, and apparent motive of the crime. The results calculated from these data tend to confirm the relative vulnerability hypothesis. First, women tend to use more lethal weapons to kill their spouses than do men: 97 percent of the women, but only 78 percent of the men, used a gun or knife. The gun fractions in spouse killings are 67 percent and 62 percent, respectively—not a large difference, but one that is notable, since women typically have less experience than men in handling guns and are less likely to think of any guns kept in the home as their personal property. It is also true that women who kill their "boyfriends" are more likely to use a gun than men who kill their "girlfriends."

Table 1 focuses on killings resulting from arguments and brawls in which both the killer and the victim were males. The gun fraction increases with the age of the killer and is inversely related to the age

4. FBI, *Crime in the United States, 1978* (Washington, DC: U.S. Government Printing Office).

5. U.S. Department of Commerce, Bureau of the Census, *Statistical Abstract of the U.S., 1978* (Washington, DC: U.S. Government Printing Office).

6. FBI.

TABLE 1

Gun Use in Murders and Nonnegligent Homicides Resulting from Arguments or Brawls, Male Victim and Male Offender

Victim's Age	Offender's Age		
	18–39	40–59	60+
18–39 (in percentage)	68.0	79.6	87.2
N*	1906	368	47
40–59 (in percentage)	54.5	64.1	66.7
N	398	245	57
60+ (in percentage)	48.3	49.2	63.3
N	58	61	30

Source: FBI Supplemental Homicide Reports, 50 large cities, 1976 and 1977 combined (unpublished).
* N = the sample size, that is, the denominator of the fraction. Cases in which the age of the killer is not known are excluded.

of the victim: the highest gun fraction—87 percent—involves elderly killers and youthful victims; the lowest gun fraction—48 percent—involves youthful killers and elderly victims. Since age is highly correlated with strength and robustness, these results offer strong support for the relative vulnerability hypothesis.

Why are less vulnerable murder victims more likely to be shot than relatively vulnerable victims? A natural interpretation of this result is that intended victims who are physically strong or armed in some fashion are better able to defend themselves against homicidal assault than more vulnerable victims—unless the assailant uses a gun, the "great equalizer." The "vulnerability pattern" can then be explained as resulting from some combination of three mechanisms. (1) Homicidal attacks are more likely to fail against strong victims than weak ones, and the difference in the likelihood of failure is greater for nongun attacks than attacks with a gun. (2) The likelihood that an individual will act on a homicidal impulse depends in part on the perceived probability of success. The intended

victim's ability to defend himself acts as a deterrent to would-be killers—but this deterrent is much weaker if the killer has a gun than otherwise. (3) In the case of a planned murder, the killer will have the opportunity to equip himself with a tool that is adequate for the task. Against well-defended victims, the tool chosen will almost certainly be a gun, if one can be obtained without too much difficulty.

Each of these mechanisms is compatible with the prediction that a reduction in gun availability will cause a reduction in homicide, a reduction that will be concentrated on killings that involve a victim who is physically stronger than the killer. A number of specific hypotheses are suggested by this observation, including the following: a reduction in gun availability will reduce the male:female victimization ratio in killings of spouses and other intimates, reduce the fraction of homicide victims who are youthful males, and reduce the fraction of killers who are elderly.

Robbery

Robbery is defined as theft or attempted theft by means of force or the threat of violence.[7] The robber's essential task is to overcome through intimidation or force the victim's natural tendency to resist parting with his valuables. A variety of techniques for accomplishing this task are used in robbery, including actual attack—as in "muggings" and "yokings"—and the threatening display of a weapon such as a gun, knife, or club. Whatever the means employed, the objective is to quickly gain the victim's compliance or to render him helpless, thereby preventing the victim from escaping, summoning help, or struggling. The amount of what could be called "power"—capability of generating lethal force—the robber needs to achieve these objectives with high probability depends on the characteristics of the robbery target—victim—and in particular on the vulnerability of the target. The most vulnerable targets are people who are young, elderly, or otherwise physically weak or disabled—for example, by alcohol—who are alone and without ready means of escape. The least vulnerable targets are commercial places, especially where there are several customers and clerks and possibly even armed guards—a bank being one extreme example.

A gun is the most effective tool for enhancing the robber's power. Unlike other common weapons, a gun gives a robber the capacity to threaten deadly harm from a distance, thus allowing him to maintain a buffer zone between himself and the victim and to control several victims simultaneously. A gun serves to pre-empt any rational victim's inclination to flee or resist.[8] Wesley Skogan documented the effectiveness of a gun in forestalling victim resistance in his analysis of a national sample of victim-reported robberies:[9] only 8 percent of gun robbery victims resisted physically in noncommercial robberies, compared with about 15 percent of victims in noncommercial robberies involving other weapons.[10] Other types of resistance—arguing, screaming, and fleeing—were also less common in gun robbery than in robbery involving other weapons.

It seems reasonable to assume that, from the robber's viewpoint, the value of employing a gun tends to be inversely related to the vulnerability of the target. A gun will cause a greater increase in the likeli-

7. The perspective of this section was first developed in John Conklin's seminal work on robbery in Boston: *Robbery and the Criminal Justice System* (Philadelphia: J. B. Lippincott, 1972).

8. Ibid., pp. 110–11; Conklin analyzes a gun's usefulness in terms of the ability it provides the robber to (1) maintain a buffer zone; (2) intimidate the victim; (3) make good the threat, if necessary; and (4) ensure escape.

9. Wesley Skogan, "Weapon Use in Robbery: Patterns and Policy Implications," unpublished manuscript (Northwestern University: Center for Urban Affairs, 1978). He used the robbery incident reports collected from the National Crime Panel, which occurred during calendar year 1973. It should be noted that any analysis of victim survey data relies on the victim's impression of the nature of the weapon that was employed in the robbery. In some cases the "gun" may be a toy, or simulated; Floyd Feeney and Adrianne Weir [*The Prevention and Control of Robbery: A Summary*," unpublished manuscript (University of California, Davis: Center on Admin. of Criminal Justice, 1974] report that of 58 "gun" robbers interviewed in Oakland, 3 claimed to have used toys and 4 to have simulated the possession of a gun.

10. Richard Block [*Violent Crime* (Lexington, MA: Lexington Books, 1977)] found from studying robbery police reports in Chicago that victims who resisted with physical force typically (68 percent) did so in response to the robber's use of force. Other types of resistance typically (70 percent) preceded the robber's use of force.

hood of success against well-defended targets than against more vulnerable targets. A strong-arm technique will be adequate against an elderly woman walking alone on the street—a gun would be redundant with such a victim—but a gun is virtually a requirement of successful bank robbery. Skogan provides evidence supporting this claim: he finds little relationship between robbery success rates and weapon type for personal robbery, but a very strong relationship for commercial robbery. He reports that success rates in commercial robbery were 94 percent with a gun, 65 percent with a knife, and 48 percent with other weapons.[11]

In economic terms, we can characterize robbery as a production process with weapons, robbers, and a target as "inputs."[12] The "output" of the production process can be defined as the probability of success. This probability increases with the number and skill of the robbers, the vulnerability of the target, and the lethal effect of the weapons. For given robber and target characteristics, the "marginal product" of a gun can be defined as the increase in probability of success if the robber(s) substitute a gun for, say, a knife. The evidence presented in the preceding paragraphs suggests that the marginal product of a gun is small against vulnerable targets and is relatively large against well-defended targets. We can go one step further and define the "value of a gun's marginal product" as its marginal product (increase in success probability) multiplied by the amount of loot if the robbery is successful. Since for obvious reasons, targets with greater potential loot tend to be better defended against robbery,[13] the *value* of the gun's marginal product is even more strongly related to target vulnerability than is the marginal product of the gun. The conclusion can be put in the form of a proposition:

The economic value of a gun in robbery tends to be greatest against commercial targets and other well-defended targets, and least against highly vulnerable targets.

It makes good economic sense, then, for gun use in robbery to be closely related to target vulnerability. This is indeed the case, as demonstrated in Table 2, which is based on tabulating results of more than 12,000 robbery reports taken from victim survey data gathered in 26 large cities.

From Table 2, we see that 55 percent of gun robberies committed by adults, but only 13 percent of other adult armed robberies, involve commercial targets. Those relatively few gun robberies that were committed against people on the street are concentrated on relatively invulnerable targets—groups of two or more victims or prime-age males—while street robbery with other weapons was more likely to involve women, children, and elderly victims. Skogan

11. Skogan.

12. This perspective is further developed in Philip J. Cook, "The Effect of Gun Availability on Robbery and Robbery Murder: A Cross Section Study of Fifty Cities," in *Policy Studies Review Annual*, eds. Robert H. Haveman and B. Bruce Zellner, Vol. 3 (Beverly Hills, CA: Sage, 1979), pp. 752–53 (hereafter cited as "The Effect of Gun Availability").

13. It is obvious that commerical targets tend to be more lucrative than noncommercial and that a group of two or more victims will be more lucrative on the average than a single victim. Feeney and Weir (p. 24) report the not-so-obvious result that robberies of male victims resulted in a much higher median take ($50) than robberies of female victims (less than $20).

TABLE 2

DISTRIBUTION OF ROBBERIES (IN PERCENTAGE)

ALL ROBBERIES ACROSS LOCATIONS			
	GUN	KNIFE OR OTHER WEAPON	UNARMED
Commercial	55.1	13.3	19.1
Residence	6.4	10.4	8.5
Street, vehicle, and so forth	38.5	76.3	72.4
Total	100.0	100.0	100.0

STREET ROBBERIES BY VICTIM CHARACTERISTICS			
	GUN	KNIFE OR OTHER WEAPON	UNARMED
Male victim age 16–54	59.8	53.8	41.1
Two or more victims	10.5	5.8	3.7
All others (young, elderly, and/or female victim)	29.7	40.4	55.2
Total	100.0	100.0	100.0

SOURCE: Adapted from Philip J. Cook, "Reducing Injury and Death Rates in Robbery," p. 43. © 1980 by The Regents of the University of California. Reprinted from *Policy Analysis*, Volume 6, No. 1 (Winter 1980), by permission of The Regents. The distributions are calculated from National Crime Panel victimization survey data of 26 cities.

NOTE: All incidents involved at least one male robber age 18 or over. Entries in the table reflect survey sampling weights.

provides further detail for commercial robberies, reporting that the likelihood that a gun is present in such robberies is only 44 percent for commercial places that have only one employee, but 68 percent for commercial places with two or more employees.[14]

What is the causal process that produces these patterns in gun robbery? There are two plausible explanations, both compatible with the evidence presented in the preceding paragraphs: (1) robbers who aspire to well-defended, lucrative targets equip themselves with a gun in order to increase their chance of success or (2) robbers who happen to have a gun are more tempted to rob lucrative, well-defended targets than robbers who lack this tool. In short, the question is whether the weapon is chosen to suit the task or, rather, the available weapon helps define the task. There is doubtless some truth in both explanations.

The first explanation suggests that the observed relationship between gun use and target choice is the result of differences between the kinds of people that rob lucrative targets and those who commit relatively petty street robberies—a difference reminiscent of John Conklin's distinction between "professionals" and "opportunists."[15] Victim survey evidence does suggest that gun robbers as a group have more of the earmarks of professionalism than other armed robbers: besides the fact that they make bigger "scores," gun robbers are older, less likely to rob acquaintances, and less likely to work in large groups of three or more. The factors that determine a robber's choice of weapon have some tendency to persist: a cohort of adult

14. Ibid., calculated from figures in his Table 3.

15. Ibid.

men arrested for gun robbery in the District of Columbia showed a greater propensity to use guns in subsequent robberies than the corresponding cohort of nongun robbery arrestees.[16]

It seems reasonable to hypothesize, then, that robbers who engage in planning and who seek out big scores will take pains to equip themselves with the appropriate weapon —usually some type of firearm. The frequency with which other less professional robbers use guns, and hence the kinds of targets they choose, may be more sensitive to the extent to which such people have access to guns and are in the habit of carrying them, for whatever reason. Increased availability of guns may then result in some target switching by this group—substitution of more lucrative, better-defended targets for more vulnerable targets. Increased gun availability may also result in weapon substitution for a given type of target, implying an increase in the fraction of street robberies committed with a gun; that is, guns will be put to less valuable uses, as guns become "cheaper." These hypotheses can be stated more precisely as follows:

16. Philip J. Cook and Daniel Nagin, *Does the Weapon Matter?* (Washington, DC: Institute for Law and Social Research, 1979). The results cited here are based on 541 adult male gun robbery arrestees and 761 nongun robbery arrestees. This cohort, which was arrested in 1973, was tracked through 1976 through Prosecutor's Management Information System (PROMIS). The robbery re-arrest rate for the gun cohort was 43 percent, of which 58 percent were gun robberies. The robbery re-arrest rate for the nongun cohort was 45 percent, of which 40 percent were gun robberies. The two cohorts had the same re-arrest rate for burglary (13 percent), but the nongun cohort was much more likely to be re-arrested for assaultive crimes (22 percent, as opposed to 13 percent for the gun cohort); see Table 9 of Cook and Nagin.

An increase in gun availability in a city will (1) increase the fraction of noncommercial robberies commited with a gun and (2) increase the fraction of robberies committed against commercial and other well-defended targets.

In an earlier study of robbery patterns across 50 cities,[17] I found some confirmation for the first of these two predictions; controlling for other robbery-related variables, the fraction of robberies committed with a gun increases with the density of gun ownership in a city. A 10 percent increase in the fraction of households that owns guns is associated with approximately a 5 percent increase in the rate of gun robbery.

Conclusions

The preceding evidence demonstrates the existence of an important vulnerability pattern in weapon choice in homicide and robbery. Guns give assailants the power to succeed in killing or robbing relatively invulnerable victims who would have a good chance of fending off attack with a less lethal weapon. If some potential killers were deprived of guns, the criminal homicide rate would be reduced. The reduction would be concentrated among the least vulnerable types of potential victims—law enforcement officers, people with bodyguards, husbands of homicidal women, youthful men, and so forth. If robbers were deprived of guns, there would be a reduction in robberies against commercial places and other well-defended victims. In general, a reduction in gun availability would change the distribution of violent crimes, with greater concentration on vulnerable victims.

17. Cook "The Effect of Gun Availability."

SERIOUSNESS: THE OBJECTIVE DANGEROUSNESS PATTERN

Recall that I am concerned with three dimensions of violent crime: the distribution, the seriousness, and the number of incidents. The vulnerability pattern suggests that gun availability will in certain respects influence the distribution of robberies and homicides across different categories of victims. I now turn to the seriousness dimension of violent crime. "Seriousness" in this discussion will be defined as the degree of injury to the victim. A violent or potentially violent confrontation, as in robbery, rape, or assault, can result in a range of possible outcomes, from no physical harm up to serious injury or death of the victim. The likelihood that the victim will be killed is influenced by the lethal effects of the weapon used by the perpetrator. The evidence on this "objective dangerousness" pattern is presented first for serious assaults, and subsequently for robbery.

Serious assaults

The fraction of serious gun assaults that result in the victim's death is much higher than for assaults with other weapons. Richard Block, for example, found that of all aggravated assaults resulting in injury to the victim—and reported to the Chicago Police—14 percent of the gun cases, but only 4 percent of the knife cases, resulted in the victim's death.[18] In part, this difference is the result of differences between gun and knife attacks in intent and capability. An assailant who intends to kill his victim, and who has some chance to prepare, is more likely to equip himself with a gun than an assailant who merely intends to hurt his victim. Furthermore, an attack that is intended to kill is more likely to be successful if perpetrated with a gun than with a knife or other weapon—especially against victims who are capable of defending themselves. But differences in intent and capability are not the whole story.

Franklin Zimring has demonstrated that a large proportion of murders are similar to serious assaults in that the attacks are unsustained[19]—the assailant does not administer the coup de grace, the blow that would ensure the death of his victim. Indeed, the victim was shot only once in about two thirds of the gun homicides in Zimring's Chicago samples. These cases differ very little from serious assaults: for every death resulting from a single wound in the head or chest, Zimring found 1.8 victims with the same type of wound who did not die[20]—victims who were clearly not saved by any differences in the gunman's intent or capability, but rather just by good luck with respect to the precise location of the wound.

Evidently, some proportion of gun murders are not the result of a clear intent to kill; given that the majority of murders are the immediate result of altercations, often involving alcohol and rarely much thought, it seems unlikely that many killers have any clearly formulated "intent" at the time of their attack. The assailant's mental state is characterized by an impulse—to punish, avenge an insult, or stop a verbal or physical attack—backed by more or less

18. Ibid., p. 33

19. Franklin Zimring, "The Medium is the Message: Firearm Calibre as a Determinant of Death from Assault," *J. Legal Studies,* I(1): 97–124 (Jan. 1972); and idem, "Is Gun Control Likely to Reduce Violent Killings?" *Univ. Chicago Law Review,* 35:721–37 (1967).

20. Ibid., computed from Table 7, p. 104.

cathexis. The immediate availability of a gun makes these circumstances more dangerous than would a less lethal weapon because an unsustained attack with a gun—a single shot—is more likely to kill than an unsustained attack with another weapon.

Zimring buttressed the conclusions from his first study, which compared knife and gun attacks, with a later study comparing large and small caliber gun attacks. Even after controlling for the number and location of wounds, he found that .38 caliber attacks were more than twice as likely to kill as .22 caliber attacks.[21] It appears, then, that weapon dangerousness has a substantial independent impact on the death rate from serious assaults.

Zimring's seminal work in this area supports several important propositions, including:

1. A restrictive gun control policy that causes knives and clubs to be substituted for guns will reduce the death rate in serious assault.

2. A gun control policy that focuses on handguns may increase the death rate from gun assault if shotguns and rifles are substituted for handguns as a result.[22]

3. In setting prosecution and sentencing priorities for aggravated assault cases, gun assaults should be viewed as more serious than assaults with other weapons, ceteris paribus, since there is a higher probability of the victim's dying in the gun assaults. This is Zimring's "objective dangerousness" doctrine.[23]

Richard Block extended Zimring's work on instrumentality by comparing death rates in aggravated assault and robbery cases. He concludes that "the relative fatality of different weapons in violent crime may be a technological invariant— . . . the probability of death given injury and a particular weapon remains relatively constant and unrelated to the type of crime committed."[24]

The notion that the number of deaths per 100 injuries is a "technical" constant, largely determined by the lethality of the weapon, is not supportable, however. Zimring demonstrated that the type of weapon was one important determinant of the outcome of serious attacks, but did not claim it was the only determinant. Presumably the weapon-specific death rates in such attacks will differ across jurisdictions and vary over time depending on the mix of circumstances, the quality of medical care, and so forth. Arthur Swersey presents an interesting case in point.[25]

Swersey reports that the number of assaultive—as opposed to felony—gun homicides in Harlem increased from 19 in 1968 to 70 in 1973, and then fell back to 46 in 1974. Much of the change between 1968 and 1973 was from an increase in intentional killings resulting from disputes involving narcotics activities. The importance of changes in the intent of violent perpetrators during this period is indicated by the fact that the death rate in gun attacks doubled between 1968 and 1973, and then fell back in 1974. Swersey concludes that more than 80 percent

21. Ibid., 1972.

22. This implication has been pointed out by Gary Kleck, "The Assumptions of Gun Control" (Florida State University, 1980) (unpublished).

23. "In the generality of cases, how likely is it that conduct such as that engaged in by the offender will lead to death?" Zimring, p. 114.

24. Block, p. 32.

25. "A Greater Intent to Kill: The Changing Pattern of Homicide in Harlem and New York City" (Yale School of Organization and Management, 1980) (unpublished).

TABLE 3

LIKELIHOOD OF PHYSICAL ATTACK AND INJURY IN ROBBERY (IN PERCENTAGE)

	GUN*	KNIFE†	OTHER WEAPON	UNARMED
Noncommercial robbery**				
Victim attacked	22.1	39.4	60.4	73.5
Victim required medical treatment††	7.2	10.9	15.5	11.1
Victim hospitalized overnight	2.0	2.6	2.7	1.6
Number of cases (not in percentage)	892	841	1060	1259
Commercial robbery				
Victim required medical treatment	4.8	10.8	17.9	5.1
Victim hospitalized overnight	1.5	3.5	6.0	0.4
Number of cases (not in percentage)	2307	288	117	570

SOURCE: National Crime Panel victimization surveys of 26 cities. This table is excerpted from Philip J. Cook, "Reducing Injury and Death Rates in Robbery," Table 2. © 1980 by The Regents of the University of California. Reprinted from *Policy Analysis*, Volume 6, No. 1 (Winter 1980), by permission of The Regents.
NOTE: All incidents included in this table involved at least one male robber age 18 or over. Entries in the table do not reflect the survey sampling weights, which differed widely among the 26 cities.
* Many robberies involve more than one type of weapon. Incidents of that sort were classified according to the most lethal weapon used.
** Robberies occurring on the street, in a vehicle, or near the victim's home.
† Only about one third of the injured gun robbery victims were actually shot. Two thirds of the injured knife robbery victims were stabbed.

of the rise and fall in Harlem homicides was due to changes in the number of deliberate murders. He finds a similar pattern for the rest of New York City.[26]

Swersey's findings do not undermine Zimring's position. Zimring did not deny that some killings were unambiguously motivated, or that the importance of intent in murder was subject to change over time, or that it might be more important in Harlem than in Chicago. In any event, Swersey's results are useful in documenting these possibilities.

My conclusions can be briefly stated. The likelihood of death from a serious assault is determined, *inter alia*, by the assailant's intent and the lethal nature of the weapon he uses. The type of weapon is especially important when the intent is ambig-

26. Swersey also notes several other indications of an increasing fraction of deliberate murders in the homicide statistics for New York City as a whole. During the 1970s, the clearance rate declined for homicide, as did the fraction of homicides occurring on the weekend and the fraction involving family members.

uous. The fraction of homicides that can be viewed as deliberate—unambiguously intended—varies over time and space, but is probably fairly small as a rule. The fraction of gun assaults that results in the death of the victim is one indication of the relative prevalence of deliberate gun murders.

Robbery

The principal role of a weapon in robbery is to aid the robber in coercing the victim—either by force or threat—to part with his valuables. If the threat is sufficiently convincing, physical force is not necessary. For this reason, it is hardly surprising that the use of force is closely related to the weapon type in robbery, being very common in unarmed robbery and rare in gun robbery. Table 3 documents this pattern for both commercial and noncommercial robberies committed by adult males. As shown in this table, gun robberies are less likely than other armed robberies to involve physical violence and, furthermore, are less likely to injure the victim.[27] These patterns are compatible with the notion that violence plays an instrumental role in robbery—that it is employed when the robber believes it is needed to overcome or forestall victim resistance and that this need is less likely to arise when the robber uses a gun than otherwise.

There is evidence, however, that this "instrumental violence" pattern can account for only a fraction of the injuries and deaths that result from robbery. Three observations are relevant in this respect. First, over two thirds of victims injured in noncommercial gun robberies do not resist in any way—even after the attack;[28] similarly, 20 out of 30 victims killed in gun robberies in Dade County between 1974 and 1976 did not resist the robber. Second, the likelihood that the victim will be injured in an armed robbery is much higher if the robbery is committed by a gang of three or more than otherwise; since victims are less likely to offer resistance to a group of three or four robbers than to a lone robber, this result is clearly incompatible with the "instrumental violence" hypothesis. Third, judging from re-arrest statistics for a large cohort of adult robbery arrestees in Washington, D.C., it appears that robbers who injure their victims tend to be more violence prone than other robbers.[29]

These findings are different aspects of an "excess violence" pattern: much of the violence in robbery is not "necessary," in the sense of being an instrumental response to anticipated or actual resistance by the victim. Rather, it is motivated by objectives or impulses that have little to do with ensuring successful completion of the theft. In particular, the high incidence of violence in street robberies committed by larger groups—which typically have a low "take"—is best viewed as a form of recreation, and the gratuitous violence against the victim may be just part of the fun.

Given these findings, it is useful to attempt a distinction between "robbery with intent to injure" or kill and robbery without such intent—in which violence would only be used to overcome victim resistance. The latter form of robbery dominates the statistics—most victims are not in fact injured, and the likelihood of injury is less with guns than with other weapons. However, the more violent strain of robbery, involving an intent to injure, apparently accounts for a high percentage of the serious injuries and deaths that do occur in the robbery context. Furthermore, the incidence of excess violence in robbery is subject to change over time, as Zimring demonstrated in his study of robbery murder in Detroit.[30] He found a sharp discontinuity in 1972 in the fraction of victims killed in armed robbery: after 10 years of stable weapon-specific death rates, this fraction doubled between 1971 and 1973 for gun robberies and increased even more during this period for other armed robberies.

27. Other sources on this pattern include Conklin; Skogan; and Philip J. Cook, "A Strategic Choice Analysis of Robbery" in *Sample Surveys of the Victims of Crimes*, ed. Wesley Skogan (Cambridge, MA: Ballinger, 1976) (hereafter cited as "A Strategic Choice Analysis of Robbery").

28. Philip J. Cook, "Policies to Reduce Injury and Death Rates in Robbery," *Policy Analysis*, 6(1):36 (winter 1980) (hereafter cited as "Policies to Reduce Injury and Death Rates").

29. Cook and Nagin, p. 39.

30. Franklin Zimring, "Determinants of the Death Rate from Robbery: A Detroit Time Study," *J. Legal Studies*, 6(2):317–32 (June 1977).

Are gun robberies more dangerous than other armed robberies, in the sense of being more likely to result in the victim's death? Victims are killed in a higher fraction of gun robberies than others: based on victim surveys and homicide data in eight cities, I calculated that there are 9.0 victim fatalities for every 1000 gun robberies, compared with 1.7 victim fatalities per 1000 nongun armed robberies.[31] Furthermore, it appears that the type of weapon plays an independent role in determining the likelihood of robbery murder; in a cross-sectional analysis of 50 cities, I found that the fraction of robberies resulting in the victim's death is closely related to the fraction of robberies that involve firearms.[32] Thus the objective dangerousness pattern applies to robbery as

31. Cook, "Policies to Reduce Injury and Death Rates," p. 39.
32. Cook, "The Effect of Gun Availability," p. 775. The regression equation is as follows:

$$\frac{\text{Robbery murders}}{1000 \text{ robberies}}$$

$$= \underset{(1.16)}{1.52} + \underset{(2.38)}{5.68} \ \frac{\text{Gun robberies}}{\text{Robberies}}$$

A closely related result uses the per capita, rather than "per robbery," murder rate:

$$\frac{\text{Rob. murders}}{100,000} = \underset{(.232)}{-.284} + \underset{(.089)}{.907} \ \frac{\text{Gun robs.}}{1000}$$

$$+ \underset{(.072)}{.136} \ \frac{\text{Nongun robs.}}{1000} .$$

(Numbers in parentheses are the standard errors of the ordinary least squares regression coefficients.) The data for 50 cities are 1975–76 averages. The second equation has an $R^2 = .82$, suggesting that robbery murder is very closely linked to robbery. Inclusion of the assaultive murder rate in this equation as an independent variable does not affect the other coefficients much—and the coefficient on the murder variable is not statistically significant. I conclude that robbery murder is more robbery than murder.

well as assault, for reasons that remain a bit obscure.

Why does the presence of a loaded, authentic gun in robbery increase the probability of the victim's death? My studies of robbery murder in Atlanta and Dade County[33] indicated that in at least half of the cases the killing was deliberate: for example, the victim was tied and then executed, or shot several times from close range. But insofar as intent could be ascertained from police reports, it appears that these intentional killings were not premeditated, but rather decided on during the course of the robbery. Perhaps the explanation for why these spontaneous decisions are more likely to occur when the robber is holding a gun is related to Marvin Wolfgang's suggestion: "The offender's physical repugnance to engaging in direct physical assault by cutting or stabbing his adversary, may mean that in the absence of a firearm no homicide occurs."[34]

Two conclusions can be inferred from the preceding discussion:

1. A reduction in gun availability will increase the robbery injury rate,[35] but reduce the robbery murder rate.

2. Given the excess violence pattern in robbery, the robbery cases in which the victim is injured should be allocated special emphasis in establishing criminal prosecution and sentencing priorities.[36] In a high proportion of these crimes, the attack that caused the injury was not instrumental to the robbery, but

33. Cook, "Policies to Reduce Injury and Death Rates."
34. Marvin Wolfgang, *Patterns in Criminal Homicide* (Philadelphia: University of Pennsylvania, 1958), p. 79.
35. See Skogan.
36. Cook, "Policies to Reduce Injury and Death Rates."

rather was a distinct act. A relatively severe judicial response to such cases might act as a deterrent to excess violence in robbery.

Coercion and assault

Does the instrumental violence pattern in robbery have any parallel in assault? I suspect the answer is yes, but I know of no empirical evidence.

Some unknown fraction of assault cases are similar to robbery in that the assailant's objective is to coerce the victim's compliance—the assailant wants the victim to stop attacking him, physically or verbally, or stop dancing with his girlfriend, or get off his favorite barstool, or turn down the stereo. And, as in the case of robbery, the probability of a physical attack in such cases may be less if the assailant has a gun than otherwise because the victim will be less inclined to ignore or resist a threat enforced by the display of a gun. It may also be true that the assailant would be more hesitant to use a gun than another weapon to make good his threat. If this reasoning is correct, than a general increase in gun availability may reduce the number of assault-related injuries.

INCIDENCE: THE SUBSTITUTION PATTERN

The preceding evidence suggests that gun availability has a substantial effect on the distribution and seriousness of violent crime. The third dimension of the violent crime problem is incidence—the number of violent confrontations and attacks. For each of the crimes under consideration—assault, robbery, and homicide—a reduction in gun availability to criminals would presumably cause a reduction in the number of incidents involving guns. But for each crime there is a real possibility that the number of incidents involving weapons other than guns would increase as a result of the reduction in gun availability. If this weapon substitution does occur, the net effect of reduced gun availability on crime rates could be either positive or negative.

First, consider the crime of assault. In an environment in which a high percentage of the violence-prone people carry guns, it is possible that a sort of mutual deterrent is created, whereby a rational person would think twice before picking a fight. A protagonist that is foolish enough to start a fight in such an environment may be persuaded to back off if his intended victim pulls a gun. When physical attacks do occur, they are likely to be perpetrated with a gun and to be serious. This line of argument may explain why the Bartley-Fox Amendment in Massachusetts—an anticarrying law that was apparently quite effective—may have resulted in an increase in the rate of aggravated assaults—the gun assault rate went down substantially following implementation, but the non-gun assault rate increased even more.[37] A legal intervention that is successful in getting guns off the streets may encourage relatively harmless fights with fists and broken bottles. Definitive results in this area are hard to come by, in part due to the difficulty in measuring the assault rate in a consistent manner over time or across jurisdictions.

My cross-sectional analysis of robbery in 50 cities found that one measure of gun availability—the

37. Glenn L. Pierce and William J. Bowers, "The Impact of the Bartley-Fox Gun Law on Crime in Massachusetts," unpublished manuscript (Northeastern University: Center for Applied Social Research, 1979).

density of gun ownership—was statistically unrelated to the overall robbery rate when other causal factors were taken into account.[38] By way of illustration, the two cities with the highest robbery rates—Detroit and Boston—differed markedly in gun ownership. Boston was one of the lowest, and Detroit was above average. The same study demonstrated that the fraction of robberies committed with a gun was closely related to the density of gun ownership in the city. Apparently robbers tend to substitute guns for other weapons as guns become readily available, but with little or no change in their rate of commission.

If guns were less widely available, the criminal homicide rate would fall. This prediction is justified by three distinct arguments developed in this article: (1) knives and clubs are not close substitutes for guns for implementing a decision to kill, especially when the intended victim is relatively invulnerable; (2) Zimring's "objective dangerousness" results demonstrate that a reduction in gun use in serious—but ambiguously motivated—assaults will reduce the homicide rate, and (3) my results on robbery murder in the 50-cities study indicate that the fraction of robberies that result in the victim's death is closely related to the fraction of robberies involving guns. A final bit of evidence comes from evaluations of the Bartley-Fox Amendment, which suggest that it reduced the criminal homicide rate in Massachusetts.[39] The tough new handgun law in the District of Columbia has also apparently been effective in this regard.[40] It should be noted that a

38. Cook, "The Effect of Gun Availability."
39. See the article by Pierce and Bowers in this issue.
40. See Jones's article in this issue.

crackdown focused on the least lethal type of gun—small caliber handguns—might not have the desired effect on criminal homicide if perpetrators substituted large caliber handguns or longguns.

My conclusion is that effective gun control measures are unlikely to reduce the total number of violent confrontations and attacks, but may well reduce the criminal homicide rate.

CONCLUSIONS

The type of weapon matters in violent crime, both in terms of its seriousness and its distribution. If robbers could be deprived of guns, the robbery murder rate would fall, the robbery injury rate would rise, and robberies would be redistributed to some extent from less to more vulnerable targets. The assaultive murder rate would decline, with the greatest reductions involving the least vulnerable victims. The overall assault rate might well increase. These predictions are based on common sense and a variety of empirical observations. None of this evidence is conclusive, but it is the best that is currently available.

Is it reasonable to suppose that moderate gun control measures have the potential to discourage some violent criminals—potential or active—from obtaining guns? No doubt there are some active criminals and other violence-prone people who have the incentive and resources required to acquire a gun even in the face of substantial legal barriers. But such determined people do not figure importantly in the violent crime statistics—indeed, most assaults and robberies do not even involve guns now, despite the fact that guns are readily available in most jurisdictions. A gun control measure that increases the average cost and hassle of a youthful urban male acquiring his first handgun may at least delay acquisition for a year or two—with noticeable effect on the gun crime rate. A vigorous crackdown on carrying concealed weapons may have a similar beneficial effect.

Not all of the predicted effects on violent crime of a reduction in gun availability are attractive. None of these predictions can be made with a high degree of certainty. But it is not unreasonable to suggest that a moderate, vigorously enforced program for regulating the sale and use of guns would save a substantial number of lives. Gun control is not "the solution" to America's violent crime problem, but perhaps it should be one aspect of the effort to find a solution.

State Programs for Screening Handgun Buyers

By PHILIP J. COOK and JAMES BLOSE

ABSTRACT: Three to five million handguns change hands each year. Almost half the states—including 64 percent of the population—require that buyers be screened by the police, with the objective of preventing certain groups of potentially dangerous people—felons, fugitives, ex-mental patients, drug addicts, and so forth—from obtaining handguns. These state systems operate within the federal framework created by the Gun Control Act of 1968, which requires that most all interstate transactions in firearms be handled by federally licensed dealers or manufacturers. The states' main problems are (1) weak federal regulation of licensees, (2) incomplete state criminal history files, and (3) the difficulty of regulating hand-to-hand transactions in used handguns. States that wish to increase the effectiveness of their screening systems will probably have to assume responsibility for regulating retail dealers and will have to institute civil liability for dealers and individual gun owners, together with a more comprehensive registration system, to make the screening system more difficult to circumvent.

Philip J. Cook is an associate professor of public policy studies and economics, Duke University. His research has focused primarily on the criminal justice system and other aspects of social regulation. He has collaborated with Mark H. Moore on a series of studies relating to gun control.

James Blose is a researcher specializing in criminal justice programs. He has held positions with several state and local agencies, most recently as the acting director of the Statistical Analysis Center, Massachusetts Committee on Criminal Justice.

NOTE: Research for this study was supported by the Ford Foundation and the Center for the Study and Prevention of Handgun Violence.

DURING the 13 years since enactment of the Gun Control Act of 1968, Congress has given short shrift to the gun control issue. A number of bills have been introduced since then, but none were enacted. The agency assigned the task of enforcing the Gun Control Act, the Treasury Department's Bureau of Alcohol, Tobacco, and Firearms (BATF), has been funded at a level that has guaranteed a lack of vigorous enforcement. In the federal arena, anti–gun control forces have been supremely effective in blocking the public majority's demand for more stringent regulation of firearms. These facts are well known and have moved pro–gun control commentators to public despair. Not as well known is the fact that many states have enacted legislation, much of it during the last decade, that goes rather far beyond the federal legislation in regulating the transfer and possession of handguns. In this article, we document and assess this increasingly important role for the states in gun control, with a focus on the nature and reliability of state systems for screening handgun buyers.

In the first major section, we characterize the primary alternative approaches for controlling firearms. The second major section focuses on one of these approaches—screening buyers through a gun permit or application to purchase system, whereby felons and other people judged too dangerous may be prevented from acquiring a gun. Almost two thirds of the U.S. population resides in states that have enacted a screening system of this type. These state systems differ in a number of respects, but share the problems of inadequate criminal history files and widespread circumvention of the screening requirement. The third major section discusses one set of proposals for reducing the rate of circumvention—those embodied in Senator Kennedy's Handgun Crime Control Act of 1979. In a concluding section, we argue that despite the apparent ease with which screening systems can be circumvented, such systems may be capable of effecting a modest reduction in gun violence rates.

STRATEGIES FOR CONTROLLING GUNS

Firearms are an important part of American life. About half of all U.S. households possess at least one gun, usually acquired for a legitimate purpose such as hunting, target shooting, self-defense, or collecting.[1] Relatively few of these guns will ever be used against people. The ideal gun control measure would reduce the use of firearms against people —except possibly in self-defense against criminals—while preserving legitimate uses and imposing minimal costs on legitimate gun owners, taxpayers, and the criminal justice system.

The most important program we have for reducing the use of firearms against people is, of course, the criminal justice system's (CJS) efforts to deter violent crime and incapacitate violent criminals. Traditionally the CJS has treated robberies, rapes, and assaults committed with deadly weapons as more serious than otherwise similar crimes that were committed without such a weapon. In recent years several states have enacted sentencing provisions that distinguish between the use of firearms and other deadly weapons in violent crime, stipulating

1. James D. Wright and Linda L. Marston, "The Ownership of the Means of Destruction: Weapons in the United States," *Social Problems*, 23(1):93 (Oct. 1975).

especially severe penalties for firearms use.[2] If the CJS and other institutions of social control were effective in keeping criminal violence rates low, then other approaches to controlling criminal gun use would be of relatively little value. But the U.S. has been afflicted with violent crime in epidemic proportions for more than a decade.

Given the failure of criminal law enforcement efforts to contain violent crime, it is arguably worthwhile to attempt to preempt the use of guns against people by regulating the transfer and use of firearms. Our focus in this article is on one of the important gun control strategies: a permit or application to purchase system designed to discourage dangerous people from obtaining firearms. A brief review of alternative strategies serves as a useful background for this focus.

The basic notion motivating most gun control legislation is as follows: the danger that a particular gun poses to the community differs widely depending on the type of gun, the characteristics of its owner, and the place and manner in which the gun is stored or transported. Gun control ordinances discriminate on each of these dimensions. Some types of guns are subjected to more stringent regulation than others; some people are proscribed from owning guns, while others remain entitled; some uses of guns, for example, carrying concealed, are subjected to much more stringent regulation than other uses. Through discrimination policies of this sort it may be possible

to reduce the gun crime problem while preserving most people's entitlement to own most types of guns and use them for sporting or other legitimate purposes.

First, federal and state laws regulate some types of firearms more stringently than others. The first important federal legislation that had this effect, the National Firearms Act of 1934, "was a concerted attack on civilian ownership of machine guns, sawed-off shotguns, silencers, and other relatively rare firearms that had acquired reputations as gangster weapons during the years preceding its passage."[3] Specifically, this act imposed a $200 tax on each transfer of one of these weapons, and required that owners register them with the Bureau of Alcohol, Tobacco, and Firearms (BATF).

There are other important examples of discrimination between types of firearms: the federal Gun Control Act of 1968 bans the importation of short-barreled or low-quality handguns—often referred to as "Saturday Night Specials"—although it does not ban the domestic manufacture of such guns. A number of state ordinances regulate handguns of all sorts more stringently than longguns. The reason for this last distinction is readily apparent: despite the fact that there are about three times as many longguns as handguns in circulation, handguns dominate the gun crime statistics, accounting for more than three quarters of the gun murders and assaults and more than 90 percent of the gun

2. For a normative discussion of this new development in the criminal law, see Philip J. Cook, "Reducing Inquiry and Death Rates in Robbery," *Policy Analysis* 6(1):21–45 (winter 1980). See also Colin Loftin's article in this issue.

3. Franklin Zimring "Firearms and the Federal Law: The Gun Control Act of 1968," *Legal Studies*, IV(1):138 (Jan. 1975). Information on state laws in subsequent sections is taken from James Blose and Philip J. Cook "Regulating Handgun Transfers" (Duke University, 1980) (unpublished).

robberies. If current rates of handgun violence persist, the approximately 2 million new handguns sold this year will eventually be involved in almost 600 thousand acts of violent crime[4]—a rate of involvement that vastly exceeds the corresponding rate for rifles and shotguns. The most extreme response to the special problem of handguns is the District of Columbia's recent ordinance— implemented in 1977—that bans the sale and acquisition of handguns.

Another important dimension of the "gun problem" is location. Most states impose no special requirements on people who keep their guns at home or place of business, but every state except New Mexico imposes some sort of restriction on carrying a concealed gun. In most states, carrying a concealed gun by a civilian is either prohibited or else requires a special license. A number of states also require such a license for carrying a handgun openly, and 21 states require it for carrying a handgun in a car. Massachusetts has the most extreme carrying law: under the Bartley-Fox Amendment, carrying a handgun without a license,

4. This estimate is calculated as follows. The National Crime Panel victimization survey report for 1977 [*Criminal Victimization in the United States, 1977* (U.S. Department of Justice, Law Enforcement Assistance Administration)] reports some data on gun use in robbery, rape, and assault. On the assumption that 90 percent of the gun rapes and robberies, and 80 percent of the gun assaults, involved handguns, then the survey-based estimate is that there were about 565,000 handgun crimes in 1977. If the rate of handgun sales, the handgun stock, and the handgun violence rate remain at current levels, then this year's "cohort" of new handguns will eventually be involved in this many crimes—a straightforward result of these steady-state assumptions. If the crime rate and/or handgun stock increases, then this year's cohort of new handguns will be involved in a still higher number of violent crimes.

or a longgun without a special identification card, is punishable by a minimum prison term of one year, without possibility of parole or suspension.

We now turn to a review and assessment of strategies for discouraging potentially dangerous people from acquiring firearms.

REGULATIONS GOVERNING FIREARMS TRANSFERS

As a group, violent criminals differ in a number of respects from the population at large. Most robbers and murderers are youthful (age 15–30) males. To a vastly disproportionate extent they live in large cities and have serious criminal records. A 20-year-old male felon from Detroit is more likely, by several orders of magnitude, to use a gun in violent crime than a 50-year-old Iowa farmer.

The current structure of federal and state regulations on gun transfers is motivated by the objective of making it difficult for certain violence-prone people to obtain guns without substantially increasing the "effective price" of guns to other people.[5]

The federal gatekeeper[6]

States began regulating firearms transactions in the nineteenth century, and New York's Sullivan Law— which was and is one of the most stringent state gun control measures—was enacted as early as 1911.

5. The term "effective price" was coined by Mark H. Moore, "Managing the 'Effective Price of Handguns: A Conceptual Basis for the Design of Gun Control Policies" (Kennedy School of Government, Harvard, 1977) (unpublished).

6. Information on state and federal laws in this and subsequent sections is extracted from Blose and Cook.

By the 1960s, many of the more urban states had nontrivial regulations governing handgun transactions. State regulations on transfer were, however, readily circumvented by individuals through mail order purchase. The first federal effort to close this gaping loophole in state regulation was a 1927 ban on the use of the U.S. mails to ship concealable weapons. The Gun Control Act (GCA) of 1968 went much further, requiring that all shipments of firearms in commerce be limited to federally licensed dealers, manufacturers, and importers.[7] Furthermore, an unlicensed individual may only purchase a firearm in his state of residence or—in the case of longguns only—in a contiguous state, if state laws permit. Licensed dealers are required to see identification that gives the buyer's name, address, and age before transferring a firearm. Anybody who knowingly sells a gun to an out-of-state resident is criminally liable.

In addition to these restrictions on interstate commerce, the GCA sought to aid states in the effective enforcement of state and local ordinances by requiring federally licensed dealers to obey all applicable state and local ordinances regarding firearms transactions. The federal licensee is thus established by the GCA as the main agent for the implementation of state and local regulation of firearms commerce. Given the importance of this role, it is surprisingly easy to obtain a federal dealers license, and some 170,000 people are currently licensed. Applicants must have a place of business and must meet certain minor requirements to be eligible for a license, as well as pay a

license fee of $10 per year. BATF's limited resources and the fact that about 23,000 new people receive licenses each year ensure that the typical applicant is not carefully investigated.[8] A recent study of federal licensees in the New Haven area found that 64 percent lacked a required state or local license and 69 percent were not bona fide businesses.[9] Thus a substantial majority of federally licensed dealers operate in violation of federal law.

The GCA does not forbid the sale of a firearm by someone who lacks a license. The license requirement applies only to those who are in the business of selling firearms. In practice, the legal line has been drawn at five guns per year. Beyond the requirement that nondealers do not knowingly sell to a nonresident, federal law does not regulate sales by nondealers.

State gatekeepers

Over half the states regulate firearms commerce to a significant degree. Most of the states that lack regulations of this sort are in the western central region, from Texas, New Mexico, and Arizona up to Idaho and Montana. Unlike the federal GCA, most state laws make a sharp distinction between handguns and longguns, with less stringent regulation of the latter.

Fourteen states require that handgun dealers obtain licenses from either local or state authorities, and

7. There are several exceptions, but none are important.

8. Rex Davis, testimony in *Hearings* before the Subcommittee on Crime, House Judiciary Committee, 4 May 1978, p. 28.

9. Samuel S. Fields et al., "Compliance of Federal Firearms Licensees with Federal, State and Local Laws and Standard Business Practices" (unpublished, 1980). One incentive for nondealers to acquire a dealer's license is that the license allows them to purchase guns by mail order.

an additional eight require such a license for all dealers in firearms. While most of these states have adopted the federal practice of a nominal license fee, a few have fees sufficiently high to discourage people from seeking a dealers' license unless they are seriously in the business of selling handguns. North Carolina's annual license fee is $50; Delaware's is $50; South Carolina charges $100 every two years and also requires that a $10,000 bond be posted; Georgia requires $25 per year and a $1000 bond. High fees, by keeping the number of licensed dealers relatively low, should make it easier for BATF and state and local authorities to regulate dealer activities relatively carefully. Indeed, any state that requires dealer licensing is in a position to supplement BATF's rather meager regulatory resources.

The Gun Control Act stipulates several categories of people that are legally denied the right to receive or possess a gun, but has no effective provision for discouraging such people from purchase—they need only sign a false statement of their eligibility before a dealer or buy from a nondealer. Twenty-three states now have laws that go a major step beyond the GCA by requiring that police be notified and be given a chance to check up on a handgun purchaser before the transfer is made—or, in two states, immediately after the transfer. These 23 states include almost two thirds—64 percent—of the U.S. population. Thus a police check prior to handgun purchase is now the norm. Three of these states apply a similar requirement to longguns.

State regulations governing handgun transfer differ in several important respects, including the type of response required from the police

to legalize a handgun transfer. There are three basic systems in effect by which police are involved in handgun transfers. The first is the open-ended licensing system adopted by Illinois. The Firearms Owner Identification card is required for the purchase of any firearm, whether from a dealer or nondealer. The identification card is valid for five years and can be used to buy any number of guns during that period—hence "open-ended." Purchase is subject to a brief waiting period of three days for handguns and one for longguns. New Jersey has a similar open-ended license system for longguns.

The "permit to purchase" system, in effect in eight states,[10] requires that a permit be issued by local police to the prospective buyer before the handgun is actually transferred. Unlike the Illinois system, a new permit is required for each gun. The alternative "application to purchase" system—in 12 states—[11] differs from the permit system in one important respect: in the application system, silence implies consent. If the police do not take explicit action to block the sale during the waiting period, then the transfer is automatically authorized. The waiting periods range up to 15 days in Tennessee and California, but some states have such short waiting periods that it seems doubtful they actually have a chance to check most of the applications. Indeed, two states, South Carolina and North Dakota, only require that the police be notified after the handgun transfer, with the presumption that if the sale involves an ineligible purchaser this "notification of purchase" system gives the

10. HI, IA, MA, MI, MO, NJ, NY, and NC.
11. CA, RI, IN, PA, MD, AL, CT, MN, OR, WA, SD, and TN.

police a chance to arrest the buyer and confiscate the gun.

The GCA does not regulate sales by nondealers, except to proscribe them from knowingly selling to a nonresident. Many state laws, however, do not distinguish between dealers and nondealers in regulating transfers. All of the "purchase permit" states require a permit for purchase from a nondealer. States that lack any requirement for a police check on handgun transfers may still place legal restrictions on knowingly transferring a handgun to a youth or other member of a proscribed category. However, regulations governing transfers by nondealers are very difficult to enforce, especially when the buyer is not required to have a permit or license.

Who is excluded?

While the main purpose of the GCA was to create a federal regulatory environment in which the states would have a real choice concerning gun control, the GCA also established a national minimal level of regulation on gun possession by designating certain categories of people as ineligible to possess a firearm. In terms of numbers, the most important category of ineligibles designated by the GCA is illegal aliens, of which there are something like 4 million.[12] About 2.3 million adult males—and a relatively few females—are excluded because of a prior felony conviction;[13] those under indictment for a felony, and fugitives from justice, are also excluded. About 1.2 million adults are excluded because they have been committed involuntarily to a mental institution at some time.[14] The only other important proscribed category is persons with a history of "substance abuse," an ill-defined category that includes somewhere between one-half million—the estimated number of heroin addicts—and 30 million—the estimated number of users of illegal drugs.[15] All of these groups are banned from acquiring or possessing any type of firearm. In addition, it is illegal for dealers to sell handguns to youths less than 21 years old, or longguns to youths less than 18, although federal law does not prohibit possession by youths—it is legal, in federal law, at least, for a parent to transfer a gun to his child.

The individual states are, of course, permitted to extend firearms prohibition to other groups, and many have done so. The most popular state prohibitions for handgun possession are for violent misdemeanants and alcohol abusers.

In most states that regulate handgun transfers, the presumption is that the transfer will be authorized unless the relevant authority finds evidence that the purchaser has a characteristic that places him in one of the proscribed categories. This type of system could be characterized as a "permissive screening system without discretion." North Carolina, on the other hand, has a permissive system—most applications are approved—with considerable discretion; the county sheriff's instructions from the state law are simply to

12. This is the figure currently used by the Immigration and Naturalization Service (INS) (telephone interview with Linda Gordon, Chief, INS Statistics Branch, 4 Dec. 1979).

13. This estimate is based on prison admission statistics, modified to reflect recidivism and the ratio of prison admissions to convictions. See Blose and Cook, pp. 40–41.

14. See Blose and Cook, pp. 39–40.

15. *National Survey on Drug Abuse: 1977, Vol. I, Main Findings* (National Institute of Drug Abuse), p. 20.

issue handgun purchase permits to applicants of "good moral character" who need the handgun for defense of the home. Some jurisdiction, most notably New York City and Boston, have highly restrictive systems, with discretion, in which applicants must have an important need for a handgun and must be able to demonstrate that need to the satisfaction of local authorities.

In regulating gun transfers and possession, the proscribed categories can be defined broadly or narrowly. The fraction of potentially dangerous people who are included in the proscribed group will, of course, increase as the definition is broadened, but establishing a broader definition also has obvious costs. The "correct" definition of the proscribed group is ultimately a value judgment, but one that should be informed by empirical analysis of individual characteristics that are predictive of involvement in violent crime. There are also practical considerations of cost and feasibility to be considered, as discussed next.

Feasibility and cost

A thorough investigation of an applicant's background would involve interviews with character witnesses and a wide-ranging search of federal, state, and local records, as is done for high-level security clearances issued by the federal government. Needless to say, this type of investigation is very expensive and is not warranted for screening handgun buyers. Jurisdictions that have adopted some sort of permit or application to purchase system for handguns usually limit their investigation to checking state and local criminal records. Such records may help to identify substance abusers and public drunks, as well as felons

and violent misdemeanants, but they are far from complete. Before discussing the quality of these criminal history records, we briefly discuss other public records that could potentially be used in an investigation.

First, there are no useful files on illegal aliens; the Immigration and Naturalization Service keeps records on some illegal aliens, but they are a small fraction of the total.

Second, there are no federal files on mental commitments, and state files are often inaccessible to police. Some states have computerized registers, and in a few of these—for example, New York and Illinois—the registers are checked in the course of a handgun license investigation. In other states—for example, Maryland and North Carolina—such registers are kept, but are not open to police investigations. County court records include information on involuntary mental commitments, but these are decentralized and expensive to search.

Third, the substance abusers are usually only identifiable if they have been arrested for a drug-related offense. The federal government keeps no substance abuser records with a name reference capability. Some states may have files on clients of drug treatment programs, but these would not ordinarily be open to police investigators.

In the absence of other information sources, handgun permit investigations are limited to criminal files. The most comprehensive set of criminal records is kept by the Identification (ID) Division of the FBI. This division has for many years been the national repository for fingerprint records submitted by law enforcement agencies. The fingerprints of 22 million persons are currently in the criminal file, including, according to the FBI, 95 percent of all known offenders.[16] Although this is the most comprehensive available source of criminal history information, handgun permit investigators do not make use of it. The FBI's regulations require that any license investigation request be accompanied by a set of fingerprints and that the state criminal records bureau conduct a check prior to the ID Division's search. The current turnaround time for FBI searches is 22 working days. These features of an FBI check make it too costly and time-consuming for a handgun permit investigation.

Every state keeps centralized criminal history files, and most states, including at least 83 percent of the U.S. population, have an operational computerized system or are in the process of developing one.[17] Whether the system is automated or manual, it is no better than the information supplied to it by local law enforcement agencies and courts. An extreme example of an inadequate state file is Mississippi's, which has only 50,000 records; Arizona, with about the same population, has 750,000 records. Felony arrests are reported to the respective state bureaus at rates of about 90 percent in Texas, 60 percent in North Carolina, and 30 percent in Maine.

It appears that local police departments are generally more likely to submit fingerprints to the FBI's ID Division than to their own state bureau, and as a result the FBI's files are more complete than the sum of all state files. In Massachusetts, for example, the state Bureau of Identification is sent only about 30 percent of the arrest cards that are sent to the FBI by Massachusetts police agencies, even though reporting to the state bureau is mandatory and reporting to the FBI is not. Reporting of court disposition data tends to be even more incomplete than arrest reporting. Since applicants are ordinarily being screened on the basis of their conviction record, rather than their arrest record, the lack of disposition information poses further problems for investigators.

Given the incompleteness of readily available public records, some applicants who are in fact not eligible to possess a gun will be approved. This problem should be kept in proper perspective, however; we suspect that most felons and other ineligibles who obtain guns do so not because the state's screening system fails to discover their criminal record, but rather because these people find ways of circumventing the screening system entirely. In North Carolina, for example, it appears that less than 40 percent of handgun buyers bother to apply for the permit required by law.[18] Under these circumstances, developing a more intensive and reliable screening process is probably not worth the additional cost.

The cost of existing state screening systems differs depending on the thoroughness of the record check, the extent to which records are

16. Information on the Identification Division was obtained from telephone interviews with Special Agent Kenneth Arnold of the ID Division on December 6 and 18, 1979, and from "An Assessment of the Uses of Information in the National Crime Information Center and Computerized Criminal History Program" conducted for the U.S. Office of Technology Assessment by the Bureau of Governmental Research and Service (University of South Carolina, 1979) (unpublished).

17. Blose and Cook, Appendix B, documents the statements in this paragraph.

18. Philip J. Cook and Karen Hawley, "North Carolina's Pistol Permit Law," *Popular Government* (May 1981).

computerized, and other factors. We obtained per unit cost estimates for five states, which ranged from $1.90 for Illinois—which has a completely automated system—to $5.30 for Indiana—which is entirely manual.[19] By way of comparison, a FBI ID Division name check cost $2.51 in 1978, while a fingerprint check cost $4.21.

In summary, most of the U.S. population is required by state laws to submit to a police check before acquiring a handgun. State and local officials screen applicants primarily on the basis of criminal record checks. Such checks utilize records that are far from complete. Most jurisdictions screen out a very small percentage of applicants, but we believe that that is primarily because ineligible people are less likely to submit to this screening process than are eligible people.

REDUCING ILLEGAL SALES

A permissive screening system is difficult to enforce in part because such a system is compatible with a high volume of gun commerce and a high density of gun ownership. In this environment it is difficult to suppress illegal transactions that circumvent the screening system. The most important sources of guns to people who wish to avoid undergoing a police check are the black market (supplied by thefts), the secondhand market (supplied by nondealers), and the under-the-counter sales by licensed dealers.[20] The first of these is a traditional criminal

law enforcement problem; the latter two can be dealt with to some extent through regulation. The two basic regulatory problems, then, are to achieve better control of the "gatekeeper's" activities and to force more gun transactions to go through the "gate." One set of proposals for achieving these objectives was recently embodied in the Handgun Crime Control Act of 1979, submitted to the U.S. Congress by Senator Kennedy and Congressman Rodino.

The Handgun Crime Control Act (HCCA) proposed to increase the federal dealers license fee from $10 to $500 for handgun dealers, a change which would greatly reduce the number of licensees and would facilitate oversight of their activities. Perhaps more important, the HCCA would establish civil liability for dealers in cases where they knowingly transferred a handgun to an ineligible person and the gun was then used in a tortious manner. The HCCA required that all handgun transactions be channeled through a licensed dealer, who would be responsible for ensuring that the buyer was entitled to possess a handgun. Individuals who sold their guns illegally would be liable for any damage caused with the gun by the new owner.

Enforcing this owners' liability provision would require that police be able to trace a gun to its most recent legal owner. The GCA requires that licensed dealers keep records of all sales and that manufacturers and importers keep records of shipments by serial number. BATF traces firearms—at the request of law enforcement agencies —by first contacting the manufacturer and then the licensed retail dealer. This system is about 90 percent successful in identifying the

19. Telephone interviews with various state officials.

20. See Mark Moore, "Keeping Handguns From Criminal Offenders," in *Gun Control*, special editor Philip J. Cook, *The Annals* of the American Academy of Political and Social Science, 455:92–109 (May 1981).

first owner for guns manufactured since 1968,[21] but it is much more difficult to trace subsequent owners if the gun has been transferred since its original sale.

Twenty states, which contain about half the U.S. population, have strengthened federal regulations by requiring that all handgun transactions be reported to and kept on file by the appropriate officials. These state registration systems are generally a natural extension of the purchase permit and application to purchase systems in these states. If this transfer system were followed faithfully, most handguns would eventually be registered to their owners. Four states, Hawaii, Michigan, Mississippi, and New York, have instituted a more comprehensive system in which every handgun must be registered with the authorities by the owner. Kennedy's HCCA would establish a national registration system managed by the manufacturers.

While there is no chance that Congress will enact anything like the HCCA in the foreseeable future, this bill is worthy of careful study by state legislators who are concerned with developing more effective methods for depriving dangerous people of guns within the context of a permissive screening system. Owner and dealer liability, together with a comprehensive registration system, may provide sellers the necessary incentive to play by the rules of a purchase permit or application to purchase system.

ARE PERMISSIVE SCREENING SYSTEMS WORTHWHILE?

The national "inventory" of handguns currently numbers 30 to 40 million, and 3 to 5 million handguns change hands each year.[22] About one quarter of all households now possess at least one handgun. The corresponding figures for longguns are much higher. The permissive screening systems—permit or application to purchase—as explained previously, are intended to discourage a relatively small number of people from obtaining guns without seriously interfering with this high level of commercial activity in firearms. Many commentators see this objective as naive. There has been no convincing empirical demonstration that a police check on handgun buyers reduces violent crime rates, though neither is there any convincing evidence to the contrary.[23] It is known that such screening systems are widely circumvented and, furthermore, that state criminal record files are sufficiently incomplete in that a felon who did choose to submit to the required police check before buying a handgun would have a sporting chance of having his application approved. Finally, a considerable fraction of people who commit violent crimes are legally entitled to own guns, at least under the federal GCA restrictions. Permissive screening systems are not very costly, but if they are not effective, then they are not worthwhile.

But we are not convinced that permissive screening systems are lacking in beneficial effect. It seems plausible that a permissive screening system could increase the effective price of a handgun to vio-

---

21. Testimony of Richard Davis, "Treasury's Proposed Gun Regulations," *Hearings* before the Subcommittee on Crime of the Committee on the Judiciary, U.S. House of Representatives, May 4 and 18, 1978, p. 32.

22. See Blose and Cook, pp. 32–36.

23. The literature on this subject is contradictory and unpersuasive. The main contributors are: Martin S. Geisel, Richard Roll, and R. Stanton Wettich, Jr., "The Effectiveness of State and Local Regulation of Handguns: A Statistical Analysis," *Duke Law J.*, 1969:647–76; and Douglas R. Murray, "Handguns, Gun Control Laws, and Firearm Violence," *Social Problems*, 23(1):81–93 (1975).

lence-prone teenagers and convicted felons enough to discourage some of them from obtaining guns, at least for a while. The average "career" of a robber is very short, as indicated by the fact that most robberies are committed by men in their late teens or early twenties; a gun control system that delayed youthful robbers from obtaining a gun for just one year, on the average, would cause a substantial reduction in the gun robbery rate. Similarly, a gun control system that was sufficiently effective to delay gun acquisition by homicidal people for a few weeks or months would prevent some gun murders. Determined people will eventually find a way of circumventing even the most tightly managed screening system, but not all dangerous people are so determined to obtain a gun—and there is some-

thing to be gained by just delaying those who are.

Our view, then, is that permissive screening systems hold some potential for causing modest reductions in firearms violence rates. The state systems of this sort that are currently in effect could be strengthened by instituting liability and registration provisions and by establishing stricter regulations of gun dealers. These controls on gun commerce can be implemented without substantial assistance from the federal government, which is an important consideration given that Congress is unlikely to act in this area any time soon. Over half the states have judged it worthwhile to supplement federal regulation of commerce in firearms, and it is at the state level that innovations in gun control will continue to arise.

ANNALS, AAPSS, **455**, May 1981

Keeping Handguns From Criminal Offenders

By MARK H. MOORE

ABSTRACT: Gun control policies must strike a balance between conserving legitimate use of handguns and reducing criminal use. Current federal law seeks to accomplish this objective by discriminating between safe and unsafe gun owners —allowing the former and prohibiting the latter from owning guns. An important practical problem soon arises: containing guns within the entitled sector. Analysis of the current supply system suggests that gun offenders acquire guns from many different sources: purchases from licensed dealers, private transfers, thefts, and black markets. Among these, legitimate purchases seem most important in supplying assaulters, and thefts seem to be the most important in supplying armed robbers. The "black market" turns out to be difficult to distinguish from the other sectors. To the extent it is distinct, it seems to be populated primarily by small-scale, impermanent enterprises, rather than durable firms. Analysis of how existing institutions might be deployed against this system leads to the conclusion that local enforcement capacities and federal regulatory efforts are the most important operational capacities to develop. Federal criminal investigation capabilities are important only for limited purposes.

Mark H. Moore is the Guggenheim Professor of Criminal Justice Policy and Management at the Kennedy School of Government, Harvard University. He was formerly director of planning and evaluation for the Drug Enforcement Administration of the U.S. Department of Justice. He is currently engaged in a collaborative analysis of gun control policies with Philip J. Cook of Duke University.

NOTE: Research reported in this article was supported by the Ford Foundation.

FOR DECADES, gun control policy in the United States has struggled with a fundamental dilemma. On one hand, intuition and empirical evidence suggested that widespread gun availability intensified violent crime. This offered some justification for generally reducing gun availability. On the other hand, most guns seemed to be used for legitimate purposes, and those who owned the guns seemed to value them highly. Thus potential gains in reducing crime could be secured only at the price of inflicting losses on those who wished to use guns for self-defense, recreation, or collecting.

It is the genius of our governmental system that it handles value conflicts such as these by searching for policies that protect some of all the expressed values. Thus the history of gun control policies is a continuing search for instruments that strike a balance between protecting legitimate uses of guns and reducing harmful uses. Sometimes the focus has been on the guns themselves. We have distinguished "safe" from "unsafe" guns and sought stringent controls—even bans—over particularly dangerous guns. Gun control policies have focused on "gangster-type weapons," "Saturday night specials," and handguns. Weapons such as .22 rifles and shotguns are only occasionally proposed as targets of regulation. Other times, gun control policies have focused on particular uses of guns. Particularly harsh penalties are advocated for those who use guns in crimes; tighter restrictions on gun use are imposed in cities than in rural areas; and possession of guns is treated more leniently than carrying them in city streets. In short, whether gun control policies are aimed at the guns or the uses, the basic thrust of our policies is to discriminate among guns and uses in an effort to protect legitimate uses while cutting down on bad uses.

DISCRIMINATING BETWEEN SAFE AND UNSAFE GUN OWNERS

Probably the most obvious discriminatory policies, however, are those that seek to distinguish safe and responsible gun owners from less reliable people and that entitle the former and proscribe the latter from acquiring, possessing, or carrying guns. This idea is embodied in the Gun Control Act of 1968, which establishes classes of proscribed users —convicted felons, adjudicated mental defectives, drug abusers, and minors. Such policies have great intuitive appeal. It makes sense to keep guns—particularly handguns —out of the hands of criminals. The practical value of such policies, however, depends fundamentally on two factors: (1) how precisely the line between safe and unsafe gun owners can be drawn and (2) how effectively guns can be contained within the entitled sector. If many gun crimes are committed by people who did not appear dangerous before they committed the offense, or if guns migrate easily from entitled to proscribed users, then the real effects of discriminatory policies will be less substantial than we might hope.

Drawing the line between safe and unsafe gun owners presents many challenging issues. Among them are the following: (1) whether the presumption should be that people are safe and responsible unless clear evidence or irresponsibility exists, or that people are unsafe unless they can present evidence of competence and good character; (2) how deeply conceivable extensions of the current line would cut into the current population of gun offenders at what price in terms of prohibiting gun ownership among people who would not have committed gun crimes; (3) what characteristics of people can be practically and conveniently observed, given current record-keeping procedures and statutory guarantees of privacy; and so on. Many of these issues are usefully addressed in the article by Philip J. Cook and James Blose in this issue.

No matter where the line is finally drawn, however, one must eventually confront the practical problem of policing the line and containing handguns within the entitled sector. This is hardly a trivial problem. In any given year, several million handguns change hands through sales, gifts, loans, and thefts. The transactions are managed by a wide variety of institutions ranging from commercial enterprises, through informal private arrangements, to more or less well-organized criminal activities. Deployed against this complex system is a relatively limited network of federal, state, and local enforcement organizations. To make the most of the limited control capabilities, it is important to develop some sense for the relative importance of the varied sources in supplying criminal offenders.

CURRENT CONCEPTIONS OF SOURCES OF GUNS TO OFFENDERS

Three more or less well-developed ideas dominate current conceptions of the sources of guns to offenders. One view is based on the observation that states with relatively lax gun control laws tend to supply states with tighter gun control policies.[1] Put more directly, a larger fraction of guns used in crimes in Boston were originally purchased out-of-state—and specifically in loose-control states, such as South Carolina and Florida—than is true of guns used in crimes in Dallas—which were bought primarily in Texas.[2] This fact clearly suggests the difficulty of protecting "local options" in establishing gun control policies, and establishes some federal interest in the gun control area. But to some, the finding suggests a great deal more. The interstate flow of handguns used for crime conjures up an image of well-organized interstate gunrunning operations that buy handguns cheaply in South Carolina, Florida, and Texas and sell the guns expensively—and exclusively to criminals barred from legitimate markets—in cities such as New York, Chicago, and Washington.

The mere fact of interstate migrations of handguns need not imply the existence of such operations, of course. The pattern we observe could be the result of a simple southern/rural to northern/urban migration that carries guns along as personal possessions and cultural practices. The people carrying the guns interstate need not be economically motivated, organized in large stable firms, nor inclined to sell to criminals. Moreover, focusing on the interstate flow of guns ignores the fact that while this is part of the problem for some states—including those that contain a large fraction of the nation's violent crime—interstate gun flows are a negligible problem for many other states, and

1. Bureau of Alcohol, Tobacco and Firearms, *Project Identification: A Study of Handguns Used in Crime* (Washington, D.C.: U.S. Department of the Treasury, 1976).
2. Ibid., pp. 11–17.

even states that import many guns used for crime also have a problem of intrastate flows of guns to crime.

A second view is based on a different observation about guns for crime. Zimring has observed that "new guns"—that is, those sold new at retail within the last few years—are "over-represented" among criminal guns when compared with their estimated share of the total stock of handguns.[3] The most direct and powerful implication of this finding is that reductions in the flow of guns will produce a greater effect on crime than equal reductions in the existing stock. This is good news for those who would like to impose restrictions on production, since it suggests that such efforts will be more effective sooner than would be true if all guns were equally likely to end up in criminal uses. But again, this important fact is stretched still further. Some use this fact to support the hypothesis that the most troublesome source of supply is commercial dealers. Since new guns are overrepresented, and since new guns are more likely to have come into the hands of the offender directly from a dealer, it seems most important to crack down on licensed dealers.

The reasoning here is, again, pretty loose. To say new guns are overrepresented is not the same as saying they are the most important source of supply to criminal offenders. Since the vast majority of the guns are old, they can be significantly underrepresented among criminal guns and still account for very large fractions of all these guns. Furthermore, a new gun is one that was sold at retail in the last five years. Five years is plenty of time for a gun to be privately resold, lent, or stolen. Thus while some positive correlation may exist between the age of a gun and the probability that its current possessor bought it from a licensed dealer in a commercial transaction, the correlation will be far from perfect. In any event, the fact that new guns are overrepresented among criminal guns falls short of establishing the proposition that licensed dealers should be the dominant focus of regulatory and enforcement efforts.

A third view is based on the idea that there is something special about people who commit crimes with handguns and that, as a result, they will patronize a specialized black market catering to their special needs or characteristics. Sometimes the argument is that since offenders want untraceable guns, they seek out people who deal in stolen guns, are specialists in removing identifying marks, ask no questions about the purchaser, and create no records of the transaction. Other times the argument is that people who commit gun offenses commonly associate with people who deal in stolen goods including guns, and that they naturally purchase guns from such people, since it is inexpensive, convenient, and relatively safe. Such views find empirical support in Brill's finding that stolen guns figured prominently among criminal guns in New York City.[4]

While this third view also seems plausible, one can, again, raise objections. Since many crimes are committed by people who did not intend

---

3. Franklin E. Zimring, "Street Crime and New Guns: Some Implications for Firearms Control," *J. Criminal Justice*, 4:95–107.

4. Steven Brill, *Firearm Abuse: A Research and Policy Report* (Washington, D.C.: Police Foundation, 1977), pp. 106–7.

to commit a crime at the time they acquired the gun, it may be unreasonable to suppose that criminal gun purchasers take special precautions in arming themselves. Moreover, since licensed dealers and private individuals can be tricked by purchasers—or actively collude with them—gun purchasers may be able to find anonymity and untraceable guns in sectors that do not resemble black markets. Finally, if people want stolen or untraceable guns they can always steal them themselves. In short, the basic assumption in this third view—that there will be a specialized black market in guns—may turn out to be false. Since the demand for criminal guns can be met in other ways, a specialized black market may not arise.

This review of current conceptions and knowledge reveals confusion about the sources of guns to criminal offenders. The purpose of this article is to begin a more systematic investigation by bringing some conceptual order and empirical evidence to bear. The first step is to identify various sectors and mechanisms that transfer handguns and to make rough estimates of the volume of transfers managed within the sectors and their vulnerability to proscribed or criminally motivated gun owners. This step is important because it fixes conceptions about possible sources of supply and aids our quantitative intuitions about their relative importance. The next step is to present a small amount of empirical information about proximate sources of supply for criminal offenders. Although the evidence is too weak to allow a confident assessment about the relative importance of the varied sources of supply, it does check and give some emphasis to the more general discussion of sources of supply. Finally, we will consider how existing control efforts are deployed against the various sources of supply. To the extent that important sectors are ignored or underemphasized, a prima facie case for some redeployment can be developed.

POTENTIAL SOURCES OF SUPPLY

For our purposes, four possible sources of supply to offenders will be distinguished and analyzed: federal licensees, private transferors, thefts, and the black market. As one might expect, currently available information will support precise estimates of neither the volume of transfers in these sectors, nor the proportion of the transfers involving proscribed or criminally motivated persons. For purposes of policy design, however, this imprecision need not be a problem. In fact, a healthy degree of uncertainty in our estimates is useful, since it urges us to diversify control efforts. Diversification is sensible not only because we are currently uncertain about which sectors are most important, but also because whatever the current reality is, we expect it to change as control efforts are tried. After all, the supply system is interdependent and reacts to specific control efforts. Consequently, if we were to focus our attack narrowly in accord with precise estimates of the relative importance of given sectors, we would soon find out that the problem had changed. In effect, since both uncertainty and the expectation of dynamic adjustments counsel a broadly diversified control effort, we can tolerate substantial uncertainty in our estimates.

Federal licensees

The federally licensed retail sector probably accounts for the largest number of transactions. If we assume that most newly produced or imported guns move through this sector, and that inventories held by dealers are either small or constant, then we can guess that approximately 1.5 to 2.0 million transfers of new guns occur each year in the sector.[5] This establishes a lower bound for transfers in this sector. There may be more. The reason is that some portion of the resale activities may be conducted by federally licensed retail dealers. After all, many of the people holding federal licenses are essentially private collectors, rather than large retail dealers. And even large retail dealers typically sell used guns as well as new guns. So it seems reasonable to guess that some 1.5 to 2.3 million handgun transfers occur in this sector.

An important question is how many of the transfers involve proscribed persons. If compliance with federal law were perfect, of course, the answer would be none. But there is little reason to believe that compliance is perfect. Dealers can be easily deceived by their customers. They may even collude with them to overlook disqualifying characteristics. Even close investigation might fail to disclose such acts. We also know, however, that there is only about a 10 percent chance that a dealer will be investigated in any given year. It seems reasonable to assume, then, that federally licensed dealers are vulnerable to proscribed persons.

The quantitative question, of course, is how vulnerable federally licensed dealers are. The Bureau of Alcohol, Tobacco and Firearms (ATF)

conducted detailed reviews of the activities of licensed dealers in Washington, Boston, and Chicago in 1977. Nearly 70,000 transfers were reviewed. The estimated rate of illegal sales and questionable purchases varied from 0.6 percent—in Washington, D.C.—to 4.0 percent—in Chicago.[6] If we apply these numbers to our estimates of 1.5 to 2.3 million transfers in this sector, we can calculate that some 9000 to 90,000 transfers involving proscribed people occur each year in the federally licensed sector.

Private transfers

The private transfer sector is probably the next largest sector. Two different methods can be used to generate rough estimates of the annual number of private transfers. One method takes advantage of a 1968 survey of gun owners which indicated that about 34 percent of current gun owners acquired used guns in private transfers.[7] If we assumed that this proportion were constant over time, then we could compute the annual number of transfers by multiplying the number of new guns sold each year by 0.34.[8] If the num-

6. "Interim Report: Analysis of Operation CUE (Concentrated Urban Enforcement)" (Washington, D.C.: Bureau of Alcohol, Tobacco and Firearms, Feb. 1977), pp. 187, 191.

7. George D. Newton and Franklin E. Zimring, *Firearms and Violence in American Life* (Washington, D.C.: National Commission on the Causes and Prevention of Violence, 1968), pp. 13–14.

8. The reason is that all of these new guns would contribute new gun owners who would respond in a survey that they acquired new guns from a retail dealer. In order for the proportion of such responses to remain constant, then, some people who were previously in this group would have to sell to a different group who would then respond that they had bought an old gun from a private source. Note that this is not a behavioral requirement. It is a mathematical

5. Franklin E. Zimring, "Firearms and Federal Law: The Gun Control Act of 1968," *J. Legal Studies*, IV:133–98 (1975).

ber of new handguns sold, then, were 1.5 to 2.2 million, this method would suggest that some 500,000 to 700,000 guns were exchanged in private transfers.

Unfortunately, there is no particular reason to assume that the proportion of gun owners claiming a given source would be constant. In fact, it seems quite likely that at the time this survey was taken, the world of gun ownership was changing rapidly. Specifically, annual sales of handguns were increasing. If new gun purchases from retail dealers were in fact increasing dramatically, the method just described would produce an inflated estimate of the number of private transfers. The reason is that the survey data would be asking people about sources of guns in a period when retail sales had been modest—thereby producing an inflated estimate of what the fraction who acquired their guns in private transfers would soon be. Then, the error would be compounded by applying this inflated rate of private transfers to a dramatically increasing number of new retail purchases. Thus the estimate of 500,000 to 700,000 is likely to be high.

An alternative method for estimating the number of private transfers yields a lower bound. This estimate is based on an analysis of how often guns are re-registered in states and cities that require registration. In Chicago from 1968 to 1977, 623,000 guns were registered. Of this number 60,000 were re-registered.[9] Since re-registrations indicate transfers, a simple calculation suggests that the

annual rate of gun transfers in Chicago was approximately 1.0 percent. Since people may be careless about reporting changes, and since the existence of the registration system may deter transfers, this estimate is likely to be low as an estimate of a national rate of private transfers. Still, if one applies this rate to an estimated 30 to 40 million handguns currently in private hands, one can calculate that 300,000 to 400,000 handguns change hands each year.[10] Taken together, the two methods suggest that somewhere between 300,000 and 700,000 old guns change hands in private transfers each year.

How many of these handguns end up in the hands of proscribed or criminally motivated people is even more uncertain. In principle, of course, this sector is extremely vulnerable to proscribed persons, since the private transferors are under no federal obligation to avoid transfers to proscribed individuals.[11] Moreover, there is virtually no regular scrutiny of this activity, and it is hard to imagine how such small-scale, intimate events could be brought under public scrutiny. In practice, however, the vulnerability of this sector may be determined by the "social proximity" of legitimate current owners to proscribed individuals. If people in the "underworld"

requirement imposed by our assumption of a constant proportion of people reporting different sources of handguns.

9. These numbers came from an interview with an official of the Bureau of Gun Registration in Chicago, IL.

10. The estimate of 30 to 40 million handguns comes from calculations that reconcile production and importation data with national survey data on handgun ownership.

11. The rules governing the conduct of dealers in the Gun Control Act of 1968 apply only to federally licensed dealers. There is also a requirement that everyone "engaged in the business of selling" guns must acquire a federal license. Unfortunately, "engaged in the business of selling" is not defined. Court interpretations have been varied, but it seems fairly clear that a private person selling or trading a few guns a year is not a "dealer" under the meaning of the act.

have few friends or relatives in the "straight world" who own guns, it may be hard for chains of "private transfers" to develop that start in legally entitled sectors and end up in proscribed sectors. The social distance may simply be too great. On balance, then, it is unclear whether the private transfer sector is more or less vulnerable to proscribed persons than the federally licensed sector: once approached, private transferors may yield to proscribed persons more easily than licensed dealers, but it requires more personal connections and initiative to make the approach.

Thefts

The third transfer mechanism is thefts. For analytic purposes, it is useful to distinguish between thefts from manufacturers, shippers, licensed dealers, and individuals. Data gathered by ATF on thefts from manufacturers and shippers are sufficient to indicate that thefts from these sources are a relatively insignificant part of the problem.[12] The greater problems lie with licensed dealers and private owners. Two different surveys of licensed dealers have been undertaken by ATF to determine the number of handguns stolen. A 1975 survey of 30,000 licensed dealers in the Midwest revealed that handguns were stolen from these dealers at an annual rate of about 1 handgun for every 10 dealers.[13] A more recent survey of a

sample of 328 licensed dealers drawn from all licensees indicated an annual rate of handgun thefts of approximately 1 handgun for every 25 dealers.[14] If these rates are applied to the population of 170,000 federal licensees, one can calculate that approximately 7000 to 17,000 handguns are stolen from federal licensees each year.

Estimates of the number of handguns stolen from private individuals can be generated by two different methods. First, for those cities or states with comprehensive gun registration systems, we can ask what fraction of the guns are reported stolen each year. This is an imperfect method, since we do not really expect the registration system to be comprehensive, nor do we expect perfect reporting on the theft of weapons. Still, on the basis of data from New York City, Brill estimates a reported theft rate of 253 per 100,000 handguns.[15] If we assumed that New York City's experience were typical of the rest of the United States, we could calculate that some 100,000 to 115,000 handguns were stolen from private individuals each year.

Second, we can investigate the burglary reports from selected cities and determine the fraction of household burglaries that yielded a stolen handgun. Table 1 presents available data from several cities. The differences in the fraction of burglaries resulting in a loss of a handgun may reflect many factors, and knowledge of these factors may be very important in estimating a true national estimate of the yield of handguns in burglaries. For our purposes, how-

12. See data reported in Mark H. Moore, "The Supply of Handguns: An Analysis of the Potential and Current Importance of Alternative Sources of Handguns to Criminal Offenders," mimeographed, pp. 52–55 (May 1979).

13. "Handgun Crime Control—1975–1976," Hearings Before the Sub-Committee to Investigate Juvenile Delinquency of the Committee of the Judiciary, U.S., Senate 94th Congress, 1st sess., p. 2004.

14. "Firearms Theft Study," Bureau of Alcohol, Tobacco, and Firearms, mimeographed (1979), p. 6.

15. Steven Brill, *Firearm Abuse: A Research and Policy Report*, Police Foundation (Washington, DC: 1977), p. 104.

TABLE 1

FRACTIONS OF RESIDENTIAL BURGLARIES YIELDING A HANDGUN: SELECTED CITIES AND YEARS

CITIES AND YEARS	NUMBER OF RESIDENTIAL BURGLARIES	NUMBER OF GUNS STOLEN IN RESIDENTIAL BURGLARIES	PERCENTAGE OF BURGLARIES INVOLVING THEFT OF A HANDGUN
Houston, 1976	6339	901	14.2
St. Louis, 1975	13,547	1047	7.7
St. Louis, 1976	12,410	840	6.8
Durham, North Carolina	534	37	6.9
Atlanta, 1977	12,446	699*	5.6*
Los Angeles, 1977	63,928	1422*	2.2*

SOURCES: Correspondence, Houston Police Department; supplementary data from the St. Louis Metropolitan Police Department; Philip J. Cook, "Crime in Durham" (Duke University); data collected from the files of the Atlanta Police Department; and supplementary data provided by the Los Angeles Police Department.
* Involves all firearms, not just handguns.

ever, it is sufficient to guess that the national yield lies between 3 percent and 10 percent. Applying this rate to annual numbers of household burglaries produces an estimate of approximately 60,000 to 200,000 handguns stolen each year.

Thus it seems reasonable to assume that some 65,000 to 225,000 handguns are stolen each year. The vast majority of them—60,000 to 200,000—come from household burglaries. This is an impressive number—even when compared with the volume of other more common transfers.

What makes this number even more impressive, however, is a strong presumption that virtually all stolen guns end up in the hands of proscribed or dangerous people. This is true partly because the immediate possessor of a stolen gun is, by definition, a thief. But it is also true that stolen guns are particularly attractive to people who intend to commit violent crimes with guns because they are virtually impossible to trace. Thus whether the thief keeps it for himself or transfers it to a fence, colleague, or black-market dealer for future sales, the gun has crossed more or less irrevocably into the proscribed sector.

The black market

So far, we have examined ways in which proscribed persons might arm themselves directly by penetrating the legitimate sector without the aid of intermediaries. It is possible, however, that some specialized institutions might develop to channel guns from legitimate to proscribed sectors. In fact, if we give our romantic fancies free rein, we can imagine specialized firms, operating on commercial scales, well known within the underworld, but largely invisible to the legitimate world, selling untraceable guns at premium prices to Mafia hit men and professional armed robbers. In fact, it is precisely this notion that justifies sophisticated federal criminal investigations of gun dealers. If such firms existed, it would be important to know something about the volume of transfers that flowed through them.

The fact of the matter is, however, that we know relatively little about this sector. It may be that we are ignorant because it is hard to observe illegal activity directly. But it could also be true that this sector does not exist—or at least not in the form we imagine. After all, the most important reason to believe that specialized black-market firms exist is our strong belief that a specialized demand for handguns composed of people with avowedly criminal intentions exists and that this demand cannot be satisfied through the other mechanisms and sectors we have identified.

But what our analysis of the other sectors has revealed is that all sectors are vulnerable to proscribed individuals. A licensed dealer may have an unrecorded inventory of used guns dealt under the counter. A private individual legally entitled to own a gun can transfer it to a proscribed person without risk of prosecution. And a proscribed person who wants a gun may steal it for himself or may acquire it from a friend or acquaintance who is a thief without the assistance of a specialized institution. In short, some portion of the specialized demand that could stimulate the black market can, in fact, be satisfied through the less specialized institutions already examined. If enough of that specialized demand is satisfied through the less specialized institutions, the black-market firms may not arise at all.

Moreover, as one thinks about how the illegal market might be structured, it becomes apparent that the particular characteristics of black-market firms will be decisively influenced by the characteristics of the competing supply mechanisms. This is obvious in the case where these other supply mechanisms substitute for the black-market firms. But it is also clear that these other supply mechanisms will directly shape the activities of the relatively specialized institutions that do come into existence.

Since the black-market firms will themselves be supplied by these other mechanisms, the particular way in which these other mechanisms "leak" guns to black-market firms will have an important effect on the size and longevity of black-market firms. If a shipment of 50 to 100 guns is stolen, for example, then the disposal of these guns may require the development—or short-term use—of a relatively large and durable institution. It must be capable of managing 50 to 100 illegal transactions, each with a new customer. On the other hand, if a few guns are stolen in a series of household burglaries or are purchased under the counter from licensed dealers, they may be disposed of through relatively small and impermanent operations or through a larger institution that has wide underworld contacts, but does not exist solely to supply guns—for example, fencing operations. In short, the smaller and more unpredictable the "leaks" of guns from the other sectors, the less likely will be the development of large, durable institutions dealing specifically in handguns for proscribed individuals.

Given these difficulties, it is necessary to change our approach in analyzing the black-market firm. Instead of defining it as a distinct sector and estimating its size, we shift to a more qualitative approach. We seek to answer the following question: if a person advertises himself as a criminal who needs a handgun, who responds to his demand? It could turn out to be the black-market firms we imagine. Or it could turn out to be something that resembles the other sectors we have identified. The great virtue of posing the question in this form is that review of investigative files created by ATF undercover agents will produce the empirical evidence we need to answer it. After all, the agents pose as criminals who want to buy guns and then accumulate and record information about the people who agree to do business with them.

Thus these investigative files provide a rich source of intelligence about the nature of the institutions and operations in the black market for handguns.

We have exploited this data base by examining closed investigative files for virtually all the cases that led to a charge of "dealing without license" made by ATF from 1974–76 in seven regional offices, including the cities of Atlanta, Boston, Chicago, Dallas, Los Angeles, San Francisco, St. Louis, and Washington, D.C. In reviewing these files, we sought information about the following: (1) the estimated scale of the operation and (2) sources of supply to the illegal firm. In gauging the scale of the firm, we generally could look at two relatively hard pieces of data: (1) reported transactions during the period of the investigation and (2) the size of the inventories seized at arrest. In identifying sources of supply, we usually had to rely on statements made by the dealer to the undercover agents. In some cases, however, relatively complete histories of the guns sold to the agents or seized at the end of the investigation were available. In still other cases, the statements by the illegal dealer could be corroborated by a burglary report indicating a recent theft of a gun or by a formal record indicating that the gun had been sold to the illegal dealer by a federally licensed dealer.

Now, there are many reasons to be very wary of these data. After all, one can hardly assume that ATF undercover agents encounter a random sample of all illegal dealers. In fact, one would expect the opposite. So it is hard to generalize from this sample to all illegal dealers. Beyond this structural problem are other equally damaging problems. It is not clear that the agents see all of a firm's operation, nor that the agents will record everything they see in a reliable way, nor that everything they record gets into the case file. Still, the usual justifications for using bad data as an interim measure applies here with the usual force: it is the only information available, and we need to make some guess about the nature of this wholly illegal sector.

Table 2 presents the data on the scale of the sample of "illegal firms" encountered by ATF agents. What is striking is how small the firms are. The majority of the "firms" had no inventories seized at arrest. Only a tiny fraction — 10 percent — have more than 20 guns on hand when the arrest is made. Similarly, the firms seem to make relatively few transactions over the course of a year. The majority sell at an observed rate of less than five guns per month. Even if we assume that the observed transactions represent only a small fraction of the total transactions, which is unlikely given the small inventories, one can calculate that the vast majority of the firms sell fewer than 600 guns per year.

Table 3 presents data on the sources of weapons to illegal firms. As one would expect from the analyses of other sectors, we find that the black-market firms are supplied by both thefts and legitimate purchases. In fact, the legitimate purchases loom surprisingly large as a source of supply to the illegal firms. Fully 45 percent of the firms whose sources are known were supplied by purchases from licensed dealers. This suggests that private transferors do often show up in this wholly illegal market and that they occasionally do collude with people who have openly illegal intentions.

The other striking fact in this

TABLE 2

The Scale of Black-Market Firms Encountered by ATF Undercover Investigations

Cities, Years, and Number	Rate of Observed Transactions					Inventories Seized at Arrest				
	<1 per month	1≤<2 per month	2≤<5 per month	≥5 per month	Unknown	0	1 to 5 guns	6 to 20 guns	>20 guns	Unknown
Boston, Massachusetts, 1973–75 N = 28	4	5	9	4	6	12	7	6	2	1
Connecticut, 1973–75 N = 7	1	—	5	1	—	6	1	—	—	—
Dallas/northern Texas, 1974–76 N = 12	—	—	6	1	5	6	2	—	2	2
Chicago/northern Illinois, 1974–76 N = 4	2	4	3	4	5	13	2	1	2	—
Southern Illinois, 1974–76 N = 17	1	6	4	5	1	15	—	—	2	—
San Francisco/northern California, 1975–77 N = 4	1	1	—	—	2	2	1	—	1	—
Los Angeles/southern California, 1975–77 N = 7	2	1	2	2	—	1	2	3	1	—
Atlanta, Georgia, 1974–76 N = 12	—	1	5	4	2	5	3	2	2	—
St. Louis, Missouri, 1975–77 N = 17	—	5	8	2	2	10	1	2	3	1
Washington, D.C., 1974–76 N = 23	4	4	13	1	1	17	3	3	—	—
Total	15	27	55	24	24	87	22	17	15	4
Percentage of total	10	19	38	16	16	60	15	12	10	3
Percentage of "known"	12	22	45	20	—	—	—	—	—	—

NOTE: N = number.

TABLE 3
SOURCES OF GUNS TO BLACK-MARKET FIRMS ENCOUNTERED BY ATF UNDERCOVER AGENTS

CITIES, YEARS, AND NUMBERS	THEFTS					LEGITIMATE PURCHASES	BOTH LEGITIMATE PURCHASES AND THEFTS	UNKNOWN
	FROM ALL SOURCES	FROM WHOLESALE UNITS	FROM RETAIL UNITS	FROM RESIDENCES	UNKNOWN			
Boston, Massachusetts, 1973–75 N = 28	18	2	3	7	7	10	2	2
Connecticut, 1973–75 N = 7	4	2	1	1	0	2	0	1
Dallas/northern Texas, 1974–76 N = 12	8	0	2	7	0	2	1	3
Chicago/northern Illinois, 1974–76 N = 4	10	4	2	5	0	6	2	4
Southern Illinois, 1974–76 N = 17	11	0	6	6	2	4	4	6
San Francisco, northern California, 1975–77 N = 4	2	0	1	1	0	2	1	1
Los Angeles, southern California, 1975–77 N = 7	3	1	1	2	0	4	1	1
Atlanta, Georgia, 1974–77 N = 12	2	0	1	1	0	6	0	4
St. Louis, Missouri, 1975–77 N = 17	10	0	4	1	5	6	2	3
Washington, D.C., 1974–76 N = 23	10	0	2	7	2	10	2	5
Total	78	9	23	38	17	52	15	30
Percentage of total firms with source**	54	—	—	—	—	36	10	21
Percentage of "known" firms with source	68	—	—	—	—	45	13	—
Percentage of firms with thefts of known source	—	13	33	54	—	—	—	—

NOTE: N = number.
These firms were also recorded in thefts and legitimate purchase columns.
** Totals to more than 100 percent because of multiple sources of supply for given firm.

table is the rather heavy reliance on thefts from private residences. Among firms supplied by thefts from known sources, 54 percent were supplied at least partly by thefts from private residences. This suggests that at least some of the enormous volume of guns stolen from private residences each year are transferred again, either by the thieves themselves or through a specialized institution. In fact, it seemed clear that many "gun firms" encountered by ATF agents were, in fact, generalized "fencing" operations. The "dealers" often sold appliances, jewelry, and so forth that were openly admitted as stolen, in addition to guns. Approximately 19 of the 115 firms with known sources of supply appeared to be fencing operations. Thus fencing operations seemed to account for about 10 percent of all the firms encountered and about 25 percent of all firms that were supplied at least partly by thefts.

The general picture of the black market suggested by these data, then, is one of fairly small firms. None appear to be exclusively in the business of selling guns to proscribed persons simply because there does not seem to be enough money in this business. They appear to be a mixture of (1) private transferors who occasionally sell guns to people who announce their illegal intentions, (2) thieves who happen to pick up guns in burglaries and are willing to sell them directly to other criminals, and (3) some people who operate as middlemen between gun owners and gun-stealing thieves on one hand and people who want to buy guns for openly illegal purposes on the other. Given the porousness of the "legitimate" sectors of the distribution system, this is roughly the result one would expect.

Summary: potential sources of supply

In sum, the potential sources of supply to proscribed persons are diversified. Federal licensees transfer 1,500,000 to 2,300,000 handguns a year with some 9000 to 90,000 involving proscribed persons. Private individuals transfer 300,000 to 700,000 handguns with an unknown number involving proscribed individuals. About 60,000 to 200,000 handguns are stolen each year with a large proportion of these ending up in the hands of proscribed persons. Finally, nestled among these transactions may be some relatively small, impermanent firms perfectly willing to deal with proscribed individuals, but probably not exclusively in this business. While thefts emerge from this analysis as probably the most important sector in supplying proscribed individuals, there is reason to be concerned about all of these sources, since all have significant potential to supply proscribed persons.

CURRENT PATHS TO OFFENDERS

These rough estimates of the supply potential of different sectors provide some basis for gauging their relative importance—both now and in the future as different control measures are tried. To give some focus to current control efforts, however, it is desirable to develop some exact information about how guns currently reach criminal offenders. Fortunately, a small amount of data is available to explore this issue. For a while, the Boston Regional Office of ATF conducted "forward traces" of handguns involved in criminal offenses in Boston. These investigations began with a gun seized in a crime, continued with a routine trace that revealed when and where the gun was last sold at retail and to whom, and then followed the path of the gun to the offender through interviews with private owners. The interviews, conducted by ATF agents, continued along the chain of private owners until the offender was reached, the gun was stolen, or the next owner could not be located.

Obviously, these data are flawed. The sample is small. Boston may be different from many other cities. It is biased toward paths that can be conveniently investigated. And the validity of statements by gun owners being questioned by federal agents about guns used in crimes must be considered questionable. Still, since this is the only empirical information of this type now available, it commands attention.

Table 4 presents the data in a way that allows us to see how guns reach criminal offenders in Boston. Three observations drawn from this table seem particularly important.

First, guns reach criminal offenders through many paths. The problem of containing handguns is not simply a problem of thefts, or retail sales, or private transfers. It is all of these things to varying degrees depending on the offense.

Second, private transfers do not emerge as a major sector supplying guns to offenders. Licensed dealers and thefts are more important. To a degree this is reassuring. A world in which guns migrated to proscribed people through long chains of private transfers shading almost imperceptibly into illegal transfers presents the most difficult control problem. Although we cannot be confident that this sector will not become important in the future, it is cheering to see that it need not be our highest priority now.

Third, a striking difference appears between the sources of guns used in armed robbery and those used in assaults. Slightly more than half of the assault guns reach the attackers from licensed dealers in legitimate transactions. The guns involved in armed robbery, however, reach the robbers through different routes with the predominant mechanism being theft. A nice intuitive explanation for this difference can be constructed. We know—largely from studies of homicides—that assaults are relatively likely to involve ordinary, noncriminal populations. We also know that armed robbers are much more likely to be criminal recidivists. If the existing regulations were successful in discouraging people with criminal records from acquiring guns through the licensed sector, and if these people could not easily find people to transfer a weapon to them privately, one would expect the pattern we in fact find: armed robbers—who are more often expressly and determinedly criminal—equip themselves largely through illegal markets.[16]

These data, then, lend additional support to the general implications of the analysis of the supply potential of the various sectors. Since all the sectors are important both now and in the future, we should organize a broadly diversified attack on the supply system. To the extent that we want to control street crime and keep guns from criminal recidivists, however, we should probably give greatest emphasis to controlling thefts.

16. Philip J. Cook and James Blose, "State Programs for Screening Handgun Buyers," *The Annals* of the American Academy of Political and Social Sciences, 455:80–91 (May 1981).

TABLE 4

PATHS OF GUNS TO OFFENDERS

| OFFENSE | ORIGINAL RETAIL PURCHASE | | UNBROKEN CHAINS OF PRIVATE TRANSFER | STOLEN AT SOME STAGE | OTHER OR UNKNOWN | TOTAL |
	ENTITLED PURCHASER	PROSCRIBED PURCHASER				
Homicide and rape (in percentage)	28 N = 2	0 N = 0	0 N = 0	72 N = 5	0 N = 0	100 N = 7
Assault (in percentage)	52 N = 21	2 N = 1	20 N = 8	13 N = 5	13 N = 5	100 N = 40
Armed robbery (in percentage)	8 N = 2	0 N = 0	17 N = 4	62 N = 15	13 N = 3	100 N = 24
Other, for example, drugs, burglary, gambling, drink, and weapons offenses (in percentage)	14 N = 6	2 N = 1	26 N = 11	50 N = 21	7 N = 3	100 N = 42

SOURCE: Closed ATF Investigative Case Files, Boston, MA, 1975–76.
NOTE: N = number.

THE DEPLOYMENT OF CONTROL EFFORTS

Given this strategic analysis of sources of supply, it is useful to consider which institutions could be helpful in plugging the various loopholes. At the outset we are inclined to think that federal efforts, and particularly federal criminal enforcement, will be the most important largely because ATF is the most prominent institution in this area. A systematic review of how these different sources might be attacked, however, leads to a strikingly different solution.

The licensed retail sector is the responsibility of the Bureau of Alcohol, Tobacco and Firearms of the U.S. Department of the Treasury. While in principle they could expect some assistance in regulating dealers from state and local agencies, little is forthcoming. Their few thousand agents and compliance inspectors constitute virtually the entire work force that can be deployed to regulate this sector. In practice this means that federal licensees feel little pressure from ATF regulators: fewer than 10 percent are investigated each year, and fewer than 1 percent have any action taken against them.[17] The modest pressure suggests that federal licensees could safely supply proscribed individuals in both intrastate and interstate transactions. In fact, a plausible argument can be made that the most effective way to shrink the interstate movement of guns from loose to tight states is not to focus on the gunrunners, but to use regulatory actions to clamp down on the relatively few federally licensed dealers involved in this trade. This

17. "Handgun Crime Control—1975–1976," p. 310.

suggests that ATF has an important regulatory role in controlling federal licensees.

The private transfer sector is currently no one's responsibility. To the extent one wanted to deter private individuals from transferring guns to proscribed individuals, he would have to rely on state or city laws prohibiting such transfers—federal laws would be irrelevant unless a person handled more than a few guns a year.[18] Enforcement would depend on undercover investigations in which police offered to buy guns after identifying themselves as proscribed persons. In principle, federal agents could do this—charging private sellers with "conspiracy" or "aiding and abetting" proscribed persons to possess handguns—but the cases would be difficult to develop and would yield returns that seemed small to sophisticated federal agents. Moreover, since there are only a few thousand federal criminal agents scattered throughout the country, it is difficult to believe that they would be much of a presence in controlling private transfers. A more plausible alternative would be to encourage local police departments to attack illegal gun transfers with the same vigor that characterizes current efforts against drug dealers. There are obvious difficulties with such an approach, but it is difficult to imagine alternative methods to prevent private transfers of handguns to proscribed individuals.

18. For a discussion of existing statutes regulating such transfers, see James Blose and Philip J. Cook, "Regulating Handgun Transfers: Current State and Federal Procedures and an Assessment of the Feasibility and Cost of the Proposed Procedures in the Handgun Crime Control Act of 1979" (Durham, NC: Institute of Policy Sciences and Public Affairs, 1980).

Thefts also seem to be most usefully attacked by local police departments. Since burglary and larceny are important local crimes, local police departments are already well organized to deter the offenses, apprehend the offenders, and, to a degree, attack fencing operations associated with burglaries. While one can, again, imagine a federal criminal effort to combat gun thefts, it is hard to imagine that a few federal agents could substantially increase current local capacities. Of course, even local police departments with all their resources have not been particularly successful in controlling burglaries. But still, to the extent one wanted to focus on thefts as current data indicates we should, one would have to rely primarily on local police.

Black-market firms sound as though they should be the special focus of federal criminal investigations. We can imagine sophisticated undercover investigations disclosing elaborate conspiracies. The problem is that our analysis and data suggest that the black market in guns will not have an elaborate structure. Chances are that the black-market firms will be small, impermanent, and hard to distinguish from private transferors and thieves disposing of stolen goods. In fact, the most elaborate operations are likely to be generalized fencing operations. Few gun dealers may be worth a federal case. The best approach is likely to be high volume, relatively unsophisticated undercover investigations aided by patrol efforts and a few informants. This, again, can be mounted most easily by local police.

This quick review suggests a surprising and important conclusion: the most important institutions for containing guns in the entitled sector are local police departments—not federal agencies. They are well positioned and organized to discourage illegal private transfers, to discourage burglaries and disrupt fencing operations, and to control the black-market firms that are most likely to appear. To control federal licensees, one would have to rely on ATF, but we would be primarily interested in their regulatory programs, not their criminal enforcement program. In fact, it seems that the institution we need least in controlling transfers is a large, sophisticated federal criminal investigative capability. To the extent that we wanted ATF to take responsibility for a national program to keep guns out of the hands of proscribed individuals, then, we would urge them to develop their regulatory programs and their liaison capabilities with local police, rather than an independent criminal investigative capacity. To the extent ATF developed and maintained independent criminal investigative capabilities, they should be deployed as follows: (1) as part of the effort to mobilize local police, (2) as substitutes for local police in areas where they are unwilling to pick up the local burden, or (3) used in a very small number of cases that involved large, interstate illegal firms. They cannot hope to contain guns in the entitled sector by themselves.

Organizational and Other Contraints on Controlling the Use of Deadly Force by Police

By JAMES LINDGREN

ABSTRACT: Researchers have often suggested rule making to control the use of deadly force by police. But organizational and other constraints impede the institution of effective rules. Unlike decisions in other large decentralized organizations, a police officer's decision to fire a gun is not easily controlled by top management. The structure of police departments, the nature of the decision to fire a gun, and the pressures on the review of the use of deadly force all make reducing the unnecessary use of force difficult. In addition, as long as the density of guns in a community is high, police policymaking is further restricted. Very little can be done to reduce the use of excessive force by police in the situations where suspects are threatening officers because of the possibility that the suspect may use a gun against the police. Police departments, however, can more effectively restrict the use of force against fleeing felons.

James Lindgren is a research attorney at the American Bar Foundation and book review editor of the American Bar Foundation Research Journal. A 1974 cum laude graduate of Yale College, he attended the University of Chicago Law School, where he was associate editor of the Law Review. *After graduating from law school in 1977, he practiced law in Chicago for two years before joining the Bar Foundation. Besides criminal law, his research interests are legal ethics and estates and trusts. He is currently directing the American Bar Foundation's project,* Sentencing Guidelines of Sentencing Commissions: Aggravating and Mitigating Circumstances.

The author would like to thank Franklin E. Zimring, Philip J. Cook, J. Randolph Block, Louise Kaegi, and Elizabeth Michelman for their many helpful suggestions. The opinions and conclusions expressed in this article are the author's, not those of the American Bar Foundation, its officers or directors, or other persons or institutions associated with its work.

AMERICAN police are more heavily armed and they shoot more often than police in any other Western democracy. Indeed, the possession of a handgun is a defining characteristic of the urban American police officer and an essential part of his uniform, now and in the foreseeable future.

The simple reason for an armed police is a heavily armed general population and an even more heavily armed criminal population. Since in the short run altering these conditions is unlikely, the issue, then, is this: when and how should police use firearms?

USING FORCE EFFECTIVELY: LOOKING AT ONE SIDE

How to make the police use their guns more effectively has been treated as a one-sided issue: how to reduce the unnecessary use of firearms by police. The other side of the issue—how to increase the necessary use of firearms by police—has been largely ignored. Almost uniformly, when police are criticized for using force, they are accused of using too much force for the situation or of failing to handle the situation in a way that would not require using force.

A number of explanations for ignoring the underuse of force are possible. If an officer fails to use force when a second officer thinks force is necessary, for example, when an officer fails to back up his partner, presumably this failure is corrected within the department. Informal pressures may force the reluctant officer to change his ways, transfer to a desk job, or even leave the force. Another possible explanation for a lack of concern about the underuse of force is that police, when making mistakes in using force, may tend to err toward using excessive force rather than insufficient force. This tendency toward excessive force may result from a police subculture that some researchers have found to be extremely violent.[1] Or police may view the public as well as criminals as enemies[2] and thus may think that shifting the risk of injury to the criminal and the public is acceptable in any potentially dangerous situation.

A final possibility is unlikely: that researchers' concern only with excessive force may reflect an anti-police "liberal" bias. But not all police work is uniformly seen as too tough on crime. Excessive leniency is a common complaint about police activities against gambling, prostitution, organized crime, graft, and union violence. Similarly, other criminal justice decisions, for example, sentencing, bail, and the insanity defense, are often criticized for favoring criminals.

VARIANCE IN THE USE OF DEADLY FORCE BY POLICE

That police will kill citizens and that they will do so almost exclusively with guns is certain. But the rate at which they kill is not. Lawrence W. Sherman and Robert H. Langworthy, who recently examined data on homicides by police in cities with populations of 250,000 or more, speculated that approximately 3.6 percent of all homicides in this country are committed by

1. See for example William A. Westley, *Violence and the Police* (Cambridge, MA: MIT Press, 1970). See also Mona Margarita, "Police as Victims of Violence," *Justice System J.*, 5:218, 229 (1980) (hereafter cited as "Police as Victims").
2. See for example Charles W. Thomas and W. Anthony Fitch, "The Exercise of Discretionary Decision-Making By the Police," *N. D. L. Rev.*, 54:61, 91 (1977).

police.[3] Yet they also found that the frequency with which officers kill citizens varies greatly from city to city. According to at least two sources of data used by Sherman and Langworthy, in Atlanta, Detroit, and Cleveland 1.0 to 2.5 civilians are killed by police for every 100,000 people, while in San Francisco, Milwaukee, Boston, Phoenix, San Diego, Long Beach, San Antonio, Columbus, San Jose, Honolulu, and Portland, less than 0.5 civilians are killed for every 100,000 people.[4] The size of these variations raises a strong possibility that policy differences in the use of force by police may account for some of the variation in the rate at which police kill citizens.

The data presented in a recent study of shootings of and by police in Chicago from 1974 to 1978 indicated that about one third of shootings by police involved flight, mistaken identity, accident, or other situation not involving a threat to an officer from a gun or other deadly weapon at the time of the shooting.[5] Even among the cases in which the police were responding to a threat of deadly force, some undoubtedly involved situations where aggressive actions by police aggravated the dangerousness of the situation or where police used greater force than necessary.

Other studies of the police use of force, both deadly and nondeadly, have also found that police often use excessive force. For example, in a 1966 study researchers rode with police officers in Boston, Chicago, and Washington, D.C., to determine how often police used force excessively.[6] Presumably, most of the situations in which force was used did not involve the use of a gun. They concluded that the police used force excessively in 35 percent of the incidents in which they used force.[7] If the Washington data are excluded, according to the researchers police in Chicago and Boston used excessive force in 46 percent of the incidents in which they used force. Of course, these figures probably substantially overstate the problem. Because excessiveness is in the eye of the beholder, it is reasonable to assume that researchers who rode with police to look for excessive force found what they were looking for.

CONTROLLING THE POLICE USE OF GUNS: ORGANIZATIONAL CONSTRAINTS

The defining function of the police, as Egon Bittner has argued, is "the distribution of situationally justified force in society."[8] Even if a policeman is called to mediate a domestic quarrel or to quiet a noisy party, the threat that police might use force motivates "calling the cops" and that same threat helps enforce whatever solution—temporary or otherwise—the police are able to achieve. But this is not their only function. Police departments are noted for the range

3. Lawrence W. Sherman and Robert H. Langworthy, "Measuring Homicide by Police Officers," *J. Crim. L. Criminology*, 70:546, 553 (1979).

4. Ibid., p. 556. Several other cities had rates above 1.0 or below 0.5 on one measure of killings by police, but not on the other.

5. William Geller and Kevin Karales, "Split-Second Decisions: Shootings of and by Chicago Police," preliminary draft (Chicago, IL: Chicago Law Enforcement Study Group, 1980).

6. Robert J. Friedrich, "Police Use of Force: Individuals, Situations, and Organizations," *The Annals* of the American Academy of Political and Social Science, 452:82–97 (Nov. 1980).

7. Ibid., p. 90.

8. Egon Bittner, *The Functions of the Police in Modern Society* (Washington, DC: U.S. Government Printing Office, 1970).

of activities performed, from information gathering to service to order maintenance to law enforcement.[9]

Horizontal undifferentiation, vertical differentiation, and rule making

The scope of police duties and discretion is vast, and the structure of police departments strongly contributes to this discretion. First, although some police duties are assigned to certain divisions of officers, the range of tasks left to the officer on the street is large. Thus, because most tasks are not divided and delegated to specific divisions of officers, police departments can be described as "horizontally undifferentiated," a characteristic that in itself tends to promote decentralized decision making.[10] Some reformers have called for altering the police structure to provide for greater specialization.[11] This has usually been suggested in order to reduce costs by using cheaper personnel for less challenging tasks or to give better, more expert service. But according to traditional management theory, an additional tendency of specialization would be to centralize control in top management.[12] Yet without such reforms, the horizontally undifferentiated structure of most police departments makes decision making more decentralized.

Second, police departments are hierarchically structured with many levels of decision making. This vertical differentiation is another characteristic that contributes to decentralized decision making.[13] Decisions in most police departments can be made by the state legislature, the city council or legislative body, the mayor, perhaps a police board, the police chief, several levels of supervisors at police headquarters, several levels of supervisors at the station house, and the officer on the street. In addition, Congress, the president, the federal executive branch, the federal courts, and the state and local courts may make policy decisions affecting the use of guns by police. The effects of such an organizational structure have been summarized by one management theorist: "Vertical differentiation also facilitates decentralization. The larger the number of supervisory levels in an organization, the more areas of responsibility will be subdivided and delegated."[14]

Thus these first two characteristics of the structure of police departments—vertical differentiation and a lack of horizontal differentiation—contribute to decentralized decision making. But according to traditional management theory, decentralized decision making does not mean a loss of control from the top. In a study of 254 government agencies, Marshall W. Meyer concluded that "vertical differentiation leads simultaneously to decentralization and rules that largely determine decisions in advance."[15] Similarly, one

9. James Q. Wilson, *Varieties of Police Behavior* (Cambridge, MA: Harvard University Press, 1968), pp. 16–19.

10. Dennis S. Mileti, David F. Gillespie, and D. Stanley Eitzen, "Structure and Decision Making in Corporate Organizations," *Soc. Soc. Res.*, 63:723, 736 (1979).

11. For example, Norval Morris and Gordon Hawkins, *The Honest Politician's Guide to Crime Control* (Chicago, IL: University Press, 1970), pp. 87–109.

12. See Mileti et al., pp. 726, 736.

13. See Marshall W. Meyer, *Bureaucratic Structure and Authority: Coordination and Control in 254 Government Agencies* (New York, NY: Harper & Row, 1972), pp. 51–55, 102–5 (hereafter cited as "Bureaucratic Structure"); but see Mileti et al., p. 738.

14. Mileti et al., p. 726. Here they are summarizing the literature; their own study casts doubt on these assertions.

15. Meyer, "Bureaucratic Structure," p. 104.

study of 63 large corporations suggested that in decentralized companies "power and influence are not relinquished by top management. . . . New decision makers are not added for influencing policy decisions, but rather information. . . . The new decision makers are excluded from any real position of or sharing in real power."[16]

The movement to use rules and procedures to control police behavior on the street has been led by Kenneth Culp Davis. Davis has applied principles developed in the law of administrative agencies to the criminal justice system, arguing that discretion must be confined and structured with open rules, open procedures, and open precedents.[17] The primary academic attacks on this approach to controlling police discretion have contested the legitimacy of rules that would provide for selectively enforcing the substantive criminal law. For example, Ronald J. Allen states that an official police policy not to arrest for marijuana possession would be impermissible legislation.[18] Davis counters that it is better for the police to openly make decisions not to enforce certain statutory crimes as a matter of policy than for individual officers to make such decisions ad hoc.[19] Both Davis and Allen appear to support rule making in areas not involving selective enforcement, such as the police use of force. Thus the problems of police rule making to control the use of force are problems not of the legitimacy of making rules, but of making rules effective.

The picture that traditional management literature paints is that of an organization easily controlled from the top. Even in decentralized organizations where the people in the lower levels of the hierarchy participate in decisions, top management is able to control all important decisions by rules and procedures. Unfortunately, this picture looks little like the reality facing police departments trying to control the use of firearms. Setting rules and procedures is much less effective in controlling the police use of force than might be supposed theoretically from the management literature, and it is important for policymakers to know why.

The decision itself

We have already seen two characteristics of police departments—vertical differentiation and a lack of horizontal differentiation—that usually contribute to decentralized decision making. The third factor limiting police rule making to control the use of force is that, unlike some other police decisions, the locus of the decision to use a gun is the bottom level of the hierarchy: the officer on the street.[20] Only rarely is an officer specifically ordered to fire a gun. At those rare times, the order usually comes from the officer's immediate supervisor who is also on the scene. That the decision to fire a gun is made at the lowest level in the hierarchy is not just a reason for rule

16. See Mileti et al., p. 738.

17. Kenneth Culp Davis, *Discretionary Justice: A Preliminary Inquiry* (Baton Rouge, LA: Louisiana State University Press, 1969), p. 225; and idem, *Police Discretion* (St. Paul, MI: West Publishing, 1975), pp. 143–48.

18. Ronald J. Allen, "The Police and Substantive Rulemaking: Reconciling Principle and Expediency," *U. Pa. L. Rev.*, 125:62 (1976); and idem, "The Police and Substantive Rulemaking: A Brief Rejoinder," *U. Pa. L. Rev.*, 125:1172 (1977).

19. Kenneth Culp Davis, "Police Rulemaking on Selective Enforcement: A Reply," *U. Pa. L. Rev.*, 125:1167 (1977).

20. Contemporary Studies Project: Administrative Control of Police Discretion, *Iowa L. Rev.*, 58:892 (1973).

making, it is an impediment to rule making.

Fourth, the decision to fire a gun is unreflective. Unlike the decisions of administrative agencies, which form the basis for Davis's recommendations, a police officer deciding whether to use a gun usually lacks the time to consider the decision, to gather and check facts, to review policies and precedents, and to seek help from a supervisor if in doubt. Albert Reiss has recently argued that the decision to use a gun is not a split-second decision, that the decision is actually a series of smaller decisions that culminate in the decision to pull the trigger.[21] I agree with Reiss to the extent that no decision is truly a split-second decision; but some decisions are made more quickly than others. The decision to hire an officer or relocate a station house can be made with greater reflection and care than the decision to fire a gun.

Scholars often draw a distinction between operational decisions and policy decisions. Operational decisions are delegated to the lower levels in the hierarchy.[22] They are usually considered so unimportant that those making only operational decisions are said to lack "real power."[23] Policy decisions, on the other hand, are the important decisions, and they are reserved for management.[24] If the decision to fire a gun can be treated as an operational decision, it is a unique one: the officer exercises real power with serious and immediate consequences.

Reviewing the use of force

Fifth, the review of the decision to use deadly force is unlike review within an administrative agency. Not only is review of the decision to fire a gun usually impossible before the decision is carried out, but even the post hoc review is distorted by outside pressures. When a police department reviews the use of a gun to shoot a citizen, it needs to justify its actions to that citizen, his family, and the public. It usually can do nothing to mitigate or correct the direct results of any particular mistake in using guns. The reviewers may be more interested in protecting the public image of the department than in controlling the use of guns.[25] One would expect that the department would not punish minor violations of rules that result in serious harm. Informal punitive sanctions are also not likely to be applied to the extent that a police subculture, especially in the officer's own station house, generally supports the use of violence by police officers.

Where shots are fired by police but no harm is done, the department has its best opportunity to review the decision to use a gun, because there may be no one pressuring the department to justify its actions. Technically, a wrongful shooting at a citizen constitutes an assault in most jurisdictions, but it is unlikely that citizens will criticize the police without injuries to citizens.

Criminal and civil actions to punish wayward officers are also ineffective at controlling excessive violence by police. In the small number of cases that have reached court, juries have on the whole been sympathetic to police officers charged with using excessive force. Only the most egregious and usually malicious inci-

21. Albert J. Reiss, Jr., "Controlling Police Use of Deadly Force" *The Annals* of the American Academy of Political and Social Science, 452:122–34 (Nov. 1980).

22. See Mileti et al., p. 738; but see Thomas and Fitch, p. 87.

23. See Mileti et al., p. 738.

24. Ibid.

25. Reiss, p. 125.

dents are likely to be directly punished with this method.

Thus, contrary to its effect in other large organizations, decentralization in police departments significantly impedes the control of police gun use by rule making. The locus of decision making is the lowest level in the hierarchy, the decision to fire a gun is unreflective, the results of gun misuse are immediate and uncorrectable, and the review process is distorted both by pressures to justify the use of force in particular cases and by the support of the police subculture and most juries for the use of force.

GUN OWNERSHIP: ANOTHER CONSTRAINT ON RULE MAKING

The organizational constraints are not the only limits on police rule making to control the use of force. Most community characteristics that might lead to the use of force by police are largely beyond anyone's control, especially in the near future. No one expects a significant reduction in the crime rate, and even if Congress were to outlaw handguns—which it is not likely to do—such a change would take years to substantially decrease the availability of guns. Preliminary data by Sherman and Langworthy show simple correlation coefficients of .25 to .54 between a city's gun density and its rate of killings by police.[26] It is easy to make too much of this moderately strong relationship because the figures do not distinguish other cultural influences that would increase both gun density and shootings by police. The same attitudes that lead people to purchase firearms would likely cause a more frequent use of

those firearms by both police and citizens. Determining the effect of the simple fact of gun ownership on killings by police is impossible from this data.

Gun ownership influences policymaking in another way. As long as gun density is high, certain types of police activity are difficult to control and reduce by rules. Oversimplifying things a bit, there are two types of situations in which police use their guns: (1) when a criminal flees an officer, and (2) when a criminal "comes toward" an officer, that is, threatens to attack an officer.

In the first situation—that of the fleeing felon—police policymaking may potentially reduce the unnecessary use of guns by police. But in the second situation—that of the criminal coming toward the officer—little can be done to control the police use of guns. Any threatening movement indicating that the criminal might be about to use a gun, or even a glint from a piece of metal, may signal to the officer that he must fire his gun or risk being fired on himself.[27] The justification of self-defense, even if later found to be mistaken, will in practice be available to any officer who can point to any fact that indicated a risk of being shot.

If 30 years from now gun control has succeeded in severely reducing gun density, then police rule making might reach farther than it does today.[28] It might more effectively control the use of guns when a felon

---

26. Sherman and Langworthy, p. 557.

27. Edward Ronkowski, Jr., "Uses and Misuses of Deadly Force," *De Paul L. Rev.*, 28:701, 718–19 (1980).

28. Franklin E. Zimring, "Handguns in the Twenty-First Century: Alternative Policy Futures," *The Annals* of the American Academy of Political and Social Sciences, 455:1 (May 1981).

comes toward an officer, as well as when a felon flees. Police would still wear guns on duty because they would need them to meet and top any threat of force. But when a suspect reached for his pocket or showed a glint of metal, he would probably be reaching for a knife instead of a gun. An officer might be required to wait before firing until he saw a gun or until a felon with a knife was close enough to strike.[29] In any event, the use of force could be more carefully tailored to the threat because an assumption in most hostile situations that a suspect is about to use a gun would be false.

Nevertheless, even today rules controlling the use of force against fleeing felons can be made more effective. In most states today police are justified in using force in two basic situations: (1) self-defense or the defense of the life of another person and (2) the arrest of a fleeing felon.[30] In some states force may not be used in stopping a felon fleeing the commission of just any felony; to justify the police using force, the felon must be fleeing a felony involving the use or threat of force. Note that the felon's threat of force may be only in the commission of the crime and may not necessarily continue during flight. Thus police may use guns to arrest a fleeing felon even if he, like most felons, shows only a desire to flee.[31]

Some states define a forcible felony as including certain enumerated crimes. Police departments ought to look very hard at the dangers involved in those crimes. In Illinois, for example, burglary is defined by statute as a forcible felony and thus justifies the use of firearms in making an arrest.[32] Data recently reported by the Chicago Law Enforcement Study Group can be used to call this definition into question.[33] Although burglary accounted for nearly 15 percent of incidents of civilians shot by police—second only to armed robbery—it accounted for only 2 percent of incidents of police officers shot by civilians. Stated another way, in burglary situations, the ratio of civilians shot by police to police officers shot by civilians is 36 to 1. This compares with a 6-to-1 ratio for armed robberies or nondomestic disturbances, a 5-to-1 ratio for situations of a person with a gun, a 4-to-1 ratio for traffic offenses, and a 3-to-1 ratio for domestic disturbances. A New York study of the reasons for criminals killing police lends inferential support to this analysis. It concluded that every police officer killed by a burglar since 1844 was killed because the burglar was trying to protect himself.[34]

How, then, can a legislature or police department[35] control the use of force in the fleeing felon situation? It could restrict the scope of the fleeing felon rule in one of two ways. First, the use of force could

29. As expected, guns are much more lethal to police officers than knives. See Margarita, "Police as Victims, " p. 223.

30. See generally Ronkowski; and Lawrence W. Sherman, "Execution Without Trial: Police Homicide and the Constitution," *Vand. L. Rev.*, 33:71 (1980).

31. Mona Margarita, "Killing the Police: Myths and Motives," *The Annals* of the American Academy of Political and Social Science, 452:63–71 (Nov. 1980) (hereafter cited as "Killing the Police"); and idem, "Police as Victims, p. 229.

32. Ill. Rev. Stat., ch. 38§2–8 (1980).
33. Geller and Karales.
34. Margarita, "Killing the Police," p. 69.
35. It has been argued that police departments rather than legislatures are better suited to making rules for police activities. See Thomas and Fitch, p. 91; and Carl McGowan, "Rule-Making and the Police," *Mich. L. Rev.*, 70:659, 672 (1972).

be restricted to life-threatening situations, as some police departments have already done.[36] This would allow the use of deadly force when the suspect is coming toward the officer, but as for fleeing felons, only those who continue to threaten to use force would be legitimate targets of police fire.

Alternatively, a police department or the legislature could undertake a study of the risks to police, felons, and bystanders in various situations. If, as in Chicago, the study suggested that burglary was of little danger to police, and presumably bystanders, but of considerable risk to burglars, then the scope of the fleeing felon rule could be restricted by excluding burglary from the list of felonies for which deadly force may be used to make an arrest.

CONCLUSION

Whatever strategies for controlling the use of deadly force are developed should deal with the organizational and other considerations I have discussed in this article. For example, if a police department were to design a system to review the police use of guns, the system should include the following three characteristics, among many others[37]: (1) every shot fired would be reviewed; (2) burdensome paperwork would be imposed on the officer as part of the review process;

and (3) review would take place "downtown," at police headquarters.

If every shot were reviewed, as it is now in some police departments, review would often occur in situations where there would be little need to justify departmental actions to the public. This would not ensure that the purpose of the review would be controlling the use of force—rather than self-justification—but it would make such a serious review possible. Also, because there are many more shots fired than citizens injured, the scope of behavior subject to review would be much wider.[38]

The second feature—burdensome paperwork—merely increases the negative consequences the officer encounters when he fires a gun. In a sense, this increase in the bureaucratic cost an officer faces when he fires a gun is at the heart of this review system. Raising costs to discourage gun use makes sense only if one accepts the assumption discussed at the outset of this article, that controlling the police use of firearms is a one-sided issue: reducing excessive force. Otherwise, increasing bureaucratic costs would merely waste resources and distort decision making.

The third feature of such a review system—a review downtown—should eliminate the effects of friendship on the review and should mitigate somewhat the effects of a police subculture supporting violence.

Any particular review system, however, is not the whole answer. Because the unnecessary use of force is a chronic problem, perhaps it cannot be solved, but only reduced at the margin. Rather than talking about this or that strategy, a combination of approaches should be tried and evaluated.

36. See Marshall W. Meyer, "Statistical Analysis of Los Angeles Police Department Officer Involved Shootings, 1974–1978/79," in *Officer Involved Shootings*, part 4 (Los Angeles Police Department: Board of Police Commissioners, June 1980), p. 18.

37. See David J. Brent, "Redress of Alleged Police Misconduct: A New Approach to Citizen Complaints and Police Disciplinary Procedures," *U. San Francisco L. Rev.*, 11: 587, 612–20; and Samuel G. Chapman, *Police Firearms Use Policy*, Presidents Comission on Law Enforcement and Administration of Justice, pp. 19–41.

38. Ibid.

The police use of force has often been debated in the political realm, with interested persons and groups lining up either for or against the police. Unfortunately, this public debate has polarized police management into defending the department. What those who so strongly attack the police use of force fail to realize is that the single most important ally they have is the police department's top managers, for the use of deadly force by the police is best understood as a management problem. If only the citizen critics and the police hierarchy can join forces, then good management can make good politics.

The Bartley-Fox Gun Law's Short-Term Impact on Crime in Boston

By GLENN L. PIERCE and WILLIAM J. BOWERS

ABSTRACT: By making the illicit carrying of a firearm punishable with a one-year "mandatory" prison term, the Massachusetts (Bartley-Fox) gun law intervenes at what appears to be a critical juncture—from the standpoint of deterrent effectiveness and political feasibility—in the chain of decision that leads from the acquisition of a gun to its use in a crime. Drawing on FBI crime data, we employed interrupted time series techniques and multiple control group comparisons to examine the impact of the law on gun and nongun assault, robbery, and homicide. First, the law substantially reduced the incidence of gun assaults, but produced a more than offsetting increase in nongun armed assaults. Evidently, the law prevented some individuals from carrying and using their firearm, but it did not prevent them from becoming involved in assaultive situations and resorting to other weapons. Second, the law resulted in a reduction in gun robberies, accompanied by a less than corresponding increase in nongun armed robberies. In effect, weapons substitution effect for armed robbery was relatively less than for armed assault. Third, the law reduced gun homicides with no increase in nongun homicides. Thus the gun law produced a net decline in the incidence of criminal homicide. Finally, the timing of the law's impact suggests that it was the publicity about the law's intent rather than the severity or certainty of the punishments actually imposed under the law that was responsible for the observed reductions in gun-related crimes.

Glenn L. Pierce is the associate director of the Center for Applied Social Research at Northeastern University, Boston, Massachusetts.

William J. Bowers is director of the Center for Applied Social Research at Northeastern University, Boston, Massachusetts.

NOTE: The data for this article were provided by the Boston Police Department (BPD) and the Uniform Crime Reporting (UCR) branch of the Federal Bureau of Investigation (FBI). We wish to thank Philip J. Cook and Joe Garner for their critical insights.

A COMPREHENSIVE gun control strategy designed to reduce the incidence of gun-related crime would need to address the successive decision points leading to the use of a gun in crime: the decision to acquire a gun, the decision to carry it, and the decision to use it for criminal purposes. Existing gun control efforts have typically focused on one of these decision points at the exclusion of the other two.[1]

The approach that casts the broadest net is the one that attempts to restrict the acquisition of guns. This includes laws that regulate or limit the importation, manufacture, sale, transfer, ownership, and/or possession of firearms. Such laws will, in principle, reduce the pool of potential gun offenders; fewer people will be in a position to carry a gun or to use it for criminal purposes.

Opponents of acquisition control laws argue that, in practice, such laws will not stop serious criminals—presumed to be responsible for most gun crime—from acquiring, carrying, and using guns. Instead, they say, such laws will deprive law-abiding citizens of the guns they want and need for sport and self-protection. A testimony to the perceived need for guns is the estimated 85 to 125 million firearms in the hands of the American public—easily one gun for every two adult citizens and more than one for each household.[2]

At the other end of the spectrum are approaches aimed narrowly at the decision to use a gun for criminal purposes. Gun-use laws, commonly referred to as "weapon enhancement" statutes, typically impose an additional term of imprisonment for crimes committed with a gun. Michigan's "felony firearms statute" which adds a mandatory two years to the sentence imposed for offenses such as aggravated assault, armed robbery, forcible rape, and criminal homicide when they are committed with a gun is an example of this approach.[3]

A law of this kind is more attractive politically; it specifically targets the "criminal element," those who have been convicted of violent felony offenses. Consequently, organized gun interests have not strenuously opposed such statutes in states like California, Florida, and Michigan. But the effects of these weapons enhancement laws are doubtful. The most thoroughly studied of these statutes—the Michigan felony firearms law—shows no solid evidence of having reduced gun-related crime.[4] The problem with this approach may be that it targets too narrow a group of potential offenders who are too committed to criminal activity and too dependent on guns in such activity.

Perhaps the optimal approach from the standpoint of both deterrent effectiveness and political feasibility is the one that targets the decision

NOTE: This article is a revised version of a report entitled *The Impact of the Bartley-Fox Law on Gun and Non-Gun Related Crime in Massachusetts* by the present authors released in April 1979 by the Center for Applied Social Research, Northeastern University, Boston, Massachusetts, and supported by the National Institute of Justice, Contract No. 76-NI-99-0100.

1. The recent New York state gun law that became effective in 1980 is an exception that focuses on both carrying and use of a firearm.

2. James Wright, "The Recent Weapons Trend and the Putative 'Need' for Gun Control" (Presented at the American Sociological Association, 1980).

3. Colin Loftin and David McDowall, " 'One With a Gun Gets You Two': Mandatory Sentencing and Firearms Violence in Detroit," *The Annals* of The American Academy of Political and Social Science, 455:150–67 (May 1981).

4. Ibid.

to carry a gun outside of the home or place of business. It may be that a substantial proportion of those who become involved in gun-related crimes carry guns but do not anticipate the specific situations that will precipitate their use and do not have the time or presence of mind when confronted with these situations to weigh the punishment if caught against the immediate advantage of using a gun.

The Massachusetts legislature took this approach when it enacted the Bartley-Fox gun law, which mandated a one-year minimum prison term for the unlicensed carrying of firearms. The law was explicitly intended to reduce the incidence of gun-related crime as well as the illicit carrying of firearms. Thus when David Bartley, one of the law's framers, first submitted the bill to the Massachusetts House of Representatives, he stated that the purpose of the law was to halt "all unlicensed carrying of guns . . . and to end the temptation to use the gun when it should not even be available."

The law is unlikely to be effective against those who decide to carry a gun for a specific, short-term purpose, such as robbing a bank. The target group is rather those who carry guns on their persons or in their cars without specific criminal purpose in mind, but as a matter of life-style—those Beha has called the "casual carriers."[5] The cumulative risk of apprehension for such people may be substantial over an extended period of time, especially if police

5. James A. Beha, III, "And Nobody Can Get You Out: The Impact of a Mandatory Prison Sentence for the Illegal Carrying of a Firearm on the Use of Firearms and the Administration of Criminal Justice in Boston, Part I–Part II," *Boston University Law Review*, 57 (1977).

employ proactive search-and-seizure tactics.

The law confronted this group with a dramatic apparent increase in the legal risk associated with carrying a gun without a license. A concerted campaign for two months prior to the law's effective date characterized the impending consequences in the following terms, "If you are caught with a gun, you will go to prison for a year and nobody can get you out." Carrying without a license had previously been punished with a fine or suspended sentence, and only occasionally with a brief incarceration.

For its intended impact on gun-related crime, this kind of law may be said to rely upon a derivative deterrent effect. That is, by increasing the punishment imposed for one offense—carrying a gun without a license—the law is intended to reduce the incidence of other crimes: gun assaults, gun robberies, and gun homicides.

The Massachusetts gun law could, conceivably, have still further deterrent effects on gun assault, gun robbery, and gun homicide if offenders were charged for carrying without a license and had a year added to the sentence imposed for assault, robbery, or homicide.[6] Such

6. Since the punishments imposed for aggravated assaults, armed robbery, and criminal homicide are, respectively, more severe in that order (quite apart from the use of a gun), a flat or constant increment in punishment when a gun is used may be expected to reduce gun assaults most, gun robberies next, and gun homicides least. The proportional addition to (marginal utility of) the additional punishment corresponds to this ordering of the three crimes. The fact that homicides are largely assault and robbery precipitated adds a derivative deterrent component for gun homicides. And, the fact that punishments for the nongun versions of assault, robbery, and homicide remain unaltered, adds a weapons displacement component for all three crimes,

an application of the law follows the model of a weapons enhancement statute. The available evidence suggests, however, that the approach will have little or no impact on gun-related crime.[7] Moreover, the publicity surrounding the implementation of the law gave no indication that it would be applied in this way, nor has this approach been adopted in subsequent practice to any noticeable degree.[8]

The Bartley-Fox Amendment became effective on 1 April 1975. Gun-related violent crime rates fell dramatically in Massachusetts between 1974 and 1976, suggesting that Bartley-Fox had an extraordinarily large deterrent effect. But before we accept this conclusion, it is necessary to rule out other possible explanations for the observed reductions in gun violence. Our rather extensive analysis of violent crime patterns in Massachusetts and other jurisdictions has convinced us that the Bartley-Fox law, and/or the publicity that attended its implementation, was indeed a highly effective deterrent—at least in the short run. The remainder of this article summarizes the evidence that has led us to this conclusion. We begin with an analysis of aggravated assault patterns, followed by robbery and then homicide. The discussion focuses

on Boston, with only very brief synopses of our results for other jurisdictions in Massachusetts.

ARMED ASSAULT

A large proportion of assaults are the result of spontaneous arguments, which the antagonists are unlikely to have foreseen. Gun assaults may typically be committed by those who are carrying guns without criminal intent and find themselves provoked or threatened. A law that dramatically increases the punishment for illicit carrying may cause a substantial proportion of these casual carriers to leave their guns at home, and thus may produce a substantial reduction in gun assaults.

To the extent that armed assault is situationally provoked rather than purposeful and preplanned, the removal of guns from the situations in which assault occurs cannot be expected to reduce the overall number of assaults. In assault-provoking situations, those involved will presumably resort to whatever weapons are available at the scene. Hence a reduction in the public's propensity to go armed with guns may increase the number of nongun assaults. Indeed, with fewer guns being carried into assault-prone situations, potential assaulters may feel less restrained, and hence the increase in nongun assaults could more than offset the decrease in gun assaults.

Our analysis of armed assault focuses on the complementary issues of deterrence and weapon substitution. The presentation of our results is organized into three parts: (1) an intervention point analysis, using Box-Jenkins techniques, to examine when and if the level of gun and nongun armed assaults change; (2) a control group comparison of changes in Boston against those in

---

at least for potential offenders with a relatively high level of criminal intent. In effect, although punishments applied to carrying and to use may operate through different deterrence mechanisms, they lead, at least according to the logic of deterrence theory, to similar patterns of expected impact.

7. Loftin.

8. David Rossman, *The Impact of the Mandatory Gun Law in Massachusetts*. (National Institute of Law Enforcement and Criminal Justice, Law Enforcement Assistance Administration, United States Department of Justice, 1979).

selected control jurisdictions; and (3) an analysis of the impact of the law on citizen reporting.

Intervention point analysis

The analysis draws upon statistical techniques originally formulated by Box and Jenkins[9] and more recently elaborated by Deutsch.[10] These statistical techniques are used in conjunction with monthly crime data to model the pre–Bartley-Fox history of gun and nongun armed assaults in Massachusetts. The parameters of the models, usually referred to as ARIMA models (Auto-Regressive-Integrated-Moving Average models) are estimated using a program (ESTIM) developed by Stuart Deutsch.[11] This procedure enables us to characterize the pre–Bartley-Fox history of gun and nongun armed assaults in terms of their long-term trends, seasonal cycles, and moving average and/or autoregressive components.[12] This information is then used to predict what future course of gun and nongun armed assaults would be if all factors affecting these two types of crime remained constant. We can test whether the actual observed crime trends after the gun law exhibit statistically significant departures from the predicted future of the crime time series based on its history prior to the policy intervention.

A major advantage of this method is that the techniques are capable of incorporating the type of seasonal cycles that is often found in crime data. This is particularly important because seasonal fluctuations can obscure or be mistaken for immediate or short-term effects of a policy intervention. When regular seasonal cycles are observed in the data, as has been the case with monthly assault statistics in Massachusetts, the information from Deutsch's ESTIM program is used to deseasonalize the data. After this step, the future of the time series is predicted in terms of its trend and ARIMA components.

For gun assault, we found that a statistically significant downward shift occurred in March 1975—the month prior to implementation of Bartley-Fox.[13] Since implementation was preceded by a vigorous publicity campaign of several months duration, it is not surprising to find evidence that the law began to influence behavior even before it was officially in effect. Our analysis found that the downward shift that oc-

9. G.E.P. Box and G.M. Jenkins, *Time Series Analysis: Forecasting and Control* (San Francisco, CA: Holden-Day, 1977).

10. S. J. Deutsch, "Stochastic Models of Crime Rates," *ISYE Report Series*, 77(15) Atlanta: Georgia Institute of Technology, 1977).

11. Deutsch.

12. For a detailed description of the estimation procedure used in this section, see Glenn L. Pierce and William J. Bowers, *The Impact of the Bartley-Fox Law on Gun and Non-Gun Related Crime in Massachusetts* (Boston, MA: Center for Applied Social Research, Northeastern University, April 1979), Appendix A.

13. This is not at all a necessarily surprising result. The Bartley-Fox law was preceded by a dramatic, and not completely accurate, two-month publicity campaign, designed to educate the public concerning the new consequences citizens faced for violating the Massachusetts gun law. Under these circumstances, it is quite possible that this publicity preceding the gun law's introduction on 1 April 1975 resulted in what Zimring has termed an "announcement" effect by creating in the minds of citizens and potential gun offenders the impression that the new law was actually in force prior to its effective date. If this were so, we might indeed expect the gun law, or more accurately its publicity, to have affected gun and nongun related assaults as early as February 1975.

curred in March was sustained in subsequent months.

The same type of analysis yielded a statistically significant increase in nongun armed assaults in Boston, beginning in May 1975. We interpret this result as reflecting a tendency for people to substitute other weapons for guns in assault situations following implementation of the law.

A similar set of analysis for the remainder of Massachusetts demonstrated similar, though less pronounced, effects.[14]

Control group comparisons

As noted, intervention point analysis, by incorporating information on the pre–Bartley-Fox history of gun and nongun armed assaults, controlled for the effect of ongoing trends that might otherwise obscure or be mistaken for an impact of the law, or its publicity. These methods, however, do not control for those instances where exogenous events or socioeconomic factors intervene and result in departures from prior trends in crime. The Bartley-Fox law, of course, represents one such event, but the issue is to isolate the effects of the law from the effects of other possible factors.

To address this issue, we introduce control groups into our analysis. The importance of obtaining adequate control groups for this type of analysis is well articulated by H. Laurence Ross. He observes that "the literature of quasi-experimental analysis asserts that causal conclusions based only on the comparison of conditions subsequent to a supposed cause with those prior to a supposed cause are subject to a wide variety of rival explanations."[15] The control group design employed here allows us to compare the level of violent crime in Boston over time with the levels of crime in comparable jurisdictions over the same period.

The logic of this type of analysis is, of course, strengthened to the extent that an investigator can select control groups that are truly similar. That is, we want to be able to identify control jurisdictions that would be subject to the same exogenous factors or shocks—except for the Bartley-Fox law—as those in Boston, Massachusetts.

Since Boston's population has averaged approximately 600,000 inhabitants over the last decade, as control jurisdictions we have selected cities in two size categories: 250,000 to 500,000 inhabitants and 500,000 to 1,000,000 inhabitants for the United States, the North Central region, and the Middle Atlantic states. There are no cities in this population range in New England other than Boston; the Middle Atlantic states have no cities with 500,000 to 1,000,000 residents. In addition, we have drawn on the set of all cities within a 750-mile radius of Boston and that are equal to or larger than Boston in population: Washington, D.C.; Baltimore; Philadelphia; New York; Cleveland; and Detroit. The Eastern Seaboard cities are especially important because they represent a set of cities which are linked by a highway network that some previous work indicates may influence the flow of new

14. Glenn Pierce and William Bowers, "The Impact of Bartley-Fox Gun Law in Massachusetts" (To be published in *Crime and Delinquency*, 1982).

15. H. Lawrence Ross, "Deterrence Regained: The Cheshire Constabulary's Breatholyser Blitz," *J. Legal Studies*, 4(L):244 (Jan. 1977).

firearms.[16] The North Central cities were selected because of their similarity to Boston as northern industrial cities.

In addition to these control groups, we also selected Chicago as a control jurisdiction. Chicago serves a dual purpose because (1) it is a northern industrial city, although somewhat farther away than the other individual cities selected; and (2) along with Boston and Washington, D.C., it was chosen by the Alcohol, Tobacco, and Firearms Commission to be one of the sites for the Project CUE, an experimental program designed to reduce the illegal sale of firearms. This program was initiated in Boston and Chicago in July 1976 and in Washington, D.C., in February 1976. Thus Chicago—and Washington, D.C., to a lesser extent—becomes a useful reference point for measuring the impact of an alternative intervention (Project CUE) whose effects could be confounded with the Bartley-Fox law.[17]

Table 1 presents the comparison group analysis for Boston and its control jurisdictions. Three sets of annual statistics are presented in this table: (1) gun assaults per 100,000 inhabitants, (2) nongun armed assaults per 100,000 inhabitants, and

16. Franklin Zimring, critical review of Rossman et al., *The Impact of the Mandatory Gun Law in Massachusetts* (Office of Research and Evaluation Methods, National Institute of Law Enforcement and Criminal Justice, Law Enforcement Assistance Administration, 1980).

17. Since CUE was an undercover operation explicitly directed at reducing illegal sale of guns, it, therefore, did not affect the existing pool of illegally owned firearms. It is somewhat doubtful that this program would impact gun-related crime in Boston during 1976. However, if CUE did have a fairly immediate impact, it ought to show results in both Boston and Chicago. Thus Chicago serves as a control for the potentially confounding of Bartley-Fox and Project CUE.

(3) the percent gun assaults of all armed assaults for the years 1974, 1975, and 1976. This last measure, because it combines both potential deterrent and displacement effects, is a particularly sensitive indicator of the law's impact.

Turning to the analyses of gun assaults in Boston, we first examine Boston's change in gun assaults between 1974 and 1975 compared with the changes occurring in the selected comparison jurisdictions.[18] Between 1974 and 1975, Boston showed a 13.5 percent decline in gun assaults, a decrease greater than that occurring in any of the central jurisdictions. Indeed, of the control jurisdictions, only Chicago showed a decline in gun assaults approaching that of Boston: 8.2 percent versus 13.5 percent. In the following year, 1975 to 1976, however, Boston showed a slight increase in gun assaults while a number of the control groups showed declines. Over the two-year period following Bartley-Fox—1974 to 1976—Boston showed an overall decline in gun assaults of 11.7 percent. Unlike the first year change, 1974 to 1975, where Boston showed the greatest decrease, 4 of the 13 control jurisdictions—Philadelphia, Washington, D.C., Cleveland, and Chicago— showed a two-year decline greater than that of Boston.

The pattern of these results—a one-year decline greater than that occurring in the control jurisdictions followed by a slight upturn in gun assaults—raises the question of whether the duration of the Bartley-

18. Examinations of these changes on an annual basis potentially make the 1974 to 1975 change a conservative test because the Bartley-Fox law was implemented on 1 April 1975, with March as the empirically determined intervention point for gun assaults (Table 1).

TABLE 1

Gun Assaults, Nongun Assaults, and Percentage of Gun Assaults of Armed Assaults in Boston in Comparison to Cities Grouped Regionally and for Selected Eastern Seaboard and North Central Cities

Regions	Gun Assaults per 100,000			Nongun Armed Assaults per 100,000			Percentage of Gun Assaults of Total Armed Assaults		
	Rate, 1974	1974–75, Percentage Change	1974–76, Percentage Change	Rate, 1974	1974–75, Percentage Change	1974–76, Percentage Change	1974	1974–75, Percentage Change	1974–76, Percentage Change
Boston	101.4	−13.5	−11.7	290.0	31.1	40.4	25.9	−27.6	−30.4
Comparison cities grouped regionally: 250,000–500,000 inhabitants									
United States without Massachusetts	108.1	6.7	3.1	181.3	9.3	17.5	37.4	−1.5	−8.7
North Central states	101.6	13.8	15.2	154.2	5.2	13.6	39.7	4.8	.8
Middle Atlantic states	57.4	4.8	−7.4	181.1	15.0	16.1	24.1	−6.9	−16.1
Comparison cities grouped regionally: 500,000–1,000,000 inhabitants									
United States without Massachusetts	111.7	1.9	−7.5	178.5	3.4	5.0	38.5	−.9	−7.7
North Central states	120.9	7.6	−1.4	131.6	8.5	12.0	47.9	−.4	−6.6
Selected eastern seaboard and north central cities									
New York	113.7	5.9	−.8	359.5	10.0	12.4	24.0	−2.8	−4.3
Philadelphia	80.3	−4.5	−21.3	158.7	−6.4	−17.3	33.6	1.3	−3.3
Baltimore	165.0	12.2	−5.2	493.2	−1.0	−7.5	25.1	9.3	1.9
Washington, D.C.	142.0	3.9	−16.1	233.6	−.5	6.5	37.8	2.7	−14.3
Detroit	139.9	11.3	15.6	318.9	−.9	−1.2	30.5	8.3	11.2
Cleveland	244.0	−3.4	−13.3	135.7	3.8	−13.6	64.3	−2.6	2.0
Chicago	123.5	−8.2	−26.0	249.6	2.3	−5.9	33.1	−7.1	−15.4

Fox impact was short-termed, lasting perhaps less than a year. We do not, however, believe this is the case. First, we shall present evidence shortly that indicates that the Bartley-Fox law's effect on the actual incidence of gun assaults may have been particularly obscured by a concomitant effect of the law on citizen's reporting of gun assaults to police. Second, the remaining comparison group analysis for Boston, with regard to nongun armed assaults and the percentage of armed assaults in which guns were used, provides strong evidence for the proposition that the impact of Bartley-Fox extended through 1976, the final year of this analysis.

Looking at nongun armed assaults, we find that Boston shows a 31.1 percent increase between 1974 and 1975 and a 40.4 percent increase over a two-year period, 1974 to 1976. Importantly, these increases are more than twice those exhibited by any of the control jurisdictions. It should be noted that Boston's increase in nongun armed assaults may not have been entirely a function of displacement effects. Indeed as noted, some control jurisdictions showed increases in nongun armed assaults of 17 and 16 percentage points. Thus it is possible some of Boston's 40.4 percent increase in nongun armed assaults would have occurred as part of an ongoing increase in assaults. This also suggests, however, that Boston might have experienced an increase in gun assaults in 1975, rather than the decline that actually occurred following Bartley-Fox.

Examination of the measure that combines potential deterrent and weapon substitution effects shows that the weapon-related character of armed assaults in Boston changed following Bartley-Fox. Between 1974 and 1975—the first year following Bartley-Fox—the percent that guns represented of all armed assaults in Boston dropped from 25.9 percent to 18.8 percent. This decrease was almost four times greater than that shown by any of the control jurisdictions. In the two-year period—1974 to 1976—Boston showed a 30.4 percent decline in the percentage that gun assaults represent of armed assaults versus a maximum 16.1 percent decline occurring in the control group.

A similar analysis of the remainder of Massachusetts, not reported here, demonstrated qualitatively similar findings.[19]

Review of the impact on assault findings reveals a strong pattern of evidence supporting the hypothesis that the Bartley-Fox law reduced the likelihood of gun assault in Massachusetts. When the first year—1975—following the introduction of the law was examined, we found that relative to each of the control jurisdictions in both Boston and non-Boston Massachusetts communities, (1) gun assaults decreased, (2) nongun armed assaults increased, and (3) the percent that gun assaults represent of all armed assaults declined. In the two years following Bartley-Fox—1974 to 1976—this same pattern of results held up with one exception: between 1974 and 1976 gun assaults in 4 of Boston's 12 control jurisdictions showed larger declines than Boston had exhibited. Thus in 5 of 6 possible comparisons made, the results consistently indicate that the gun law affected the character of armed assault in Massachusetts.[20]

19. Pierce and Bowers.
20. This refers to the comparisons made with each of three indicators we have examined for the gun law impact: (1) gun assault, (2) nongun assault, and (3) the percent that gun assault represents of all assaults in the first year (1974–75) and in the two years (1974–76) following the Bartley-Fox law.

The statistics in Table 1 suggest the rather surprising conclusion that the weapon substitution effect of Bartley-Fox was larger than the deterrent effect—that is, the increase in nongun assaults more than compensated for the reduction in gun assaults. However, closer scrutiny of these data have convinced us that deterrent effects of the law are underestimated in Boston. Implementation of the Bartley-Fox law and its attendant publicity appears to have increased the likelihood of citizens' reporting gun assaults. We present the evidence for this conclusion in the next section.

Impact on citizen reporting: more refined measurement of gun assaults

As Richard Block has noted, the citizen's decision to notify the police of a crime is based, in part, on a victim's "calculation of the benefits derived from notification and the costs incurred."[21] For example, a victim may think he has something to gain by reporting an assault if he believes that the police can actually catch and punish an offender.

The Bartley-Fox law may have altered the likelihood that citizens will report gun crimes, particularly gun assaults, to the police. Compared with robberies or murders, assaults are a relatively ambiguous category of offenses. That is, in some cases it may not be altogether clear to the average citizen whether a legally punishable assault has actually occurred. Particularly in cases where a victim has been threatened with the visible display of a deadly weapon, but where no injury has occurred, the citizen may not be sure that such an action constitutes a criminal assault that the police and courts will take seriously. The Bartley-Fox law may have signaled the public that any crime involving a gun was serious and would be treated as such by the criminal justice system.

We would expect that any tendency of the law to increase citizens' reporting of gun assaults would be concentrated on the less serious forms of gun assault that involved threats rather than injuries. Empirical research bears out this observation. Richard Block found that assault victims who have been hospitalized or have received medical attention are significantly more likely to report the crime to the police than victims who were not injured.[22] Thus more accurate estimates of the deterrent effect of the gun law on assaultive behavior—unbiased by possible changes in citizens' reporting behaviors—could be obtained by isolating for analysis those gun assaults where an injury has been incurred.

This line of analysis cannot, however, be pursued using the FBI's Uniform Crime Reports (UCR) statistics because the UCR definition of an armed assault combines into one category: (1) assaults that involve only threats or attempts to inflict "bodily harm" on a victim and (2) assaults in which the victim actually has been injured. With statistics based on the UCR definition of assault, then, it is not possible to separate gun assaults that are threats from those that result in injury.

Fortunately, the Boston Police Department's (BPD) computerized crime statistics provide more refined categories of gun assaults than

21. Richard Block, "Why Notify the Police: The Victims Decision to Notify the Police of an Assault," *Criminology*, 4(2):555 (Feb. 1974).

22. Block.

TABLE 2

GUN ASSAULTS WITH BATTERY AND WITHOUT BATTERY IN BOSTON FOR THE PERIOD 1974 TO 1976

	NUMBER AND PERCENTAGE CHANGE	1974	1975	1976	1974–76, PERCENTAGE CHANGE
Gun assaults involving battery	Number	329	289	207	—
	Percentage change	—	−12.2	−24.9	−37.1
Gun assaults without battery	Number	266	236	339	—
	Percentage change	—	−10.3	+43.6	+27.4
Proportion of gun assaults which involved battery	Proportion	55.3	55.0	37.9	—
	Percentage change	—	−.5	−31.1	−31.5

are available in the UCR data. Specifically, using BPD data, we can independently examine gun assaults with battery and gun assaults without battery. Under Massachusetts law, assault with battery indicates that some type of force has been used on the victim. In the case of a gun assault, this would mean that the victim had in some manner been struck with either a bullet or a gun. In contrast, an assault without battery simply means that an offender has attempted to injure or has threatened to injure his victim, but has not inflcted any physical harm. Table 2 presents BPD statistics on gun assaults involving battery and those without battery.

The top row of figures in Table 2 presents the annual number of gun assaults with battery in Boston from 1974 through 1976. This is the category that research suggests should be less subject to changes in reporting behavior. Notably, while UCR Boston gun assault statistics (Table 1) show only a 11.7 percent decline between 1974 and 1976, BPD gun assaults with battery—that is, those most likely to involve injury—show a 37.1 percent decline over this same period. Thus the subcategory of gun assaults with bat-

tery showed a decrease in the two years following the introduction of the Bartley-Fox law more than three times the decrease exhibited by the UCR gun assault statistics, which groups gun assaults both with and without battery into one category.

Note further that in the two years after the introduction of the law, the number of gun assaults without battery actually increased and that the increase was concentrated between 1975 and 1976. Thus it would appear that the pattern of reported gun assaults in Table 1, especially the increase between 1975 and 1976 in Boston, occurs in the category of assaults without battery, which is more subject to reporting biases. Although the specific dynamic underlying the increase in incidence of less serious forms of gun assault in Boston is unclear, it seems likely that the increase is a result of some change in citizens' willingness to report gun assaults.

If we rely on Boston's battery gun assault statistics for our estimate of the deterrent impact of the gun law in Boston, we find, as noted previously, that Boston showed a 37.1 percent decline in the level of gun assaults between 1974 and 1976. It is important to note that using this revised estimate of the gun law's impact, we find that Boston's two-year decline in gun assaults is 30 percent greater than exhibited by any of Boston's control jurisdictions in Table 1.

Conclusions of the assault analysis

The introduction of the Bartley-Fox gun law had a twofold effect on armed assaults in Massachusetts. First, the law substantially reduced the incidence of gun assaults in Boston and other Massachusetts communities. Importantly, the decline in gun assaults in Boston appears to have started one month prior to the introduction of the law—suggesting that offenders initially were responding to the publicity attendant with the gun law implementation. Second, the gun law also apparently resulted in a substantial increase in nongun armed assaults. Thus while the law appears to have deterred some individuals from carrying and/or using their firearm, it appears not to have encouraged these individuals to avoid assaultive situations.

The law also appears to have increased the likelihood of citizens reporting less serious forms of gun assaults to the police; at least in Boston this phenomenon tended to obscure the deterrent effect of the law on gun assaults.

ARMED ROBBERY

As with our analysis of the Bartley-Fox law's impact on armed assaults, the armed robbery analysis will examine the dual questions of deterrence and weapon substitution. Specifically, we shall examine whether the gun law resulted in a reduction in gun robberies and whether this change was offset by corresponding increases in robberies with other types of weapons.

The analysis will also compare the relative magnitude of potential deterrence and weapon substitution effects for robbery with those observed in the assault analysis. To the extent that robbery is more often the result of planned purposeful action than is assault, we would expect a law like Bartley-Fox to have less deterrent impact on robbery because this law is specifically aimed at the carrying rather than the using of a firearm. Under these circumstances, individuals who carry firearms with a specific use in mind have relatively less to lose than offenders who are not planning to assault or to rob someone. Quite simply, although the costs are the same in terms of the gun law—a one-year prison term—the benefits of carrying a gun are less for the person who carries a gun, but who has no specific anticipated use for it.

Compared with assault, we also expect the magnitude of the displacement effects to be less. The logic behind this hypothesis is straightforward.[23] Robbery with a gun is generally a much easier task than robbery with other types of deadly weapons, unless an offender chooses to rob highly vulnerable targets. However, there is also a disincentive to switch to more vulnerable targets because these also tend to be much less lucrative, for example, a street robbery of an elderly person is generally much easier but also less lucrative than a robbery of a drug store.

Control group comparisons

Data restrictions prevent our conducting an intervention point analy-

23. Philip J. Cook, "The Effect of Gun Availability on Violent Crime Patterns," *The Annals* of The American Academy of Political and Social Science, 455:63–79 (May 1981).

sis of gun and nongun armed robberies. The UCR program only began classifying armed robbery into gun and nongun categories in 1974. The Box-Jenkins statistical techniques employed in the analysis of gun and nongun armed assaults require a minimum of five years of monthly preintervention data in order to model pre–Bartley-Fox crime trends.[24]

The available data are sufficient, however, for a comparison group analysis. As in the assault analysis, we examined the law's impact on (1) gun robbery, (2) nongun armed robbery, and (3) the percent that gun robbery represents of all armed robbery for Boston.

Table 3 presents annual statistics for Boston and its control jurisdictions on gun assaults, nongun armed assaults, and the percent that gun assaults represent of all armed assaults. When we initially examined Boston's first-year (1974 to 1975) post–Bartley-Fox change in gun robbery, there appeared to be little evidence of an immediate deterrent effort of the law. Indeed, between 1974 and 1975, gun robberies declined by only 1.8 percent in Boston. However, when Boston's first change in gun robberies—1.8 percent—is compared to the changes occurring in the control jurisdictions, we find that in 9 of the 12 sets of control jurisdictions, gun robberies increased more than they did in Boston. Thus although the law failed to reduce the level of gun robbery in Boston between 1974 and 1975, it may have been responsible for suppressing what would have been a substantial increase.

This impression is reinforced when the two-year (1974 to 1976) post–Bartley-Fox change in gun robbery is examined. Between 1974 and 1976, Boston showed a 35.5 percent decrease in gun robberies. Boston's two-year post–Bartley-Fox decline was exceeded by only 2 of the 12 control groups: Philadelphia, 36.7 percent, and Chicago, 43.5 percent.

The preceding interpretation, of course, remains quite tentative because several of Boston's control jurisdictions showed declines in gun robbery, similar to or greater than those exhibited by Boston. As in our armed assault analysis, however, we do not analyze the effect of the Bartley-Fox law on gun robberies separately from the analysis of the law's potential effect on nongun armed robberies.

Indeed, analysis of Boston's nongun robbery statistics (Table 3) reveals strong evidence indicating substantial first-year (1974 to 1975) displacement effects. In the first year following the Bartley-Fox law, we find nongun armed robberies in Boston increased by 35.4 percent between 1974 and 1975—an increase of 40 percent greater than that occurring in any of the control jurisdictions.

One measure—the fraction of robberies involving guns—incorporates both the potential deterrent and displacement effects of the law, and hence is an especially sensitive

---

24. Two independent studies analyzed the impact of the Bartley-Fox law on armed robbery in Boston, using the Box-Jenkins techniques: Stewart Deutsch, "The Effect of Massachusetts Gun Control Law on Gun Related Crimes in the City of Boston," *Evaluation Quarterly*, 1(4) (1977); and Richard A. Hay, Jr., and Richard McCleary: "Box-Tiao Time Series Models for Impact Assessment," *Evaluation Quarterly*, 3(2) (May 1979). Armed robbery, however, is not a necessarily useful indicator of the Bartley-Fox law's impact on crime. Indeed, to the extent that deterrent effects of the law on gun robberies are offset by weapon substitution effects of the law on nongun armed robberies, we would expect to find no net effect of the law on armed robberies.

TABLE 3

GUN ROBBERIES, NONGUN ROBBERIES, AND PERCENTAGE OF GUN ROBBERIES OF ARMED ROBBERIES IN BOSTON IN COMPARISON TO CITIES GROUPED REGIONALLY AND FOR SELECTED EASTERN SEABOARD AND NORTH CENTRAL CITIES

Regions	Gun Robberies per 100,000			Nongun Armed Robberies per 100,000			Percentage of Gun Robberies of Total Armed Robberies		
	Rate, 1974	1974–75, Percentage Change	1974–76, Percentage Change	Rate, 1974	1974–75, Percentage Change	1974–76, Percentage Change	1974	1974–75, Percentage Change	1974–76, Percentage Change
Boston	363.4	−1.8	−35.5	319.7	32.4	+6.3	53.2	−14.0	−23.2
Comparison cities grouped regionally: 250,000–500,000 inhabitants									
United States without Massachusetts	194.2	4.9	−11.8	74.2	−.8	−3.9	72.4	1.5	−2.4
North Central states	181.1	4.0	−20.9	73.0	−18.0	−19.5	71.3	6.5	−.5
Middle Atlantic states	179.7	17.5	−5.5	145.4	6.7	−4.1	55.3	4.3	−.5
Comparison cities grouped regionally: 500,000–1,000,000 inhabitants									
United States without Massachusetts	249.9	7.3	−12.1	80.9	5.3	−4.1	75.5	.5	−2.2
North Central states	300.9	24.3	.1	83.6	18.5	−.8	78.2	1.0	.2
Selected eastern seaboard and north central cities									
New York	326.4	6.5	8.4	391.2	9.8	−4.9	45.5	1.6	1.8
Philadelphia	229.6	−5.1	−36.7	99.9	9.4	−17.9	69.7	−4.4	−8.3
Baltimore	422.1	−5.1	−30.0	184.0	−4.0	−15.1	69.9	−.3	−6.1
Washington, D.C.	570.4	12.1	−13.2	90.6	6.6	−10.9	86.3	.6	−.4
Detroit	767.6	22.3	32.4	38.7	19.6	32.3	95.2	.1	0
Cleveland	492.9	25.9	−2.0	59.8	16.9	5.5	89.2	.8	−.8
Chicago	414.9	−20.6	−43.5	136.6	.0	−5.8	75.2	−6.1	−14.2

indicator of the gun law's impact. When this measure is examined, Boston unambiguously shows the greatest post–Bartley-Fox change in the weapon-related character of armed robbery. In the first year following Bartley-Fox—1974 to 1975—the percent that gun robbery represents of all armed robbery declined in Boston by 14 percent—a decline twice that shown in any of the control jurisdictions. In the two-year period—1974 to 1976—following Bartley-Fox, Boston showed a 23.3 percent decline versus a maximum 14 percent decline—Chicago—shown in any of the control jurisdictions.

Conclusions on armed robbery

The introduction of the Bartley-Fox law appears to have resulted in a short-term reduction in gun robberies throughout the city of Boston, Massachusetts. The decrease in gun robberies also appears to have been accompanied by an increase in nongun armed robberies. The magnitude of the displacement effect for armed robbery appears to be less than we observed for armed assault.

Finally, due to data contingencies and time limitations, our conclusions with regard to robbery are more tentative than they are for assault: (1) historical data on gun robbery is unavailable prior to 1974 and (2) a refined analysis of the impact of the Bartley-Fox law on the reporting of gun robbery using BPD data has not yet been conducted.

CRIMINAL HOMICIDE

To the extent that homicide is a function of an offender's premediated willful intention to kill his victim, we would have little reason to expect that the Bartley-Fox law would deter gun-related homicides. The assumption is that an offender who is willing to risk the legal sanction for murder would also be willing to risk the sanction for a Bartley-Fox offense. On the other hand, if as Richard Block proposes, homicides occur not primarily as a result of an offender's planned determination to kill, but rather as something that sometimes happens as the unanticipated consequence of other criminal or life-style activities,[25] then the introduction of the gun law might have a derivative deterrent effect on gun homicide. That is, the gun law might prevent some gun-related homicides by affecting the decisions that potential offenders make regarding whether or not to carry a firearm, and/or whether or not to use a firearm to commit a robbery or an assault.

Indeed, we have already observed that the Bartley-Fox law appeared to reduce gun-related assaults and robberies throughout Massachusetts. Thus we should not be surprised if gun-related homicides also show a decline following the Bartley-Fox law.

There also appears to have been an increase after the law in nongun armed assaults and, to a lesser extent, nongun armed robberies. However, for at least two reasons, we also do not expect to find similar displacement effects for criminal homicides: (1) we would expect to find that an increase in nongun armed assaults or robberies did not result in a proportionate increase in nongun criminal homicides because guns are likely to be more deadly than other types of weapons and (2) offenders who switch from

25. Richard Block, *Violent Crime: Environment, Interaction and Death* (Lexington, MA: Lexington Books, 1977).

TABLE 4

GUN HOMICIDES, NONGUN HOMICIDES, AND PERCENTAGE OF GUN HOMICIDES OF ALL HOMICIDES IN BOSTON IN COMPARISON TO CITIES GROUPED REGIONALLY AND FOR SELECTED EASTERN SEABOARD AND NORTH CENTRAL CITIES

Regions	Gun Homicides			Nongun Homicides			Percentage of Gun Homicides of All Homicides		
	Rate, 1974	1974–75, Percentage Change	1974–76, Percentage Change	Rate, 1974	1974–75, Percentage Change	1974–76, Percentage Change	1974	1974–75, Percentage Change	1974–76, Percentage Change
Boston	70	−21.4	−55.7	64	0.0	−20.3	52.2	−11.5	−27.6
Comparison cities grouped regionally: 250,000–500,000 inhabitants									
All United States cities except Boston	3140	−6.5	−23.0	1379	+9.3	−0.7	69.5	−4.9	−8.2
North Central cities	470	−9.1	−26.1	139	+3.4	−5.7	77.2	−9.7	−9.1
Middle Atlantic cities	164	−0.6	−28.0	171	−1.3	−11.6	49.0	+6.9	−10.4
Selected eastern seaboard and north central cities									
New York	794	9.1	−2.5	822	0.2	3.0	49.1	4.3	−2.9
Philadelphia	248	−24.2	−32.7	171	−4.1	−13.5	59.2	−9.8	−10.5
Baltimore	204	−23.5	−45.6	90	15.6	−4.4	69.4	−13.5	−18.9
Washington, D.C.	170	−14.7	−30.6	106	−16.0	−33.0	61.6	0.6	1.3
Detroit	510	−14.7	−3.5	200	−13.5	−12.5	71.8	−0.4	2.8
Cleveland	254	−15.7	−34.6	52	42.3	−11.5	83.0	−10.5	−5.7
Chicago	668	−17.4	−25.0	301	−11.3	2.7	68.9	−2.2	−10.2

guns to other deadly weapons may generally be those offenders who are least intent upon physically harming their victims. Thus an increase in the use of other deadly weapons by these offenders might very well not result in an increase in homicides.

Comparison group analysis

As in the robbery and assault analyses, we will compare homicide trends for Boston with those in selected control jurisdictions. We have selected as our control jurisdictions grouped into communities of 250,000 to 1,000,000 inhabitants for the Middle Atlantic states, the North Central states, and all United States cities, except Boston. In addition, we also included the selected Eastern Seaboard and North Central cities included in the assault and robbery analyses.

Criminal homicide statistics for Boston and the control jurisdictions are presented in Table 4. We first examine the impact of the Bartley-Fox law on gun-related homicide. In the first year—1974 to 1975—following the gun law's implementation, gun homicide in Boston declined by 21.4 percent—a decrease greater than any of the jurisdictions experienced except Baltimore. In the two years—1974 to 1976—after Bartley-Fox, gun homicides in Boston declined by 55.7 percent—a decrease greater than that exhibited by any of the control jurisdictions. Thus it appears that the Bartley-Fox law in the short-term prevented some gun-related homicides in Boston.

We, of course, want to address the issue as to whether the Bartley-Fox law also produced displacement effects similar to those observed for nongun armed assaults and to a lesser extent nongun armed robberies. How-

ever, when nongun criminal homicides for Boston are examined we find that in the two years—1974 to 1976—following Bartley-Fox, nongun homicides actually dropped in Boston by 20.3 percent. Moreover, only one of the control jurisdictions—Washington, D.C.—exceeded this decline while several other jurisdictions experienced decreases in nongun criminal homicide ranging between 1.5 percent and 13.5 percent. Thus we find no evidence suggesting a displacement effect of the Bartley-Fox law on nongun criminal homicide.

The pattern of impact where gun homicides appear to have been deterred while nongun homicides do not appear to have increased has important implications because it suggests that the Bartley-Fox law may have had an overall effect of reducing incidence of criminal homicides in Boston, at least in the short run. Indeed, if the gun homicide and nongun homicide statistics in Table 4 are added together, we can see that the overall level of criminal homicides showed a greater decline in Boston—38.8 percent—than in any of the control jurisdictions in the two years following the introduction of the gun law.

Finally, further evidence of the Bartley-Fox law's impact on criminal homicide in Boston is available when the percent of gun homicides (Table 4) is studied. Here we find that between 1974 and 1976, Boston showed a greater decrease in this measure than any of the control jurisdictions.

Criminal homicide conclusion

The Bartley-Fox law appears to have in the short run deterred some gun-related criminal homicides in Boston, but the law does not appear to have resulted in an increase in nongun criminal homicides. We conclude that the gun law caused an overall decline in the incidence of criminal homicide in the first two years of its implementation.

CONCLUSION

This analysis has focused on the Bartley-Fox law's impact on armed assault, armed robbery, and homicide. For each type of crime, we independently examined the law's impact on gun-related offenses and nongun-related offenses in Boston.

Introduction of the gun law had a twofold effect on armed assaults. First, the law substantially reduced the incidence of gun assaults. Second, it resulted in a substantial increase in nongun armed assaults. Thus while the law appears to deter some individuals from carrying and/or using their firearms, it did not prevent them from using alternative weapons in assaultive situations.

Introduction of the Bartley-Fox law also resulted in a short-term reduction in gun robberies, and a concomitant increase in nongun armed robberies. However, the magnitude of the weapons substitution effect for armed robbery appears to be less than what we observed for armed assault.

The law also deterred some gun-related criminal homicides in Boston, but did not result in a corresponding increase in nongun criminal homicides. Thus the gun law produced an overall decline in the incidence of criminal homicide.

Our analysis also suggests that the law may have achieved its effect primarily through its "announced" intent, rather than its actual implementation. Importantly, in the assault analysis where the effects were most pronounced, we observed that the decline in gun assault in Boston started one month prior to the effective date of the law—suggesting that offenders, at least initially, were responding to the publicity attendant with the introduction of gun law rather than mandatory imposition of its sanctions. Hence, we conclude that the observed reduction in gun crime was the result of an announcement effect,[26] rather than the product of sanctions actually imposed—the traditional definition of a deterrent effect. In research presently underway, we address the matter of separating the announcement and deterrent effects of the law.

For this reason, we draw no conclusions about the effect of the "mandatory" nature of the law. That is, the observed effects of the law do not depend on its having been applied in a mandatory fashion. At this point in our analysis, we simply know that it was advertised as imposing a "mandatory one-year prison term."

26. It should be noted that if gun assault, gun robbery, and gun homicide rates for 1974 in Boston were abnormally high, the results shown in Table 2–5 would tend to exaggerate the deterrent effect of the Bartley-Fox law. That is, the subsequent reduction in these rates could be "a regression to the mean" or a return to levels more consistent with the previous history of these offenses. However, this appears not to be the case, at least for gun assault and gun homicide. For example, linear projections of gun homicides and gun assaults based on the year 1970 through 1973 yield predicted 1974 levels of 81 and 97.1 for gun homicides and gun assaults, respectively, versus their observed levels of 70 and 101.4. A more detailed analysis of this issue will be presented in our subsequent work (Pierce and Bowers).

ANNALS, AAPSS, **455**, May 1981

The District of Columbia's "Firearms Control Regulations Act of 1975": The Toughest Handgun Control Law in the United States—Or Is It?

By EDWARD D. JONES, III

ABSTRACT: The District of Columbia's Firearms Control Regulations Act of 1975 went into effect on 24 September 1976. It was the outgrowth of three more restrictive legislative proposals that had been introduced in 1975 and had two legislative objectives: (1) to reduce the potential of firearms-related crimes and (2) to monitor more effectively firearms' trafficking. In July 1980, the U.S. Conference of Mayors' study reported its evaluation of the effectiveness of this act and stated that the act significantly reduced firearm and handgun crime. This report met largely with opposition. This article, in addition to relating the provisions and legislative history of the Firearms Control Regulations Act, analyses the deficiencies in the Conference of Mayors' research methods and assumptions and also discusses any beneficial effects and weaknesses of the act. However, it can only be concluded that further research on firearms control effectiveness in the District of Columbia is clearly needed to develop demonstrably effective public policies against criminal misuse of handguns.

Edward D. Jones, III, received his degree from the University of Chicago and was formerly with the U.S. Department of Justice.

NOTE: Points of view or opinions expressed in this article are those of the author and do not necessarily represent the official position or policies of the U.S. Department of Justice.

THIS article discusses the District of Columbia's "Firearms Control Regulations Act of 1975" and offers a critique of a recent United States Conference of Mayors' assessment of the act's effectiveness in reducing violent crime in the District. The next section describes the Firearms Control Regulations Act's provisions, legislative history, and objectives, as elaborated in the legislative debate, and continues with an examination of the appropriateness of the assumptions and research method of the U.S. Conference of Mayors' study. This section also presents additional evidence pertaining to the effectiveness of the Firearms Control Regulations Act. Finally, the concluding section offers several suggestions for future research on the effectiveness of the Firearms Control Regulations Act.

FIREARMS CONTROL REGULATIONS ACT

On 24 September 1976, the District of Columbia's (D.C.) Firearms Control Regulations Act of 1975 went into effect as D.C. Law 1–85. The purpose of the law was "[t]o protect the citizens of the District from loss of property, death, and injury, by controlling the availability of firearms in the community."[1] Toward this end, the Firearms Control Regulations Act prohibited the purchase, sale, transfer, and, with one exception, possession of handguns by D.C. residents other than law enforcement officers or members of the military. The exception with respect to possession involved owners of handguns and longguns—rifles and shotguns—who had registered their fire-

1. Council of the District of Columbia, "Notice: D.C. Law 1-85— 'Firearms Control Regulations Act of 1975' " (Washington, DC, 24 Sept. 1976).

arms under the District's 1968 registration law.[2] To be in compliance with the Firearms Control Regulations Act, handgun and longgun owners were required to re-register their firearms within 60 days following the effective date of the act. After that date, handguns were "unregisterable," but longguns could be registered if they were newly acquired, in person, from a licensed dealer in the District.[3]

The Firearms Control Regulations Act also required all firearm re-registrants and future purchasers of rifles and shotguns to file with the Metropolitan Police Department an "Application for Firearms Registration Certificate" and be screened to determine eligibility to possess. An applicant was required to be 21 years of age or older, with the exception that an individual between 18 and 21 years of age could qualify if his parents or legal guardian assumed civil liability for damages resulting from the applicant's use of the prospectively registered firearm. In ad-

2. D.C. Code Ann. Tit. 22, §§3201–3217, Arts. 50–56 (D.C. Police Regulations).
3. Federal law provides that a nonresident may purchase a rifle or shotgun in a contiguous state if his home state has enacted "enabling legislation" permitting its residents to make such purchases. See U.S. Department of the Treasury, Bureau of Alcohol, Tobacco and Firearms, *Your Guide to Firearms Regulations, 1978* (Washington, DC: U.S. Government Printing Office, 1978), pp. 126–27. The District of Columbia has not enacted such legislation. Therefore, District residents may only purchase rifles and shotguns from licensed dealers in the District. The Firearms Control Regulations Act strengthened dealer license requirements, and in the 1976 Revenue Act, the annual dealer license fee was increased from $29 to $300. The result of these actions, along with the ban on handgun sales, according to an official of the Metropolitan Police Department's Firearm Registration Section, is that there are only five retail firearm dealerships in the District.

dition, an applicant was required not to have had a history of behavior—evidenced through conviction, indictment, or other official processing—that would enhance the likelihood of the firearm's misuse. Such behavior included crimes of violence, weapon offenses, use of narcotics or dangerous drugs, alcoholism, mental health problems, and negligence in a firearm mishap. Finally, a registrant was required to provide two full-face photographs and fingerprints, pass a vision test, evidence no physical disability that would preclude safe firearm use, and pass a written test pertaining to knowledge of firearms laws and the safe use of firearms.[4]

Finally, the Firearms Control Regulations Act established possession responsibilities for firearms registrants. The owner was required to have the certificate of registration in his possession whenever in possession of the registered firearm; to report immediately to the chief of police in writing, and to return within 48 hours the certificate to the Metropolitan Police Department whenever the firearm was lost, stolen, destroyed, or transferred; to maintain the firearm in his residence unloaded and disassembled or bound by a trigger-locking device; and not to transfer, for any reason, a firearm to anyone other than a licensed firearms dealer. The penalty for violation of these requirements or others of the Firearms Control Regulations Act is a fine of up to $300 or a jail term of up to 10 days.[5]

Legislative history

The Firearms Control Regulations Act, which amended Police Regulations of the District of Columbia, was passed by the Council of the District of Columbia on 29 June 1976 by a vote of 12 to 1 and was signed by Mayor Walter Washington on 23 July 1976. Under the provisions of the District's 1974 "Home Rule" charter, the Firearms Control Regulations Act had to be submitted to the Congress of the United States for a 30-legislative-day review, during which a "Resolution of Disapproval" could be introduced. If passed, then the Firearms Control Regulations Act would be overturned. In the absence of such a resolution, the Firearms Control Regulations Act would be law following the review period.

Apparently in an effort to disapprove the Firearms Control Regulations Act, but avoid a vote on the controversial issue of handgun control in an election year, both the House and Senate in late August 1976 passed an amendment to the District's Home Rule Charter, later signed by President Ford, that prohibited changes in the District's Police Regulations and Criminal Code until 1979.[6] However, because the District Council had enacted the Firearms Control Regulations Act prior to passage of the amendment and because the amendment did not include a retroactivity provision, the Congressional Research Service of the Library of Congress concluded in its legal opinion that the amendment did not cover the Firearms Control Regulations Act.[7] Because of

4. The written test was not administered to re-registrants during the period of registration following the effective date of the Firearms Control Regulations Act because of budgetary considerations. An August 1977 amendment to the Firearms Control Regulations Act excused re-registrants from the written test requirement.

5. The penalty for a subsequent violation is a fine of $300 and a jail term of not less than 10 days or more than 90 days.

6. United States Conference of Mayors, Handgun Control Project, "Congress Kills D.C. Gun Control Bill and Avoids Controversial Vote," *Targeting in on Handgun Control,* II(7):1(Aug. 1976).

7. United States Conference of Mayors, Handgun Control Staff, "D.C. Gun Control

election year unease, subsequent attempts in the Congress to disapprove the Firearms Control Regulations Act were not permitted by the leadership to come to a vote.

On 9 December 1976, 18 days after the 22 November deadline for re-registration, the National Rifle Association, nine D.C. residents, and two companies, as plaintiffs, were granted a preliminary injunction in D.C. Superior Court against enforcement of the Firearms Control Regulations Act, with Judge Fauntleroy finding that the plaintiffs were "threatened by or suffering from 'irreparable and immediate injury," and that the D.C. Council "had 'acted unlawfully' in legislating on gun control."[8] The effect of the preliminary injunction was to lift the prohibition on handgun possession as embodied in the Firearms Control Regulations Act and to reinstate the 1968 registration requirements as law.

On 7 February 1977, the Appeals Court for the District of Columbia lifted the preliminary injunction and reinstated the Firearms Control Regulations Act as law.[9] The law became effective on 21 February 1977, following a 14-day re-registration period for owners to register handguns that had been lawfully acquired and registered, under the 1968 registration law, prior to 24 September 1976, and between 8 December 1976 and 7 February

1977. Further, on 25 February 1977, D.C. Superior Court Judge Goodrich issued a summary judgment denying the challenge of the National Rifle Association to the Firearms Control Regulations Act and declared unconstitutional a provision of the Act that would have permitted non-residents of the District to bring handguns into D.C. for " 'any lawful recreational firearm related activity.' "[10] Finally, in August 1977, the Firearms Control Regulations Act was amended to permit licensed security agencies to register new handguns that are used during working hours by employees who are licensed to carry a handgun.[11] Since that time, the Firearms Control Regulations Act, as amended, has been law in the District of Columbia.

Legislative intent[12]

The Firearms Control Regulations Act was the outgrowth of three more restrictive legislative proposals that had been introduced in 1975.[13] The

10. Ibid.

11. United States Conference of Mayors, Handgun Control Staff, "D.C. Gun Law Amended to Exempt Security Guard Industry," *Targeting in on Handgun Control*, III(5):4(Sept. 1977); and Council of the District of Columbia, Committee on the Judiciary, "Report: Bill 2-194, the 'Firearms Control Regulations Act Technical Amendments Act of 1977' " (Washington, DC, 27 July 1977).

12. Information presented in this subsection is from Council of the District of Columbia, Committee on the Judiciary and Criminal Law, "Report: Bill No. 1–164, the 'Firearms Control Act of 1975' " (Washington, DC, 21 April 1976); and mimeographed transcripts of Legislative Meetings of the Council of the District of Columbia, dated 18 May 1976, 15 June 1976, and 29 June 1976, provided by Councilman David A. Clarke's office (hereafter cited as Council of the District of Columbia, "Transcript").

13. Bill No. 1-24, introduced by Councilman John Wilson on 11 Feb. 1975; Bill No. 1-42, introduced by Councilwoman Polly

Bill Enacted Despite Congressional Blocks," *Targeting in on Handgun Control*, II(8):1 (Sept. 1976).

8. United States Conference of Mayors, Handgun Control Staff, "NRA Wins Injunction Against District Gun Law," *Targeting in on Handgun Control*, II(10):3 (Dec. 1976).

9. United States Conference of Mayors, Handgun Control Staff, "Nation's Strictest Gun Law Takes Effect in D.C.," *Targeting in on Handgun Control*, III(2):1(Feb. 1977).

decision of the Committee on the Judiciary of the Council of the District of Columbia to report a less restrictive legislative proposal apparently was based upon considerations of constitutional law, budget impact, and political feasibility.[14] Nevertheless, it is clear from a reading of the transcripts of the legislative debate that a majority of members would have supported the more restrictive legislative proposals had those considerations not been significant constraints.[15]

From a legislative perspective, the Firearms Control Regulations Act had two objectives. The first objective was to "reduce the potentiality" of firearm-related crime and accidents,[16] and the second was to more effectively "monitor the traffic in firearms." The objectives were reflective of the failures of the 1968 registration law, most visible in a record number of homicides in 1974 and in the ease with which juveniles were obtaining access to handguns.[17]

The first objective was addressed in the Firearms Control Regulations Act by possession requirements that constrained the "easy availability" and enhanced the accountability of firearm owners, and by the ban on the future possession of the most frequently used firearm in crime, the handgun. Council members in the legislative debate were mindful of the fact that the proposed possession requirements generally would have more of an impact on law-abiding firearm owners than criminal users because criminal users likely would not attempt to re-register.[18] Nevertheless, they considered the possession requirements desirable because of their potential for reducing the number of easily accessible handguns that could be used in argumentative situations spontaneously by law-abiding citizens and with relatively greater lethal effect than other potential weapons. The requirement that residents maintain firearms in residences in an immediately inoperable condition, which was the subject of lengthy legislative

---

Shackleton on 11 March 1975; and Bill No. 1-164, introduced by Councilman Wilson on 22 July 1975, in lieu of Bill No. 1-24. See Council of the District of Columbia, Committee on the Judiciary and Criminal Law, p. 1. Bill No. 1-24 would have banned totally all handguns in the District. Bill No. 1-42 also would have banned totally all handguns in DC, but residents would have been compensated for their handguns. Bill No. 1-164 would have licensed firearm owners and provided mandatory minimum sentencing of violators. See United States Conference of Mayors, "The Analysis of the Firearm Control Act of 1975: Handgun Control in the District of Columbia" (Washington, DC, July 1980) (hereafter cited as U.S. Conference of Mayors, "Handgun Control").

14. See Council of the District of Columbia, Committee on the Judiciary and Criminal Law, p. 2; and U.S. Conference of Mayors, "Handgun Control," pp. 1–2.

15. For example, the proposed Firearms Control Regulations Act, as reported out of the Committee on the Judiciary, provided that penalties be mandatory for violation of the Act. Because the D.C. Corporation Counsel advised the Committee that "the mandatory 10 day quality would effect [sic] the jurisdiction of the Court in such a manner to make the law inappropriate" under the Home Rule charter, Committee Chairman Clarke reluctantly offered an amendment, subsequently passed, that eliminated the mandatory quality of penalties. See Council of the District of Columbia, "Transcript" (15 June 1976), p. 12.

16. Fatal firearm accidents in the District of Columbia, in relation to all fatal home and occupational accidents, are relatively infrequent. Of 931 fatal home and occupational accidents during the period 1974–79, only 0.5 percent, or five, were firearm related. See Government of the District of Columbia, Department of Human Resources, Office of the Chief Medical Examiner, *Annual Report* (Washington, DC, 1974–79).

17. See Council of the District of Columbia, Committee on the Judiciary and Criminal Law, pp. 3, 5.

18. See Council of the District of Columbia, "Transcript," (18 May 1976), p. 87.

debate,[19] reinforces this consideration and the council's notion that a handgun or other firearm was not a desirable instrument for home protection.

The second objective of enhanced control over firearm traffic was addressed in the proposed Firearms Control Regulations Act by the more stringent possession requirements, particularly the owner's responsibility to report and the prohibition on his transferring of a firearm. In addition to increased accountability standards for owners, the Firearms Control Regulations Act, in its ban on future handgun sales, purchases, and transfers, permitted the freezing of the stock of permissible, registered handguns in the District. It also led toward the eventual diminution of that stock with the death of or moving from the District by D.C. residents owning registered handguns, and with the deterioration of or voluntary, "no questions asked" turn-in of registered or unregistered handguns to the Metropolitan Police Department.

THE U.S. CONFERENCE OF MAYORS' STUDY[20]

In July 1980, the U.S. Conference of Mayors reported on its evaluation of the effectiveness of the Firearms Control Regulations Act. Its staff report concluded that "[b]ased on the regression model employed in the analysis, it has been demonstrated that the Firearms Control Act, and not chance alone or other extraneous factors, has been responsible for the significant reduction in both firearm and handgun crime."[21]

This evaluation includes a brief description of the legislative history and provisions of the Firearms Control Regulations Act, an analysis of previous research pertaining to the effectiveness of firearm controls; a tabular presentation of annual data for 1974–79 on total rates of homicide, robbery, and aggravated assault for Washington, D.C., and eight control groups—United States, the South, all cities between 500,000 and 1,000,000 in population, Atlanta, Baltimore, Cleveland, San Antonio, and San Diego—a tabular presentation of annual data for 1974–79 on firearm-related rates of homicide, robbery, and aggravated assault for Washington, D.C., and three control groups—United States, the South, and all cities between 500,000 and 1,000,000 in population—a tabular presentation of annual data for 1974–79 on suicide and accident rates for Washington, D.C., and the United States; and an analysis of annual percentage changes in incidence rates for Washington, D.C., and control jurisdictions approximately three years before—1974–76—and three years after—1977–79—the effective date of the Firearms Control Regulations Act.

The Conference of Mayors' analysis and findings received prominent coverage in the metropolitan sections of the Washington Post[22] and Washington Star.[23] The Post and Star also reported in their coverage that the National Rifle Association and Metropolitan Police Department of Washington, D.C., questioned the accuracy of the Conference of Mayors' findings. The

19. See Council of the District of Columbia, "Transcript," (15 June 1976), pp. 17–33.
20. See U.S. Conference of Mayors, "Handgun Control."
21. Ibid., p. 17.

22. Paul W. Valentine, "Study Cites Decline Over Last 3 Years in Handgun Crime," Washington Post, 28 June 1980, p. B1.
23. Charles McCollum, "Handgun Crimes Down Since New District Law," Washington Star, 28 June 1980, p. B1.

National Rifle Association contended that crime was "cyclical" and would have declined in the absence of the Firearms Control Regulations Act and that criminals would ignore the requirements of the Act and acquire handguns if they so chose.[24] The Metropolitan Police Department echoed the National Rifle Association's contention pertaining to the cyclical nature of crime and reportedly said through its spokesman that "gun-related crimes cannot clearly be attributed to gun registration" because the Conference of Mayors' study did not examine the effect of "new law enforcement tactics and programs."[25] Further, the Metropolitan Police Department spokesman noted the ease with which handguns could be obtained in neighboring jurisdictions. In particular, he reportedly said that "less than 1 percent of all firearms confiscated each year by police are registered here or elsewhere, 'so somehow or other, the illegal guns are still getting in here.' "[26]

In addition, in October 1980, Congressman John Ashbrook of Ohio reported on the findings of a Congressional Research Service evaluation of the Conference of Mayors' study that he had requested. The Congressional Research Service evaluation concluded that the study was " 'flawed by an inappropriate model' " and " '[a]lthough the Firearms Control Act may have affected the crime rate in the District of Columbia, it is our judgment, based on the information at hand,

that the study fails to establish such a relationship.' "[27]

FURTHER EVALUATION OF THE U.S. CONFERENCE OF MAYORS' ANALYSIS

Crucial factors in the sustainability of the U.S. Conference of Mayors' conclusion pertain to the appropriateness of assumptions and research method. The Conference of Mayors' study acknowledges that "confounding influences of exogenous socio-economic factors may impact the level of crime independently of any legislation"[28] and criticizes the methods of previous studies because they have not accounted for "differential enforcement policies, inaccuracy of reporting data, numbers of transient residents, interstate traffic in firearms and harshness of penalties among states and cities."[29] The U.S. Conference of Mayors' study also does not consider these "accountability" factors. Rather, the U.S. Conference of Mayors' study assumes "that violence in Washington, D.C. is subject to the same exogenous forces as is crime in other communities and regions of the country."[30]

For two reasons in particular, the U.S. Conference of Mayors' assumption is not sustainable. First, with respect to law enforcement that would have the potential of affecting firearm crime rates, three significant changes occurred in Washington, D.C., during the two years immediately preceding the February 1977 effective date of the Firearms

---

24. The latter contention was articulated by citizens nearly four years earlier as they stood for up to three hours in line waiting to reregister their handguns. See Jacqueline Bolder, "Gun Registry Goes Slowly in District," *Washington Star*, 16 Nov. 1976, p. B1.

25. Valentine.

26. Ibid., p. B3.

27. Hon. John M. Ashbrook, "United States Conference of Mayors Should Release Data on District of Columbia Gun Law Study," *Congressional Record* (Extensions of Remarks), 1 Oct. 1980, p. E4705.

28. U.S. Conference of Mayors, "Handgun Control, p. 10.

29. Ibid., p. 8.

30. Ibid., p. 10.

Control Regulations Act. In February 1976, "the Sting," the first of several undercover fencing operations in the District of Columbia, was disclosed to the public. This operation resulted in the recovery of $2.4 million in stolen property, including 52 illegal firearms, issuance of 196 arrest warrants, and the closure of more than 10,000 cases.[31] Also, in cooperation with the U.S. Attorney for the District of Columbia, the Metropolitan Police Department enhanced the efficiency with which it could process major criminal offenders, including those using firearms in the commission of offenses. Finally, the Bureau of Alcohol, Tobacco and Firearms (ATF) initiated an intensive federal enforcement effort known as Operation CUE, aimed at stemming regulatory and criminal abuses pertaining to the use of and transactions involving firearms.[32] Each of these changes in law enforcement could have had as significant an impact as the Firearms Control Regulations Act in reducing firearm-related crime in the District.

Second, with respect to interstate traffic in firearms, ATF data from Operation CUE and other investigations indicate that interstate traffic in firearms is a significant problem. For example, in a trace analysis of firearms used in crime in Washington, D.C., ATF found that in a three-month period—February through April 1976—prior to initiation of

Operation CUE, 82 percent of firearms successfully traced had been purchased interstate and that in a three-month period—February through April 1977—during Operation CUE, 79 percent had been so purchased.[33] The magnitude of those numbers, which are substantially higher than the comparable figures for the other Operation CUE cities of Boston and Chicago, and the ease with which handguns can be purchased in nearby Virginia,[34] albeit in violation of federal law, would dictate that interstate traffic in firearms be an important factor in an analysis of firearm control effectiveness in the District.

With regard to research method, the U.S. Conference of Mayors' study is deficient in its choice and use of control jurisdictions. The appropriate control for comparison of changes in D.C. crime rates are other urban jurisdictions.[35] The U.S. Conference of Mayors' study uses five such jurisdictions, but offers no choice criterion for the cities studied. Further, in its use of the control jurisdictions, it only employs the control cities for analysis of total crime rate changes, not firearm-related crime rate changes. As the following analysis of Washington, D.C., and other urban jurisdiction firearm-related crime rates shows, Washington, D.C. did not have "the greatest decrease in crime rates in all three categories."[36]

---

31. Metropolitan Police Department, *Fiscal Year 1976 Annual Report* (Washington, DC, 1977), p. 6; and Earl Byrd, "Area Drive Cuts Gun-Related Crime 24%," *Washington Star*, 26 Aug. 1977, p. C1.

32. U.S. Department of the Treasury, Bureau of Alcohol, Tobacco and Firearms, *Concentrated Urban Enforcement: An Analysis of the Initial Year of Operation CUE in the Cities of Washington, D.C.; Boston, Massachusetts; and Chicago, Illinois* (Washington, DC, 1978).

33. Ibid., p. 107.

34. Michael Isikoff, "Gun Control Shot With Holes: Weapons Bought With Relative Ease in Virginia Gun Shops," *Washington Star*, 21 Dec. 1980, p. A1.

35. For a discussion on the desirability of analyzing cities in firearm effectiveness research, see Edward D. Jones, III, and Marla Wilson Ray, *Handgun Control: Legislative and Enforcement Strategies* (Washington, DC: National Institute of Justice, 1981).

36. U.S. Conference of Mayors, "Handgun Control," p. 4.

TABLE 1

FIREARM INCIDENTS AS A PERCENTAGE OF TOTAL INCIDENTS FOR SELECTED JURISDICTIONS,
AVERAGES OF YEARS 1974–76 AND 1977–79

	ROBBERY		PERCENTAGE OF CHANGE	AGGRAVATED ASSAULT		PERCENTAGE OF CHANGE
	1974–76	1977–79		1974–76	1977–79	
United States	44.1	40.7	−7.7	24.6	22.9	−6.9
Washington, D.C.	50.5	44.1	−12.7	35.3	29.6	−16.1
Baltimore, Maryland	36.1	31.6	−12.5	23.9	22.6	−5.4
Boston, Massachusetts	28.0	24.0	−14.3	19.4	14.1	−27.3
Cleveland, Ohio	57.2	53.4	−6.6	61.3	59.1	−3.6
Denver, Colorado	44.2	46.4	+5.0	36.1	36.8	+1.9
Milwaukee, Wisconsin	60.3	51.4	−14.8	73.1	74.8	+2.3
New Orleans, Louisiana	61.8	60.1	−2.8	46.7	44.7	−4.3
St. Louis, Missouri	48.1	49.9	+3.7	26.6	26.3	−2.3
San Francisco, California	30.5*	30.7	+0.7	18.6*	14.0	−24.7
Seattle, Washington	38.9	29.1	−25.2	33.3	24.4	−26.7
Maryland						
Greenbelt	33.3	41.3	+24.0	30.6	20.0	−34.6
Hyattsville	70.7	56.7	−19.8	9.2	21.7	+135.9
Mount Rainer	40.9	35.3	−13.7	13.1	13.2	+0.8
Takoma Park	69.2	56.3	−18.6	13.5	9.0	−33.3
Virginia						
Alexandria	45.7	37.8	−17.3	15.5	12.1	−21.9
Arlington County	58.3	46.6	−20.1	13.2	15.7	+18.9
Falls Church	62.8	53.7	−14.5	10.1	3.8	−65.3
Fairfax County	54.8*	44.5	−18.8	21.7*	12.0	−44.7

SOURCE: Federal Bureau of Investigation, Uniform Crime Reporting, "Return A Record Card" (Washington, DC, 1974–79) (unpublished data).
* 1975–76.

Further evidence

Table 1 provides data on firearm-related robbery and aggravated assault for urban jurisdictions "comparable" to Washington, D.C., and for suburban jurisdictions proximate to Washington, D.C. The choice of urban jurisdictions shown was suggested by an analysis of the District of Columbia's Office of Budget and Management. It found that nine cities, comparable in size to Washington, D.C., all experiencing population declines between 1960 and 1975, were "more similar in terms of density, percent of the population on welfare, percent of housing built before 1940, the rate of increase in the daytime population, and the proportion of the total metropolitan population residing in the central city" than comparably sized cities

with population increases.[37] Because of their similarity to Washington, D.C., the set of urban jurisdictions shown is appropriate for comparison of changes in relative frequency of firearm use in robbery and aggravated assault.

Looking at urban jurisdictions, Boston, Milwaukee, and Seattle experienced greater percentage declines in the frequency of firearm use in robbery than did Washington, D.C., and Boston, San Francisco, and Seattle experienced greater percentage declines in the frequency of firearm use in aggravated assault. This contradicts the findings of the

37. Government of the District of Columbia, Office of Criminal Justice Plans and Analysis, Statistical Analysis Center, *Crime and Justice Profile: The Nation's Capital* (Washington, DC, Oct. 1979), pp. 46–47.

Conference of Mayors' study. However, each of the states in which these cities are situated, except for Washington state, also effected change in its firearm control laws during the period of analysis.[38] Certainly, each of these cities and Washington, D.C., evidenced impressive decreases in the percentage frequency of firearm use in robbery and aggravated assault. Nevertheless, a more thorough analysis than provided by the Conference of Mayors study, and one beyond the scope of this study, is required to sort out the relative effects of these different firearm control systems and changes on firearm-related robbery and aggravated assault incidents.

Looking at suburban jurisdictions, three Maryland jurisdictions[39] and all Virginia jurisdictions evidenced greater decreases in the frequency of firearm use in robbery than Washington, D.C., and two Maryland jurisdictions and three Virginia jurisdictions evidenced greater decreases in the frequency of firearm use in aggravated assault. Again, an explanation is beyond the scope of this study. The data illustrate the need for further research on the determinants of the incidence of firearm-related robbery and aggravated assault in proximate jurisdictions of metropolitan areas.

Crime data measure very complex interactions between offender and victim. For analysis of firearm control effectiveness, the choice of total or firearm-related crime incidents or rates is important, reflecting consideration of issues pertaining to an offender's attack intentions, the substitutability of weapons, and the differences in weapon lethality. Studies by Cook and Nagin, Seitz, and Zimring[40] suggest that firearm accidents, homicides, and aggravated assault likely reflect "ambiguous" intentions of offenders, whereas robbery likely reflects "single-minded" intentions of offenders. This dichotomy is analytically important, especially when looking at the different circumstances of homicide.

Table 2 presents data on the circumstances of handgun homicide in Washington, D.C., and Baltimore, Maryland, for 1974 and 1978. Between the two years, the incidence of handgun homicides decreased by 35.8 percent in Washington, D.C., and by 46.1 percent in Baltimore. Note, for each city, the differences between the two years in the percentage of total handgun homicides accounted for by particular circumstances. In 1974, "within family" handgun homicides accounted for 9.8 percent of total handgun homicides. In 1978, this percentage decreased to 4.5 in Washington, D.C.,

38. In 1974, Massachusetts enacted a mandatory minimum sentence for unlawful carrying of a handgun; in the same year, Wisconsin enacted a two-day waiting period for handgun purchases; and in 1976, California increased its "waiting period" between purchase and acquisition of a handgun from 5 to 15 days. See Jones, III, and Ray, Appendix II.

39. Because of data constraints, the Maryland jurisdictions are relatively small. Prince Georges County, Maryland, which is slightly smaller than DC and contiguous to it, provided two years of data for robbery. Comparing 1974 and 1978, firearm robberies as a percentage of total robberies declined 20.9 percent; for the District for those two years, the decline was 14.6 percent.

40. See Philip J. Cook and Daniel Nagin, *Does the Weapon Matter: An Evaluation of a Weapons–Emphasis Policy in the Prosecution of Violent Offenders* (Washington, DC: Institute for Law and Social Research, Dec. 1979), pp. 6-8; Steven Thomas Seitz, "Firearms, Homicides, and Gun Control Effectiveness," *Law & Society Review*, 6(4): 595–613 (May 1972); and Franklin E. Zimring, "Is Gun Control Likely to Reduce Violent Killings?" *Univ. Chicago Law Review*, 35:721–37 (1968).

TABLE 2

CIRCUMSTANCES OF HANDGUN HOMICIDE IN WASHINGTON, D.C., AND BALTIMORE, MARYLAND, 1974 AND 1978 (IN PERCENTAGES)

CIRCUMSTANCE	WASHINGTON, D.C.		BALTIMORE, MD	
	1974	1978	1974	1978
Within family	9.8	4.5	9.8	13.5
Outside family, total	44.3	37.5	29.0	28.8
Lovers and triangle	5.2	3.6	5.7	5.7
Argument over money and property	2.9	2.7	2.1	2.9
Other arguments	36.2	31.2	21.2	20.2
Crime-related murders, total	31.6	40.2	31.6	22.1
Felony murder	27.6	39.3	22.3	20.2
Suspected felony murder	4.0	0.9	9.3	1.9
Justifiable homicide, total	9.1	6.2	7.8	14.4
Felon killed by private citizen	3.4	0.9	2.6	5.8
Felon killed by police	5.7	5.3	5.2	8.6
Circumstances unknown	5.2	11.6	21.8	21.2
Grand total	100.0	100.0	100.0	100.0
Number of incidents, (not in percentages)	174	112	193	104

SOURCE: Federal Bureau of Investigation, Uniform Crime Reporting, "Supplementary Homicide Reports" (Washington, DC, 1974 and 1978) (unpublished data).

but increased to 13.5 percent in Baltimore. Washington, D.C., evidenced a greater percentage decline than Baltimore in "outside family," argumentative homicides. With respect to "crime-related murder," Washington's percentage increased by about nine points while Baltimore's fell by about nine points. Finally, Washington's percentage for "justifiable homicide" fell, primarily due to the decline in private citizen justifiable homicide, while Baltimore's almost doubled.

The results for Washington, D.C., are consistent with the hypothesis that the Firearm Control Regulations Act had a beneficial impact on handgun homicide. First, by constraining availability of handguns in the home and requiring registered handguns to be immediately inoperable, the act would tend to reduce the relative frequency of "within family" and "outside family" handgun homicides. This is consistent with the data. Second, for the same

reasons the act would tend to have the effect of reducing justifiable homicides involving private citizens. Finally, the act did not address per se felony murder, except to make it more difficult for criminals to re-register and eliminate one possible source of handguns—the federally licensed dealer in handguns in the District. However, other evidence suggests that criminal offenders easily acquire handguns through alternative sources, namely, private transfer and theft[41] or by

41. See D.E.S. Burr, "Handgun Regulation (Final Report)," prepared for Florida Bureau of Criminal Justice Planning and Assistance (Orlando, FL: Florida Technological University, 1977); and Mark H. Moore, *The Supply of Handguns: An Analysis of the Potential and Current Importance of Alternative Sources of Handguns to Criminal Offenders* (Cambridge, MA: Harvard University, May 1979). During the period 1974–79 there were 1613 reported offenses involving stolen firearms in the District of Columbia. Six percent of these offenses involved robbery, 34 percent burglary, and 60 percent larceny. See Metropolitan Police Department, "Monthly Return

interstate purchase.[42] Because a criminal in the District is unlikely to seek a private transfer involving a registered handgun and because the act affected directly neither the criminal's likely alternative sources for handguns nor his "single-minded" intention to engage in criminality, the impact of the act is not inconsistent with a higher percentage of handgun "crime-related murder."

CONCLUSIONS

This article has described the provisions and legislative history of the Firearms Control Regulations Act and has offered a critique of its effectiveness as evaluated in a study by the U.S. Conference of Mayors. Because of deficiencies in its research method and its use of unrealistic assumptions, the U.S. Conference of Mayors' conclusion is questionable. This is not to say that the Firearms Control Regulations Act did not have a beneficial effect in reducing handgun crime in the District of Columbia. In fact, the homicide data presented in this article suggest that the Firearms Control Regulations Act may have been responsible, in part, for the reduction in handgun fatalities that

result from arguments among acquaintances and family members.

Nevertheless, these data also show, in the increase in the percentage of handgun homicides that are felony related, that the Firearms Control Regulations Act is no panacea for crime. This is illustrated further by the highly publicized December 1980 felonious handgun murder of Washington, D.C., cardiologist Dr. Michael Halberstam, for which the alleged assailant used a .38 caliber revolver taken in a burglary in nearby suburban Virginia.[43]

Further research on firearm control effectiveness in the District of Columbia is clearly needed for the development of public policies that will be effective in stemming the criminal misuse of handguns. Such research must analyze the effect of other factors, such as narcotics use, and their influence on the incidence of the use of firearms in crime. Further, it must identify sources of supply of illegal firearms to criminal offenders and develop tactics that will result in the successful interdiction of those sources. Finally, the challenge for public policymakers is to have the courage to implement demonstrably effective prevention tactics and to provide for tough sanctions that will deter the criminal misuse of handguns.

---

of Offenses Known to Police: Return—A (Calendar Year City-wide Data)" and "Percentage of Property Stolen in Robbery, Burglary, and Larceny (Calendar Year City-wide Data)" (Washington, DC, 1974–79).

42. See Isikoff.

43. Benjamin Weigen, "Suspect in Halberstam Slaying is Ordered Held Without Bond," *Washington Post,* 11 Dec. 1980, p. B1.

ANNALS, AAPSS, 455, May 1981

"One With A Gun Gets You Two": Mandatory Sentencing and Firearms Violence in Detroit

By COLIN LOFTIN and DAVID MCDOWALL

ABSTRACT: Mandatory sentences for crimes committed with a gun are a popular policy because they promise a reduction in gun violence at a relatively low cost. In this article we present some results of a study of the implementation of such a law in Detroit, Michigan. Two major questions are discussed: (1) what effect did the Michigan gun law have on the certainty and severity of sentences; and (2) did the gun law reduce the number of serious violent crimes in Detroit? We find that, although the law required a two-year mandatory sentence for felonies committed with a gun and the prosecutor followed a strict policy of not reducing the gun law charge, there was little change in the certainty or severity of sentences that could be attributed to the effects of the gun law. Only in the case of assault was there a significant change in the expected sentence. Also serious violent crimes—murder, robbery, and assault—follow patterns over time that lead us to conclude that the gun law did not significantly alter the number or type of serious crimes in Detroit.

Colin Loftin is an assistant professor in the Department of Sociology and the Center for Research on Social Organization at the University of Michigan. His Ph.D. is from the University of North Carolina at Chapel Hill, and his research interests are in the area of social control and social organization.

David McDowall is a Postdoctoral Fellow at the Center for Research on Social Organization at the University of Michigan. His Ph.D. is in sociology from Northwestern University. His research interests are in the areas of quantitative methodology and criminology.

IN DECEMBER of 1976, billboards and bumper stickers in the Detroit area announced that "One With a Gun Gets You Two." This unusual publicity campaign, sponsored by the Citizens Committee to Deter Crime, informed the public about a new gun law that required two-year mandatory sentences for felonies committed while in possession of a firearm. The state representative who introduced the legislation described the purpose of the publicity campaign in an interview quoted in the Detroit News:

By January 30, every violent felon in the state will realize that if he is convicted of committing or attempting to commit a crime with a gun, he will be behind bars for at least two years without hope of parole or suspension of that sentence.[1]

Wayne County Prosecuting Attorney, William Cahalan, who had frequently advocated more certain sentences as a way to control crime,[2] gave his support to the publicity campaign and declared that in Wayne County there would be no plea bargaining on the Michigan gun law. The prosecutor warned potential offenders to "Leave the gun at home if you set out to commit a felony after December 31, or count on at least two years in prison if you're caught and convicted."[3]

Any dramatic change in gun control policy may provide insights, but this one was especially interesting, not only because it involved Detroit, a city with one of the most serious gun crime problems in the country, but also because it promised the simultaneous introduction of two complementary strategies:

mandatory sentence enhancement and a constraint on plea bargaining. It is widely believed that prosecutorial discretion dilutes the effects of mandatory sentences. Since a charge reduction can avoid or soften the mandatory sentence, it provides a powerful inducement to plead guilty. In this case, we had an opportunity to observe what would happen if this hole were plugged by a prohibition on charge bargaining.

As the law went into effect in January of 1977, we began a study of its impact on the processing of cases in the Detroit Recorder's Court and on crime patterns in the city. This article is the first attempt to estimate the preventive effects of the law.[4]

Two questions are fundamental to our inferences about the impact of the law on crime. First, what was the impact of the law on the certainty and severity of sanctions for gun offenses in Detroit? Although the intent of the law and the policy of the prosecutor were to increase the magnitude of sentences, especially the probability of incarceration for serious crimes committed with a gun, it is by no means certain that the mere introduction of the law would have this effect. A more likely outcome, in fact, would seem to be an uneven and varied response from the complex organization of police, defendants, attorneys, and judges who ultimately produce criminal sanctions.[5]

4. The research reported here was supported in part by grants 78-NI-AX-0021 and 79-NI-AX-0094 from the National Institute of Law Enforcement, and T32-MH14598-05 from the National Institute of Mental Health. Points of view or opinions stated are those of the authors and do not necessarily represent the official position or policies of the U.S. Department of Justice.
5. A consistent finding of studies of legislative and administrative attempts to change criminal sanctions is that the organization

1. Detroit News, 1 Dec. 1976, p. 8-A.
2. William L. Cahalan, "Certainty of Punishment," J. Urban Law, 51:163–70 (1973).
3. Detroit News, p. 3-A.

The nature of the organizational responses to the gun law are interesting in themselves and are the focus of much of our continuing research, but more important for present purposes is the fact that knowledge of the actual changes in sanctions provides a set of specific predictions that can be used in estimating the preventive effects of the gun law.

The second question is, What were the patterns of gun crimes and other crimes before and after the gun law went into effect? Since different theories of the preventive effects of the law make quite different predictions about the changes in crime patterns, we can use this information to select the model or models that best fit the data.

In the sections that follow, we will describe some of the background that is necessary to understand the nature of the Michigan Felony Firearm Law and the organizational context in which the gun law was implemented in Detroit. Next we summarize the findings of our analysis of sanction data and crime data. The final section considers several interpretations of our findings. Our major conclusion is that although the gun law had selective effects on the sanctions delivered by Recorder's Court, the crime patterns best fit a model in which there were no reductions in serious violent offenses, such as murder, robbery, or assault, which could be attributed to the gun law.

BACKGROUND

The two most interesting features of the Michigan Felony Firearm Law are that it mandates a "flat" two-year sentence for possessing a firearm while committing a felony and that the Wayne County prosecuting attorney, as a matter of policy rather than of law, refused to drop charges made under the gun law in exchange for a guilty plea. Specifically, the gun law creates a new offense, committing a felony while in possession of a firearm, and mandates a two-year prison sentence to be served preceding and consecutively to the sentence imposed for the underlying felony. In addition, the gun law prohibits parole, probation, or suspended sentences.[6] Unlike Massachusetts' Bartley-Fox Law, which imposes a one-year mandatory sentence for carrying a firearm in violation of the state's firearm laws, the Michigan gun law does not apply to offenses such as carrying a concealed weapon or illegal possession of a firearm, since these are considered to be "included" offenses. The fact that the gun law places no new restrictions on the ownership and use of guns is fundamental. It is the major reason for the popularity of this type of gun control strategy.

The prosecutor's no-reduced-charge policy, while not a part of the law, is no less real in its application. Our data indicate that with few exceptions, the prosecutor initiated and enforced policies that prevented his subordinates from bargaining the gun charge.[7]

---

absorbs much of the effort, and the change is irregular, if it occurs at all. See, for example, Michael L. Rubinstein and Teresa J. White, "Alaska's Ban on Plea Bargaining," *Law and Society Review*, 13(2):367–83 (winter 1979); Joint Committee on New York Drug Law Evaluation, *The Nation's Toughest Drug Law: Evaluating the New York Experience* (New York: The Association of the Bar of the City of New York and Drug Abuse Council, 1977); and Thomas Church, Jr., "Plea Bargains, Concessions and the Courts: Analysis of a Quasi-Experiment," *Law and Society Review*, 10:377–401 (1975–76).

6. M.C.L.A. 750.227b; M.S.A. 28.424(2).
7. For a description of some of our evidence on this, see Milton Heumann and Colin

The year before the gun law went into effect was a very bad year for law enforcement in Detroit. A list of only those events that made national news includes the laying off of nearly 1000 police officers; a massive backlog of cases awaiting disposition in Recorders Court; attacks by street gangs on spectators at the bicentennial fireworks display and a Cobo Hall rock concert; the use of the Michigan State Police to patrol the city's freeways because of attacks on stalled motorists; a federal investigation of narcotics trafficking that implicated top police executives; and a suicide by one such executive and an extended educational leave by another. Finally, in September, the mayor fired the police chief.

While this series of events unfolded, the violent crime rates in Detroit soared. In spite of the fact that other cities of comparable size experienced a decline of five percent in violent index crimes, Detroit experienced a five percent increase. Armed robbery rates increased by 7 percent in Detroit while they fell by an average of 13 percent in her sister cities. Worst of all, the homicide rate reached 49.7 per 100,000, just below the peak of 52.4 that occurred in 1974.[8]

As 1977 began and the gun law went into effect, a virtual criminological miracle occurred. Detroit went for six days without a murder, something that had not happened for 10 years. At first people attributed it to the weather or to chance. William Hart, the new police chief, said that it was a "million-to-one shot."[9] But then it happened again, and this time the interval between murders was seven days.

By the summer, the newspapers were celebrating a 20 percent decline in index crime led by a spectacular 30 percent decline in murders. Mayor Young ran for and won reelection on a record that included a "20 percent reduction in major crime." Though some skeptics persisted, 1977 seems to have been a genuine turning point in the fortunes of the city. The easing of the crime problem, the improvement of the national economy, the opening of the Renaissance Center, and many other factors came together to create a mood of optimism that continues, even in the face of new economic problems.[10]

Not surprisingly many observers have suggested that the gun law was responsible, at least in part, for the decline in crime.[11] The timing of

---

Loftin, "Mandatory Sentencing and the Abolition of Plea Bargaining: The Michigan Felony Firearm Statute," *Law and Society Review*, 13(2): 401–7 (winter 1979).

8. Most of the crime data are from U.S. Department of Commerce, Bureau of the Census, *Statistical Abstract of the United States: 1976* (Washington, DC: U.S. Government Printing Office, 1976), Table 256; and idem (1977), Table 277. The 1974 murder rate was calculated from data in the Uniform Crime Report, *Crime in the United States: 1974* (Washington, DC: U.S. Government Printing Office, 1974), p. 109; and City of Detroit, Department of Health, *1974 Fact Book*, mimeographed (Detroit, 1975).

9. *Detroit Free Press*, 25 March 1977, p. 2-A.

10. One of the most skeptical comments appeared in the *Detroit Free Press* on 14 August 1977, but on 5 January 1978, the *Free Press* rebuked its own "stationhouse cynicism" and encouraged a more constructive attitude toward the positive trend in crime.

11. Some interesting and thoughtful analysis by the Wayne County Prosecutor and two physicians who are associated with the Emergency Surgical Service of the Detroit General Hospital can be found in: William L. Cahalan, *Annual Report, Prosecuting Attorney, Wayne County*, mimeographed (Detroit, 1977), p. 2; and Charles E. Lucas and Anna M. Ledgerwood, "Mandatory Incarceration for Convicted Armed Felons: A Trauma Prophylaxis," *J. Trauma,* 18(4): 291–92 (1978).

major events makes this a natural inference, but as we shall see, a closer look at the patterns and a statistical analysis of the crime data do not support this view.

The Court's Response to the Gun Law

Data on sanctions are derived from a study of the impact of the gun law on the legal process in the Detroit Recorder's Court.[12] For that study we coded detailed information on 8414 cases that were disposed of by the court during 1976, 1977, and 1978. In this article, we will analyze only those cases in which the original charge was one of the following: (1) murder, first or second degree; (2) armed robbery; (3) felonious assault; or (4) other aggravated assaults. These charges were selected because they are comparable to the offense that will be discussed in the next section.

Our interest is in the average sentence given to persons who have been charged with an offense.[13] To estimate the effect of the gun law, we have used a modified multiple regression analysis in which we estimate (1) the effect of the contrast between offenses committed with a gun and those committed without a gun; (2) the effect of the contrast between offenses committed in the

preintervention period with those committed in the postintervention period; and (3) an interaction between the weapon contrast and the time-period contrast.

This method of analysis allows for a weapon effect and a time trend that may be unrelated to the impact of the gun law, but assumes that changes in expected sentences that are unique to the gun cases reflect the impact of the gun law. This is a very important, but, we think, reasonable assumption. There were many extraneous factors that influenced the court during the study period. Especially important was a "crash program" to reduce the case backlog that occurred very close to the time that the gun law went into effect. However, there is no reason to think that any of these factors would influence gun cases selectively. If this reasoning is correct, the estimate of the interaction effect provides us with an estimate of the impact of the gun law on sentencing that is unconfounded with such extraneous factors.

The measure of the magnitude of the sentence requires some explanation. Although such things as indeterminate sentencing, suspended sentences, "good-time" sentence discounts, and life sentences create operational problems in arriving at a numerical value for the length of a sentence, the concept that we want to measure is clear. We want a single value that reflects the amount of time a defendant can expect to spend in prison.

To deal with these problems we created a measure of expected minimum sentence following these conventions:

1. Cases in which the defendant was not incarcerated—for example, acquitted, dismissed,

---

12. Recorder's Court has jurisdiction over all felonies committed in the city of Detroit from arrest to final disposition. For a recent description of case processing in Recorders Court, see James Eisenstein and Herbert Jacob, *Felony Justice: An Organizational Analysis of Criminal Courts* (Boston, MA: Little, Brown, 1977); see also, Heumann and Loftin, pp. 393–40.

13. More precisely, our interest is in the expected value of sentences among defendants charged with a particular offense. We can think of this as the product of the probability of conviction and the expected value of the sentence given conviction.

suspended, or probated—are coded zero. In these cases the defendant was charged with an offense, but no time was actually served.[14]

2. All minimum sentences were discounted for good-time using the same procedures used by the Michigan Department of Corrections. We simply calculated the maximum amount of good-time and subtracted it from the minimum sentence.

3. All life sentences, and minimum sentences that were greater than 10 years after they had been discounted for good-time, were coded as 10-year sentences. This corresponds to the policy of the Michigan Department of Corrections as prescribed by statute. The parole board has jurisdiction over cases after 10 calendar years of incarceration.

This variable roughly corresponds to expected length of sentence, but more precisely it is the length of time to first possible release.

For purposes of the analysis presented here, we have grouped cases according to the original charge: murders, armed robberies, felonious assaults, and other aggravated assaults.[15]

Table 1 presents parameter estimates for our basic sentencing model. We use a maximum likelihood estimator referred to as TOBIT (truncated probit) analysis because the expected minimum sentence has a lower limit of zero, with a substantial number of cases falling at this point. Given this distribution, the assumptions for ordinary least squares estimation will not be met, and the TOBIT procedure is appropriate.[16] In this particular analysis, the choice of estimator does not affect the general conclusions that are reached. It does have a substantial influence on estimates of the magnitude of effects, but we reached the same conclusions using ordinary least squares.

The data indicate quite clearly that for murders and armed robberies there is no statistically significant change in expected minimum sentence that is selective for the gun cases. That is, the interaction terms, which measure the change in sentence that occurred only for gun offenses, are not statistically significant. In contrast, for felonious assaults and other assaults, the expected minimum sentence increased for gun cases more than for nongun cases. This interaction is statistically significant and can, according to the logic of our design, be attributed to the gun law.

Two important points should be made about the selective impact of the gun law on assault cases. First, the pattern of change is consistent

14. Of course, we do not assume that all defendants are guilty. We simply assume that the probability of being guilty of the charge is unrelated to other variables in the analysis.

15. Since cases frequently have multiple charges, we have used the following "case defining" charge conventions: (1) a case is designated a murder if one of the original charges is first- or second-degree murder; (2) an armed robbery if one of the charges is an armed robbery and there is no charge of murder or criminal sexual conduct; (3) a felonious assault if this is one of the original charges and there is no charge of another type of assault, armed robbery, criminal sexual conduct, or murder; and (4) an other aggravated assault if the original charges included as-

sault with intent to commit murder, assault with intent to commit great bodily harm, or assault with intent to commit armed robbery and there is no charge of murder, criminal sexual conduct, or armed robbery.

16. See James Tobin, "Estimation of Relationships for Limited Dependent Variables," *Econometrica*, 26(1): 24–36 (Jan. 1958).

TABLE 1

TOBIT ESTIMATES FOR SENTENCING MODEL BY ORIGINAL CHARGE

	INTERCEPT	GUN/ NO GUN	PRE/ POST	INTER- ACTION
Murder, n = 1143				
TOBIT				
Expected sentence =	897	−26	+406	−57
$\hat{\beta}/S\hat{\beta}$	(4.82)*	(−.13)	(1.55)	(−.18)
Armed robbery, n = 2768				
TOBIT				
Expected sentence =	−227	+637	+310	−7
$\hat{\beta}/S\hat{\beta}$	(−2.30)*	(5.63)*	(2.33)*	(−.05)
Felonious assaults, n = 1282				
TOBIT				
Expected sentence =	−677	−215	−6	303
$\hat{\beta}/S\hat{\beta}$	(−11.17)*	(−2.37)*	(−.08)	(2.51)*
Other aggravated assaults, n = 1484				
TOBIT				
Expected sentence =	−820	+234	−146	+487
$\hat{\beta}/S\hat{\beta}$	(−7.32)*	(1.63)	(−.91)	(2.38)*

NOTES: Variables are coded: 1 if gun present, 0 if no gun; 1 if postintervention, 0 if preintervention; and interaction is the product of these two variables. An asterisk indicates that the ratio $\hat{\beta}/S\hat{\beta}$ is greater than two. Under the null hypothesis, the probability of obtaining a value this large or larger is less than .05. TOBIT = truncated probit.

both with theoretical expectations and our field experience in Recorders Court. Before the gun law went into effect, the "going rate" for offenses such as murder and armed robbery was substantial. The average sentence for cases originally charged with armed robbery in the preintervention period was about six years. Few such cases received probation or suspended sentences. On the other hand, for felonious assault, suspended sentences and probation were the most common disposition, and for those cases that received a sentence, the average was only about six months.[17] The mandatory two-year sentence could easily be absorbed by the relatively long sentences that were typical for murders and robberies. The sentencing judge could simply shave a couple of years off the murder or robbery sentence, making the net sentence the same as it had always been. This, of course, was not so easy for assaults. The lower going rate in the preintervention period forced a substantial number of these sentences to a higher level after the gun law went into effect.[18]

Second, the pattern of the results is not an artifact of the way we measure the sanctions. We obtained the same pattern when we used the minimum sentence and excluded the life sentences and extremely long sentences—which would have been outliers in the analysis—and when we modeled the probability of serving any sentence at all.

17. The exact values for the average minimum sentence given defendants who were originally charged with armed robbery was 2340 days; for those charged with felonious assault, it was 198 days. Note that the charge is the original charge, not necessarily the charge on which the defendant was sentenced. Cases that were not convicted of some offense were excluded from these calculations.

18. Heumann and Loftin, pp. 393–40.

ANALYSIS OF CHANGES IN CRIME VOLUME

We turn now to the question of the extent to which the Michigan gun law has been effective in altering the patterns of violent crime. Our research strategy is to specify simple models that might represent the impact of the gun law on crime in Detroit, then to compare the actual crime patterns with the models. Inferences about the effects of the gun law will depend on the fit between the models and the observed crime patterns.

There are two mechanisms by which a gun law such as this might reduce gun-related crime: deterrence and incapacitation. Since we have demonstrated that the law had very limited impact on the length of sentences and the probability of incarceration for gun-related offenses, it seems reasonable to focus on possible deterrence mechanisms.

The initial publicity given the gun law and its implementation by the Wayne County prosecutor was intended to send a clear signal to potential offenders that they now faced the threat of more severe legal sanctions than previously. If the signals were received and believed by the relevant population, there is the possibility that some would be deterred from committing an offense and others might substitute another weapon. Given our results on sentencing in Recorder's Court, we would expect any change to be a result of the initial publicity campaign and the change in the charging behavior of the police and prosecutor, not a result of changes in the expected sentence.

If the dominant effect of the gun law were deterrence without weapon substitution, gun offenses would go down beginning about January 1977,

the month the gun law went into effect. More precisely, if the publicity campaign were primarily responsible for transmitting the threat of a change in sanctions, the effect would be abrupt and would begin in December 1976, which was when the publicity campaign began.[19] Alternatively, if the charging behavior of the police and the prosecutor were the primary transmission mechanism, the effect would begin gradually, increasing over time as information diffused among potential offenders. In contrast, offenses committed without a gun, which would not be influenced by the gun law, would remain unchanged.

If the dominant effect were deterrence with weapon substitution, we would expect gun offenses to decline just as in the pure deterrence model, but offenses committed without a gun would be expected to rise, either gradually or abruptly—depending on the transmission medium—as offenders substituted other weapons for guns.

In the real world we might find a combination of the pure deterrent effect and the weapon-substitution effect. In any case, the expected impact on crime patterns would be similar: gun offenses would decline

19. The bill establishing the gun law was signed into law on 11 Feb. 1976. See *Detroit News*, 12 Feb. 1976, p. A3. But no article about the law appeared in the Detroit newspapers between 12 Feb. 1976 and 1 Dec. 1976 when the publicity campaign was announced. See "Ad Drive to Spell Out Jail-for-Gunman Law," *Detroit News*, 1 Dec. 1976, p. 8A. The nongun assaults include assaults with weapons other than a gun, aggravated assault without a weapon, and simple assaults. Other combinations produce results that are not substantially different from those presented subsequently. For both the assault and the robbery series, there were three missing observations, which we replaced with forecasted values.

FIGURE 1
HOMICIDES

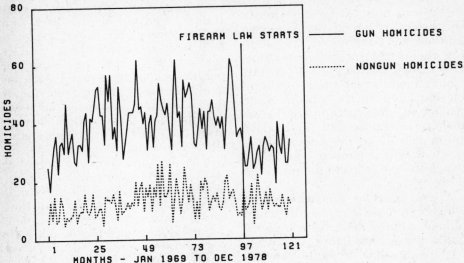

MONTHS - JAN 1969 TO DEC 1978

and nongun offenses would remain stable or would rise slightly.

For our statistical analysis, we collected time series data on homicides, robberies, and assaults. These data are depicted in Figures 1 through 5. For homicides, we were able to obtain monthly data for eight years prior to implementation and two years after;[20] for robbery and assaults, we have 10 years of data

20. The homicide series was constructed by examining death certificate data obtained from the Office of Vital and Health Statistics of the Michigan Department of Public Health. Homicides occurring in Detroit were classified by month of occurrence and by whether or not the death was the result of an assault with a firearm. Following the International Classification of Diseases, homicide includes all deaths purposely inflected by other persons, except those due to legal intervention and the operation of war. The homicide codes are E960-969. Of these E965, assaults by firearm and explosives, were considered to be gun homicides. See U.S. Department of Health, Education and Welfare, *Eighth Revision, International Classification of Diseases*, vol. 1 (Washington, DC: U.S. Government Printing Office, 1967).

before implementation and four years after. As is evident from the figures, we were able to classify homicides and assaults according to whether they involved a gun or not, but we were forced by available data to treat robberies differently. Figure 2 presents monthly series of armed and unarmed robberies for the entire study period. In Figure 5, we present yearly series for gun and nongun robberies for 49 years. Unfortunately, only three of these are in the postintervention period. Figure 4 is a short—1975–79—monthly robbery series of gun and nongun robberies. None of the robbery series is completely satisfactory, but they complement each other and provide important information about Detroit robberies.[21]

21. In Figure 5, there seems to be some minor errors in the weapons codes, which are a result of changes in the codes during the study period. In creating the five-year monthly series, we excluded the unknown weapon category and grouped all weapons other than firearms into the nongun category. This included the following: blackjack, knife,

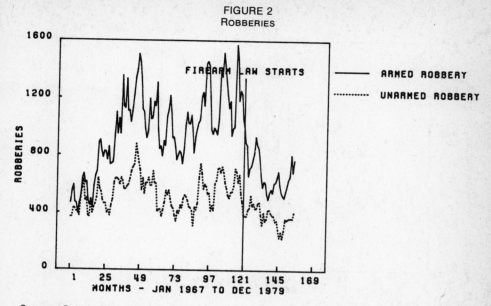

FIGURE 2
ROBBERIES

SOURCE: Detroit Police Department, Records Section, *Computerized Monthly Report* (Jan. 1967–Dec. 1979).

The data in the figures reflect the dramatic decline in violent crime in Detroit, which occurred at about the time the gun law was implemented. Between 1976 and 1977, homicides declined by 31 percent, robberies by 27 percent, and aggravated assaults by 2.5 percent. These are the reductions that were widely noted by law enforcement officials and the press and served to generate considerable enthusiasm for the gun law.[22] Close

inspection of the data, however, suggests several patterns that are inconsistent with the hypothesis that the gun law contributed to the decline. First, the decline in all three offenses began months before the gun law went into effect. The peak month in 1976 was July, the month of the widely publicized youth gang incidents. The general downward trend in offense levels begins at this point, which was five months before the gun law went into effect and four months before the publicity campaign began.

Second, only for homicides was the change significantly greater for gun offenses than for offenses committed without a gun. Armed robberies fell dramatically in 1977, but so did unarmed robberies. The best comparisons for robberies are Figures 4 and 5 in which the monthly and yearly series of gun and nongun robberies are compared. It is apparent that both gun and nongun

---

missile, blunt object, other sharp object, and miscellaneous. Differences between the monthly and the yearly series are a result of differences in the way these categories are grouped. In Figure 3, nongun assaults include assaults committed with a weapon other than a gun as well as aggravated assaults without a weapon and simple assaults. Other combinations produce the same results as those reported subsequently.

22. Index property offenses also fell: burglary by 30 percent, larceny by 12 percent, and auto theft by 21 percent. See Detroit Police Department, Records Section, *Computerized Monthly Report* (Dec. 1977).

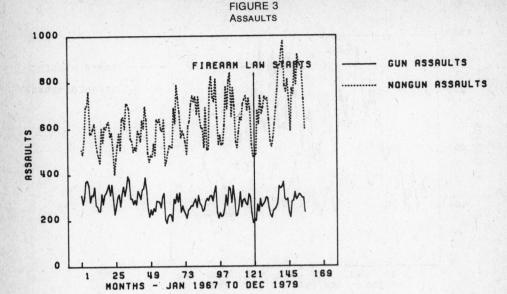

FIGURE 3
ASSAULTS

SOURCES: Information Systems Bureau of the Detroit Police Department (1975–79); and Uniform Crime Reporting Section of the FBI (1967–75) (combined computer tape data).

robberies declined with a very similar pattern. For assaults (Figure 3) the patterns are quite contrary to what would be expected if the gun law had a deterrent effect. Both gun and nongun assaults remain about the same in the postintervention period, though there is a slight increase for nongun assaults.

This type of visual inspection of time series, while interesting, can be misleading because of the presence of trend, drift, seasonality, and autocorrelation, which may be confounded with the effects of the gun law. To avoid these problems we use statistical models based on the work of Box and Jenkins.[23] In general terms, the procedure starts with the development of a noise model to account for trend or drift, seasonality,

and autocorrelation in the time series. Having specified an appropriate noise model to control the effects of these series characteristics, an intervention model is added to represent the effect of the gun law. If there is a change in the series at the point of intervention, the intervention model will have statistically significant effects.

Donald T. Campbell and his collaborators have argued that interrupted time series designs, such as the one that we use here, are among the strongest of quasi-experimental research designs.[24] However, as with any research design, there are possible threats to the validity of inferences from it. No doubt the most serious of these threats is history, the possibility that events occurring at the same time as the intervention

23. G.E.P. Box and G. M. Jenkins, *Time Series Analysis: Forecasting and Control* (San Francisco, CA: Holden-Day, 1976); and G.E.P. Box and G.C. Taio, "Intervention Analysis with Applications to Economic and Environmental Problems," *J. Am. Statistical Association*, 70: 70–92(March 1975).

24. Donald T. Campbell and Julian C. Stanley, *Experimental and Quasi-Experimental Designs for Research*, (Chicago, IL: Rand McNally, 1966); and Thomas D. Cook and Donald T. Campbell, *Quasi-Experimentation: Design and Analysis Issues for Field Settings*, (Chicago, IL: Rand McNally, 1979).

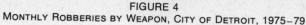

FIGURE 4
MONTHLY ROBBERIES BY WEAPON, CITY OF DETROIT, 1975–79

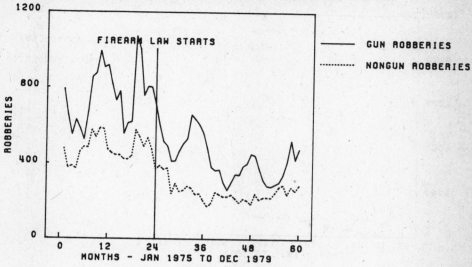

SOURCE: Detroit Police Department, Records Bureau, *Annual Report* (1931–79).

were responsible for observed changes in the level of crime. To minimize this possibility, we will compare gun offenses and nongun offenses and, as was the case with the analysis of the sanctions, assume that an effect that is unique to gun offenses can be attributed to the gun law. Of course, this strategy does not completely rule out alternative explanations, but it does make them much less plausible.

For each series, we considered three intervention models: an abrupt temporary change model, a gradual permanent change model, and an abrupt permanent change model. While more complex models are possible, these three seem reasonable and do not require elaborate assumptions about impact patterns. Taking advantage of arithmetic relationships between the models, we were led to the abrupt permanent change model as the most appropriate for each of the series.[25]

25. Discussion of the types of intervention models we considered may be found in

Specific information on the time series analysis is presented in the appendix to this article. The conclusions derived from that analysis are generally consistent with what was suggested by Figures 1 through 5. Homicide with a gun is the only offense that experienced a statistically significant decline after the gun law went into effect. Gun homicides went down abruptly at a rate of almost 11 per month, while none of the other violent offenses ex-

Leslie J. McCain and Richard McCleary, "The Statistical Analysis of the Simple Interrupted Time-Series Quasi-Experiment," in Thomas D. Cook and Donald T. Campbell; in David McDowall, Richard McCleary, Errol E. Meidinger, and Richard A. Hay, Jr., *Interrupted Time Series Analysis*, University Papers on Quantitative Applications in the Social Sciences (Beverly Hills, CA: Sage, 1980); or in Richard McCleary and Richard A. Hay, Jr., with Errol E. Meidinger and David McDowall, *Applied Time Series Analysis for the Social Sciences* (Beverly Hills, CA: Sage, 1980). These sources also provide introductions to Box-Jenkins modeling in general.

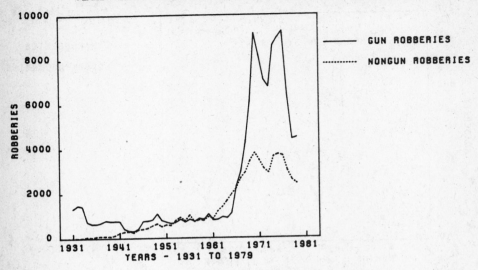

FIGURE 5
YEARLY ROBBERIES BY WEAPON FOR THE CITY OF DETROIT, 1931–79

SOURCE: Information Systems Bureau of the Detroit Police Department.

perienced a shift in level that could be attributed to the gun law.

At first we thought the decline in homicides might reflect a change in gun assaults that could be linked to the change in sentences for assaults in Recorder's Court.[26] Now that we have examined the assault series, this interpretation no longer fits the facts. Since there was no significant change in gun assaults that might explain the decline in gun homicides, we believe that the decline in gun homicides occurred because of factors that were not directly related to the gun law.

These patterns are quite different from the predictions of the deterrence models, and we can think of no reasonable version of that theory that would accommodate them.[27] For that reason we are led to our current working hypothesis, which is that the gun law did not significantly alter the number or type of violent offenses committed in Detroit.

DISCUSSION

Why did the gun law fail to reduce gun crime in Detroit? One likely reason is simply that the gun law was too weak an intervention to produce a measurable effect on crime patterns. Our investigation of

---

26. Colin Loftin and David McDowall, " 'One With a Gun Gets You Two': Mandatory Sentencing and Firearms Offenses in Detroit" (Presented to the 75th Meeting of the American Sociological Association, New York, NY, 25 Aug. 1980).

27. We should note two issues raised by Philip J. Cook, special editor of this volume,

in response to an earlier version of this article. First, if the gun law encouraged weapon substitution, it is possible that there would be no discernible change in either gun or nongun series taken one at a time. But if some combination of them, such as the ratio or proportion were modeled, the effect might be statistically significant. Second, if the gun law stimulated the reporting or the recording of gun offenses, this would tend to mask any decline in offenses which might have been caused by the gun law. One way to test this hypothesis would be to examine trends for offenses in which there is serious injury and therefore a consistently high probability of reporting and recording. We have not been able to find this type of data and therefore cannot conduct the test.

the impact of the gun law on Recorder's Court has repeatedly demonstrated the ability of the organization to moderate and soften the force of the gun law. Not only was there no change in expected sentences for murders and robberies, the changes that did occur in assaults were far short of the expected two-year increase that the legislature and the public intended. Though statistically significant, the effects that we found were small in magnitude, only about one month for felonious assault and four months for other assaults.[28]

Another factor is that the scope of the gun law is very narrow, focusing only on the commission of a felony while in possession of a gun, without influencing the carrying of a gun. Cook[29] has noted that the value of a gun to an offender is great in the commission of a crime where there is a high likelihood of armed resistance. Given the high density of guns in Detroit, it may be that the threat of a two-year prison sentence is just too weak to have an impact.

Another possibility, not inconsistent with the others, is that not enough time has passed in order for the effect to be discernible. If the effect were quite small, which would be in line with what we know about the change in sanctions, more time would be necessary for our statistical models to show an impact. The length of our postintervention series is sufficient to detect even relatively small changes. If, however, the effect were very slight, it is possible that our models could miss it.

Mandatory sentencing or sentence enhancement for crimes committed with a gun are politically popular because they offer an apparent means of controlling gun violence without imposing direct costs on legitimate gun owners. In principle, the costs are borne completely by criminals and by the criminal justice system in the form of longer sentences, more litigation, and so forth.

The Detroit experience indicates, however, that the benefits may be more apparent than real. If the policy does not reduce gun violence, and at the same time diverts attention and resources from alternative policies, its costs are clearly greater than its benefits.

Perhaps the problem lies in the fact that the sentence enhancement was not great enough, or that there was not enough constraint placed on the court. It is always possible to devise new schemes that would plug the holes and, at least in theory, prevent the court from moderating sentences. Again, however, the Detroit experience suggests otherwise. This is a tough gun law. There were no obvious loopholes in its formulation, and the prosecutor's policy of enforcing it was not just a "grandstand" act. The policy was enforced and cases were vigorously prosecuted. Any scheme that would stand a better chance of producing more change in average sanctions would have to be very different from the Michigan law.

If the gun law had reduced gun offenses, there would be cause for celebration. We would have found something analogous to a criminological wonder drug, a low-cost policy that would save lives and prevent violence. Unfortunately, the evidence suggests a harsher reality. The costs of reducing gun violence will be greater, perhaps much greater than we might have hoped.

---

28. See Table 1. The size of these effects varies with the estimation procedure. We cite the ordinary least squares estimates here because they are the easiest to interpret.

29. Philip J. Cook, "The Role of Firearms in Violent Crime: An Interpretative Review of the Literature, With Some New Findings and Suggestions for Future Research" (Unpublished paper, Nov. 1980).

APPENDIX: DESCRIPTION OF TIME SERIES ANALYSIS

GUN HOMICIDES

Based on our preliminary identification, we estimated an ARIMA(1,0,0) $(1,0,0)_{12}$ noise model for the gun homicide series. Parameter estimates and diagnostic statistics for the model are presented in the first part of Table 1.

The results of the intervention analysis are presented in the second part of Table 1. Our estimate for the change parameter in the model (ω_o) is very large, indicating a dramatic decline of almost 11 gun homicides per month in Detroit in the postintervention period.

TABLE 1

GUN HOMICIDES
Noise model
ARIMA (1, 0, 0) (1, 0, 0)$_{12}$:
$a_t = (1 - \emptyset_1 B)(1 - \emptyset_{12} B^{12}) Y_t - \theta_0$
$\hat{\theta}_0 = 38.23$ 95% c.i. = 34.30 to 42.16
$\hat{\theta}_1 = .5002$ 95% c.i. = .3410 to .6594
$\hat{\theta}_{12} = .2755$ 95% c.i. = .0903 to .4606
Residual mean square = 64.443 w/df = 118
Q = 20.452 w/df = 22
P > .50
Intervention model
$Y_t^* = a_t + \omega_0(I_t)$
I_t = 0 for observations 1–96
= 1 for observations 97–120
$\hat{\omega}_0 = -10.857$ 95% c.i. = -17.107 to -4.607
Residual mean square = 59.902 w/df = 117
Q = 17.39 w/df = 22
P > .50

ARIMA = Autoregressive Integrate Moving Average.
c.i. = confidence interval.

NONGUN HOMICIDES

Perhaps because of its relatively low level throughout most of the period, the nongun homicide series presented analytical difficulties. A floor effect constrained the series variance, and the noise model was determined by just six extreme observations. Although logarithmic transformations are known to help in situations such as this,[1] a transformation did not fully remove the problem here. Therefore in addition to transforming the series, we treated the influential observations as missing and forecast replacements for them. After replacing the observations, only the series mean needed to be estimated for the noise model (Table 2, first part).

In contrast to the gun homicides, the intervention component for the nongun homicides was very small, both statistically and substantively zero (Table 2, second part). We thus conclude that there was no change in Detroit nongun homicides in the postintervention period.

1. Richard McCleary and M. C. Musheno, "Floor Effects in Time Series Quasi-Experiments," *Political Methodology* (forthcoming).

TABLE 2

Noise model
  ARIMA (0, 0, 0)
    $a_t = Y_t - \theta_0$
    $\hat{\theta}_0 = 2.5181$ 95% c.i. $= 2.4580$ to 2.5783
    Residual mean square $= .1076$ w/df $= 118$
    $Q = 27.86$ w/df $= 24$
    $P > .25$
(Observation 1 was dropped, and observations 5, 9, 55, 57, and 61 were forecast in this model.)

Intervention model
  $Y_t^* = a_t + \omega_0(I_t)$
    $I_t = 0$ for observations 2–96
    $I_t = 1$ for observations 97–120
    $\hat{\omega}_0 = -.0008$ 95% c.i. $= -.1566$ to $.1550$
    Residual mean square $= .1086$ w/df $= 117$
    $Q = 27.86$ w/df $= 24$
    $P > .25$

ARMED ROBBERIES

In order to produce a constant variance throughout the armed robbery series, we first logarithmically transformed it. After transformation, we identified and estimated an ARIMA$(0,1,0)(3,0,0)_6$ noise model.[2]

The estimate of the intervention parameter was statistically insignifi-

2. Those familiar with Box-Jenkins techniques will recognize this model as quite unusual, both because of the six-month seasonal pattern and because of the high order of the process. However, both the parameter estimates and the diagnostic statistics (Table 3, part one) indicate that the model is appropriate, and we were unsuccessful in attempting to fit simpler ones.

TABLE 3

Noise model
  ARIMA (0, 1, 0) (3, 0, 0)$_6$
    $a_t = (1 - B)(1 - \emptyset_6 B^6 - \emptyset_{12} B^{12} - \emptyset_{18} B^{18}) Y_t$
    $\hat{\emptyset}_6 = -.2119$ 95% c.i. $= -.3781$ to $-.0457$
    $\hat{\emptyset}_{12} = .2041$ 95% c.i. $= .0385$ to $.3696$
    $\hat{\emptyset}_{18} = -.2414$ 95% c.i. $= -.4024$ to $-.0804$
    Residual mean square $= .0130$ w/df $= 152$
    $Q = 28.48$ w/df $= 22$
    $P > .10$
(This model was initially estimated with a trend parameter, but the trend was not statistically significant and was dropped.)

Intervention model
  $Y_t^* = a_t + \omega_0(I_t)$
    $I_t = 0$ for observations 1–120
    $= 1$ for observations 121–156
    $\hat{\omega}_0 = .0676$ 95% c.i. $= -.1540$ to $.2893$
    Residual mean square $= .01304$ w/df $= 151$
    $Q = 28.48$ w/df $= 22$
    $P > .10$

cant, indicating that there was no discernible change in the series in the period following introduction of the gun law (Table 3, second part). This is a very important finding. Although it appears obvious from Figure 2 in the preceding article that rob-beries went down in the postintervention period, all of this effect can be attributed to the factors in the noise model. When they are controlled, there is no change in the level of the series.

UNARMED ROBBERIES

The unarmed robbery series also required an initial log transformation in order to produce a constant variance. After transformation, we identified and estimated an ARIMA $(1,1,0)(1,0,0)_{12}$ noise model. The estimates and diagnostic statistics for this model are presented in the first part of Table 4.

As with armed robberies, our estimate of the intervention parameter was not statistically significant (Table 4, part two), and we conclude that there was no change in unarmed robberies following the introduction of the felony firearm law.

TABLE 4

UNARMED ROBBERIES (SERIES TRANSFORMED BY NATURAL LOGARITHM)

Noise model
  ARIMA $(1, 1, 0)$ $(1, 0, 0)_{12}$
  $a_t = (1 - B)(1 - \emptyset_1 B)(1 - \emptyset_{12} B^{12})Y_t$
  $\hat{\emptyset}_1 = -.2983$ 95% c.i. = $-.4548$ to $-.1418$
  $\hat{\emptyset}_{12} = .6289$ 95% c.i. = $.4975$ to $.7604$
  Residual mean square = .0127 w/df = 153
  Q = 28.75 w/df = 23
  P > .10
(This model was initially estimated with a trend parameter, but the trend was not statistically significant and was dropped.)

Intervention model
  $Y_t^* = a_t + \omega_0(I_t)$
  $I_t = 0$ for observations 1–120
     = 1 for observations 121–156
  $\hat{\omega}_0 = .0700$ 95% c.i. = $-.2535$ to .1134
  Residual mean square = .0127 w/df = 152
  Q = 29.97 w/df = 23
  P > .10

GUN ASSAULTS

We identified and estimated an ARIMA$(0,1,1)(0,1,1)_{12}$ noise model for the gun assault series. Parameter estimates and diagnostic statistics are presented in the first part of Table 5. The intervention component was again statistically insignificant (second part, Table 5), and we thus conclude that Detroit gun assaults were unaffected in the postintervention period.

TABLE 5

GUN ASSAULTS

Noise model
  ARIMA (0, 1, 1) (0, 1, 1)$_{12}$
  $(1 - \theta_1 B)(1 - \theta_{12} B^{12})a_t = (1 - B)(1 - B^{12})Y_t$
  $\hat{\theta}_1 = .7583$ 95% c.i. $= .6564$ to $.8602$
  $\hat{\theta}_{12} = .8835$ 95% c.i. $= .8380$ to $.9290$
  Residual mean square $= 408.1450$ w/df $= 141$
    $Q = 18.40$ w/df $= 23$
    $P > .50$
(This model was initially estimated with a trend parameter, but the trend was not statistically significant and was dropped.)

Intervention model
  $Y_t^* = a_t + \omega_0(I_t)$
    $I_t = 0$ for observations $1-120$
       $= 1$ for observations $121-156$
  $\hat{\omega}_0 = -.3335$ 95% c.i. $= -1.1788$ to $.5118$
  Residual mean square $= 410.0650$ w/df $= 140$
    $Q = 19.40$ w/df $= 23$
    $P > .50$

NONGUN ASSAULTS

As for the gun assault series, we identified and estimated an ARIMA $(0,1,1)(0,1,1)_{12}$ noise model for the nongun assaults. The parameter estimates and diagnostic statistics for this model are presented in the first part of Table 6.

Again, the intervention estimate is not statistically significant (Table 6, second part), indicating no change in nongun assaults following the introduction of the firearm law.

TABLE 6

NOGUN ASSAULTS

Noise model
  ARIMA (0, 1, 1) (0, 1, 1)$_{12}$
  $(1 - \theta_1 B)(1 - \theta_{12} B^{12})a_t = (1 - B)(1 - B^{12})Y_t$
  $\hat{\theta}_1 = .7229$ 95% c.i. $= .6116$ to $.8342$
  $\hat{\theta}_{12} = .8590$ 95% c.i. $= .8075$ to $.9105$
  Residual mean square $= 3951.0100$ w/df $= 141$
    $Q = 31.10$ w/df $= 23$
    $P > .10$
(This model was initially estimated with a trend parameter, but the trend was not statistically significant and was dropped.)

Intervention model
  $Y_t^* = a_t + \omega_0(I_t)$
    $I_t = 0$ for observations $1-120$
       $= 1$ for observations $121-156$
  $\hat{\omega}_0 = .0244$ 95% c.i. $= -.0600$ to $.1088$
  Residual mean square $= 3971.5100$ w/df $= 140$
    $Q = 31.10$ w/df $= 23$
    $P > .10$

CALL FOR PAPERS

1982 ANNUAL MEETING

ACADEMY OF CRIMINAL JUSTICE SCIENCES

March 23-27, 1982

THE GALT HOUSE

Louisville, Kentucky

THEME:

**Interdisciplinary Contributions to
Criminal Justice**

Persons interested in participating
should write for an abstract format. Contact:
Robert G. Culbertson, Ph.D., President,
Academy of Criminal Justice Sciences
401 Schroeder Hall
Illinois State University
Normal, Illinois 61761

DEADLINE DATE FOR ABSTRACTS: SEPTEMBER 10, 1981

Book Department

INTERNATIONAL RELATIONS AND POLITICS

BARRY RUBIN. *Paved With Good Intentions: The American Experience and Iran.* Pp. xii, 426. NY: Oxford University Press, 1980. $17.50.

Today there is a spate of books relating to the shah's Iran and the American government of his time. The Iranian Revolution, the hostages, and America's predicament merge in this. Some of these books are such hasty journalistic attempts at mixing fact and opinion, however, that they are difficult to appraise. Perhaps the best current approach is an extensive use of the press, combined with congressional hearings, oral interviews, and certain factual volumes. This combination is the trove that Dr. Rubin uses in the present work. While the Freedom of Information Act has helped in extracting some classified material, much relevant information is still locked, such as that of the Nixon-Kissinger and Carter years. Nevertheless, Rubin has winnowed his sources and produced a very readable, timely, and reasonably authentic volume.

Background upon the development of the American–Iranian relationship is quite well done. Particularly solid is the period through World War II and the Mosadeq years, culminating in the CIA catalytic action in getting the Iranian public to choose between the shah and Mosadeq. While the United States had no illusions about the slender-reed nature of the shah's strength of character, the strategic imperatives of the time impelled continued American support. An indecisive though intelligent man, formed by a tyrannical father, simply proved in the long run to be incapable of leading his people into the modern world. He lacked the reforming ruthlessness of an Ataturk, he was burdened by a voracious family, and unpunctured dreams substituted for reality. The tragedy for both countries was that America, although tarred with the association, really proved unable to influence the shah's domestic courses. The foundations were being eaten away while the shah was proclaimed by American policymakers as a pillar of Middle Eastern stability. The United States had placed all its chips upon one essentially unstable, physically deteriorating man. It did not even know he was ill, although presumably through their consulted doctors the French did.

The folly of the Nixon–Kissinger policy in building up the shah as a surrogate and in giving him access to unlimited, advanced arms is clearly depicted by Rubin. Similarly, depicted is the studied reluctance to face the consequences, extending into the Carter administration. When the crash came, America was surprised by the depth of the hostile forces in Iran, which true to their culture, believed this country was responsible for the shah's every adverse action. Despite embassy warnings, the shah's medical treatment in the United States sparked the hostage crisis, as the Iranian revolutionaries deemed America was preparing a coup against them.

This book gives clear summations of the stages in American–Iranian relations and surveys the ground swells of Iranian discontent. Rubin is adept at presenting both sides of differing viewpoints. There is , despite the references and bibliography, a tendency at pertinent sectors of the narrative to omit footnotes where they could be useful. Over 100 interviewees are claimed, but only a handful are cited, for the others are said to be off-the-record talks. These aspects can be frustrating. Yet for a needed preliminary survey and analysis of an important topic in America's interest, the book is an excellent compendium.

A final thought: the shah is gone, but still one muses. Has superpower America learned the futility of building a strategic policy, not upon indigenous forces, but upon the survival of a single, imperfect man who may momentarily hold the panoply of power?

ROY M. MELBOURNE
University of North Carolina
Chapel Hill

BRUCE A. ACKERMAN. *Social Justice in the Liberal State*. Pp. xii, 392. New Haven, CT: Yale University Press, 1980. $17.50.

Bruce Ackerman takes a proper liberal state to be neither the result of a contract, as suggested by John Rawls, nor the consequence of a utilitarian legislature, nor a night watchman guarding natural rights, as offered by Robert Nozick. Rather than imaginary contract or natural right, he takes liberalism to be essentially a way of talking about power. Dialogue is the basic machinery. We are asked to go back to Plato, but our dialogue is to be given special parameters. The three restrictions are what Ackerman calls Rationality, Consistency, and Neutrality.

His notion of Rationality is the requirement that every question about the legitimacy of someone's power must be responded to by the power holder. He must give "a reason that explains why he is more entitled to the resource than the questioner is." The requirement of Consistency is that the reasons offered in defense of holding power must be consistent with all other such defenses offered by that individual. The Neutrality principle forbids counting a reason if it makes the assertion that one citizen is better than another.

Can conversation save us? Even Neutral, Rational, and Consistent conversation seems a thin support for the foundation of a liberal state. However, with Socrates as patron saint, and with an author whose intelligence and style are delightful, the results are surprisingly rich. We are given both artificial and actual examples of how liberal dialogue can reach conclusions on an enormous variety of problems. These neatly constructed dialogues consider problems that run from the distribution of wealth to genetic manipulation, abortion, infanticide, education, affirmative action, the place of the family, inheritance, population control, civil disobedience, contracts, and law. The dialogues depend critically on a stock question and answer: the question, "Why should you get it rather than I?"; and the answer, "Because I'm at least as good as you are." The principle of Neutrality is to solve almost all problems; when it cannot, a limited use of lottery and of majority rule is available.

Has he discriminated between three rivals—contractarianism, utilitarianism, and liberal dialogue? Not convincingly. I leave with the notion that the method of dialogue may well be used to produce a contract as its product, a contract that has social utility as its goal. While Ackerman argues impressively in favor of the method of dialogue, he had denied us neither a series of contracts as its product, nor the goal of individualized patterns of utility. Even as a method we need to know more of the mechanism by which anyone may challenge anyone else. Beyond a small town meeting, this is complicated. The role of representatives is unclear. The use of force against irrational citizens is not explained.

Ackerman claims Socrates "as the emblem upon the liberal standard." Is this the Socrates who stood outside of government, but recognized its legitimacy? Ackerman is even closer to the nineteenth-century anarchist, William Godwin. He has the same charming and flattering assumption that man is more properly persuaded by reason than by power. Certainly he is right that this is one basic part of liberalism. Moral dignity requires it. But with the charm of anarchism, there comes the matter of its weakness.

Ackerman has constructed an analysis of liberalism that uses Platonic dialogue to reach results diametrically opposed to Plato. His Neutrality principle does not apply to this book; despite my criticisms, it is the best recent study of liberalism, and I look forward to his future work on it.

SIDNEY AXINN

Temple University
Philadelphia
Pennsylvania

WALTER L. ADAMSON. *Hegemony and Revolution: A Study of Antonio Gramsci's Political and Cultural Theory.* Pp. x, 304. Berkeley, CA: University of California Press, 1980. $20.00.

Professor Adamson's full-length study of Antonio Gramsci's *Prison Notebooks*, the first in English, is a first-rate piece of intellectual history that is well crafted, widely researched, and buttressed with copious notes and a selected bibliography. Gramsci experts will not discover anything new or startling in this book about the West's most original twentieth-century Communist thinker, but its lucidity and depth make it a valuable addition to the literature of Marxism-Leninism.

In Adamson's view, "Gramsci's theory is enormously provocative and speaks to a number of problems in contemporary political theory." His purpose, therefore, is to reveal the intricate network of closely interwoven themes of the *Notebooks*, such as the crucial concept of hegemony and the role of intellectuals in politics, and to draw out the implications of his theory of the state while depicting the historical context that framed Gramsci's innovative writings. In pursuit of this purpose, Adamson, employing a straightforward style, goes a long way toward elucidating what formerly had been clear only to a handful of political theorists and philosophers. Most of the book's closely argued analysis compels assent, and some of it compels genuine admiration by the incisiveness of its explanations and the precision in conceptualizing difficult ideas.

Although the detailed analysis of the book verges on the tedious in places, that is the price of a comprehensive survey of such a complex subject. In his conclusion, Adamson endeavors to set Gramsci's political theory in historical perspective. Here he notes that most of the major themes in the *Notebooks* "were developed between 1930 and 1933 in the prison compound at Turi." It is Adamson's judgment that "Gramsci's political understanding did develop with substantial continuity from a thematic basis already well established in 1918." Respecting the theorist's originality, it is suggested that Gramsci anticipated Eurocommunism in his stress on the need for "prefigurative institutions," such as worker councils, cooperatives, and cultural associations. Adamson is perhaps on more speculative ground when he denies that Gramsci's "totalitarianism" implied "the kind of political repression and control which the word has more recently acquired." Finally, Adamson is convinced, more than most of his critics are likely to be, that by making certain revisions in classical Marxism, especially in the concept of hegemony, Gramsci helped to create a "coherent, democratic, and historically serviceable political theory within the Marxist tradition."

With considerable skill, Adamson has managed to compress as much vital information in a small compass as a silicon chip. Given the book's overall level of excellence, one hesitates to take issue with its conclusions. Yet many scholars will do so, concentrating no doubt on the far-ranging value judgments set forth at the end of the book. Certainly the book is a valuable conceptual effort at clarification of an important thinker's seminal ideas. And because of Adamson's philosophical and methodological virtuosity, he has managed to combine intensive textual exegesis with the kind of acute analysis of meaning that few scholars today can match—no small feat.

FRANCIS M. WILHOIT

Drake University

Des Moines

Iowa

STEVE J. HEIMS. *John von Neumann and Norbert Wiener: From Mathematics to the Technologies of Life and Death.* Pp. xviii, 547. Cambridge, MA: The M.I.T. Press, 1980. $19.95.

Professor Heims' book is a chronological double biography of the early childhoods and major scientific contributions of John von Neumann's work in building quantum mechanics from an axiomatic basis, game theory, and the theory of automata and of Norbert Wiener's work on stochastic processes and cybernectics, and their contrasting social functions.

The book presents a number of facets or qualitative dimensions pertinent to characterizing a scientist's relation to technology and society, and locates both Wiener and von Neumann in each dimension. They both provide dichotomies on the costs and benefits, economic and social, of technological development based on human nature.

For von Neumann, new technology is always basically beneficial, even if sometimes hazardous; people simply have to adapt to the inevitable march of progress. Wiener regards most technological developments as harmful, not intrinsically, but because their control is in the hands of institutions and individuals prone to use them in ways harmful to the human community as a whole. The former demonstrates the view from his emphasis on the fixity of human nature and the use of the utility function for decision making. The latter's view lies in his emphasis on learning, communicating, and the fulfillment of human possibilities. His model for decision making includes an explicit ethical dimension.

Another separate facet discussed throughout the chapters is the relation of technologies to time scales as experienced by both men. Wiener's emphasis concerning the element of time is ecological, and von Neumann's reflects the race against time. A final dimension is that of social function: von Neumann's function can be likened to that of postindustrial man; and Wiener's function fits that traditionally performed by conscious Quakers, even though he functioned in the world of high technology and approached every issue intellectually.

Heims also uses the book to express his dissident views concerning nuclear armament. He laments the reckoned use of scientific manpower and knowledge in the weapons department as part of the indispensable arsenal (Hiroshima and Nagasaki episodes) for furthering "national interest." He raises some practical life–or–death questions about armament or disarmament races. Questions that would challenge not only the readers of the book but also the government officials, politicians, intellectuals, policymakers and ordinary citizens worldwide, to identify their own positions on the either–or question of disarmament.

Heims didactically suggests that even a small minority with a strong commitment to nuclear disarmament can provide the needed momentum to the progress of the new cultural transformation. He laments the purposeful contradition of SALT treaties as nothing more than agreements between the two super-powers on how to engage in further armament.

Some alternative institutions to resolve the slow but sure likelihood of world catastrophe are suggested. These alternative institutions can be utilized to initiate the process of transition in the 1980s from a world terrorized by nuclear threats to one in which nuclear weapons play no major role in governing. But the economic rewards for participation in these institutions are usually lower than those offered by mainstream institutions.

The publication of this book is timely at this juncture of a stalled SALT II treaty. Heims echoes a message to policymakers and scientists in particular that if the human race cannot learn from the history of Hiroshima and Nagasaki, then it is condemned to repeat it. I commend this book to every citizen of the world because it has a message for everybody and deserves our unflinching attention if we are to survive as a human race.

JOHN B. ADESALU

Loyola College
Baltimore
Maryland

THOMAS B. LARSON. *Soviet-American Rivalry.* Pp. xii, 308, NY: W. W. Norton, $13.95.

Thomas Larson, a former American diplomat and author of several books on Soviet politics, introduces this present work on Soviet-American rivalry as differing in two respects from other studies in the same field: it examines all relevant elements in this rivalry, that is, economic, political, ideological, and military, as well as simply diplomatic, on the basis that such rivalry goes far beyond issues subject to diplomatic regulation; and it is written from an "outside," rather than partisan, point of view. By and large, both aims are satisfied, although the assertion about the need for objectivity is perhaps more a reflection on the quality of much American literature on the subject than it is on the special merits of this particular author.

This is a judicious but not a very exciting book, and it does not develop any new slants or interpretations on what is an already familiar and much-debated area of interest. Larson offers instead essentially a workmanlike and comprehensive synthesis of knowledge on the development of the two super-powers from the end of World War II until the mid-1970s. His method of approach is historical, applying throughout a direct bilateral comparison between the U.S.S.R. and the United States concerning the different elements in their rivalry. These are treated separately in consecutive chapters with the result that a fairly balanced overview is formed of their respective positions as world powers after three decades since the defeat of fascism ushered in a fundamentally changed structure in international relations.

The principal value of this book is therefore to underline the connection between the domestic and external aspects of East–West conflict, although traditional diplomatic studies are in any case generally regarded as outdated and too one-dimensional an explanation of U.S.S.R.-U.S. rivalry. Their rivalry is viewed by Larson as all-embracing, as it "involves the viability of the two states, of the social systems they champion and of the position in the world to which they aspire," for which reason areas where there is no direct competitiveness—notably the U.S.S.R. and the United States as representing rival economic and political models—are included in the discussion.

This hypothesis does, however, lead too often in the actual treatment here to little more than a descriptive comparison of the two countries. The interlinkage between economic, social political–institutional, ideological, military, and diplomatic factors is invariably assumed without this being subject to more careful scrutiny, which would have added significantly to the lessons to be drawn from East–West developments. Such inter-linkage is obvious in the case of economic competition between the two powers because their strength here is crucial to their military capacity, a theme referred to again later in the book, but otherwise the specific connection between the various factors tends to be neglected.

Some of the best insights are provided not so much over the broad patterns as on particular items, such as in the skeptical assessment of the importance of arms limitation and in basic limitations on freedom for maneuver enjoyed by the U.S. and Soviet leaderships, which Larson sees as the main, though not the sole, reason for the strong degree of consistency in Soviet and American foreign policy during this period. In this sense, Larson's historical approach puts the vagaries of Carter's presidency and the prospects for different initiatives by Reagan into a suitable context. Indeed, events since 1975, as the chronological end of this study, have not greatly altered the picture of East–West relations outlined by Larson, except that the full consequences of the Soviet invasion of Afghanistan still remain to be seen.

Considering the broad scope of this book, it is the last chapter on the future of Soviet-American rivalry that occasions special interest. Here, Larson is necessarily cautious because of the uncertain impact of short-term episodes, but so far as long-term trends are concerned, he presents various interesting, though not surprising, conclusions. Drawing on his main point that there has been a shift in the balance of power between the two states, favoring the U.S.S.R. and reducing substantially the U.S. economic, military and technological superiority after the War, Larson projects a continued gradual closing of the gap between American and Soviet production capabilities and their greater economic rivalry, all the more as near parity in military strength has promoted a neutralization in that area. A continued decline in U.S. political influence, with the increase in Communist systems in different parts of the world, though not always firmly pro-Moscow in allegiance, is also seen as likely. At the same time, despite the growth of ideological fragmentation within both camps, serious challenges to Soviet and American world leadership —possible contenders mentioned are China, Japan, and the European Community—are not regarded as viable for different reasons in the foreseeable future.

Altogether, Larson's survey provides a handy compendium on the subject and useful background to current developments in international affairs.

GEOFFREY PRIDHAM
University of Bristol
England

ERNEST W. LEFEVER. *Nuclear Arms in the Third World: U.S. Policy Dilemma.* Pp. xiv, 154. Washington, DC: The Brookings Institution, 1979. $9.95. Paperbound, $3.95.

Books on the possible spread of nuclear weapons are topical these days, and this relatively concise Brookings Institution study provides a good amount of detail on the problem in the "third world"—although Israel, South Korea, Taiwan, Brazil, and Argentina, among the most important cases in the book, do not fit too well into the "third world" category.

Lefever's presentation of the data is generally consistent with what one expects of Brookings publications, exhaustively researched and carefully compiled. His tone is nonetheless one of realpolitik pessimism, suggesting that the spread of weapons-related technology—and of weapons—is largely unstoppable, indicating that it is already an accepted fact that such weapons have spread to Israel. Here he may mislead the reader, by relying on relatively sensational *Time* magazine reports as reliable proofs and sources.

While the reader can thus obtain the outlines of the analytical and strategic debate for each of these countries from this volume, the tone of Lefever's "bottom line" for such cases may be too predeterminedly pessimistic, suggesting almost that it was always naive and hopeless to try to head off nuclear proliferation. If we wished to be more optimistic, we might note that any similar book published 10 years earlier would perhaps have had chapters on nine other countries, including Japan,

Italy, West Germany, Sweden, Brazil, India, and Israel, only one of which definitely then went ahead to make bombs—calling them "peaceful nuclear explosives"—most of which have instead definitely committed themselves not to make bombs.

As a sign of how rapidly events move along, the book makes no reference at all to the nuclear weapons possibilities in Iraq—currently one of the two most worrisome proliferation threats in the nonaligned third world—while the pessimistic section on Iran's nuclear program has been very much overtaken by events.

Analysts writing on nuclear weapons spread may be tempted to pessimism, because the maintenance of a nonproliferation regime is not easy. Yet such pessimism could be misleading if it stems from an iron law assumption that all weapons have tended to spread. Much of the world today knows that nuclear weapons are different, so different that old attitudes and old tendencies can no longer be allowed to govern.

GEORGE H. QUESTER
Cornell University
Ithaca
New York

MELVIN SMALL. *Was War Necessary? National Security and U.S. Entry into War*. Pp. 311. Beverly Hills, CA. Sage Publications, 1980. $18.00. Paperbound, $8.95.

Though admitting that his assertions are "overdrawn" and that, considering the realities of the time, the actions of the respective presidents "are defensible," Melvin Small nonetheless (somehow!) concludes that none of the six international wars fought by the United States between 1783 and 1950 were "necessary." That is, in "historical hindsight" the reasons for our entry into these conflicts do not satisfy Small's confused conception of what "national security" should be and should have been.

For Small, who denies he is a pacifist, "almost all wars are products of mis-calculation" and "most, *if not all*, wars should be avoided." National security is variously defined as (1) an overt attack or imminent danger of attack on our national territory, bases, vessels, or formal allies, and (2) "limited to a direct military attack on our own soil or on the soil of a near neighbor." Small is undisturbed by—and unaware of—the critical differences between his two definitions; after all, says Small, "*no matter how* we define national security, we cannot justify American entry into most [sic] of her international wars."

Three classes of threats to national security are distinguished: (1) direct military, (2) economic, and (3) threats to national honor. The last class, present in all six conflicts, does not justify war for Small, since he is "suspicious" of claims "that a failure to stand up to a stronger bully . . . can be translated into a threat to national security." Indeed, "fighting for national honor when . . . the best you can do is to tie or even lose is folly." As for economic factors, which allegedly loomed large only in World War I: they do "not . . . justify the loss of one citizen in war." That leaves only direct military threats. Certainly we can dismiss Polk's "rape of Mexico" and the War of 1812 when Washington was put to the torch ("One can sympathize with the British"), but what about Pearl Harbor? Well, World War II "was probably inevitable," but it was still unnecessary for the United States. There was "not a serious military threat to the United States. At Pearl Harbor "Japan *merely* destroyed our fleet"; it could have been avoided had we made "an amoral settlement with Tokyo."

The book is devoid of footnotes. It is wordy, stylistically defective, and negligently proofread: for example, there are 11 "I's" on page 25; "hitler" on page 17; and Charles—instead of Robert—Osgood is erroneously cited as the author of *Ideals and Self-Interest in America's Foreign Relations*. The language is "loose": Jefferson "jockeyed for position"; Canning "pulled the rug from under"; General Pershing could not apprehend Pancho Villa because "Mexico was a pretty big place and all

Mexicans looked alike." Finally, the book is endowed with such carefully crafted scholarly insights as "Americans think that every nation has its price." *Was War Necessary?* was clearly unnecessary. It is destined for a richly deserved obscurity.

DUNCAN L. CLARKE

The American University
The National War College
Washington, D.C.

CHARLES W. YOST. *History and Memory: A Statesman's Perceptions of the Twentieth Century.* Pp. 352. New York: W. W. Norton, 1980. $14.95.

Charles W. Yost is one of America's most experienced and wisest diplomats. He is also one of the least known and least appreciated. This book, which is described much more accurately by its subtitle than by its title, provides ample evidence of his common sense and wisdom, but it will do little to gain greater recognition for the man or greater acceptance of his ideas.

Yost was a Foreign Service officer for nearly 40 years, from 1930 to 1971, with a two-year interlude in 1933–35. He served under seven presidents, from Herbert Hoover to Richard Nixon. In his long career, he notes, he was "destined . . . to experience three wars, attend four celebrated international conferences, hold ten foreign posts, including five as chief of mission, and serve the last of these years at the United Nations, first as deputy to Adlai Stevenson and Arthur Goldberg and eventually as Principal U.S. Representative."

Many of his views reflect his liberal inclinations, which presently seem to be out of favor. He believes that "the military and political threat of the Soviet Union as a great power is no doubt exaggerated," and he finds many evidences of "American misreadings of Soviet intentions." He deplores "the extravagant and fundamentally nonsensical militarization of the planet." He foresees increasing turbulence in the Third World—"not only its own problem but ours"—and "an acrimonious series of confrontations between de-

veloped and developing countries." His main general warning seems to be "that mankind cannot much longer afford government, either in the political or the economic sphere, as disorderly, as careless, as inequitable, as shortsighted, as most governments have been and still are today."

While Ambassador Yost frequently refers to his own experiences and gives his impressions of men and events, most of his book is an impersonal commentary on "the bewildering panorama of our times." Five chapters are devoted to the causes, course, and aftermath of world wars I and II, and one each to communism, the democracies, and the Third World in the post–World War II era. The last three chapters contain reflections on such diverse subjects as "The Scientific Revolution," "Life-styles, Visions, and Moods," and "The Next Twenty Years: What Is to Be."

Like the man himself, this book is solid, sensible, perceptive, reserved, and unspectacular. It provides many vignettes of the twentieth century and many recommendations for a reversal of present national and international trends. Unfortunately, there is little prospect that either the nation or the world will move in the direction of the preferred world order that this experienced and concerned diplomat believes to be essential for mankind's survival under conditions of freedom and dignity.

NORMAN D. PALMER

University of Pennsylvania
Philadelphia

AFRICA, ASIA, AND LATIN AMERICA

JONATHAN R. ADELMAN. *The Revolutionary Armies: The Historical Development of the Soviet and the Chinese People's Liberation Armies.* Pp. x, 230. Westport, CT: Greenwood Press, 1980. $22.50.

This comparative study of the two major Communist armies is especially welcome because it breaks from the rather excessive tendency of recent years for scholarly examination of military institutions and politics to focus on third-world armies, and often on the smaller ones at that. Armies with small officer corps facilitate methodological neatness for the analyst, but however useful the models they afford, they cannot substitute for occasional direct appraisal of the military systems that most influence world politics.

Professor Adelman's study emphasizes the differences between the principal Communist armies over the similarities, especially the differences, of their roles in their respective countries' political and social systems. Both armies were created in the midst of Communist revolutions and grew to be multimillion mass forces; both began by operating at relatively primitive levels of military technology; and both responded early to serious external and internal threats to their countries' revolutions; but Adelman finds the similarities not going far beyond these points. The People's Liberation Army has played a consistently much greater role in society, economic development, and party affairs than the Soviet army. Whereas in 1956, for example, seven of ten PLA marshals were elected to the Chinese Politburo, from 1921 to 1940 no professional military man was a member of the Soviet Politburo, and few have played large political roles since. Overall, the Soviet army has never been presented as a role model for the entire society as the PLA has.

Adelman surveys possible explanations of the contrasts in terms of differing levels of military technology between the Russian and Chinese armies, the differing international political environments in which the armies have operated, the differing pre-Communist political cultures of the two countries, and the countries' differing levels of economic development. He finds that these factors "provide some useful guidance," but he locates the principal source of the contrasts between the two great Communist armies elsewhere, in their differing experiences during their formative civil wars. "Although often neglected by scholars, the civil wars had a profoundly formative impact in both countries." In Russia, the Communists had to employ during the civil war a politically unreliable army, whose officer corps had largely been tsarist and whose whole membership was torn by mass desertions; the Communist party was always a thin stratum within the army. In China, the prolonged civil war drew the army and the party closely together, intertwining military and civil leadership.

This emphasis on contrasting civil war experiences as the basic source of contrasts between the Soviet army and the PLA is convincingly developed through chapters on the comparative effectiveness of the two armies, on their officer corps, on army–party relations, and on army–society relations. Occasionally, it is true, Adelman's insistence on differences rather than similarities as the key to understanding the two armies leads him to exaggerate the differences. The chapter on comparative military effectiveness uses four indicators of battlefield capabilities: desertion, treason, mobilization of manpower, and the nature of the armies' campaigns. While Adelman spends part of the chapter on the early years of the Chinese Communist Army and notes in the 1920s problems of desertion and treason similar to those that wracked the Soviet army during the civil wars, essentially he is comparing the Chinese Communist Army of the late 1930s and early 1940s with the Soviet army of 1919–21. It is not remarkable, then, that he should conclude that "the state of the Chinese army was far superior to that of the Russian army at the end of their respective civil wars." He is comparing an army that had a quarter of a century to build cohesion with one less than five years old.

Thus while Adelman complains that too much of the literature on armies in politics and society "possesses a static bias," not dealing with changes over time as fully as it might, he does not always handle the chronological dimension satisfactorily himself. Nevertheless, this is a book to be recommended. Adelman set a large task for himself—and he had to rely on sources outside the Chinese language for the PLA—but in a field so often characterized by cautious choice of subject and methodology, his ambition itself is commendable, and his book is full of information and insight.

RUSSELL F. WEIGLEY
Temple University
Philadelphia
Pennsylvania

JAMES N. KARIOKI. *Tanzania's Human Revolution*. Pp. 229. University Park, PA: The Pennsylvania State University Press, 1979. $12.95.

In the contemporary world dominated by the competition between two superpowers and their radically divergent economic and political systems, Nyerere's Tanzania represents a nonaligned stance of stature and authenticity in Africa comparable to that of Tito's Yugoslavia in Europe. The Tanzanian case is of special interest to those concerned with Third World change and development because it represents a self-consciously African solution to the problems of economic and political construction, in contrast to the Western-oriented capitalist and Eastern-oriented scientific socialist directions of its near neighbors in eastern Africa. Tanzania is similar to Yugoslavia as well in that its unique form of African socialism is closely associated with the creativity of its leader, President *Mwalimu* Nyerere, the "Teacher," whose writings represent an intellectually stimulating and refreshing rethinking of the Third World postcolonial predicament.

This work draws heavily from these official documents, many published in Nyerere's *Freedom and Unity*, and may thus serve as an introduction to the wider issue of African political consciousness for the general reader, since it proficiently establishes the subcontinental historical context of the Tanzanian case, but because of its overreliance on official sources will not prove informative to the reader of continuing interest in the Tanzanian experiment.

Of the four central chapters of the book, two are directed to a discussion of the key *Ujamaa* concept, and two focus on the Tanzanian one-party theory of democracy. With respect to the latter issue, the book presents a familiar defense of systems of representative government in one-party states, which holds that multiparty states, with the institutionalized opposition to the government, breed factionalism and disunity and thus represent an undesirable luxury for states following rigorous paths of national development.

Ujamaa is the framework within which Tanzania "grapples directly with the practical substance of human equality, freedom and unity," the three principles which underly its concern with the "welfare of man." As the basis for this "anthropocentric philosophy," various dimensions of an indigenous African socialist attitude were summed up by Nyerere; these included traditional mutual respect between persons, a collective attachment to and possession of land, acceptance of a universal obligation to work, and the fundamentality of generosity and hospitality. As the antithesis of capitalism, which undermines equality, and communism, which abrogates freedom, *Ujamaa* ensures both of those values within the spirit of "family unity," to which the term literally refers.

Following the 1967 Arusha Declaration, Tanzanian socialism assumed the radical stance of "self-reliance," which included the nationalization of all key industries and plantations and the organization of the nation on the basis of "*Ujamaa* villages," which were to form the basis for a rural-oriented development. In hand with the priority given to the rural peasantry, the incipient urban elite were checked by the prohibition of economic activity by government and party leaders and the establishment of the basis for a popular system of education that supported community-level primary education at the expense of specialized higher education.

On the crucial subject of the *Ujamaa* villagization program, Karioki's reliance on official texts proves especially unfortunate. We are told, for instance, that "group work . . . *would* almost certainly allow for greater productivity and greater services in the community, with a consequent benefit to all members" (my emphasis) when this is precisely the issue in question.

Karioki regrettably ignores the evidence that does exist with regard to the problems facing the villagization program and denies the coercion involved in the mass resettlement of entire districts by suggesting that the program represents a "voluntary alternative to individual settlement." Surely, a realistic assessment of such programs need not tarnish the Tanzanian image of imaginative Third-World leadership.

In sum, this work is a useful exercise as an "official history," but lacks critical perspective and tells us little about the actual processes involved in the creative venture described by its title, since in the end we know much about Nyerere's thoughts and little about "Tanzania's Human Revolution." Certainly, we know nothing more about the major question of whether the principles of socialism can be realized under conditions of poverty and low productivity through centrally organized community action. We await the African response.

JOHN G. GALATY
McGill University
Montreal
Canada

WALID KHALIDI. *Conflict and Violence in Lebanon: Confrontation in the Middle East*. Pp. 217. Cambridge, MA: Harvard Studies in International Affairs, 1979. $12.95. Paperbound, $6.95.

Conflict and Violence in Lebanon is an interpretive political essay on the Lebanese civil war of 1975–76 and subsequent developments in Lebanon up to 1978. Its author is uniquely equipped to write such a study. Professor Khalidi is a Palestinian; a recognized scholar of Middle Eastern affairs; a professor of political science at the American University of Beirut and a visiting professor at Harvard; head of the Institute of Palestine Studies; and long a resident of Lebanon.

The book traces the political history of Lebanon from World War II, when compromises made by traditional sectarian leaders gave the fragile new state a lease on life that lasted more than three decades, until the outbreak of the civil war in 1975, which has almost ended it. Khalidi describes the interaction between and among all of the diverse factors that produced the civil war: the sectarian political maneuvers and compromises among Lebanon's leaders; foreign pressures and involvements; and the effects of the Palestinian presence and Palestinian policies in Lebanon. By the end, it is clear that there have been no real winners or losers.

One of the most valuable contributions of the book is Khalidi's analysis of the internal dynamics and policies of each party to the dispute inside Lebanon—mainly Muslims, Christians, Palestinians, and Syrians—and how these interacted to produce events in the war. Khalidi sees at the base of intra-Lebanese violence and conflict a crisis of group and religious identity. Interestingly, he does not see the conflict as a Muslim-Christian clash, as have many others; rather, the sectarian dimension involves the influential Maronite Christians on the one hand and non-Maronite Lebanon on the other.

In Khalidi's view, the final solution of the Lebanese question is, without doubt, related to the delicate Palestine question, especially in the south of Lebanon, but Lebanon cannot wait for that solution. In the meantime, understanding and deliberations among all parties involved inside Lebanon is necessary to reconstruct a country torn by the consequences of a bloody civil war and which has lost tens of thousands of victims.

The idea of a partition of Lebanon is unacceptable to Khalidi, who believes "it can be a disastrous experience," as evidenced by the partition of India in 1947 and Cyprus in 1974. What is needed to bring a resolution to this crisis is "a clean break with the past on the basis of truly democratic participation which alone can guarantee social justice for the greatest number, irrespective of sectarian affiliation."

Much of the valuable information in the book is the fruit of Khalidi's daily experience of Lebanese life during the ongoing crisis and personal interviews with top Palestinians, Lebanese, and other officials and leaders. However, he sometimes depends too much on the Western press to cover internal Lebanese and Palestinian events when local sources might have been more revealing. The book would have given us an even more valuable insight into Lebanese politics if Khalidi had devoted more time to the social and economic structure of Lebanon.

LOUAY BAHRY

University of Tennessee
Knoxville

CHONG-LIM KIM, ed. *Political Participation in Korea: Democracy, Mobilization and Stability.* Pp. xvi, 238. Santa Barbara, CA: ABC-Clio Press, 1980. $26.50.

The origins of this valuable volume are to be found in a survey conducted in Korea in 1972. This was followed by a conference on political participation at the University of Washington where papers were read based on these data as well as other perspectives. Nine of the participants at that conference, chosen for their behavioral methodology, contributed the 10 chapters that make up this edited work.

It is impossible within the space of a short review to do justice to each contribution contained herein. But clearly the backbone of this book consists of those chapters that are based upon the 1972 survey data. These contributions suggest that higher voter turnout in rural areas, rather than urban areas, not only distinguishes Korean political participation from the "normal" pattern, but also forms the basis for what Kim terms a mobilization model to explain this. The government has been able to mobilize pro-regime voters who are more tradition-oriented rural residents as well as older citizens, females, and those in low-status occupations. Conversely, those voters who exhibit modern values—and who tend to live in urban areas—are less easily mobilized and are more likely to oppose the government.

This socioeconomic model of voting behavior is persuasive. If support or opposition is determined in this way only, then as modernization and urbanization continue as rapidly as they have in Korea, it becomes clear that the basis of government support is eroding. Naturally, other considerations also affect voting choice, but if a government remains in power due mainly to mobilized voting, where many voters defer to authority rather than making a conscious political choice, then it is unlikely to be responsive to its citizens. If so, the long-term prospects for political stability in Korea are tenuous where the government which tends to be unresponsive to its citizens is at the same time losing its socioeconomic basis of support in a political tradition that has not as yet permitted a peaceful transfer of power to the opposition.

A few quibbles remain. The exclusively behavioral focus on the one hand ensures a degree of uniformity among the contributors, but on the other hand the jargon at times serves more to confuse than enlighten and seems almost tautological in places. In addition, the use of the same data base by a number of the contributors makes some of the chapters too repetitive.

Overall, this volume confirms much of what students of Korea have intuitively suspected for some time. The models presented provide new insights on Korean political participation and at the same time allow for comparisons with other political systems. It has certainly achieved Kim's aim to lay the groundwork for further research on Korean political participation.

WAYNE PATTERSON

Saint Norbert College
De Pere
Wisconsin

DANIEL C. LEVY. *University and Government in Mexico: Autonomy in an Authoritarian System.* Pp. xiv, 173. NY: Praeger Publishers, 1980. $19.95.

Daniel Levy is a research associate in the Higher Education Group of the Institution for Social and Policy Studies of Yale University. Although his research interest extends to private education, as well as public, this study deals only with public higher education in Mexico. Specifically, it treats the question of university autonomy in educational policy and administration. Major attention is given to the huge National Autonomous University of Mexico, but the study also embraces the state universities and the technical institutes, both those that are regional and the large National Polytechnic Institute in Mexico City.

It is not easy to analyze the autonomy of higher education in view of the unique character of Mexican authoritarianism, operating through the official Partido Revolucionario Institucional and through the mechanism of transmission of power from one president to another within a kind of revolutionary "family" system, as Frank Brandenburg has described it. As Levy sees it, the Mexican government has pursued, with only minor deviations, policies that allow the universities' structure to operate with great autonomy, especially in the case of the National University. This relationship stands out in contrast to the situation in many of the other Latin American universities in recent years, characterized by extensive government intervention.

Five chapters analyze policymaking in its distinctive aspects. Chapter 3 treats policy in respect to university reform; chapter 4 deals with appointive autonomy; chapter 5 discusses academic autonomy; chapter 6, financial autonomy; and chapter 7, entitled "Autonomy and Authoritarianism," summarizes Levy's conclusions.

UNAM (the National University) comes off well in respect to autonomy in all respects. Student admissions continue to be controlled by the University Council, made up of students and professors. The appointment of rectors is made by a governing board chosen by the University Council. On the score of financial autonomy, the conclusion is somewhat equivocal. Autonomy exists in formulation of budget proposals and in control of the distribution of the approved budget. One unique aspect of financial autonomy is that "defenders of autonomy" have successfully insisted "that government continue as the predominant financier," rather than relying more on student fees.

The picture of autonomy is less clear in the state universities, the Polytechnic Institute, and the regional technical institutes. In general the technical institutes are controlled by government to a larger extent. In the case of the state universities, the situation varies from state to state. The federal government, while subsidizing these universities, has not intervened in the appointments to the overall university council (ANUIES) and has left the appointment of rectors to the states. Some state universities enjoy a high degree of autonomy in all respects, either through university councils or through governing boards elected by these councils. In other cases, state governments intervene more directly.

This generally excellent contribution to our literature on Latin American universities gives us a well-balanced and documented view of the degree of autonomy of public higher education in Mexico. It leaves unanswered, of course, the question of how permanent the conditions described may turn out to be.

HAROLD EUGENE DAVIS
The American University
Washington, D.C.

ROBERT BOETTCHER with GORDON L. FREEDMAN. *Gifts of Deceit: Sun Myung Moon, Tongsun Park, and the Korean Scandal*. Pp. xii, 402. New York: Holt, Rinehart and Winston, 1980. $14.95.

ROBERT T. OLIVER. *Syngman Rhee and American Involvement in Korea, 1942–1960: A Personal Narrative*. Pp. x, 508. Seoul, Korea: Panmun Book Co., Ltd., 1978. No price.

Methodically and with no sparing of persons at any level, Boettcher and Freedman tell of the singularly applied corruption of the Korean apparatus by the late President Park Chung Hee who ruled and manipulated Korea with both political and economic success as an ally of the United States and the free world. He used the scare tactic of the threat from North Korea with constant success, from the day of his first coup to the hour of his liquidation by his own most intimate collaborators. The charade so well concealed his method that patriotic Americans of all ranks, as well as Koreans, accepted his presence as the least of many evils.

Apart from setting forth the simplistic details of Park's initial takeover from Prime Minister Chang Myon, the strange restoration of South Korean "democracy," and its denouement, the authors detail the winnowing process of the KCIA, which was created by Park's nephew-in-law, Lieutenant Colonel Kim Jong Pil, as a merger of all three areas of intelligence. This KCIA thereafter invaded and eroded all aspects of Korean life at the pleasure of Park and his junta, before and after the alleged democratic restoration.

Surfacing early in this Sargasso Sea of total power corruption was Sun Myung Moon as a self-designated messiah, with Bo Hi Park his "John the Baptist" and Korea as the chosen nation. Lieutenant Colonel Pak, a model "Moony," was first assigned as assistant military attache to Washington and brought "the master's" message to America. His role began innocently enough with the coming of the Little Angels from Korea, a troupe of young girls performing Korean songs and dances. This troupe was the first of many front groups sent to establish and legitimatize the Unification Church, beginning early in the 1960s when most Christian Koreans knew nothing of Moon's church.

With the creation of the Korean Cultural and Freedom Foundation, a highly publicized friendship front, Bo Hi Pak could moonlight no longer. He was given an early retirement from the army, a diplomatic visa, and full opportunity to further the increasingly sinister apparatus of the Unification Church in the United States.

The sequence of what became known as "Koreagate" Boettcher tells step by step. It is the story of Ambassador Kim Dong Jo, the former Japanese informer turned congressional briber extraordinary; of Tongsun Park, the playboy and influence buyer; and of those many Americans caught innocently or guiltily in the web of blackmail and intrigue. These men traded in "futures": rice and other nonmilitary aid, such as Food for Peace and the Peace Corps, and—most critical—military aid and support for Park Chung Hee.

Tongsun Park slid smoothly into the Washington scene, a young Korean businessman who gave wonderful parties. His new acquaintances were a cross section of Capitol Hill legislators and lobbyists and military, State Department, and other civil servants who found themselves accepting his hospitality. These were joined even by Old Korea Hands of the A-OK, pre-independence era—all witness to the Tongsun Park charm and lavish blend of Korean and American razzle-dazzle. Boettcher shows him as a single-minded seeker after wealth—no matter the risks or the means. In his case, the results amply justified the risks. No man in modern times has demonstrated more skills as a successful knave.

However, all other protagonists were pikers beside the Reverend Sun Myung Moon, the most successful practitioner alive today of the art of transforming the illusion of power into real power. The third thread of the Boettcher–Freedman account, the bottom line of this modern morality play, concerns the appalling success of the Reverend Moon, who proclaims his own divinity while demonstrating again the total evil that can be achieved by mind-control techniques. Programmed indoctrination of young people into slavery is more dangerous to the future goals of any civilized society than even the threat of nuclear power.

And yet, the attorney general of the United States has never had the courage to challenge Moon's awesome defense battery of American lawyers flaunting the First Amendment.

The reader is left with the strong impression that Koreans are as skillful in corruption as they are at worthy activities of the modern world. Upside-down lessons can be learned by legislators, lobbyists, and such individuals as seek to influence others, for good or ill. Koreans, Americans, Japanese, and indeed all who value the human condition could well spend some time reading and reflecting on this book.

Much has been written about Syngman Rhee, his lifelong fight to free his native land, his single-minded patriotism, his relationships with the generals, the presidents, the State Department and the United Nations; his alleged stubbornness and tyrannical use of power; and much of what has been written is false, or so slanted as to falsify the facts. Here, at last, is a personal biography to set at rest all rumor, fake reporting, and oversimplifications about the man who did his best to defy and defeat the Marxist takeover in East Asia. To Syngman Rhee, all who would force or pressure him into any kind of collaboration with communism were his personal enemies as well as enemies of his country and of the Free World. His unyielding refusal to go along with conciliation, even when urged by all the powers that were ostensibly his allies, earned him the reputation of a stubborn old tyrant with whom no one could work. Later events have vindicated most of his beliefs. Today, looking at current events, he could say, "I told you so!" which would have pleased him not at all. He wanted the eyes of the world powers open in his day.

There could be no more classic case study of such major political confrontations as we have today than is this narration of events in Korea during the 20-odd years the book covers. Dr. Oliver would have made a noteworthy contribution to the historical record even if all he had done was to edit the correspondence he had with Syngman Rhee while serving as adviser and low-key publicist to him and for Korea. But he has done more. He has undertaken the monumental task of choosing from his sources, laying events and decisions on the line, risking judgment from others, and, inescapably, making a few himself. He does not justify; nor does he in this book serve as an apologist for Syngman Rhee, except to

put the record straight. He was in daily contact in person or by letter with Dr. Rhee during all of this time. No one can question the genuineness of his sources—they are primary.

During the 20 years since 1960, the raw records have had time to mellow, the crisis immediacy has retreated into the past, and the heat of the day-to-day confrontations has cooled. However, I am sure it took courage for Dr. Oliver to re-open his files and re-live events. This task would not have been one of emotion remembered in tranquility, but rather a renewed sense of frustration and rage that the Free World seems to have learned so little of statecraft in 20 years. However, the fact that a uniquely qualified author put it off so long provides an advantage, since now, on the eve of a change in U.S. foreign policy, the Korean experience may constitute a telling lesson.

Syngman Rhee was a gentleman, in the eighteenth-century sense, of fair play, honor, self-control, and noblesse oblige—this is all apparent in the lines of his letters written in utter confidence to a friend and associate. He was also a tough pragmatist and a coldly realistic political activist: compromise with basic principles does not work. Communism and the four freedoms are mutually exclusive. You cannot compromise with cholera, as he wrote at one time; nor with a cobra, as he said to me early in our acquaintance, before he went back to Korea to become its first president. On the other hand, while he was a Wilsonian Democrat by training, he saw clearly the dilemmas of democracy. He wrote:

The greatest weakness of democracy is the dependence of the popularly elected leaders on widespread public approval. They cannot do anything that a majority does not currently support. This makes them timid. Instead of asking themselves which course is right, they ask what programs will best win votes. . . . the policies of democratic nations are undependable. . . . What leaders promise today they may find it expedient to abandon tomorrow.

From the beginning of the Korean involvement, Rhee and U.S. political leaders were at cross-purposes on one vital issue: the United States did not want another war. The "police action" concept, the "containment" of Marxism—this was the choice of the Western powers during this time, carefully encouraged by such disingenuous allies as India and the United Nations. To Rhee this was disaster, blindness, and deadly day-to-day frustration. The shilly-shallying at Panmunjom, the shifts in United Nations' actions and attitudes, the whole unhappy road of appeasement, "peaceful settlement," diplomacy rather than force—all created finally a picture that weakness was the word for Western policy, that constant pushing and shoving would achieve Communist goals if persisted in—and there is nothing so persistent and so consistent and so never-changing as Marxists' goals. Staying power is their middle name, and Syngman Rhee knew it with every bone in his body. For him appeasement was impossible.

In October of 1945, after decades of exile, Syngman Rhee finally returned to Korea. Soon after he returned, I—then inspector general of U.S. forces in Korea—arranged to meet Dr. and Mrs. Rhee at various points in their first swing around Korea. On one occasion, I witnessed him hold 10,000 and more Koreans spellbound in the hot sun while he spoke, giving them back their country with his sincerity, his authority, and his demonstrated courage and steadfastness. It was an impressive demonstration, only one of many. He had the Korean people solidly on his side, and he never lost their allegiance.

In 1954, by sheer obstinacy and disdain for the prevailing political winds, Rhee had brought his country through the Korean war, had obtained material aid for rebuilding devastated South Korea, and had forced the United States to commit itself to Korean defense and major economic aid; but he had failed to convince the United States to push the Communists back up and off the Korean peninsula. And this "sin of our fathers" for which we are paying today looks as if it will be repeated tomorrow.

From this distance of 20 and more years, Oliver looks back and voices a few personal conclusions—though he keeps the stream very clear in his day-to-day reportage of events as they took place. One conclusion, not given as his own but to which he clearly subscribes, is that the Vietnam War might never have taken place if the U.N. had persisted until victory in Korea. And yet another conclusion is that "allowing the Red Chinese to win in Korea . . . helped Mao Tse Tung consolidate his control over the mainland."

There emerges from these letters of Dr. Rhee's a portrait of an honest, able, devoted, tireless patroit and statesman; very human, very straightforward, very much like an American in his training and viewpoint, but an American of the eighteenth century, rather than the twentieth. Our own founding fathers would have felt at home with him; our statesmen of his time, quite evidently, did not.

GEORGE FOX MOTT
Mott of Washington & Associates
Washington, D.C.

DAVID SCOTT PALMER. *Peru: The Authoritarian Tradition*. Pp. xvi, 134, NY: Praeger Publishers, 1980. $18.95. Paperbound, $9.95.

This is an unusual book. It is designed as one of a series of textbooks on the politics of Latin American countries, in this case by one of the leading students of contemporary Peru. As such, we are presented with considerable background material on Peruvian political history and economic development, with emphasis on such themes as Peru's Spanish heritage, dependency, social mobilization, and the impact of U.S. policy. There are, as well, two perceptive chapters covering the rise and decline of Peru's military reform experiment (1968–80). A large number of helpful tables are included on such matters as inflation, elections, and union membership, most of them longitudinal.

At the same time, and unusually for a text, the book seeks to be extensively comparative with other Latin American countries, again over time and again very substantially through the copious use of tables. Thus we have almost a dozen tables showing the degree of dependency of Latin American countries—as measured by such indicators as the size of U.S. investments—as well as other tables denoting the capacities of central governments—as measured by government revenues, for example—levels of social mobilization, and the like. There are, in addition, graphs that characterize levels of institutionalization and authoritarianism in Latin America over time, among others. The result is that we get more cross-national data on Latin American political and other developments than in almost any other book of its size.

What we do not get is very much analysis of the institutions and processes of Peruvian politics—except for the military and the Alianza Popular Revolucionaria Americana (APRA)—other than indirectly. Thus one does not find any explicit discussion of the powers of the Peruvian president relative to other institutions or political actors, nor of the impact of such groups as labor, students, or the Church on politics.

What we have, then, is a handy compendium and interpretation of Peruvian political—and to some extent economic—development, including a good capsule analysis of the recent period of military rule, plus a series of tables and graphs of interest to any student of Latin American political development. While useful as the only extant text on Peruvian politics, for many the greater utility of this book will be the compilations of data, both on Peru and on other countries, often covering subjects and time periods not handily available in any other one place.

ROBERT H. DIX

Rice University
Houston
Texas

JOSEF SILVERSTEIN. *Burmese Politics: The Dilemma of National Unity*, Pp. xii, 263, Rutgers University Press, 1980. $23.00.

This book deals with Burmese politics with respect to relations between the central valley majority and the 30 percent frontier populations resident in adjacent hill areas. The first half of the book describes the traditional patterns of frontier relations under Burma's kings and the British colonial control. Border peoples such as Karens, Shans, Kachins, and Chins exercised limited autonomy under both systems, but British control was the less oppressive of the two. The authority of Burmese kings was supported by divine kingly symbols under the Shiva tradition borrowed from India, a factor lacking in recent decades. The latter half of the book deals with the deterioration of frontier peoples' relations within the newly independent government of Burma. From 1945 to 1947, Burma's national leaders were involved in negotiations with the returned wartime government from Simla and India and later with Premier Clement Attlee in London. The emerging constitution of 1947, which Silverstein describes in detail, undertook to provide a pattern of federated relationship with the four principal frontier people, which proved to be unworkable after a decade of trial efforts under U Nu.

Silverstein tends to attribute much of the deterioration to the tragic assassination in July 1947 of General Aung San, who had been the articulate advocate of "national unity" coupled with "diversity." He even devotes an entire chapter to comparing Aung San and Nu, the latter being a literary personality with limited administrative capacities. From 1948 to 1950, Nu's government encountered rebellion crises involving the Communists, the PVO veterans, and the Karens, and it was unable thereafter to deal effectively with frontier relations. Nu's efforts as ruler ran aground in 1958, and he was eventually replaced by Ne Win's military dictatorship in 1962. Ne Win's ruling tactics involved the arbitrary suppression of political opposition within Burma proper, the discouragement of private industry, and the isolation of the country from all outside contacts. In the face of overt oppression, the neglected peoples of the frontier turned to open rebellion, which degenerated into a situation of semi-anarchy in time. Communist rebels established limited contacts with China militarily, but northeastern people generally became increasingly dependent on income derived from opium and heroin sales via China and Thailand. Ne Win's periodic dispatch of army contingents into the frontier areas accomplished nothing constructive.

At the end of the 1960s, Ne Win made a faltering effort to abandon army dictatorship in favor of rule under a Socialist-type constitution, which became operable in 1973–74. The army-infiltrated ruling party of fewer than 300,000 members selected a representative council of 450, which promptly designated Ne Win as civilian president. Nu and other released prisoners of 1971 staged an abortive two-year rebellion along the northern Thailand border. The ruling council has met periodically to review operational problems, and to eliminate subversive tendencies and widespread corruption in government. Border relations with China improved after 1975, but the 120-member Soviet embassy in Rangoon dominated the diplomatic scene. Silverstein fails to mention Ne Win's recent efforts to encourage foreign trade and investment, which proved particularly attractive to the Japanese. A pipeline has been completed connecting interior oil fields with the restored Syrian refinery located across the river from Rangoon. Rice exports have also expanded. Persons interested in Burma's recovery problems should read relevant articles in the *Far Eastern Economic Review* and Robert Shaplen's Burma chapter in *A Turning Wheel* (1979). Frontier area problems will have to await the recovery of Burma proper, both governmentally and economically.

JOHN F. CADY
Ohio University
Athens

FRANS J. SCHRYER. *The Rancheros of Pisaflores: The History of a Peasant Bourgeoisie in Twentieth Century Mexico.* Pp. xvi, 210. University of Toronto Press, 1980, $20.00.

This book is a new and fine piece of historical revisionism on the Mexican revolution, written by an anthropologist about the village he learned to know and love during the year he spent in the field. This book deals with the problems raised by the historical documents collected in local archives, as they forced Schryer to question some basic assumptions long accepted as evidence.

More than a monograph, it is a reexamination of the last century of Mexican history.

This case history reveals some new factors in the Mexican revolution by focusing on the small and medium-sized landowners, the rancheros. Schryer argues that the rancheros of central Mexico constituted a significant political force during and after the revolution and that they helped to determine both the direction and the outcome of this event. The rancheros were provided with a unique opportunity for upward social mobility and found in the upheaval a fantastic opportunity to jump on the back of the landless masses in order to destroy the huge estates, the haciendas.

This argument, strongly presented, gives us an analysis of the agrarian reform very far from the classical one, and it is a good thing. At the same time, Schryer gives emphasis to the rancheros, following the fine tradition of Luis González and David Brading. This class of small landowners, which emerged here in the middle of the nineteenth century, earlier in the Bajío and in the west, was numerically larger than the hacendados and constituted a local upper class. Unlike the absentee landlord, they resided on their small hamlets or at the village; they managed their own farms and business. Like the hacendados, they employed wage laborers and rented to sharecroppers, but they shared the dress, speech, and customs of all the peasants. That is why Schryer speaks of "peasant bourgeoisie," and it is easy to understand why that bourgoisie has been ignored or misunderstood.

Those Mexican "kulaki" are not as spectacular as the hacendados, and their regions did not experience violent clashes between absentee landlords and landless peasants. Mediocre wealth, mediocre clashes, not between classes but between ranchero familes, did not call the attention of the scientist before Luis González did in his famous *Pueblo en vilo, microhistoria de San José de Gracia"* (1969).

Schryer takes the position that if a regime largely composed of "petit bourgeois" elements did come to power in 1917, then the peasant bourgoisie must have constituted a major part of it. I agree: the Carrera Torres brothers, the Cedillos brothers, the Santos brothers of Tamaulipas and San Luis, the Figueroa brothers in Guerrero, the Zapata brothers in Morelos, and so many more in Veracruz, Sinaloa, and Nayarit were all rancheros and played an important role during and after the revolution.

A careful analysis of the class structure of the region (Sierra alta de Hidalgo) provides the basis for a reinterpretation of the revolutionary party that came out of the revolution and celebrated in 1979 its fiftieth anniversary. This party, until recently, represented the patronage structure, the political tactics, and the style of the rancheros. This region is representative of other parts of Mexico that are characterized by the absence of large-scale latifundium and by the presence of rancheros before 1920.

Because of this absence of local agrarian conflict, the ranchero upper class was not threatened by the revolution and was able to direct it locally. Then those revolutionaries were able to wield considerable influence in the government because their rustic attire enabled them to pass as genuine peasants and defenders of the rural proletariat to leftist politicians of urban centers. This explains the paradox of so many harsh caciques, depicted as agrarian leaders. Now Schryer opens one's eyes to the existence of that invisible class that played such an important role in the Mexican revolution.

JEAN MEYER
Colegio de Michoacán
Zamora
Mexico

MARGARET STROBEL. *Muslim Women in Mombasa, 1890–1975.* Pp. xiii, 258. New Haven, CT: Yale University Press, 1979. $19.50.

One of the most exciting developments in cultural anthropology and related social science disciplines is the crucial emergence of women's studies. This is indeed a refreshing trend, a drastic departure from past conventional research, teaching, and publication in anthropology where men dominate. This book is a significant and substantive contribution to efforts by female anthropologists to research and publish on women's role in culture and society. According to Dr. Strobel, "This study resulted from the convergence of my interests in African history and my participation in the women's movement in the late 1960s and the 1970s. As I began my research I realized how little study had been devoted to African women, particularly from a historical perspective. Since then new information has appeared, including important materials by African women themselves, yet much remains to be done." In nine well-researched and well-organized chapters, Strobel has succeeded in fulfilling her stated aim of enhancing knowledge on the changing role of women in Mombasa society.

Among the topics explored are the following: women, weddings, and Swahili culture; the development of Mombasa society; slavery and male–female relations in coastal society; the impact of female education on the traditional role of women; the "marginalization" of women's tasks; women's collectivities and sex, class, and ethnicity.

This book has theoretical, methodological, and applied anthropological significance. The concepts of "tradition" and "change" have been critically assessed by Strobel, using Kenyan society as a unit of analysis. Her brilliant exposition of the concepts of class, ethnicity, and sex in anthropology and history is a model for future research. She concludes, in her study, that "Class, ethnicity, and sex all influenced a women's position, options, behavior, and consciousness. The complex interaction of these factors over time prevented women from identifying exclusively with any particular division and organizing accordingly." Strobel's interviews and participant observation in Mombasa society reflect objectivity, empathy, and intellectual integrity. This study offers fresh insight and tremendous information on Mombasa society and culture, useful to planners and administrators of change in Kenya and in third world societies in general.

The only negative comment is Strobel's lack of comparative data from other third world societies in her exposition of basic themes and concepts, which could have enriched her discussion and broadened our basic understanding of the changing role of women in general. Overall, however, she and her publisher are to be congratulated for this very important publication.

MARIO D. ZAMORA
College of William and Mary
Williamsburg
Virginia

EUROPE

F. L. CARSTEN. *The Rise of Fascism.* Pp. 279. Berkeley and Los Angeles, CA: University of California Press, 1980. $18.50

This book presents, in less than 300 pages, a clear, well-written account of exactly what its title states. The narrative element is predominant and is firmly based on extensive study in the sources in English, French, German, and Italian. Carsten is not a *homo unius linguae*, as some writers on this subject have been. Mr. Carsten combines the necessary language skills with the personal experience of his youth spent in the Berlin of the Weimar Republic. He spent his later life in Britain.

Carsten is a disciple of Ranke. He aims to present, *sine ira et studio*, a narrative description that depicts events and persons "the way they actually were." He is eminently successful in achieving this goal.

But Carsten also presents interpretations of the events. He is not the servant of any ideology or *parti pris* in formulat-

ing his interpretations, but seeks to present commonsense lessons for the use of mankind. He is thus seeking to learn from history what Edmund Burke described as "prudence" in the broad eighteenth-century English meaning of the term. In treating such a recent and highly ideological and emotional subject as the rise of fascism, this is probably the most fruitful approach.

Although Carsten in his descriptions respects the individuality of the Fascist movement in each country, he also attempts to draw general conclusions about the elements they had in common: a new, more virulent nationalism; an anti-Semitism more motivated by racial and economic factors than by religious resentments; an appeal not only to the middle and especially the lower-middle class, but also to the lower classes in social revolutionary terms; an anti-intellectual romanticism and quasi-religious mysticism that glorified "the leader," "the soil," and "the national community"; and the claim to speak for youth and its aspirations for a glorious future.

In addition to the treatment of the rise of Fascist movements in the larger European countries, the work also includes detailed accounts of the similar developments in such smaller countries as Austria, Hungary, Romania, Belgium, and Finland. These latter are generally not as well known as the former, but they often included unique and significant local variations. The final chapter is devoted to the neo-Fascist movements since 1945, such as the National Democrats in West Germany, the *Movimento Sociale Italiano*, and the National Front in Britain.

H. F. MACKENSEN
Fairleigh Dickinson University
Teaneck
New Jersey

SHEILA FITZPATRICK. *Education and Social Mobility in the Soviet Union 1921–1934.* Pp. x, 335. Cambridge, NY: Cambridge University Press, 1979. $32.50.

Thanks to the benevolence of several English and American institutions, Fitzpatrick was able to examine archival collections of the Russian Commissariat of Education and the collections of certain other Soviet archives and repositories. She reminds us that the aim of the Soviet Union was to industrialize and to create its own elite by promoting and educating workers, peasants, and their children. She discusses the formulation of educational policy, the institutional rivalries, and the positions of different bureaucratic interest groups. The educational strategy during the First Five-Year Plan, she says, was "to educate" as many peasants as possible in the shortest time in order to produce a proletarian intelligentsia. For this purpose, educational opportunities for the peasant were greatly expanded.

In a brief introductory chapter (3–17) on "Education and Soviet Society," Fitzpatrick comments on the initial educational objectives of the Bolsheviks, the Marxist legacy, Stalin's position on education, and conflict with the "Right Opposition." This is followed by discussion of the "new Soviet School," the problem of ideology and political consciousness, the teaching cadres, the pedagogical method, and the conflict between the exponents of the "new" and the "old" school. Fitzpatrick provides us with a brief account of the variety of educational institutions and of the problems of access to higher education and employment.

Of special interest is the chapter entitled "Professors and Soviet Power" in which Fitzpatrick tells us how professors, most of whom in the Civil War years looked upon the new regime "with deep hostility," ultimately came to accept it. In this connection, she discusses Marxism and the social sciences, the teaching of ideology, professional organizations, salaries, and privileges. Other important topics discussed include the recruitment for higher education, the 1924 student purge, the cultural revolution and the administrative reorganization of education (1929–30), "class war" in rural education, and the impact of collectivization on the schools. The two final chapters in the book assess the educational policies introduced

in 1931–34, social mobility and education under Stalin, and the new social elite. Also included in a short statement on the teaching of history and the destruction of the Pokrovsky school, which she says resulted "not only in poor Marxism but poor history." Fitzpatrick says that the Bolsheviks fulfilled the promise of the revolution, that is, by giving the opportunity to workers and peasants "to rise into the new ruling elite of the Soviet state." She concludes that the objective adopted in 1928—to create a new elite, or "proletarian intelligentsia" —was a "major political achievement" that had a lasting impact "on the nature of the Soviet regime and leadership." The educational strategy during the first Five-Year Plan to produce a proletarian intelligentsia by educating as many peasants as possible in the shortest possible time was also successful. Fitzpatrick lauds Stalin for this "bold and imaginative policy."

This is a stimulating work on education and social mobility in the Soviet Union and adds a great deal to our understanding of the Soviet Union, its society and politics. I might suggest, however, that the use of Soviet statistics, especially in reference to social classes and categories, could have been more cautious. It seems to me that the genesis of the Soviet intelligentsia still remains problematic.

WAYNE S. VUCINICH
Stanford University
California

JERRY F. HOUGH. *Soviet Leadership in Transition.* Pp. xi, 175, Washington, DC. The Brookings Institution, 1980. $11.95. Paper bound, $4.95.

United States foreign policy reflects domestic values, attitudes, and objectives, as it should. But it must also be shaped in the light of external realities, and it is here that Hough's new book makes its contribution. Seldom has a more useful book appeared at a more opportune time. In compact form it provides detailed and objective evidence on the individuals and groups in the USSR who will operate the system during the

1980s. It therefore offers a rational basis for anticipating Soviet positions toward the outside world, and thus for designing the best possible U.S. policies toward the USSR.

As a tough-minded political scientist, Hough seeks to identify the backgrounds and outlooks of that part of the Soviet population whose abilities, interests, and influence will have a significant bearing on Soviet foreign policy. His analysis rests on primary evidence in Soviet sources, on-the-spot contacts in the USSR, and a wide range of Western scholarly research. The result is a well-written monograph presenting a substantial body of meticulous research by a painstaking scholar.

Because a series of drastic events have fallen on the peoples of the USSR since 1900, individuals of different ages have been shaped by sharply contrasting life experiences. The Brezhnev-Kosygin generation, for example, came to maturity under Stalin, bore the brunt of World War II, and held responsible positions during the Khrushchev era. This generation is leaving the stage, and those who succeed them will reflect notably different education and life experiences. A 45-year-old in 1980 was only 18 when Stalin died in 1953. There are many millions of Soviet professional men and women in their twenties and thirties who have only come to maturity since Khrushchev was ousted in 1964. Their outlook and attitude grow out of education and life experiences that have generated new expectations; how will a new Party leadership respond to them?

After describing the formative experiences that have shaped Soviet generations, Hough focuses on three groups: the political and administrative elite, the military, and the foreign policy establishment, examining their attitudes, values, and special perspectives. He also provides an incisive sketch of the economic and political problems that will complicate the Soviet situation in the 1980s. The labor force will stop growing and energy supplies will be strained. Economic growth will be modest at best, while powerful interest groups struggle to maintain their claims on resources. The clumsy bureaucratic mechanism

needs reform, but the system's directors feat that decentralization would erode their controls.

His final 20-page chapter offers cautious observations on the current prospects for succession at the top and on the implications for United States foreign policy. Since even the Soviet leaders specifically involved cannot yet be sure what will happen, Hough wisely refrains from making specific predictions. He goes on, however, to comment on the ways that U.S policy can perhaps influence the evolution of Soviet policy. Readers need not agree with all his views in order to find their own judgments sharpened in the light of Jerry Hough's analysis of the changes now underway in the USSR.

HOLLAND HUNTER
Haverford College
Pennsylvania

MICHAEL KEATING and DAVID BLEIMAN. *Labour and Scottish Nationalism.* Pp. xii, 215. Atlantic Highlands, NJ: Humanities Press, 1980. $37.50.

Keating and Bleiman examine the origin of modern Scottish nationalism in the nineteenth century, the agitation for home rule before and shortly after World War I, and the shifts in the British Labor party's attitude toward devolution since then.

They aver that the Scottish coalition of radicals, crofters, and later trade unionists, to World War I, and the cooperative movement after it, all endorsed home rule. After about 1924, enthusiasm dimmed. Settlement of the land question caused the crofters to disappear as a major political force. The economic recession after 1924 thrust home rule far down the list of Labor's priorities. The slump, furthermore, convinced most Scottish workers that their financial interests lay in national—British—organizations rather than local ones.

The authors argue convincingly that Scottish nationalism declined during the 1930s, a period when some authors state that it reemerged. The birth of the Scottish National party signified that decline, not its growth.

Nationalist sentiment also lay dormant during World War II. Tom Johnston, as secretary of state for Scotland, demonstrated that by working within a British administration he could perhaps do more for Scotland than a separate assembly could. His "administrative devolution" revived Scottish agriculture and industry, and his policies became a model for the Labor party.

That party in 1959, for the first time in its history, repudiated the notion of a Scottish parliament. With the reemergence of Scottish nationalism, however, the party waffled. Accepting in principle Scottish devolution from 1974 on, it never figured out how to implement it without alienating the English and Welsh. Failure of the Scottish referendum shelved the question.

During this narrative, several major points emerge. First, devolution has had more appeal to the Scots during periods of economic prosperity than economic hardship. Second, the British Labor party has held, and still holds, an ambivalent attitude toward devolution, its adherence to Scottish democracy running counter to its emphasis on central planning. Finally, the Scottish trades unions from the 1920s on tended to dislike devolution because they feared their wages and working conditions might suffer as a result of it.

This book should, but does not, contain a glossary. The authors introduce so many British and Scottish organizations and thereafter identify them only by their initials, that a reader unfamiliar with them all becomes confused. This caveat aside, the authors write lucidly about the historical relation of Scottish nationalism to the labor movement and the Labor party.

FRANKLIN B. WICKWIRE
University of Massachusetts
Amherst

DALE KENT. *The Rise of the Medici: Faction in Florence, 1426–1434.* Pp. viii, 389. New York: Oxford University Press, 1978. $37.50.

In September 1433, Cosimo de' Medici and members of his merchant-banking family, as well as several intimate associates, were exiled from Florence by a Signory, or government, dominated by a conservative aristocratic faction. Exactly 12 months later, the Signory passed into the hands of pro-Mediceans who invited them to return to Florence. The Medici in turn exiled their political opponents and established their mastery over the republic by manipulating its constitution. Medici domination over the republic lasted until 1494, but it was soon renewed to take the form finally of a grand duchy.

Curiosity about just how such a momentous reversal of family fortune and of urban politics could have taken place caused Dale Kent to seek an answer by focusing on the few years immediately preceding the final confrontation between the factions. Although the general outlines of the story were known, especially through the contemporary account of Giovanni Cavalcanti, Ms. Kent, exploiting the uniquely rich collections of largely unpublished letters, chronicles, and memoirs extant in Florence, was able to refine to the utmost the composition of the two fractions, the networks of association and patronage in each, and the conflicting interests which set them against each other.

In Florence, a city of 37,000 inhabitants in 1427, some 2000 males, belonging to 325 families, were eligible to hold major offices. The city, however, was actually governed according to the wishes of a restricted ruling group: the two competing factions involved only one sixth of the individuals, one third of the families of those eligible. The "webs of patronage and association" of each faction consisted of three interrelated elements, reinforced by economic interest: blood relationship, "the most natural determinant of political action," in the feudal sense; neighborhood, a basic administrative unit especially important for deciding the burden of taxes; and friendship, a category reconstructed from often enigmatic and allusive references in the correspondence.

The Medici faction is characterized as a planned association, based more upon individual than familial ties and interests, composed of men on the rise economically and politically, more aggressive and ambitious, more easily led and organized. The opposing faction, on the other hand, was a group of conservative aristocratic families, accustomed to exercising power and proud of their nobility, but which had passed the peak of their prosperity; their traditional consorterial structure made united action in defense of perceived interests more difficult. Confusion is not lacking: 10 of the 93 families involved in the confrontation were split, with a member or members crossing over because of personal differences reinforced by interest.

The Medici, who had begun their political involvement early in the century, are said to have used the crisis of the war with Lucca, 1429–33, to move into important offices. They and their partisans practically directed the war effort, and Medici money was crucial in financing the war. Just *how* the war, which was disastrous for Florence, clearly the loser, enhanced the Medici reputation, however, is not explained by Kent.

As remarkable as the rise of the Medici was the failure of the conservative faction to take advantage of their victory in 1433. A strange sense of fair play prevented them from reforming the purses containing the names of eligible officeholders in order to eliminate persons hostile to their regime. Medici partisans were able to protect the interests of their exiled leaders, and the Medici return was prepared simply by the drawing by lot of a Medicean majority of Priors in August 1434.

This book is clearly exhaustive and definitive, within the parameters fixed by Kent. The reader in search of Medicean Renaissance grandeur will not find it here. There is little drama, aside from the story of the trip into exile of the aged and ailing Averardo de' Medici and the passing temptations of the respective parties to resort to force of arms. There is no attempt to relate the struggles within the ruling class to the fate of Florentine society as a whole. But it is a masterful and meticulous analysis of nuances and shifts in the balance of power in a crucial decade that saw the rise of the Medici as first citizens of the Florentine republic.

REINHOLD C. MUELLER
University of Venice
Italy

MARGARET WADE LABARGE. *A Baronial Household of the Thirteenth Century*. Pp. 235. Totowa, NJ: Barnes & Noble, 1980. $22.50. Paperbound, $9.95.

The reissue of Professor Labarge's monograph with its excellent bibliography is particularly valuable in view of the proliferation over the last 15 years of works on popular history that assume we know all about the nobility. We do not, and historians have recently begun filling in the gaps in our knowledge of noble life, thought, finances, and political behavior. Professor Labarge's conclusions about the efficiency of the household of the countess of Leicester correspond well with those of recent historians stressing the fundamental competence and strength of the European nobility of the Old Regime.

The basic argument of Professor Labarge's work, which is based upon the household accounts of the countess of Leicester for seven months in 1265, is that the administrative machinery of a baronial household was successfully structured to meet the needs of a wandering and wealthy nobility. Great noblemen were, she shows, regularly en route, traveling from one castle to another, carting with them their furniture and belongings, bringing dozens of men, women, and horses in their train. The castle was not, for them, a home—the out-of-doors made them feel far more comfortable—but a stopping place, a necessary shelter against winter, a stronghold. Movement and style—upon which she elaborates at length—required a staff organized in the logistics of transport and supply. Stocking numerous castles around England with wine from Bordeaux each year, for instance, was not a simple task. The household was the instrument allowing the great nobility to live at their society's technological limits on shelter, clothing, transport, the exercise of power, and the production of food.

This is a delightful little book, eminently readable and suggestive, even in the areas of noble thought, where I would have appreciated greater elaboration. If, for instance, as Labarge claims, nobles were regularly on the road, if they regularly transformed the interiors of their castles, if the numbers of persons and horses present at any castle were regularly shifting, if the very structure of the household sprang from motion, how did the nobleman conceive himself? Did he see himself as the sun spinning around the earth? Did he take strength in the elegant and dancelike mastery of chaos? What were the ideological underpinnings of the great nobleman and how did they relate to the circumstances of his daily life?

WILLIAM A. WEARY
Abington Friends School
Jenkintown
Pennsylvania

J. M. LEE. *The Churchill Coalition, 1940–1945.* Pp. 192. Hamden CT. Archon Books/Shoe String Press, 1980. $20.00.

This slender volume is a valuable reconnaissance of the manner in which the coalition presided over by Winston Churchill managed a devastating conflict and governed Britain during World War II. Its several introductory chapters, which outline the character of the "Great Coalition," are a good deal more revealing of the administrative devices that characterized Britain's organization for war than they are of the men and women who participated in the effort. Subsequent chapters deal with different aspects of governmental policy—strategy and mobilization, economy and production, social reform and reconstruction, and diplomacy and working with the Americans. Somehow the managerial tasks of government were related to the traditional machinery of administration and normal outlets for political expression. Many members of the House of Commons were given bureaucratic roles to play despite conventional restrictions against members taking "offices of profit" under the Crown, The mobilization

of the economy drew into government service many new talents, and the effect, particularly in the building of the Welfare State, had lasting consequences.

Lee makes clear the shallowness of the notion that Churchill turned over the conduct of domestic affairs to major Labour politicians like Bevin, Attlee, and Morrison while he concentrated on grand strategy. Particularly in the area of reconstruction and social reform he was skeptical. His fascination with experimentation in weapons technology did not extend to use of social science research in pursuing social policy. He gave low priority to reconstruction questions, despite the fact that the experience of mobilization provided an agenda that his "home front" ministers found difficult to ignore. As the war moved toward a close, despite the efforts of Beaverbrook and Bracken to prod Churchill into an even more reactionary stance, the coalition worked out a minimum basis for the reconversion to peacetime, whatever the political complexion of postwar Britain.

The most provocative section of this monograph is the chapter on diplomacy. Acknowledging the close relationship between Churchill and Roosevelt that has claimed so much attention, Lee nevertheless shows how that relationship became strained as the Americans demoted British standing and moved toward greater American-Russian agreements. Tensions developed within the British War Cabinet over Churchill's faith in Anglo-American understanding, particularly as Anglo-American differences became abundantly evident over such major issues as how to handle Britain's debts incurred to purchase war supplies and how to secure the needed level of American aid in the transition from war to peace.

On balance, the coalition was characterized by a strong sense of constitutional orthodoxy. Many of the normal rules of parliamentary government were suspended for the duration, and the executive was given supreme authority. But ministers and members of Parliament alike, as the war drew to an end, were insistent on the return to normal processes of statute making and to the restoration of parliamentary supremacy. British institutions, Lee argues persuasively, were sufficiently adaptable to be able to use the technology of modern warfare without substantial social unrest. The cost of survival, inevitably, was a massive loss of overseas capital and a diminished international standing.

HENRY R. WINKLER

University of Cincinnati
Ohio

STEPHEN WHITE. *Political Culture and Soviet Politics.* Pp. xii, 234. New York: St. Martin's Press, 1979. $22.50.

Stephen White defines political culture "as the attitudinal and behavioral matrix within which the political system is located. The political culture, that is to say, both expresses and influences the patterns of political belief and behavior within a given political system." One of the main objectives of White's book is to establish the relationship between behavioral patterns and beliefs within the general framework of Soviet political culture. White criticizes the psychocultural approach to the study of Soviet political behavior, and he applies what might be termed as a historical-sociological approach to the interpretation of political culture in the USSR.

After a chapter in which the general evolution of the concept of political culture is examined, several chapters are devoted to the discussion of Russia's historical past, with particular emphasis on the features of tsarist Russia's social structure that were different from those existing in most other European states of the same period and that the Bolsheviks could easily adapt to their purposes. These include a highly centralized tsarist political system, an economic system in which government regulation and public ownership of resources was extensive, and a social and political life that had a long tradition of "collectivism."

In the remaining five chapters, White discusses the changing political culture and subcultures prevalent in contemporary Soviet society and the means of political socialization with the help of which the government and the party intend to turn Soviet citizens into conscientious builders of a new Communist society. Much attention is devoted in the book to the discussion of the system of party-political education. Regrettably, no mention is made of the impact of the Soviet school on the formation of the "new" Soviet man. The success of the Soviet system of political indoctrination is judged, in the book, on the basis of sociological data obtained from Western studies conducted among émigrés and refugees from the USSR. The findings of Western sociologists have established a paradoxical fact that former Soviet citizens have a love–hate relationship with their native country: they favor public ownership of heavy industry and means of communication, but they reject collective farming. They approve of the Soviet system of education and welfare; they recognize the achievements of the Soviet state and they support a political system in which the government exercises a great measure of control over the destiny of the nation. Yet they abhor the secret police, they decry the frequent abuse of power by the authorities, and they yearn for a better life and more personal freedom.

This book is certainly well researched and most conclusions are substantiated and well documented. Yet it appears that White fails to elucidate the main thesis of the book, since the influence of political culture on Soviet politics is hardly discussed and the correlation of behavior and belief in Soviet political culture remains at best hypothetical. White's study reminds the reader of the difficulty of surveying public opinion in a closed and tightly controlled society, and it makes one aware of the fact that conventional research techniques are not always adequate for the purpose of studying social structures that are based on a set of values different from those accepted in the West.

N. N. SHNEIDMAN

Erindale College
University of Toronto
Ontario

UNITED STATES HISTORY AND POLITICS

PAUL BLUMBERG. *Inequality in an Age of Decline.* Pp. xv, 290. New York: Oxford University Press, 1980. $15.95.

Inequality in an Age of Decline, by Paul Blumberg, professor of sociology at Queens College and the Graduate Center of the City University of New York, suggests that neither the concepts of "class convergence"—indiscriminately accepted by many social and political commentators in the fifties—or "class stability"—the traditional viewpoint of the left—adequately portrays the dynamics of the social system of the United States; rather, American society is experiencing what Blumberg labels "class divergence." To wit, Blumberg argues that while rapid inflation has resulted in a lower standard of living for most, including those of us who labor in the halls of academe, the upper class has fared reasonably well through it all, more-or-less maintaining their bundle of economic privileges. Or more succinctly, inflation is not an equal debacle for all, even in egalitarian America. Indeed, the members of the upper class have profited through the higher rate of return on their investments. From this perspective, the phenomenon of inflation has remained true to form: what is one man's burden is another man's gain. A recent article in the *New York Times* substantiated that purveyors of Cadillacs, fur coats, and other "fine" items that most of us only carry on wish games about, continue to enjoy a "brisk" business.

Back to the book under review. *Inequality in an Age of Decline* is well written and organized; however, I failed to find within its pages anything particularly novel or terribly perceptive. In short, what is asserted has been advanced many times before, standard litany stuff. For instance, despite the common wisdom, Blumberg is not alone in suggesting that the advance of automation in manufacturing probably requires less-skilled workers, rather than those possessing skills. Needless to say, pushing a button now and then does not require any awesome mastery of mental or manipulative skills. Nor is the author revealing anything new when he writes that wealth and income in America are unequally distributed. And we are all aware that over the last several decades the United States has annually suffered a trade deficit and that American industry is finding it increasingly difficult to effectively compete with overseas entrepreneurs, although on this score Blumberg provides us with a nice case study of the demise of the American steel industry. Nor is Blumberg sharing any gold rings when he writes that Americans are becoming more pessimistic about their own future and the future well being of American society.

Being a political scientist, I was particularly interested in Blumberg's renditions of what would be the political ramifications resulting from an American society increasingly characterized by scarcity. Certainly, he is on mark when he suggests that there will be more conflict, primarily because of a shrinking economic pie, and probably he is correct in asserting that once again economic, rather than social and life-style, issues will constitute the primary focus of the political agenda. But if I have correct reading of American history, I do not share his faith that the organized labor movement will abandon its business-as-usual approach and become the vanguard of social democratic change.

In conclusion, this is an interesting and informative work, free of excessive jargon, which can be read with profit by both the academician and concerned layman. Yet if one wants to gain a deeper understanding of the politics of scarcity, additional reading is in order.

NELSON WIKSTROM
Virginia Commonwealth University
Richmond

HARRY C. BOYTE. *The Backyard Revolution.* Pp. xvi, 271. Philadelphia, PA: Temple University Press, 1980. $14.95.

If this book purports to be a treatise in political science, it fails woefully. The term "backyard revolution" connotes a political movement aimed at changing the way in which policy decisions are made. In order to show the change, one must first show how policy decisions are or have been made and then cite the change. This is not what Boyte does.

As a political theorist, he should have laid out the conceptual framework within which public policy has been made in this country. If he had, he would have immediately recognized that the so-called backyard demands are nothing new. The history of the United States is replete with grass-root movements, local organizational demands, and mushrooming pressures, all dedicated to the proposition that formal governmental authority is suspect and those in political position are apt to be notoriously corrupt. Therefore nothing really new is presented, even though a catchy phrase indicates that something radically different is happening in this country.

What Boyte needs to do in order to make his study useful to students of government is to develop some intellectual framework that would explain how the data he has amassed should be utilized in policymaking. For example, there is a very time-honored theory that holds that democracies abet the rise of multifaceted interest groups, which in turn promote the bargaining that occurs in the legislature as its members seek the support of these groups. The key to this theory is that there is a forum—the legislature—where the various demands from the so-called grass-roots can be voiced and honored. Without such forum the protests of the pressures become a babbling noise or, worse yet, form the material for demagogic manipulation by those adept at conning the disgruntled. Participatory democracy requires a clearly defined means by which the populace can participate in a rational manner in developing policy. Boyte is apparently unaware of the danger issuing from popular movements that are uncoordinated and disjointed. Such movements are sources of potential political energy that once loosed can cause havoc with public order and

can generate further disillusionment among the frustrated, as witness the denouement of the student revolt of the sixties.

While Boyte writes at length about the roles played by such organizations as SNCC and NOW in helping structure demands of blacks and women, he does not show how such organizations have affected party commitment or effected response by such institutions as the legislatures and the courts. It is not enough to say that Reagan "activists" overwhelmed Republican Party machinery, or that various groups such as the blacks, the young, and women superseded the Democratic bosses in 1972. What did happen was that organized groups using the party machinery got control of the party for the time being, but in so doing had to blend with other forces in the party in order to run an effective campaign. In the case of the Republicans in 1980, they did; in that of the Democrats of 1972, they did not. The reader is left in the dark concerning the relationship between citizen movements and political institutions. One is led to believe that somehow the organized denizens of the backyards of the country will bring forth, in some mystical manner, true self-government and that the people will be happy.

If the so-called neighborhood revolt is to change the political format of the way in which policy is determined, we will have to wait a bit before any realistic assessment of its effort is possible. My own feeling is that we shall wait in vain. It probably will be *plus ca change plus c'est le meme chose*.

PAUL DOLAN
University of Delaware
Newark

RICHARD GRISWOLD DEL CASTILLO. *The Los Angeles Barrio, 1850–1890: A Social History.* Pp. xiv, 218. Berkeley, CA: University of California Press, 1979. $16.95.

The 1840s were the decade that saw the United States expand from coast to coast. The highlight for expansionist Americans was the 1848 Treaty of Guadalupe Hidalgo that, among other things, brought to a land-hungry nation Los Angeles—the largest Mexican town in North America. This short volume portrays for us the interesting but sad saga of that proud, prosperous, and growing town and its inhabitants, facing together a callous new proprietor who disregarded the heritage and accomplishments of a fascinating community by moving swiftly to replace the town's uniqueness with "Eastern ways" and the national philosophy. This clash led to racial discrimination, cultural expression, and continuing violence, much of which has been discussed in other volumes. However, the cultural clash led also to creative responses to fast-changing circumstances, which allowed the heritage of proud settlers to make its way successfully through a morass of acculturation efforts, despite the fact that by 1890 only one Chicano family in ten could trace its roots back to ancestors living in Los Angeles 40 years earlier.

Herein lies the value of this thoughtful volume. It portrays, in a relatively unbiased manner, the means used by Mexican-Americans to adapt to changes imposed by a growing nation and state during the 40-year period (1850–1890) that saw an agricultural and rural country change into one worshipping cities and industrial power. While this metamorphosis was taking place, and while Los Angeles was growing and its Mexican-American inhabitants were being restricted more and more into a barrio, the people adapted to change by publicly accommodating themselves to the will of the nation, but refusing to do so privately. They retained Spanish-language newspapers, organized a variety of political and social clubs, and managed to give the inhabitants of the barrio a life apart from Anglo-American society.

This willingness to bend but not break is clearly portrayed by Castillo; the reader finds himself applauding a people refusing to change within, as did rural Mexican-American Californians during the same time span. Castillo suggests that the sense of community that enveloped barrio families saved the *pobladores* of Los Angeles, while the absence

of a community and the inevitable independence of rural people made cultural survival impossible in the countryside. This premise has been offered by others; and it appears to be sound and defensible. However, it also seems appropriate to suggest that as the Mexican-American population grows into America's largest minority nationality, it is time to expand the horizons from one barrio to an examination of the fuller picture that is the history of Mexican-Americans in a nation whose melting pot failed—thankfully—to acculturate myriad nationalities and races of people who journeyed here seeking economic opportunity, political asylum, or other freedoms that never included surrender of self for the blandness offered by a melting pot.

This volume is a thought-provoking one that deserves contemplation. It stands as a pioneering effort that merely points the way to others, offering them questions to ponder as they expand a fascinating but neglected theme that, when fully developed, will add luster to a nation composed of endless varieties of proud people who did, indeed, contribute something worthwhile to our collective history.

ARTHUR H. DEROSIER, JR.
The College of Idaho
Caldwell

JOHN FOLEY, DENNIS A. BRITTON, and EUGENE B. EVERETT, JR., eds. *Nominating A President: The Process and the Press.* Pp. xiii, 147. NY: Praeger Publishers, 1980. No price.

This book offers a slightly edited account of a conference at Harvard's Institute of Politics in which several political operatives, professional campaign managers, and technicians joined with news media executives and journalists in discussing the presidential nominating process. The conference, jointly sponsored by the *Los Angeles Times*, took place on the weekend of February 1–3, 1980, between the Iowa caucus and the New Hampshire primary. The discussions might have proved more fruitful had the conference been held after the presidential nominations were closed.

The format featured five round-table discussions, each with a separate panel and a moderator. No position papers were presented. Under these circumstances, discussions inevitably were inchoate and discursive, their coherence depending mightily on the skills of the moderator. The organization of material within each panel, presented in this book as chapters, consists entirely of large-print subheads provided by the editors. This is hardly sufficient to correct for the vast unevenness of the material.

In scrutinizing the nominating process, the panelists addressed familiar themes: the impact of television, the timing of the early primaries, and the covering of issues and their importance, as well as the need for reform. Knowledgeable as the participants were, it is difficult to find a fresh insight or any special words of wisdom in these pages.

Jonathan Moore, director of the institute, in a brief afterword, finds the results of the conference "elusive and ambiguous." His reading of the conference is that it may be too early to pass judgment on the system being tested. Moore also notes that the participants in the conference also happen to be participants in the process they have under examination. It is hard, therefore, to disagree with Moore's suggestion that the participants may have an interest in the existing system not being changed in ways that might diminish their influential roles.

Serious students of voting behavior, elections, and political parties agree that the problem of the increasingly influential role of the media in presidential nominating politics deserves the closest scrutiny by practitioners and social scientists. This small book offers little of value for these academic specialists. It is also hard to imagine what special insights the general reader might glean from this version of "inside-dopesterism." The Institute of Politics will surely want to improve upon this initial effort in the future.

JOHN C. DONOVAN
Bowdoin College
Brunswick
Maine

LESTER D. LANGLEY. *The United States and the Caribbean, 1900–1970.* Pp. ix, 324. Athens, GA: University of Georgia Press, 1980. $22.00.

This book completes Lester D. Langley's two-volume history of U.S. diplomatic relations in the Caribbean, which began with *Struggle for the American Mediterranean: United States-European Rivalry in the Gulf-Caribbean, 1776–1904.* The earlier study related the history of U.S. hostility to the European presence in the Caribbean in the nineteenth century. This one traces the course of U.S. relations with the small countries of the region during the twentieth century. Beginning with the expansion of America's Caribbean empire following the Spanish-American War, this second part of Langley's interpretive survey culminates with the disintegration of the American empire in the decade following Castro's revolution in Cuba.

The idea of an American empire—an empire founded upon the strategic importance of the Caribbean in early twentieth-century American diplomacy and expressing itself through influence upon the cultural, economic, and political development of the countries of the region—is the organizational focus of this study. The method of treatment is necessarily chronological and episodic. Writing primarily from the perspective of the makers of American policy, Professor Langley, who teaches diplomatic history at the University of Georgia, succeeds in describing the sometimes subtle differences in the U.S. approach to the various countries of the Caribbean and also the differing concerns, emphases, and methods of the successive leaders responsible for the conduct of American diplomacy. At the same time, Langley manages to explain enough of the internal politics, economic conditions, and social organization of the Caribbean nations to enable the reader to comprehend the impact of the American intrusion upon Caribbean America.

Langley's prose is clear and concise, his command of the English- and Spanish-language sources is impressive, and his conclusions are generally well founded. It is difficult to quarrel with the view that the United States functioned as an imperial power in the Caribbean or with the conclusion that this nation's bottom-line concerns in that region have been the maintenance of order and stability and the prevention of penetration by other outsiders. The proposition that the American empire was founded upon strategic considerations to a greater extent than economic ones is, of course, more debatable; but the considerable literature examining American economic intervention in the Caribbean and Central America makes it unnecessary to join that debate here.

The contention that a genuine sense of mission—the tutoring of the Caribbean peoples in economic progress, political democratization, and moral improvement—found actual expression in American policy may fairly be criticized for confusing rhetoric with reality. However, Langley's interpretation need not be accepted in all its details in order to recognize that he has got the main points right. He understands—and he forces the reader to understand—that from first to last, the North American approach to the Caribbean has been informed by a contempt for Caribbean peoples and by a presumption of their innate inferiority and incapacity. Whatever its motivation, whatever its purposes, and no matter what changes in goals and emphases it has undergone, American policy toward the Caribbean has consistently denigrated the institutions and disparaged the culture of the small countries it has sought to control. This conviction of Caribbean inferiority, even more than strategic necessity, has justified the U.S. violation of the sovereignty of its neighbors in the eyes of both its leaders and people.

This book does an excellent job of telling the story of the expression of ethnocentrism in American diplomacy and of its consequences. For that reason as well as for its lucid style and integration of extensive sources, this book is deserving of respect and of a broad readership.

THOMAS M. HILL
Department of Health and Human
    Services
Kansas City
Missouri

JAMES MELLOW. *Nathaniel Hawthorne in His Times.* Pp. xiv, 684. Boston: Houghton Mifflin, 1980. $19.95.

Nathaniel Hawthorne could be a patron saint of American repression—as a racist ("I have not . . . the slightest sympathy for the slaves"); an anti-Semite; an opponent of coeducation; a sexist who preferred conventional women as "gentle parasites" to feminist "petticoated monstrosities"; a religious reactionary; a political conservative; and a person with apparently suppressed homosexual yearnings.

In his gracefully written biography, James Mellow does not ignore such vulgar questions, but he does imply that they are too "complex" and "ambiguous" to analyze in a biography. Instead of generalities, he focuses on particularities, creating a richly detailed canvas. By succeeding in this project, however, he fails to portray Hawthorne "in his times." We do learn colorful chitchat about food and climate, quality gossip about personalities and places, lucid outlines for various stories, and charming quotes suitable for repetition at sophisticated cocktail parties, but we are given only the broadest hints about the socioeconomic context of Hawthorne's life, or the relation of his work to various cultural traditions. Even significant events within Hawthorne's personal life—if too controversial—seem to be offstage, although mentioned. Thus after some sly allusions in the text, we are startled by the footnote revelation of the possible homosexual seduction of Hawthorne in his youth and the homoerotic ties between Melville and Hawthorne.

The possibility of a civil war within Hawthorne deserves greater attention. It might, after all, unearth a central root for his fearful sense of sin, his despair and world-weariness. Although Mellow can offer the excuse that this is speculative psychohistory, just as he might say that he is not an economist or a sociologist, a book without such dimensions is more style than substance. A biography without any compelling feeling of passion, poverty, joy, hatred, and fear, or even the dull monotony of routine life, is a fundamentally false life seen from the comfortable library of a gentleman.

Thus we have a book that lacks either the political sensibilities of Van Wyck Brooks or F. O. Matthiessen, or the elaborate—if sometimes dully composed—scholarship of recent years: Nina Baym, *The Shape of Hawthorne's Career* (1976); Richard Brodhead, *Hawthorne, Melville, and the Novel* (1976); Kenneth Dauber, *Rediscovering Hawthorne* (1977); Edgar Dryden, *Nathaniel Hawthorne: The Poetics of Enchantment* (1977); Taylor Stoehr, *Hawthorne's Mad Scientist* (1978); Rita Gollin, *Nathaniel Hawthorne and the Truth of Dreams* (1979); Robert Long, *The Great Succession: Henry James and the Legacy of Hawthorne* (1979); Lea Newman, *A Reader's Guide to the Short Stories of Nathaniel Hawthorne* (1979); and Arlin Turner, *Nathanial Hawthorne, a Biography* (1980). Unlike these often homely academic studies, however, Mellow's pretty book belongs on the coffee tables of beautiful people. This is its twin virtue and vice.

DAVID DeLEON

Howard University
Washington, D.C.

LEO RANGELL. *The Mind of Watergate: An Exploration of the Compromise of Integrity.* Pp. 318. New York: W. W. Norton, 1980. $12.95.

Mark Twain once quipped: "Always tell the truth. It will gratify some and astonish the rest." Good advice when it was given, this would have been good advice to the Watergate conspirators in June 1972, the time the Watergate phenomenon, following the break-in at the Democratic convention headquarters— began to unfold. The compromise of integrity—of which Watergate is only a single but egregious instance—began much earlier than 1972, Rangell insists, although his book is primarily a "psychochronicle" of the events following in the wake of the 1972 break-in.

Rangell's book is an attempt to do two things: first, to explain the Watergate phenomenon in the context of a revised psychoanalytic theory; second, to provide a fair and accurate account and explanation of the historical events immediately preceding and following Watergate. Rangell's primary methodological assumption is that "a psychological and motivational view of history rather than a mere chronology of events supplies the cement which binds them together." Despite my admiration for what Rangell has done here, I must add the caveat that the so-called psychoanalytic cement he provides at times appears to be too filled with emotional sand to hold the events together in the comfortable, objective scholarly way one would prefer. In other words, Rangell's historical account is more convincing than his psychoanalytic explanations because he too often slips from the "neutral" language of psychoanalysis to the language of ethical preachment and name-calling. This tendency is apparent, for example, in the following excerpts: "His [Nixon's] motive was to attack, smear, accuse, kill, and not to stop at overkill"; "While delivering the killing blow, he [Nixon] can smile, gesture, pull back. . . ."; and "Richard Nixon . . . scratched and clawed and gouged his way from congressman to president."

Even the less emotionally charged psychoanalytic judgments of Rangell's can be troublesome to the dispassionate scholar seeking truth not supercharged rhetoric: "Most people live with their egos constantly checked by their superegos. Nixon's has free reign, allowing it to satisfy ambition at will."

If it were not for the fact that Rangell exhibits a historian's attention to the infinitesimal details of Watergate, we would dismiss the book as a political tract interfused with some fairly good psychoanalytic observations, occasionally overstepping the boundaries of scholarly neutrality. However, one political act after another is analyzed so carefully that one has difficulty feeling much sympathy for Nixon. In addition to participating in the cover-up of Watergate, Nixon apparently sanctioned the following: (1) 3620 B-52 bombing raids on Cambodia, disguised from Congress by a "double-entry reporting system that listed them as taking place elsewhere";

(2) asking the IRS to investigate "contributors to the McGovern campaign, as well as those who failed to contribute to Nixon's own treasure chest for re-election"; (3) spending half a million dollars in cash from his reelection campaign to "stop George Wallace, a potential opponent in 1972, from winning the governorship of Alabama"; (4) taking a mammoth income tax deduction for his presidential papers only after removing those deemed most valuable; and (5) commenting in the context of a conference called to dissuade those pressing for his impeachment that "I can go in my office and pick up the telephone and in twenty-five minutes millions of people will be dead."

Nixon was, of course, pardoned by Gerald R. Ford when impeachment was imminent. The committee recommending impeachment concluded that he was guilty of at least three impeachable offenses: (1) directing a "criminal conspiracy" to cover up the Watergate conspiracy; (2) misusing the "powers of his office"; and (3) refusing "to comply with requested subpoenas."

Rangell's account of the events and motives behind Nixon's political career is devastatingly clear. His penchant for pointing out the contradictory, political nature of Richard Nixon is equally devastating. However, his objectivity leaves something to be desired. Nonetheless, I would recommend this book to all who want to develop their powers of observation because portions of the book are unexcelled as political analysis.

STEPHEN W. WHITE
East Tennessee State University
Johnson City

WILLIAM C. WIDENOR. *Henry Cabot Lodge and the Search for an American Foreign Policy.* Pp. xii, 389. Berkeley, CA: University of California Press, 1980. $18.50.

Historians, particularly those sympathetic to Woodrow Wilson, have generally found little to like in Henry Cabot Lodge, the senator from Massachusetts who has been depicted as an imperialist, an intensely partisan Republican, and the most vindictive opponent to Wilson's "idealistic" proposal for a League of Nations. William C. Widenor's study will probably do little to make many new friends for Lodge—this is not its intention—but Widenor does show that Lodge was more than the one-dimensional figure that he has often been portrayed as. In correcting Lodge's historical image, Professor Widenor shows a critical sensibility that comes with intelligence and a thorough reading of the primary and secondary sources. More importantly, Widenor's own sense of man's limitations in an imperfect world prevents him from romanticizing Lodge's search for an American foreign policy suitable for the modern age he was entering at the turn of this century.

Widenor shows that Lodge was also an "idealist" who believed from his reading of history that America could only play a leading role in furthering the progress of world civilization if the nation's leaders recognized the importance of military power and national self-interest in international relations. Lodge, therefore, willingly accepted Washington's dictum that "if we desire peace . . . it must be known that we are at all times ready for war." Lodge feared, however, that Americans would not prove strong enough, militarily or psychologically, to fulfill their historic mission.

Widenor observes that Lodge, a holder of one of the first doctorates in history ever granted in this country, brought to his writings "the interest of a class reeling before the assaults of the magnates of the new industrialism and an immigration which appeared to recognize neither the same God nor the same values." History became for Lodge a jeremiad to reawaken the heroic qualities of the American character, which was now threatened by a "failure of nerve" and crass materialism. To ensure America's ascent into a world power, Lodge finally reached what Widenor calls a "Rooseveltian solution." Lodge wanted, Widenor writes, "a foreign policy which would bring American power and American morality into a closer relationship, a foreign policy equivalent of the practical ideals which he considered the essence of the American approach to politics." These practical ideals, if they were to be realized, depended ultimately on a strong government, unity and cohesion at home, and military preparedness.

Widenor's book is clearly controversial and for this reason engaging. For instance, he describes the kind of imperialism espoused by Lodge as eclectic, opportunistic, limited, and defensive. This characterization will surely be questioned by revisionist historians who will point out, as Widenor himself observes, that not only was Lodge a vehement supporter of the Spanish-American War—which is discussed at length in the book—but that Lodge felt that the American empire should reach from the Rio Grande to the Arctic. Issue will also be taken with Widenor's description of Lodge's role during the fight over the League of Nations. Widenor argues that Lodge's position, as well as the Republican party's policy, in the initial stages of the fight was "reservationist." Only Wilson's inability to compromise and his own political ineptness led Lodge to take an increasingly more "irreconcilable" position as the fight continued.

Readers, whether convinced or not by Widenor's eloquent portrayal of Lodge, will find this book thoughtful and subtle. Widenor is fully aware of the historical consequences of the events he discusses. Of those Americans who carried Wilson's fight for an international organization into World War II, Widenor writes, "In their devotion to atoning for the mistake of 1919–20 by constructing a new international organization for securing the world's peace, they were as blind to some of the other requisites of a lasting peace settlement as Wilson had been twenty-five years earlier. Instead of learning from their elder's mistakes, they only compounded their tragedy." There are hints here of a future book on the founding of the United Nations. If this is the case, and if this fine study of Lodge is taken as an example of things to come, Widenor's next work will be eagerly awaited.

DONALD T. CRITCHLOW
North Central College
Naperville
Illinois

WILLIAM APPLEMAN WILLIAMS. *Empire as a Way of Life: An Essay on the Causes and Character of America's Present Predicament Along With a Few Thoughts About an Alternative.* Pp. xiv, 226. NY: Oxford University Press, 1980. $14.95.

Not surprisingly, this new book by William Appleman Williams is a jeremiad, an essentially theological history that invokes doom on the American people for their pursuit of an "imperial" way of life. By "imperialism," Williams means what anyone would expect it to mean, but he extends it to include the development of economic superiority, of ethnic hegemony, of political authority, even of cultural and intellectual preeminence. He holds that as a result both of their participation in "imperialism" and of their enjoyment of its fruits, the American people have abdicated self-government, abandoned self-restraint, and saddled themselves with an unthinking demand for increased material gratifications that can only bring disaster to themselves and the rest of the world.

On some levels Professor Williams's argument is highly persuasive, and its main thesis was well exemplified in the recent presidential campaign. Nevertheless, he overdoes his argument by imputing consistency of purpose to actions that were at best confused responses to a variety of circumstances and by blaming the Americans' economic system for all of their other faults. In other respects, his work is a highly traditional and methodologically obsolete essay on the national character, novel only because it is so condemnatory. Williams has, indeed, deepened his previous efforts to explain the American society by introducing a vaguely psychological orientation: the Americans do not appear as prisoners of an economic structure so much as prisoners of mental dispositions associated with it. Still, his account of American history remains superficial, tendentious, and open to easy refutation in many of its details, while its prose is often made opaque by its burdens of allegation, insinuation, and indignation. The nation's present predicaments require a wiser form of understanding, and the American electorate has displayed more resources than this book admits.

Even so, the concluding chapters, in which Williams outlines the disastrous tendencies of our foreign policy since World War II, are often powerful in spite of their formulaic character. In particular, his account of the *hubris* displayed by our officials is frightening even when it is clearly selective, while his invocation of a world devoted to different values, vague and hortatory though it may be, also identifies the moral limits within which the United States must approach the future. Williams's history may be tendentious, but his theology is probably true in spite of his dubious scholarship.

RUSH WELTER

Bennington College
Vermont

SOCIOLOGY

MICHAEL BURAWOY. *Manufacturing Consent: Changes in the Labor Process under Monopoly Capitalism.* Pp. xvii, 267. The University of Chicago, Press, 1979. $20.00.

Contrary to Marx's belief, competitive capitalism was pregnant, not with socialism, but with monopoly capitalism. *Manufacturing Consent* is a Marxist work in industrial sociology that attempts to outline and explain the changes that occurred in the labor process when competitive capitalism gave way to monopoly capitalism. Unlike most works in sociology, *Manufacturing Consent* has a literary quality that makes it good reading. Burawoy spent a year working in the engine division of Allied Corporation as a machine operator and observed industrial behavior firsthand on the shop floor. He compared this experience with that of Donald Roy, who worked in the same shop 30 years earlier when it belonged to the small Geer Company, which was later taken over by Allied, and who documented his observations in a Ph.D. thesis.

Burawoy describes the contempt with which he was treated by other workers until he began "making out." Making out is the culture of the shop floor whereby workers attempt to achieve levels of production that earn incentive pay. To Burawoy, this made workers active participants in their own exploitation. Yet he found himself seduced by this culture which made meaningless work challenging and made time go almost too fast.

In comparing his experience at Allied with Roy's experience at Geer 30 years earlier, Burawoy observed dramatic changes. Unlike Geer, Allied was much better able to deal with competition in the marketplace through oligopolistic practices. It was also much more able to absorb losses in one department, since it could balance them against profits in other departments. This resulted in the democratization of the labor process. The despotic organization of work in which coercion prevailed was replaced by the hegemonic organization of work where consent facilitated the exploitation of workers by capital. There was a strengthening of the collective bargaining process, increased autonomy of workers, and greater constraints on managerial discretion.

Far from leading Burawoy to extol the virtues of modern capitalism, these changes lead him to despair. They seem to have a mind-numbing effect on workers, since they diminish class struggle and reinforce the capitalist relations of production as part of the given and unchanging order of things. But none of this gives Burawoy reason to believe that capitalism is the last stage of history. It only leads him to conclude that socialism is not imminent in the developed world.

The only weakness of Burawoy's work is one that it shares with all Marxist analyses of our social world—a reluctance to question the assumptions of Marxism or to go beyond Marx in giving concrete suggestions regarding the organization of the labor process under socialism.

S. B. DRURY

The University of Calgary
Canada

CLARICE FEINMAN. *Women in the Criminal Justice System.* Pp. xii, 123. New York: Praeger Publishers, 1980. No price.

Dealing with discrimination against women, this book surveys American historical experience as well as the current situation, presenting statistics and instances of segregation and exclusion. While the topic is criminal justice, some items relate only indirectly—like the appointment of a probate judge—while other subjects on point are omitted—like the deplorable treatment of rape victims.

The basic thesis is that the treatment of women in a wide range of roles—as criminals, prison guards, and police officers, lawyers and judges—can be explained by a single "massive, deep-seated, widely-held stereotype: the madonna/whore duality." Unfortunately for anlaysis of a problem as critical as sex discrimination, the link between the data and this all-encompassing explanation is often assumed rather than demonstrated.

The use of supporting facts and generalizations, moreover, is sometimes questionable. For example, the book begins by tracing to the Old Testament the madonna/whore stereotyping of women as either submissive or dangerous, omitting Biblical stories of women accepted as leaders, like the prophetess Miriam, the judge Dinah, the Queen of Sheba, and Queen Esther. Similarly, the last substantive chapter states that the first woman law professor was appointed in 1972, while in fact women have been teaching law for decades. Barbara Armstrong, for example, was full professor at Berkeley in the 1930s, and Herma Kay's full professor appointment there dates to 1960. Indeed, though nepotism rules had held back some careers unfairly, at least four other women had been appointed full professor in the 1960s—Soia Mentschikoff, at Chicago in 1962; Ellen Peters, Yale 1964; Patricia Harris, Howard 1965; and Dorothy Nelson, Southern California, 1967. These are persons whose successful careers are not to be overlooked; the four number themselves three deans, an ambassador, a cabinet secretary, a state supreme court justice, and a federal appellate judge.

More generally, we are told that women "are not well represented" in top law schools, "seldom are offered" prestigious law firm summer or permanent positions, "have made small gains" as law faculty members, have done even worse in the legal profession, and suffer from "similar patterns of discrimination [which] are evident in appointing judges."

Women indeed have long suffered invidious discrimination in legal careers, but these conclusions do not acknowledge the victories they have won. Women now comprise 33.5% percent of incoming students in accredited law schools, are admitted equally to the best schools, and are hired by firms at starting salaries up to $35,000 annually. In recent years they received preference in federal and California judicial appointments. There are now women in roles of leadership in the law, for example, in California as chief justice of the state supreme court, United States Attorney, and all three of the federal circuit judges sitting on a U.S. Court of Appeals bench this spring.

The struggle toward long-delayed equality for women in law is a continuing one that deserves study beyond that given in this book.

MARTIN LYON LEVINE
University of Southern California
Los Angeles

D. ROSS GANDY. *Marx and History: From Primitive Society to Communist Future.* Pp. xiii, 472. Austin, TX: University of Texas Press, 1979. $14.95.

RADOSLAV SELUCKY. *Marxism, Socialism, Freedom: Towards A General Democratic Theory of Labour-Managed Systems.* Pp. xiv, 237. NY: St. Martin's Press, 1979. No price.

Gandy's work is an outgrowth of a Ph.D. dissertation on Marx at the University of Texas in 1967. However, the analysis and discussion of this contribution deal chiefly with Marx and Engels. In other words, how did Karl Marx and Friedrich Engels see nineteenth-century conditions?

Marx and Engels worked on the basic assumptions of evolution from the beginning. "They easily absorbed the nineteenth century's growing fascination with evolution." For Marx, according to this work, the industrial proletariat was the historical agency of socialist revolution. During the nineteenth century, social conditions drove the European proletariat toward revolution, while in the twentieth century these conditions have largely disappeared, though some of them might reappear. In short, "Marx and Engels believed that it takes two classes to make a revolution, and one of these is always the ruling class."

Marx said in 1847: "The loss of the old society is no less for those who have nothing to lose in the old society. . . . They have rather everything to gain by the destruction of the old society. . . ." And everyone knows Marx's famous slogan of 1848: "The proletarians have nothing to lose but their chains."

Moreover, Marx and Engels focus on class and ignore status, for they are interested in social development, and the static models of the stratification theorists would have bored them. They took a close look at their own period, the epoch of competitive capitalism. "It may be summed up briefly: a revolution in Russia at the present moment (1888) . . . would be the beginning of the revolution in the whole world."

Finally, the message of *Marx and History* is strongly reminiscent of a terrestrial and secular "Bible," dealing primarily with a chosen people, the proletariat. By comparison, the celestial Bible (Old and New Testaments), although it has its own "chosen" people, nevertheless embraces all humanity and preaches love—not hatred—of one's neighbor, including proletariats.

Although the title of Selucky's book is different from Gandy's contribution, both works have been produced on the same subject. In many respects they also have much in common as regards methodology; however, the authors' conclusions are at variance. We should be grateful to the publishers for producing these two works simultaneously. In short, Radoslav Selucky's *Marxism, Socialism, Freedom* interpretation on the period in question is more conservative and brings it more up to date.

In the third part of his well-written book, Professor Selucky presents a model of democratic socialism and a new theory of labor-managed systems. Having presented his definition of socialism, "stripped it of many Utopian features," he based it on individual freedom and political democracy. "Moreover, Lenin was attacked by the social democrats not for the Soviet *form* of the postrevolution Russian state, but for its lack of democratic content." In addition, once the revolution is won, the state is no longer necessary, and therefore, the dictatorship of the proletariat is not necessary either. "Consequently, there cannot be any dictatorial form of government in a socialist state."

Finally come the following statements by Selucky:

It may be argued that my interpretation of the Marxian theory of the state does not follow the letter of Marxism. Some may even doubt if it reflects the spirit of Marxism. I do not hide my intention to revise some of Marx's and Engels' propositions and to adjust them to the needs of democratic socialism. It will be seen . . . that Marx's theory suffers much more from its author's methodological inconsistencies than from imaginary cleavages between the young and the old Marx. It was not only Lenin who changed the spirit of Marxism; some elements of Leninism are present in the original Marxist theory. . . .

. . . Though I am fully aware of the significance of particular political cultures for both the economic efficiency of labor self-management and the maintenance of political democracy, application of the theory to national traditions, customs, institutions, patterns of behavior, specific social and ethical values, religious and idealogical beliefs would require another study.

IVAR SPECTOR
University of Washington
Seattle

GERALD R. MILLER and NORMAN E. FONTES. *Videotape on Trial*. Pp. 224. Beverly Hills, CA: Sage Publications, 1979. $17.50. Paperbound, $8.95.

W. BOYD LITTRELL. *Bureaucratic Justice*. Pp. 284. Beverly Hills, CA: Sage Publications, 1979. $16.00. Paperbound, $7.95.

These two Sage publications are methodologically sound, empirical studies of controversial issues. Although one book deals largely with civil cases and the other with criminal cases, both speak to the problem of docket backlog and what to do about it.

Miller and Fontes's *Videotape on Trial* reports the findings of a series of studies dealing with juror responses to videotaped trial materials. The authors' framework, stated broadly, is one which views the trial as a communications event and which views information-processing problems as one of the leading determinants of docket backlogs.

Essentially, the authors assume—based upon actual experiences in some Ohio courts—that the use of taped depositions of witnesses to augment live trial presentations—generally, opening and closing arguments of counsel—would reduce information management problems, increase the number of cases tried, and increase the fairness of trials by editing out inadmissible testimony. The question they seek to answer, then, is whether the adoption of this innovation would produce jury decisions different from those rendered by totally live trials. Using actual jurors whenever possible, the authors videotaped reenacted, live trials to be used as "stimulus trials." The research is aimed at assessing two possible uses of videotape in the courtroom: prerecorded entire trials for presentation to juries and videotaped depositions for use in otherwise live trials.

Clearly, the authors are aware of the limitations of their findings. Notably, the findings are limited to the video technology actually used in their research and thus the impact of other production techniques remains to be examined. Also, the findings are not generalizable to criminal proceedings. Nevertheless, the findings are significant. In general, the authors find that verdicts and final awards of jurors exposed to videotaped trial presentations do not differ significantly from those of jurors viewing live presentations. Some differences in juror information processing do appear to stem from the type of medium used, for example, jurors viewing testimony on monochromatic tape recall a greater amount of testimony than jurors watching the same testimony in color. And, presumably, there are other dimensions of video technology which might make a difference and which would require careful monitoring if videotaped trials were to become widely accepted practice, for example editing techniques, types of camera shots, and so forth. The overall findings, however, are that there is little reason to preclude the use of videotape in the courtroom, that taped trial presentations do not produce jury decisions significantly different from those rendered by totally live trials and, indeed, jurors tend to remember more of the later portions of testimony when they are presented on tape than when they are presented live.

Littrell's *Bureaucratic Justice* deals with the administration of criminal justice rather than civil justice, but like *Videotape on Trial* it treats case processing and docket backlog within an organizational framework. It is within this mode of analysis then that Littrell *attempts to identify the changing relationship between legal rule and discretion forced by the shift in the organizational character of administration from "traditional" to "bureaucratic" criminal justice.*

By "traditional" administration of justice, Littrell means a system in which official conduct is legitimated by the sanctity of custom, the personage of the judge, and an administrative staff selected by the judge. In nineteenth century America, the court of the "hanging judge", Isaac C. Parker, embodied most of the characteristics of the traditional form. By "bureaucratic justice", the author means a system in which written rules replace custom and the personage of the judge as legitimating forces, civil service replaces personal appointment of administrative staff, and "specialists" administer the justice bureaucracy in accordance with written procedures and regulations. Littrell does not attempt to demonstrate or "prove" the emergence of bureaucratic justice. Rather, he assumes a gradual and uneven transformation from the traditional to the bureaucratic during the first half of the twentieth century and he assumes the dominance of the bureaucratic today.

The research is based partly on field work (interviews with detectives in three police departments and with assistant county prosecutors), partly on examination of random samples of materials and closed cases in municipal and county courts, and partly on observation. Generally, discretion exists in both traditional and the bureaucratic forms. In traditional administration discretion was necessary when rules "left off" (i.e., no longer provided a guideline under the circumstances) and commonly resulted in arbitrary exercise of authority. In bureaucratic administration, discretion is spread through the vast administrative machinery. The old problem of arbitrary decisions remains—although such decisions are smaller and less visible—but has changed in the sense that discretion is now necessary not only when rules "leave off," but becomes especially important for applying the rules themselves. This is because ambiguity in the complex application of rules necessarily results from a system in which anonymous specialists gather information, place it in files, and send it to the next office and in which no one knows exactly who has applied a rule or at what point it was applied. Unquestionably, the most revealing chapter in the book is the fifth, which presents a theory of dispositions in which it is observed that although selfish interests, that is, racial bias, workload demands, and other political considerations, can influence the charging decision there is also an "informed morality" at work in which authorities "make the crime fit the punishment", that is, after concluding that a "bad act" has been committed, authorities not only consider explicit provisions of criminal law for example, presence of a gun—but also consider questions of "fairness," "good and bad character," and the "moral seriousness of the harm" to design an accusation which fits the case. Though some readers—and I would be among them may be troubled by the social values implicit in some of the

conclusions of this bold book, I cannot but applaud this value-critical approach to policy analysis.

WILLIAM C. LOUTHAN
Ohio Wesleyan University
Delaware

RICHARD S. MORRIS. *Bum Rap on America's Cities: The Real Causes of Urban Decay.* Pp. vi, 198. Englewood Cliffs, NY: Prentice-Hall, 1980. $7.95. Paperbound.

This dogmatic title raises a suspicion that here may not be a landmark contribution to the literature on the subject. A reading fully confirms the suspicion. The title should be: *The Mess in Washington: No Cleanup in Sight*.

Morris contends that "the Nixon-Ford view about the causes of the urban crises were inaccurate [*sic*]. . . . Liberals are . . . taking a bum rap for the fiscal and economic decay of the American city. . . . Permissivism, labor unions . . . social welfare . . . and other targets of the right" are not the causes of our urban ills. The true causes originated right in our nation's capital.

Federal policies shortchange the cities at every turn: excessive prices for energy, welfare, and social security payments buy less in the cities. Grants and defense spending in the cities are less than they should be, given the income taxes cities generate. But, asserts Morris, only some cities get a "bum rap," the northeastern cities. The Sun Belt reaps a major portion of the federal "goodies" today.

This argument is supported by highly selective, poorly documented, and frequently outdated statistics. Regardless, Morris insists that if the Northeast received from Washington what is paid in taxes, all would be well.

Morris totally ignores the historical, widely recognized problems of cities: worn-out physical plants; traffic congestion and poor transportation; the flight of the middle class to the suburbs; crime; poor schools; increasing numbers of poor, uneducated families, many non-English-speaking; and so on. Many cities are poorly organized and depend far too much on highly regressive property taxes. Many cities not in the Northeast are high cost and suffer from the federal discrimination cited, San Francisco being one. Not long ago Philadelphia, New Haven, and Boston received billions in redevelopment funds. Who was discriminated against at that time?

This book, in reality, is a strong indictment of a federal system that has weakened the ability of state and local governments to finance and manage their own affairs. While Morris holds liberals blameless for urban decay, he should acknowledge that so-called liberal Democrats in national, state, and local governments have created the very programs and policies he so indignantly condemns.

JAMES R. BELL
California State University
Sacramento

ROBERT REPETTO. *Economic Equality and Fertility in Developing Countries*. Pp. xv, 186. Baltimore, MD: Johns Hopkins University Press, 1979. $14.50.

This small volume is one of the Resources for the Future books. It is about the effects of income equality—rather, inequality—on fertility within and between nations. The main thrust of the findings of this book is that income inequality within the developing countries is positively and causally related to high fertility levels.

Gains in income and the changes in living conditions that accompany them have different effects on fertility depending on the initial income of the recipients. Those who have already high income levels that increase, tend to increase their fertility; on the other hand, economic gains to financially depressed households result in reductions in fertility.

Repetto argues that different income distribution patterns imply different fertility levels for the population as a whole and that this has important implications. Rather than seeing a trade-off between rapid economic growth and equity of income distribution, he suggests that greater equity in the distribution of benefits from development leads to more rapid economic growth.

A more equitable distribution of income lowers the rate of population growth and permits faster accumulation of both physical and human capital. This in turn promotes higher productivity per worker. Lowering of fertility leads to a reduction of the dependency ratio, which leads to faster growth in output per worker. Given that there are limited substitution possibilities between labor and other inputs in production and that the labor force increase is far outpaced by increases in capital, labor's share of total output increases and encourages savings. This leads to further reductions in income inequalities, which, in turn, sustain reductions in fertility. "This sketches a process by which equalization of incomes, decline in fertility, and faster growth in output per capita interact positively. Progress in solving the problem of inequality aids the solution of the problem of population growth, and vice versa," says Repetto.

Repetto maintains that in the typical less-developed country, the most affluent 10 percent of the households enjoy 40 to 50 percent of the income, whereas the households in the lower half of the income scale typically get only 15 to 20 percent of the total income. The policy implications are quite clear. High fertility and poverty must be attacked by selective intervention to reduce economic inequality.

Repetto argues that what is true for the individual nation is also true on the international level. During the decade of the 1960s, the developed countries received more than 80 percent of the world's income, slightly more than their share at the beginning of the decade. This increase in income probably had little effect on reducing fertility in the developed countries and it certainly had almost no effect on world fertility. Eighty-five percent of all births during the decade occurred in the developing countries. Repetto says, "From the standpoint of world population growth, all this income growth in the affluent countries was virtually irrelevant." The policy implications for reducing the world fertility level are then clear. Reduce income inequality between and within the nations of the world.

The book consists of a foreword, six chapters, a reference section, and an index. I warn the reader that there is a serious logical inconsistency on p. xii of the foreword. Otherwise, the foreword is well written and informative about this study and how it came to be commissioned.

Chapter 1 presents a good introduction to the theoretical underpinnings of the study and a summary of the findings. Chapter 2 gives a conceptual framework for a test of the hypothesis that a single household's fertility responds to changes in its income. The data used for a test of this hypothesis are aggregative data from a cross-national sample of 68 developed and less developed countries for a single period in the mid-1960s. Chapter 3 constructs an alternative test of the hypothesis and uses disaggregated data from a sample of individual households in Puerto Rico in 1970. Chapter 4 is a case study of economic development and fertility change in South Korea. These three chapters, 2 through 4, using respectively aggregative, disaggregated, and historical data, bear on the main thesis of the book. Chapter 5, based on a region of rural India, explores the determinants of the existing distribution of income and the mechanisms for change. It concludes that distribution of land is the primary determinant of income distribution—land is the main asset and source of income and power in a rural community.

Chapter 6 applies the same arguments of the earlier chapters to world fertility and income distribution. Repetto also presents judicious statements about the limitations of his study and suggests that additional research is needed to investigate more directly the relationship between fertility and policies and programs that effect redistribution of the income of households.

I applaud Robert Repetto's work. I wonder though if the study should not have been titled *Economic Inequality and* . . . .

SURINDER MEHTA
University of Massachusetts
Amherst

SANDRA PERLMAN SCHOENBERG and PATRICIA ROSENBAUM. *Neighborhoods That Work*. Pp. xi, 179, New Brunswick, NJ: Rutgers University Press, 1980. $14.75.

This book examines the strategies used by members of working-class and low-income inner-city neighborhoods to improve their social environment.

Four propositions are presented that outline the components of a viable neighborhood. The neighborhood must have mechanisms to define and enforce shared standards of public behavior, it must have formed organizations, it must have ties to city resources outside the neighborhood, and it must have enduring channels for exchange between conflicting groups.

Schoenberg and Rosenbaum call for integration between local neighborhood interests and citywide interests, even when federal policies reflect conflict between them.

Families may go to a discount store ten miles away for the best buy on a television set, but they still go to the local tavern for beer and conversation. Some functions cannot be performed better on a larger scale . . . . We need to sort out those functions that should be provided on the metropolitan level and receive metropolitan support from those that are most effectively supported by local neighborhoods.

The development of social area analysis was a compromise between researchers who mapped the social characteristics of a population with no attention to a city's organizational characteristics and community researchers who studied individual neighborhoods without attention to their position within the larger aspects of city life.

The direction of planning and policy in the 1970s, according to the authors, seems to suggest that the neighborhood and the metropolitan region are seen as the two levels of the urban whole and leave the nature and future role of the city uncertain.

Defining the neighborhood as ethnic provides a basis for the exclusion of unlike people. From the stated interest in keeping the neighborhood Italian, it is a short step past defensiveness to exclusivity. O'Leary suggested in a very sensitive appraisal of the uses of ethnic identification in America in the 1970s:

> Whereas the middle and upper classes maintain isolated, legal and political jurisdictions in defense of their interests through the use of economic boundary maintenance, perhaps ethnic identification provides a political and social buttress to the limited economic resources of the working class in their defense against invasion by the lower classes in American society.

The authors have used indicators to test empirically whether the criteria of a neighborhood are being met. Their indicators include such matters as perceived decline in crime and the perception of the existence of social networks and also some unusual but effective measures, such as agreement about garbage disposals and whether visiting takes place on front porches.

These techniques have been applied to five neighborhoods in St. Louis selected because of their differences in population, age of housing, location, and symbolic and institutional heritage. These neighborhoods range from the Hill, where there is an attachment to an Italian heritage and a stable population, to the Ville, a historic black neighborhood that has experienced physical deterioration. In between are Lafayette Park and Soulard, two neighborhoods undergoing restoration, and Hyde Park, a transitional neighborhood dependent on what happens in surrounding neighborhoods.

This excellent comparative approach to the study of neighborhoods should be of interest to social scientists and planners in seeking to analyze urban problems with increased rigor. This book should also be of interest to social scientists and social workers with an interest in neighborhood revitalization and to policymakers interested in a more balanced central city.

CLAUDE M. URY

University of Colorado
Boulder

BAIDYA NATH VARMA. *The Sociology and Politics of Development: A Theoretical Study*. Pp. xvi, 219. Boston, MA: Routledge & Kegan Paul, 1980. $25.00.

The distinguished publisher, Routledge & Kegan Paul, has not served the author well by putting this work into print. An "expert" knowledge is not necessary to see that the book is hopelessly dated, completely out of touch with the important challenging works of the seventies—of whole new schools of thought like those of dependency theory, or world systems analysis, or the Marxist structuralists, or authors like Immanuel Wallerstein, or Nicos Poulantzsas, or Samir Amin, or Andre Gunder Frank. At best, this is a book of the sixties, both in terms of the major sources upon which Varma relies and in terms of the controlling ideas that he seeks to discuss. From Almond and Apter to Vidich and Weiner, Varma cites good persons whose works scholars have already chewed over and digested.

Professor Varma's declared intent is to produce "a theoretical study" of the sociology and politics of development. Even had he more modestly intended an introduction, or a summary, or a text for beginners, this book would not wash.

Varma treats us to generalizations at the level of the following: "The barriers to modernization are many"; "Classes are nominal for Weber but real for Marx"; "Hobbes Leviathan has often turned into a tyrant"; "A person, a group, or a community will not feel deprived or exploited if each has the opportunity to participate in the shaping of the plan"; and asks questions like "Modernization, for What?" This is not edifying stuff.

Varma also states that he classifies all writings about modernization into three categories. "Ideological" is where the author "consciously or subconsciously propounds a framework of inquiry which articulates some program of change." He calls the second category "Social Scientific" because "social scientists use various schemes in terms of their disciplinary interests and often claim objectivity for them." The last category is called "Activistic" because "it is the change agents who recommend this framework." Insofar as Varma stresses that he does not believe that any analysis can be completely value free and insofar as he does not exclude social scientists from being "change agents," the boundaries of his categories do not appear sturdy.

If all of this also sounds vague and general, it is. Varma claims that spelling out the ingredients of the activistic theories of modernization is the focus of this book. What is an "activistic theory?" The "important premise of the activistic theories of modernization," he tells us, "is that societies and civilizations need the active guidance of men in reaching higher levels of performance and excellence and in avoiding the catastrophic inherent in the evaluating process."

Although he provides no example of a nonactivistic theory of modernization, from here he goes on to distinguish between gradualist and revolutionary activistic approaches. How all of this fits together in any comprehensive way with "economic," "political," and "anthropological" theories of modernization and "ideological and non-ideological" theories appears very unclear.

I believe Varma when he states, "I have a commitment to democracy and a commitment to equalitarianism" and that this is why he felt that it was his "duty" to advance "a theoretical model for modernization." We are all the poorer for his lack of success.

IRVING LEONARD MORKOVITZ
Queens College
Flushing
New York

ECONOMICS

PHILLIP CAGAN and ROBERT E. LIPSEY. *The Financial Effects of Inflation.* Pp. xiv, 89. Cambridge, MA: Ballinger Publishing, 1978. No price.

CHARLES E. McLURE, JR. *Must Corporate Income Be Taxed Twice?* Pp. xvii, 262. Washington, DC: The Brookings Institution, 1979. $11.95. Paperbound, $4.95.

These two mini-books deal with several instances of institutional rigidity in the face of structural alterations in the American economy. The monograph by Cagan and Lipsey, examines how financial markets have—or have not—adjusted to inflation of the 1970s in light of the several theories economists have about this question. In general, they find that financial markets have not adjusted to the inflationary 1970s as would be expected from what the authors call the "standard theory." McLure asks the "have-you-stopped-beating-your-wife" question about double taxation of corporate profits and concludes, not surprisingly, that it should not be taxed twice.

In the decade of the 1970s, the United States experienced as much inflation as had occurred in the previous 40 years. It was the most inflationary decade in the history of the nation. Cagan and Lipsey are interested in testing various theories as to how financial markets should respond to this inflation in light of the experience of the 1970s. If inflation is a "tax on money balances and other fixed assets in dollar value," then how do wealth holders protect themselves from the ravages of inflation?

Theory suggests, according to Cagan and Lipsey, that wealth holders will shift out of money balances toward "goods that are expected to maintain their real value during inflation and can also serve as partial substitutes for the store-of-value function of money." This hypothesis of the standard theory should apply to common stocks, say the authors, but it has been more operative with land, where households and wealth holders have rushed to purchase land as a hedge against inflation. Notwithstanding this fact, the authors contend that "the market has *failed to develop* an asset that serves as a satisfactory hedge against inflation." Their most important conclusion is that "common stocks were once thought the prime asset to provide this hedge, but they have been inadequate over the past decade."

Cagan and Lipsey attempt to answer the question of why common stocks did not perform their supposed function as a hedge against inflation. Profits fell in real terms, the authors contend, and this is the primary reason why common stocks did not increase in value during the inflationary 1970s. Interest rates behaved erratically, further dampening investments in common stocks. During the inflationary 1970s, people moved their wealth into tangible assets—land, gold, collectibles, and the like. The authors do not investigate this phenomenon, but it is interesting to speculate as to why this occurred. The sharpness and magnitude of the inflationary trends in the 1970s can provide us with a clue as to why individuals behaved as they did. The fact that there was as much inflation in the decade of the 1970s as there had been for the previous 40 years signaled to individuals that they had better not trust any asset tied to the productive system of the economy. Psychologically, they retreated to very fundamental tenets of survival in the United States: acquire some land and squirrel away some tangible asset, like gold. Perhaps individuals were trying to tell economists and politicians something that was being ignored, namely, a dramatic loss of confidence in economic policy.

McLure deals with an old issue in the tax law: corporations pay a tax on their profits and then shareholders pay a tax on the dividends received from those same profits. This double taxation of the profits is said to reduce the attractiveness of individual investment in common stocks, since profits are subject to taxation twice. In this way, these two books delve into the same issue: what accounts for the sluggishness in investments in common stocks? McLure favors proposals which have appeared on the scene to deal with this issue, such as dividend relief and changing the treatment of corporate profits for purposes of taxation. However, his basic point is that a more preferable way to deal with this problem is to integrate the tax system.

True integration, as McLure defines it, means that "income earned at the corporate level, whether distributed or not, would be attributed to shareholders . . . and taxed only at the rates applicable

to the income of the various shareholders." McLure's book, based on a conference held at the Brookings Institution, proceeds to investigate the pros and cons of such an integrated tax system as well as ideas that have been tried, or are being contemplated, in other countries. In general, he concludes that the best way to eliminate the anomalies of double taxation is to move toward tax integration.

Whether these schemes would achieve their desired result is problematical. As McLure points out, England provides partial dividend relief from double taxation, yet has an investment rate lower than ours. More fundamentally, we have to ask whether wealth holders have sufficient confidence in the corporations to warrant investment in them. The same can be said for the present climate of national economic policy-making, which does not instill confidence in our ability to manage our affairs effectively.

HOWARD M. WACHTEL
The American University
Washington, D.C.

ROBERT CURRIE. *Industrial Politics.* Pp. x, 294. New York: Oxford University Press, 1979. $26.00.

Currie's objective, in this well-written and informative book, is to demonstrate that an industrial relations system is essentially a product of sociocultural antecedents. Focusing on the British system, he examines these antecedents and traces their influences and mutations over time as they establish "the concrete form and life of labour organization" emphasizing labour's perceptions, policies and priorities. In support of his own approach, Currie questions the usefulness, if not integrity, of "universalist" approaches in the social sciences, such as Hegel's universal historical process, Marx's concept of a universal proletariat, and Perlman's universality of the regulative labor organization. In doing so, the appropriateness of these universalist theories is criticized in both their internal limitations and external, cross-cultural applications. The book examines, in order, British laissez-faire ideology, corporatism, workers' control, labor sectionalism, and industrial democracy. It concludes by analyzing important, current social and political problems.

Laissez-faire, Currie observes, is fundamental to both British capitalists and labor and confers rights to each "in the defence and furtherance of self." Thus conflicts between interests are settled by power that has "in the abstract no privileges other than those which it can defend" and no merit other than existence. A laissez-faire system then is competitive and acquisition oriented. Labor organizations that reflect these characteristics are decidedly market oriented, that is, exacting the best possible price for selling labor, and even opportunistic. The development and competitive implications of industry outside of Britain in the latter 1800s implied a collective response directed and implemented—especially internationally—via the British government—a response premised upon the supremacy of state interests over those of individuals, of collectivism over laissez-faire. Corporatism is presented in *Industrial Politics* as a compromise between laissez-faire and collectivism, a movement by labor away from the former wherein trade unions now concerned about their own corporate identity, would bargain collectively with employers—a "bipartite corporatism." This corporatism, which emphasizes goals of limited groups over those of individuals and constrains conflict via collective bargaining, endures somewhat to this day.

Key events occurring around the turn of the twentieth century, especially the implementation of new industrial technology in the United Kingdom and subsequent effects on work-force organization, power relationships, union structure, and collective bargaining, are presented by Currie as leading to adjustment problems and protective barriers developed by labor. For example, the advent of collective bargaining was strongly resisted by some unions—especially in engineering. Concurrently, resistance to union political action, in-

cluding the Labour Party's "enthusiasm for 'nationalization,'" developed with such action denounced as an extension of state power. Labor's laissez-faire roots found even socialist state power unacceptable. The Labour Party became politically neutralized. Controversy over collectivism, in turn, supported interest by some in a distinctively British laissez-faire syndicalism, characterized with a dispossession of employers via the general strike followed by rule by trade unions. Distrustful of union leadership, however, many labor intellectuals understandably condemned this syndicalism.

By World War I, labor's loyalty to laissez-faire had been conspicuously confirmed in workers' rejections of any substitute ideology—notwithstanding "wartime syndicalism," its later influence on shop stewards' organization, and the development of "notions of 'workers' control.'" Currie then discusses labor's eventual disenchantment with communism and the revival of corporatism and the need to equate worker control—via unitary corporatism—with the simple need for employment while turning again to laissez-faire in promoting traditional actions to secure more money for the same work.

Following World War II, Currie contends, labor's "utilitarian, liberal-individualist tradition" resulted in "extreme sectionalism" characterized by the separation of the Labour Party and labor unions and of the union and the smaller work groups, and by growth in the shop steward's power. This sectionalism is also manifested in workers' lack of interest in participation in management under the guise of "industrial democracy." Currie observes in this behavior a desire by workers "to stay true to liberal individualism in the sense of holding no political principle that cannot be reduced to egoistic pursuit of material self-interest."

Industrial Politics concludes with an especially interesting discussion on the industrialization of politics, where the "political" is converted into the "industrial," that is, the "whole range of economic and social policies . . . is to be subsumed within 'the total package the worker is to enjoy, and therefore to bargain over." Currie observes, "Such policies are to be determined, not within the overtly political structures of society, but 'across the negotiating table between the unions and the employers.'" Who "unions" are may be unclear, but "what is clear is that the formulation of all national decisions by negotiation between 'unions' and 'employers' would represent the total assimilation of the 'political' to the industrial.'"

Clearly, Currie's work is rich in detail and is insightful. His analysis and rationale are substantially based on the uniqueness of individualism in British society. Currie presents this individualism as a consistent determinant in industrial relations and politics through time — a theme "chronologically universal." It appears then his earlier denial of cross-cultural universality may be a bit suspect. Currie's longitudinal analysis through time need not deny cross-sectional analysis at a point in time. The two approaches involve different levels of abstraction and are likely more complimentary then contradictory. Together, they can present a fuller, if not clearer, picture of reality and can facilitate understanding and the transmission of knowledge. From this, the single criticism can be derived that Currie is perhaps too ambitious in his own criticism of the "universalists." His own work, nonetheless, is substantial and significant.

DUANE KUJAWA

University of Miami
Coral Gables
Florida

LENNART J. LUNDQUIST. *The Hare and the Tortoise: Clean Air Policies in the United States and Sweden.* Pp. xii, 236. Ann Arbor, MI: University of Michigan Press, 1980. $15.00.

Professor Lundquist has written a very detailed comparative analysis of how the United States and Sweden have developed clean air policies, how they have applied them, and how they have worked. He concludes, quite correctly, that policies are developed in response to perceived political opportunities, rather than in response to the ideal utilization of resources, a lesson obvious to anyone who has read Anthony Down's book, *An Economic Theory of Democracy*.

The most valuable part of this book is the comparison of the Swedish "cooperative" approach to developing a clean air policy verses the United States' "confrontational" method of developing a policy. He starts with the political perception that the public was demanding clean air in both the United States and Sweden and then examines how the political apparatus functioned in both Sweden and the United States. Not surprisingly, it took a "crisis," real or otherwise, to get the president and congress to develop a program. And naturally, since it was a crisis, the legislators were unable to fashion a truly elegant solution to the problem. He contrasts this situation with the situation in Sweden where the reality was perceived, but much more time was spent with industry to develop a program that would allow industry to meet the perceived needs in a slower, but hopefully, more effective fashion.

While it is true that legislation was passed with much greater speed in the United States and there are some problems in the legislation, it is not clear that the Swedish solution will provide a better result. Industry in the United States as anyone who has been in Washington is aware, maintains a fairly substantial group of political operatives, familiar with Washington and possessed of expertise that the government needed to develop the legislation. Thus even though the legislation may not have been as desirable as the industry would have wanted, the industry did manage to have more than an adequate amount of input in the design of the legislation. And in keeping with American political tradition, Congress passed a law that had to be implemented by the bureaucracy. In effect, the real difference between Sweden and the United States is that the industry–government accommodation in the United States is now being accomplished at the bureaucratic level, rather than at the legislative level.

In short, this book is a fascinating

example of how a very perceptive foreign professor views the American political mechanisms' capacity to deal with a specific problem. It is a good case study for those who want to involve their students with how two governments respond to a similar probem in different fashions. My only caveat is that I think the book would have been much better had Lundquist spent more time with the people who actually did the drafting and legislating, in particular, the congressional and White House staffs who had to draft a bill that met the perceived need without offending so many political powers that it could not pass.

MARTIN LOBEL

Lobel, Novins & Lamont
Washington, D.C.

HAROLD LYDALL. *A Theory of Income Distribution*. Pp. v, 226. New York: The Clarendon Press, 1979. $32.50.

In a careful review of 200 years of economic theorizing about factor shares, Lydall explains the weaknesses he finds in the theories of classical and neoclassical economics including Smith, Richardo, Marx, Walras, Marshall, Wicksteed, and Keynes. He also examines closely the arguments of more recent writers like Kalecki, Kaldor, Pasinetti, Joan Robinson, and Hicks.

Lydall seeks greater realism by rejecting many of the assumptions of his predecessors, particularly those of perfect competition and perfect knowledge. He proposes to substitute "Entry and Product Market (EPM) competition," which combines free entry by "One Man Firms (OMFs)" with imperfect competition among firms enjoying economies of scale but facing imperfect capital markets and forced to make decisions with imperfect knowledge of both present and future. Falling cost curves bring larger firms higher profits than OMFs and faster rates of growth. Luck may help certain OMFs to begin to grow. Thereafter increasing size reduces dependence on external sources of capital and contributes to the accumulation of "private techniques" including both

production know-how and managerial skills. The influence of Steindl is apparent. A statistical chapter buttresses the argument.

Lydall describes his model as accounting for "persistent growth in the size of firms; the skewness of the size distribution of firms; the stability of that size distribution; the widespread existence of unutilized internal economies of scale; the dominant role of self-finance; the importance of practical know-how and learning by doing; and the use of fixed markup pricing rules." It also explains "why wage and profit shares are stable over considerable periods of time; why investment demand is self-renewing . . . ; why imperfect competition tends in some circumstances to magnify fluctuations; and why freer trade in manufactures under modern competition tends to reduce the aggregate profit share."

The final third of the volume is built upon much of Lydall's earlier work on the size distribution of incomes assisted by the acknowledged contributions of Kuznets, Mincer, Becker, Phelps Brown, Atkinson, and Reder, inter alia. Lydall shows why there is at first a greater degree of inequality as primitive economies improve their technology. This is followed by a trend toward greater equality as productivity-improving discoveries increase and spread to raise the output of a growing percentage of the work force.

Differences in personal incomes at any given time are explained as due to the differences in productivity of different jobs—the demand side—and differences in the ability and affort of job holders—the supply side. Individuals differ in their native abilities, their formal schooling, their on-the-job learning experience, and the "D-factor," which includes important intangibles like ambition, reliabilty, imagination, and so forth. Luck helps individuals as well as firms, especially in the beginning—job opportunities at that time, fortuitous choice among employers, where and when they enter the labor market, and soforth. Family influence is intergenerationally important and through bequests of various forms of wealth, affects property income supplements to earnings. More attention possibly should have been paid to the disparate effects on real incomes of uneven government transfers and of working wives as more of them enter the labor market.

I applaud a final section in which Lydall discusses the policy implications of his theories against a well-defined set of value premises that include as desirable goals "equality of status" and freedom of choice, both economic and political. Lydall would diminish the rights of private inheritance by heavier taxation at death, but strongly defends the personal incentive aspects of a market economy.

ROBERT B. PETTENGILL
Tampa
Florida

RUSSELL B. STEVENSON, JR. *Corporations and Information: Secrecy, Access, and Disclosure.* Baltimore, MD: *The Johns Hopkins Press, 1980.* $17.95.

In Stevenson's words, "the principal undertaking of this book is an examination of some of the more important existing rules about corporate information and an exploration of . . . changing [them] to increase the availability of that information of interested persons outside the corporation". Part I explores some of the broader issues concerning corporate information, both technological—patents, trade secrets, and industrial espionage—and economic—prices, costs, sales volume, and numbers and types of personnel. Part II discusses briefly the substance of certain laws designed to increase the availability of such information for conventional ends and some ways in which they might be improved.

Part III is the heart of the work, in which "The New Disclosure" is examined as a tool for rendering corporations more accountable to the larger society and for influencing their behavior through noneconomic mechanisms. Stevenson's position in discussing information both as an economic

factor—reducing the imperfection of the market—and as a means of social betterment seems to be that the initial burden ought to be put on the proponents of disclosure to show some social benefit from a reduction in secrecy; however, it should then lie with the proponents of secrecy to demonstrate that increased disclosure would cause a net harm to society.

The conclusions that Professor Stevenson presents in Part I are almost tentative. For example, in concluding the chapter on trade secrets and incentives to innovate, he says, "The only generalization I feel entirely safe in making about the economic impact of trade-secret protection for business—as opposed to technological—information is that we do not really understand the matter really well. Indeed, this may account for the fact that the law of trade secrets is so confused in this area." Similarly, regarding information and rivalrous competition, "On the whole it can probably be concluded that where it can be shown that there are benefits to be expected from increasing the flow of corporate information, and where a careful study uncovers no obvious ill effects for the competitive structure, it is relatively safe to proceed to alter the information rules."

Of particular interest is chapter 8, "Information and the Consumer." The benefits of information to the retail purchaser—improving the market's ability to narrow price dispersion, providing incentives for improvements in quality, and facilitating the entry of new firms—and the role of consumer product testing organizations in providing useful and reliable comparisons among competing products are recognized as is the "free rider" problem. Stevenson makes a real contribution to this discussion in asking "whether in some cases the market fails to provide as much consumer information as might be desirable simply because producers are unaware that the provision of more information would serve their own and their customer's interests." He also concludes that "the potential for disclosure as a tool for protecting consumers and improving the efficiency of the market is limited . . . by the fact that only a relatively small amount of information can be required before the capacity of the consumer to make use of it is exceeded . . . and by the fact that consumers obstinantly refuse to behave in the logical, deliberate manner in which some disclosure advocates want them to behave."

Notwithstanding all this, he makes the astonishing statement that "requirements that sellers make full disclosure of the undesirable qualities of their products or services may lead, through mechanisms that are not strictly 'economic', to the production of better products and services."

This tendency to go beyond conclusions crafted upon thorough and thoughtful analysis to highly speculative opinions is repeated frequently through Parts I and II, to the detriment of the persuasiveness of the arguments presented in Part III in favor of using corporate information to influence the behavior of corporations through political means.

Stevenson seems, even after great effort, to have barely succeeded in bearing the burden of showing some social benefit from a reduction in secrecy. At the same time, he has pointed to so many potentials for net social harm, than those who would limit disclosure should be able easily to develop arguments favorable to their view.

Therefore, much as I deplore the proliferation of regulations, I am not persuaded by the author to accept either of the two principal conclusions of the work. (1) Only by approaching the problem of rendering corporations more accountable for the social consequences of their behavior from the broader viewpoint that the disclosure mechanism can provide a vastly superior alternative to direct substantive regulation will we be able properly to balance the social interest in greater public knowledge of the internal workings of corporations against the legitimate claims of corporations to that degree of secrecy which is essential to their functioning in a competitive economy. (2) The alternative to more disclosure seems to be ever more direct government regulation of corporate behavior with its attendant loss of both economic efficiency and individual freedom.

WALTER V. CROPPER
American Society for Testing
  and Materials
Philadelphia
Pennsylvania

BEN J. WATTENBERG AND RICHARD J. WHALEN. *The Wealth Weapon, U.S. Foreign Policy and Multinational Corporations.* Pp. 127. New Brunswick, NJ: Transaction Books, 1980. $16.95. Paperbound, $6.95.

PAUL E. SIGMUND. *Multinationals in Latin America, The Politics of Nationalization, A Twentieth Century Fund Study.* Pp. 426. Madison, WI: The University of Wisconsin Press, 1980. $22.50. Paperbound, $6.50.

On the first page of this book, the authors state that the "global power puzzle" seems to demand an economic response by the United States. In the following chapter they examine the "multinational problem" by listing those conditions and events that form a backdrop to it: job export, OPEC, Third World ploys, the corruption issue, Western reversals around the world (détente), and recession. The next five chapters are devoted to a debate about multinationals and U.S. economic policy by four fictional characters: a businessman, a labor leader, a foreign policy activist, and a Third World leader. In the final chapter, "Who's Right, Who's Wrong?" the authors give us their own views on multinationals and U.S. foreign policy.

The authors draw five main conclusions. (1) There is no definitive answer to the question of who's right; they— the businessman, the labor leader, the third worlder, and the foreign activist —are all right about some things. (2) The MNC has been a force for world peace, has helped to raise the standard of living, and has spread "American ideology" aroung the world. Against these contributions, the issues of bribery, taxes, accounting, and exploitation are peripheral. After all, governments have the power to forbid them. (3) Protectionism is a political issue, a worldwide process of continual adjustment that aims at achieving tolerable temporary arrangements, a process of "impure free trade." Labor unions are entitled to a "place at the table." (4) The case made by the less-developed countries is unacceptable: they cannot get a unilateral transfer of wealth from the United States; they should live in the real world, not in a fairy-tale world. (5) Only the economic primacy of the West remains unimpaired and so the United States should use "economic tools" to preserve a political environment in which "the Western notion of freedom can best survive." But wealth weaponry is two-edged; it is a scapel, not a meat cleaver.

It is hard to know what to make of this book or why its authors felt the need to write it. The use of economic power to achieve foreign policy goals has a long tradition in U.S. history—witness, for instance, the 1812 embargo—but apparently the authors believe they are offering a new idea to policymakers when they talk of the "wealth weapon." The real question is not the use of economic power, but the modalities of its use. And here the authors leave us with only a disclaimer in the final chapter: "It is not the intention of this work to offer a detailed U.S. economic-political strategy." And so, the reader will learn nothing more about the wealth weapon than that it should be used by the United States. Moreover, anyone who has followed the debates about multinationals in the 1970s will learn nothing new in this book.

Wattenberg and Whalen have written a political tract that fails to make a cogent argument for either multinationals or the wealth weapon. It is a personal statement, unsupported by documentation, written in a breezy, all-knowing style. More than once, the authors credit Adam Smith with the notion of "comparative advantage," ignoring its true author, David Ricardo. It is hortatory in tone, substituting assertion for analysis or reasoned agreement. Incredibly, the authors state on page 3 that it "took us three years of on-and-off labor to put together this volume." So much for on-and-off labor.

What are the costs and the benefits of nationalization to national development in comparison with, or combined with, alternative approaches? What does the research of American defense of private investment show about the motivation and direction of U.S. foreign policy in the past, and what should that policy be in the future? Conversely, what does the record of Third World nationalizations indicate about the possible pitfalls of government takeovers? What is "at bay" in the last quarter of the twentieth century, the multinational corporation or the sovereignity of the nation-state? These are among the questions that Professor Sigmund addresses in the context of the U.S. investment experience in Latin America as revealed in five case studies of expropriation: the nationalization of the oil industry in Mexico in 1938, the full-scale nationalization of American companies in Cuba after the Castro revolution in 1959, the nationalization of the copper industry in Allende's Chile in 1971, the expropriation of the International Petroleum Company in Peru in 1968, and the nationalization of the oil industry in Venezuela in 1975.

These five case studies alone are worth the price of the book. Buttressed by a thorough documentation, Sigmund's analysis strikes this reviewer as eminently reasonable in substance and commendably fair in tone.

In two concluding chapters, Sigmund draws some general conclusions based on his case studies for both Latin American and U.S. policy toward foreign investment. Although nationalization remains politically appealing in Latin America, Sigmund believes that there is a growing recognition by developing countries that confrontational nationalization—as occurred notably in Chile—incurs economic costs that may considerably outweigh its potential benefits. Third World countries appear to be taking a less ideological and more economic (cost-benefit) approach to foreign investment. Instead of using confrontational approaches, they are now negotiating with multinational companies also because their bargaining strength has been significantly increased by access to information; by the competition among

American, European, and Japanese investors; and by their own institutional capacity, especially in Latin America, to negotiate effectively. In this new situation, multinational companies have some bargaining counters of their own, such as the spreading of equity risk so that expropriation will provoke opposition from many countries and financial institutions, and more basically, the continuing need by Third World countries for the technology, management, and market access that only the multinationals can provide.

This assessment leads Sigmund to recommend that the United States government maintain a watchful "low profile" in the area of expropriation. In particular, the State Department's insistence on the "prompt, adequate, and effective" compensation standard should be replaced by a "fair and equitable" standard. Multinational corporations can develop—and have developed—their own defense strategies against expropriation, and beyond the basic requirements of diplomatic protection, they do not need special government-imposed sanctions.

I heartily recommend this book to business, government, and academic readers. It brings the voice of reason to controversial issues that need to be resolved by policymakers in both the United States and Latin America.

FRANKLIN R. ROOT
University of Pennsylvania
Philadelphia

OTHER BOOKS

AALTO, PENTTI. *Classical Studies In Finland 1828–1918.* Pp. 210. Helsinki, Finland: Helsinki University, 1980. No price.

ABRAHAMSSON, BENGT and ANDERS BROSTROM. *The Rights Of Labor.* Pp. 301. Beverly Hills, CA: Sage Publications, 1980. $25.00.

ALEXANDER, YONAH and ROBERT A. FRIEDLANDER, eds. *Self-Determination: National, Regional, and Global Dimensions.* Pp. xv, 392. Boulder CO: Westview Press, 1980. $27.00.

ALGAR, HAMID. *Religion and State in Iran, 1785–1906.* Pp. xviii, 286. Berkeley, CA: University of California Press, 1980. $17.50.

AMERICAN SOCIETY OF COMPOSERS, AUTHORS, AND PUBLISHERS. *Copyright Law Symposium Number Twenty-Five.* Pp. xvi, 243. NY, NY: Columbia University Press, 1980. $17.50.

BACK, KURT W., ed. *Life Course: Integrative Theories and Exemplary Populations.* Pp. xv, 173. Boulder, CO: Westview Press, 1980. $18.50.

BAILEY, WILLIAM. *Man, Religion, and Science: A Functional View.* Pp. x, 242. Santa Barbara, CA: Wm. Bailey, 1980. No price.

BAINS, J. S., and R. B. JAIN, eds. *Contemporary Political Theory.* Pp. xv, 185. Atlantic Highlands, NJ: Humanities Press, 1981. $19.25.

BALAWDER, ALOYSINS. *The Maple Leaf and the White Eagle.* Pp. viii, 300. NY, NY: Columbia University Press, 1980. $20.00.

BARTLETT, DAVID, F., ed. *The Metric Debate.* Pp. 144. Boulder, CO: Colorado Associated University Press, 1980. $10.00.

BELL, DANIEL. *The Winding Passage: Essays and Sociological Journeys 1960–1980.* Pp. xxiv, 370. Cambridge, MA: Abt Books, 1980. $25.00.

BELL, DAVID S., ed. *Labour into the Eighties.* Pp. 168. Totowa, NJ: Croom Helm Ltd., 1980. $25.00.

BENDIX, REINHARD and GUENTHER ROTH. *Scholarship and Partisanship: Essays on Max Weber.* Pp. ix, 313. Berkeley, CA: University of California Press, 1980. $18.50.

BERLING, JUDITH, A. *The Syncretic Religion of Lin Chao-en.* Pp. xv, 348. NY, NY: Columbia University Press, 1980. $20.00.

BEST, JUDITH A. *The Mainstream of Western Political Thought.* Pp. 149. NY, NY: Human Sciences Press, 1980. $17.95. Paperbound, $8.95.

BILSKY, LESTER J., ed. *Historical Ecology: Essays on Environment and Social Change.* Pp. 195. Port Washington, NY: Kennikat Press Corp., 1980. $13.50.

BLASIER, COLE and CARMELO MESALAGO. *Cuba in the World.* Pp. vii 343. Pittsburgh, PA: University of Pittsburgh Press, 1979. $21.95. Paperbound, $5.95.

BOLLOTEN, BURNETT. *The Spanish Revolution: The Left and the Struggle for Power during the Civil War.* Pp. xxv, 664. Chapel Hill, NC: The University of North Carolina Press. 1980. $14.00.

BOTTOMS, A. E., and R. H. PRESTON, eds. *The Coming Penal Crisis: A Criminological and Theological Exploration.* Pp. xiii, 242. NY, NY: Columbia University Press, 1980. $12.50. Paperbound.

BOURGUIGNON, ERIKA. *A World of Woman: Anthropological Studies of Women in the Societies of the World.* Pp. xv, 364. NY, NY: Praeger, 1980. No price.

BRAUNTHAL, JULIUS. *History of the International World Socialism 1943–1968.* Pp.

xv, 600. Boulder, CO: Westview Press, 1980. $39.50.

BRIDSON-CRIBB, MARGARET and P. J. BOYCE, eds. *Politics in Queensland: 1977 and Beyond.* Pp. xv, 340. Lawrence, MA: University of Queensland Press, 1980. $27.25. Paperbound, $12.00.

BROMLEY, DAVID G., and ANSON D. SHUPE, JR. *"Moonies" in America: Cult, Church, and Crusade.* Pp. 269. Beverly Hills, CA: Sage Publications, 1979. No price.

BROOKS, PAUL. *Speaking for Nature: How Literary Naturalists from Henry Thoreau to Rachel Carson Have Shaped America.* Pp. xvi, 304. Boston, MA: Houghton Mifflin, 1980. $12.95.

BRUNN, STANLEY D., and JAMES O. WHEELER, eds. *The American Metropolitan System: Present and Future.* Pp. viii, 216. Somerset, NJ: John Wiley, 1980. $27.95.

BUNDY, McGEORGE and EDMUND S. MUSKIE. *Presidential Promises and Performance.* Pp. 103. NY, NY: The Free Press, 1980. $10.95.

CABLE, MARY. *Lost New Orleans.* Pp. xi, 235. Boston, MA: Houghton Mifflin, 1980. $21.95.

CALDWELL, LAWRENCE T. and WILLIAM DIEBOLD, JR. *Soviet-American Relations in the 1980s: Superpower Politics and East-West Trade.* Pp. xvi, 314. NY, NY: McGraw-Hill, 1980. $10.95. Paperbound, $7.95.

CAMPBELL, JOHN CREIGHTON. *Contemporary Japanese Budget Politics.* Pp. xv, 308. Berkeley, CA: University of California Press, 1980. $19.50. Paperbound. $6.95.

CAMPBELL, KEITH O. *Food For The Future.* Pp. x, 178. Lincoln, NE: University of Nebraska Press, 1979. $12.50.

CARLEN, PAT and MIKE COLLISON, eds. *Radical Issues in Criminology.* Pp. vii, 212. Totowa, NJ: Barnes & Noble Books, 1980. $23.50.

CARLSEN, ROBIN WOODSWORTH. *Seventeen Days in Tehran: Revolution, Evolution, and Ignorance.* Pp. 163. British Columbia, Canada: The Snow Man Press, 1980. No price.

CHAWLA, SUDERSHAN and D. R. SARDESIA, eds. *Changing Patterns of Security and Stability in Asia.* Pp. xi, 257. NY, NY: Praeger, 1980. No price.

CLARK, GRAHAMN. *Mesolithic Prelude.* Pp. viii, 122. NY, NY: Columbia University Press, 1980. $15.00.

COHEN, HOWARD. *Equal Rights for Children.* Pp. x, 172. Totowa, NJ: Littlefield, Adams & Company, 1980. $13.50. Paperbound, $4.95.

COHEN, KENNETH P. *Hospice: Prescription for Terminal Care.* Pp. xi, 302. German-town, MD: Aspen Systems Corporation, 1979. No price.

COHEN, LESTER H. *The Revolutionary Histories: Contemporary Narratives of the American Revolution.* Pp. 286. Ithaca, NY: Cornell University Press, 1980. $15.00.

DANIELS, ROBERT V. *Studying History: How & Why.* 3rd ed. Pp. xii, 125. Englewood Cliffs, NJ: Prentice-Hall, 1981. No price.

DEANE, MICHAEL J. *Strategic Defense in Soviet Strategy.* Pp. vii, 119. Washington, D.C.: Advanced International Studies Institute, 1980. No price.

DELBRUCK, HANS. *History of the Art of War Within the Framework of Political History: The Germans.* Pp. 505. Westport, CT: Greenwood Press, 1980. $39.95.

DERNBERGER, ROBERT F., ed. *China's Development Experience in Comparative Perspective.* Pp. vi, 347. Cambridge, MA: Harvard University Press, 1980. $30.00.

DIERKES, MEINOLF, SAM EDWARDS, and ROB COPPOCK, eds. *Technological Risk: Its Perception and Handling in the European Community.* Pp. xii, 141. Cambridge, MA: Oelgeschlager, Gunn & Hain, 1980. $20.00.

DOUGLAS, MARY. *Edward Evans-Pritchard.* Pp. x, 151. NY, NY: The Viking Press, 1980. $12.95.

DYE, THOMAS R. *Politics in States and Communities.* 4th ed. Pp. xvi, 492. Englewood Cliffs, NJ: Prentice-Hall, 1981. No price.

EATON, WILLIAM W. *The Sociology of Mental Disorders.* Pp. xii, 233. NY, NY: Praeger Publishers. 1980. No price.

EDEL, ABRAHAM. *Exploring Fact and Value: Science, Ideology, and Value.* Vol. 2. Pp. xxii, 369. New Brunswick, NJ: Transaction Books, 1980. $16.95.

EHRLICH, STANISLAW and GRAHAM WOOTTON, eds. *Three Faces of Pluralism: Political Ethnic and Religious.* Pp. ix, 219. England: Gower Publishing Company Ltd., 1980. No price.

ELLIOTT, CHARLES, F., and CARL A. LINDEN, eds. *Marxism in the Contemporary West.* Pp. xii, 177. Boulder, CO: Westview Press, 1980. $19.00.

ETIENNE, MONA and ELEANOR LEACOCK, eds. *Women and Colonization: Anthropological Perspectives.* Pp. ix. 339. NY, NY: Praeger Publishers, 1980. No price.

FERRELL, ROBERT H., ed. *Off the Record: The Private Papers of Harry S. Truman.* Pp. vix, 448. NY, NY: Harper & Row, 1980. $15.00.

FESLER, JAMES W. *Public Administration: Theory and Practice.* Pp. xii, 369. Englewood Cliffs, NJ: Prentice-Hall, 1980. $15.95.

FESTINGER, LEON, ed. *Retrospections on*

Social Psychology. Pp. 297. NY, NY: Oxford University Press, 1980. $12.95.

FITZGIBBON, RUSSELL H., and JULIO A. FERNANDEZ. *Latin America: Political Culture and Development.* 2nd ed. Pp. vi, 374. Englewood Cliffs, NJ: Prentice-Hall, 1981. No price.

FREEMAN, MICHAEL and DAVID ROBERTSON, eds. *The Frontiers of Political Theory: Essays in a Revitalized Discipline.* Pp. ix, 308. NY, NY: St. Martin's Press, 1980. $32.50.

FRESE, JOSEPH R., S. J., and JACOB JUDD, eds. *An Emerging Independent American Economy 1815–1875.* Pp. xiv, 207. Tarrytown, NY: Sleepy Hollow Press, 1980. $20.00.

FRY, CHRISTINE L., and contributors. *Aging in Culture and Society.* Pp. xi, 323. NY, NY: Praeger Publishers, 1980. No price.

GERBNER, GEORGE, CATHERINE J. ROSS, and EDWARD ZIGLER, *Child Abuse: An Agenda for Action.* Pp. x, 345. NY, NY: Oxford University Press, 1980. $14.95. Paperbound, $7.95.

GERTZ, ELMER and JOSEPH P. PISCIOTTE. *Charter for a New Age: An Inside View of the Sixth Illinois Constitutional Convention.* Pp. xii, 378. Chicago, IL: University of Illinois Press, 1980. No price.

GIRALDO, Z. I. *Public Policy and the Family.* Pp. xxii, 217. Lexington, MA: Lexington Books, 1980. No price.

GLENWICK, DAVID and LEONARD JASON, eds. *Behavioral Community Psychology: Progress and Prospects.* NY, NY: Praeger Publishers, 1980. No price.

GORDON, WENDELL. *Institutional Economics.* Pp. x, 354. Austin, TX: Texas Press Services, 1980. $19.95. Paperbound, $9.95.

GRINDLE, MERILEE S., ed. *Politics and Policy Implementation in the Third World.* Pp. xv, 310. Princeton, NJ: Princeton University Press, 1980. $20.00. Paperbound, $7.95.

GUREVITZ, BARUCH. *National Communism in the Soviet Union, 1918–28.* Pp. xii, 121. Pittsburgh, PA: University of Pittsburgh, 1980. No price.

GURR, TED ROBERT, ed. *Handbook of Political Conflict: Theory and Research.* Pp. ix, 566. NY, NY: The Free Press, 1980. $39.95.

GUTTING, GARY, ed. *Paradigms & Revolutions: Applications and Appraisals of Thomas Kuhn's Philosophy of Science.* Pp. viii, 339. Notre Dame, IN: University of Notre Dame Press, 1980. $18.95. Paperbound, $7.95.

HAGEN, WILLIAM W. *Germans, Poles, and Jews: The Nationality Conflict in the Prussian East, 1772–1914.* Pp. ix, 406. Chicago, IL: The University of Chicago Press, 1980. $17.50.

HAMMOND, KENNETH, GARY H. MCCLELLAND, and JERYL MUMPOWER. *Human Judgement and Decision Making: Theories, Methods, and Procedures.* Pp. xiv, 258. NY, NY: Praeger Publishers, 1980. No price.

HAG, KHADIJA, ed. *Dialogue for a New Order.* Pp. xiii, 312. Elmsford, NY: Pergamon Press, 1980. $32.50.

HARRISON, HELEN A., ed. *Dawn of a New Day: The New York World's Fair, 1939/40.* Pp. xii, 123. NY, NY: Columbia University Press, 1980. $24.95. Paperbound, $12.95.

HAYS, SAMUEL P. *American Political History as Social Analysis.* Pp. 459. Knoxville, TN: The University of Tennessee Press, 1980. No price.

HELD, DAVID. *Introduction to Critical Theory: Horkheimer to Habermas.* Pp. 511. Berkeley, CA: University of California Press, 1980. $32.50. Paperbound, $12.75.

HERSHLAG, Z. Y. *Introduction to the Modern Economic History of the Middle East.* Pp. xvi, 431. Leiden, The Netherlands: E. J. Brill, 1980. Paperbound.

HOADLEY, WALTER E., ed. *The Economy and the President—1980 and Beyond.* Pp. vi, 180. Englewood Cliffs, NJ: Prentice-Hall, 1980. $11.95. Paperbound, $4.95.

HOOKER, J. T. *The Ancient Spartans.* Pp. 254. Totowa, NJ: J. M. Dent & Sons Ltd., 1980. $29.50.

HORN, NELSON, ed. *Rights and Responsibilities: International, Social, and Individual Dimensions.* Pp. 298. New Brunswick, NJ: Transaction Books, 1980. $18.00.

HOUSE, ERNEST R. *Evaluating With Validity.* Pp. 295. Beverly Hills, CA: Sage Publications, 1980. No price.

HUGES, H. STUART. *Contemporary Europe: A History.* 5th ed. Pp. xv, 620. Englewood Cliffs, NJ: Prentice-Hall, 1981. $18.95.

IATRIDES, JOHN O., ed. *Ambassador MacVeagh Reports: Greece, 1933–1947.* Pp. xiii, 769. Princeton, NJ: Princeton University Press, 1980. $35.00.

JACKSON, ROBERT J., and MICHAEL M. ATKINSON. *The Canadian Legislative System.* 2nd rev. ed. Pp. xiv, 222. NY, NY: New York University Press, 1980. $8.95. Paperbound.

JENKINS, HUGH. *Rank and File.* Pp. 181. Totowa, NJ: Croom Helm Ltd., 1980. $25.00.

JOHNSON, GUY BENTON & GUION GRIFFIS JOHNSON. *Research in Service to Society: The First Fifty Years of the Institute for Research in Social Science at the University of North Carolina.* Pp. xv, 442. Chapel

Hill, NC: The University of North Carolina Press, 1980. $20.00.

JOYCE, BRUCE and MARSHA WEIL. *Models of Teaching*. 2nd ed. Pp. xxiv, 499. Englewood Cliffs, NJ: Prentice-Hall, 1980. No price.

JULIAN, JOSEPH. *Social Problems*. 3rd ed. Pp. xvii, 572. Englewood Cliffs, NJ: Prentice-Hall, 1980. No price.

KAY, JANE HOLTZ. *Lost Boston*. Pp. xiii, 304. Boston, MA: Houghton Mifflin, 1980. $24.95.

KEEFE, WILLIAM J., and MORRIS S. OGUL. *The American Legislative Process: Congress and the States*. 5th ed. Pp. xiii, 495. Englewood Cliffs, NJ: Prentice-Hall, 1981. No price.

KERBER, LINDA K. *Federalists in Dissent: Imagery and Ideology in Jeffersonian America*. Pp. xvi, 233. Ithaca, NY: Cornell University Press, 1980. $4.95. Paperbound.

KINLOCH, GRAHAM, C. *Ideology and Contemporary Sociological Theory*. Pp. xii, 194. Englewood Cliffs, NJ: Prentice-Hall, 1981. $15.95.

KOHN WALTER S.G. *Governments and Politics of the German-Speaking Countries*. Pp. 291. Chicago, IL: Nelson-Hall, 1980. $18.95.

KURTEN, BJORN and ELAINE ANDERSON. *Pleistocene Mammals of North America*. xvii, 442. NY, NY: Columbia University Press, 1980. $42.50.

LAWSON, KAY, ed. *Political Parties & Linkage: A Comparative Perspective*. Pp. vi, 410. New Haven, CT: Yale University Press, 1980. $35.00. Paperbound, $8.95.

LEE, MAURICE, JR. *Government By Pen: Scotland under James VI and I*. Pp. ix, 232. Champaign, IL: University of Illinois Press, 1980. $16.00.

LELOUP, LANCE T. *The Fiscal Congress: Legislative Control of the Budget*. Pp. xiii, 227. Westport, CT: Greenwood Press, 1980. $25.00.

LEVITT, MORRIS J., and ELEANOR G. FELDBAUM. *Of, By, And For The People: State and Local Government and Politics*. Pp. xvii, 328. Boulder, CO: Westview Press, 1980. $27.00. Paperbound, $12.00.

LINDSAY, BEVERLY, ed. *Comparative Perspectives Of Third World Women: The Impact of Race, Sex, and Class*. Pp. xi, 319. NY, NY: Praeger Publishers, 1980. No price.

LIPSET, DAVID. *Gregory Bateson: The Legacy of a Scientist*. Pp. xii, 360. Englewood Cliffs, NJ: Prentice-Hall, 1980. $16.95.

LONDON, KURT, ed. *The Soviet Union in World Politics*. Pp. xiii, 380. Boulder, CO: Westview Press, 1980. $27.50.

LOZOYA, JORGE, and A. K. BHATTACHARYA, eds. *The Financial Issues of the New International Economic Order*. Pp. xxiii, 229. Elmsford, NY: Pergamon Press, 1980. $20.00.

LOZOYA, JORGE and HECTOR CUADRA, eds. *Africa, The Middle-East and the New International Economic Order*. Pp. xx, 161. Elmsford, NY: Pergamon, 1980. $20.00.

MALMBERG, TORSTEN. *Human Territoriality*. Pp. xiv, 346. NY, NY: Mouton Publishers, 1980. No price.

MANDEL, NEVILLE J. *The Arabs and Zionism: Before World War I*. Pp. xxiv, 258. Berkeley, CA: University of California Press, 1980. $4.95. Paperbound.

MANSFIELD, ALAN. *Ceremonial Costume*. Pp. xvi, 304. Totowa, NJ: Barnes & Noble, 1980. $36.00.

MAYFIELD, JOHN. *Rehearsal for Republicanism: Free Soil and the Politics of Anti-Slavery*. Pp. 220. Port Washington, NY: Kennikat Press, 1980. $17.50.

MECHANIC, DAVID, ed. *Readings in Medical Sociology*. Pp. xi, 513. NY, NY: The Free Press, 1980. No price.

MEDISH, VADIM. *The Soviet Union*. Pp. xiv, 367. Englewood Cliffs, NJ: Prentice-Hall, 1981. No price.

MEDVEDEV, ROY. *On Soviet Dissent: Interviews with Piero Ostellino*. Pp. 158. NY, NY: Columbia University Press, 1980. $10.95.

MORGAN, RICHARD E. *Domestic Intelligence: Monitoring Dissent in America*. Pp. x, 194. Austin, TX: The University of Texas Press, 1980. $13.95. Paperbound, $6.95.

MOSSE, GEORGE L. *Massess and Man: Nationalist and Fascist Perceptions of Reality*. Pp. xii, 362. NY, NY: Howard Fertig, 1980. $25.00.

MURPHY, D. J., R. B. JOYCE, and COLIN A. HUGHES. *Labor in Power: The Labor Party & Governments in Queensland 1915–57*. Pp. xxv, 583. Lawrence, MA: University of Queensland Press, 1980. $42.50.

MYERS, KENNETH, ed. *NATO: The Next Thirty Years*. Pp. xxiii, 469. Boulder, CO: Westview Press, 1980. $35.00.

NELSON, DANIEL N. *Democratic Centralism in Romania*. Pp. xii, 186. NY, NY: Columbia University Press, 1980. $15.00.

NORRIS, LOUIS WILLIAM. *Values and the Credibility of the Professor*. Pp. xiii, 155. Washington, D.C.: University Press of America, 1980. $16.75. Paperbound, $8.75.

OXNAM, ROBERT B., and RICHARD C. BUSH, eds. *China Briefing, 1980*. Pp. xvii, 126. Boulder, CO: Westview Press, 1980. $14.50. Paperbound, $6.50.

PAPERT, SEYMOUR. *Mindstorms: Children,*

Computers, and Powerful Ideas. Pp. viii, 230. NY, NY: Basic Books, 1980. $12.95.

PARISH, DAVID W. *Changes in American Society, 1960–1978: An Annotated Bibliography of Official Government Publications.* Pp. xxx-ix, 438. Metuchen, NJ: Scarecrow Press, 1980. $22.50.

PERKINS, EDWIN J. *The Economy of Colonial America.* Pp. xii, 177. NY, NY: Columbia University Press, 1980. $17.50. Paperbound, $6.00.

POSAVAC, EMIL J., and RAYMOND G. CAREY. *Program Evaluation: Methods and Case Studies.* Pp. xviii, 350. Englewood Cliffs, NJ: Prentice-Hall, 1980. $15.95.

PRINGLE, ROGER. *A Protrait of Elizabeth I: In the Words of The Queen and Her Contemporaries.* Pp. 128. Totowa, NJ: Barnes & Noble Books, 1980. $10.75.

PUIG, JUAN CARLOS. *Doctrinas Internacionales Y Autonomia Latinoamericana.* Pp. 316. El Conde-Caracas, Venezuela: Universidad Simon Bolivar, 1980. No price.

ROSE, NORMAN. *Lewis Namier and Zionism.* Pp. x, 182. NY, NY: Oxford University Press, 1980. $29.95.

ROSSI, INO, ed. *People In Culture: A Survey of Cultural Anthropology.* Pp. xii, 626. NY, NY: Praeger Publishers, 1980. No price.

RUDOFSKY, BERNARD. *Now I Lay Me Down to Eat: Notes and Footnotes on the Lost Art of Living.* Pp. 189. NY, NY: Doubleday, 1980. $19.95. Paperbound, $10.95.

RAVEN, BETRAM H., ed. *Policy Studies: Review Annual.* Vol. 4. Pp. 768. Beverly Hills, CA: Sage Publications, 1980. No price.

ROBINSON, DANIEL N. *Psychology & Law: Can Justice Survive the Social Science?* Pp. viii, 221. NY, NY: Oxford University Press, 1980. $14.95. Paperbound, $5.95.

SANDLER, TODD, ed. *The Theory and Structures of International Political Economy.* Pp. xxii, 280. Boulder, CO: Westview Press, 1980. $25.00.

SARGENT, LYMAN TOWER. *Contemporary Political Ideologies.* 5th ed. Pp. viii, 199. Homewood, IL: The Dorsey Press, 1980. $8.95. Paperbound.

SOLOMON, RICHARD H., ed. *Asian Security in the 1980s: Problems and Policies for a Time of Transition.* Pp. xii, 324. Cambridge, MA: Oelgeschlager, Gunn & Hain, 1980. $20.00.

TAYLOR, CHARLES LEWIS, ed. *Indicator Systems for Political, Economic, and Social Analysis.* Pp. x, 242. Cambridge, MA: Oelgeschlager, Gunn & Hain, 1980. No price.

TAYLOR, TELFORD. *Munich: The Price Of Peace.* Pp. xiv; 1084, NY, NY: Random House, 1980. $8.95. Paperbound.

THACKERAY, FRANK W. *Antecedents of Revolution.* Pp. viii, 197. NY, NY: Columbia University Press, 1980. $15.00.

VIGUERIE, RICHARD A. *The New Right— We're Ready to Lead.* Pp. 243. Falls Church, VA: The Viguerie Company, 1980. $8.95.

WARD, JAMES A. *J. Edgar Thomson: Master Of The Pennsylvania.* Pp. xviii, 265. Westport, CT: Greenwood Press, 1980. $25.00.

WEILER, HANS N., ed. *Educational Planning and Social Change.* Pp. 211. Paris, France: International Institute for Educational Planning, 1980. No price.

WEINSTEIN, FRANKLIN B., and FUJI KAMIYA. *The Security of Korea: U.S. and Japanese Perspectives on the 1980s.* Pp. xiii, 276. Boulder, CO: Westview Press, 1980. $20.00. Paperbound. $8.50.

WEIR, ROBERT F., ed. *Death In Literature.* Pp. xiii, 451. NY, NY: Columbia University Press, 1980. $25.00. Paperbound, $10.00.

WEISS, CAROL H., and MICHAEL J. BUCUVALAS. *Social Science Research and Decision-Making.* Pp. xiv, 332. NY, NY: Columbia University Press, 1980. $22.50.

WHISKER, JAMES B. *A Dictionary of Concepts on American Politics.* Pp. xi, 285. Somerset, NJ: John Wiley & Sons, 1980. $7.95. Paperbound.

WHITFIELD, STEPHEN J. *Into the Dark: Hannah Arendt and Totalitarianism.* Pp. xii, 338. Philadelphia, PA: Temple University Press, 1980. $18.95.

WILSON, RICHARD W., and GORDON J. SCHOCHET, eds. *Moral Development and Politics.* Pp. xxii, 338. NY, NY: Praeger Publishers, 1980. No price.

INDEX

The Development of Capitalism in Colonial Indochina (1870–1940)

Martin J. Murray

This is a systematic and comprehensive analysis of the development of capitalism in Indochina. Murray supplies a historical and theoretical treatment which goes far toward explaining both the backwardness of Indochinese economic structures after seventy years of capitalist "development" and the reasons for barriers to capitalist production. $29.50

Communism in Southeast Asia

Justus M. Van der Kroef

The first comprehensive book-length study of Communism in Southeast Asia to appear in more than twenty years, this volume deals with the developments in each country of the critically important area. $25.00

Environmental Protest and Citizen Politics in Japan

Margaret A. McKean

The Japanese environmental movement absorbed several million people during the 1970s. McKean examines the causes and consequences of "citizens' movements," and she discusses the major environmental lawsuits, which served as catalysts for the emergence of thousands of citizen's movements and converted the intimidating and little-used Japanese legal system into a channel of effective participation. $28.50

Political Women in Japan
The Search for a Place in Political Life

Susan J. Pharr

A fascinating inquiry into how and why Japanese women became involved in politics. Tracing developments that led to the grant of suffrage to women in Japan during the Allied occupation, Pharr analyzes the process as reflected in the experiences of individuals and examines both the satisfactions of political volunteerism and the psychological and social costs associated with it. $17.50

Conflict and Consensus in Switzerland

Carol L. Schmid

Switzerland has long been cited as an important exception to every rule about national identity. But because most of the literature in race and ethnic relations has focused on causes of conflict and discord, majority-minority relations in Switzerland have received little attention. This is the first in-depth examination of the major sources of Swiss coexistence as well as of some of the problems now facing Switzerland. $18.50

The Taming of Fidel Castro

Maurice Halperin

"New and insightful. . . . (Halperin's) well-written narrative, based on Cuban sources and personal experiences, adds new dimensions and dispels many myths concerning Castro's personality and Cuban internal affairs." —*Library Journal* $16.95

University of California Press
Berkeley 94720

EQUALITY, MORAL INCENTIVES, AND THE MARKET
An Essay in Utopian Politico-Economic Theory

Joseph H. Carens

Countering the prevalent claim that certain inequalities are inevitable in modern societies, Carens argues that an egalitarian system, relying on powerful moral incentives, need not reduce efficiency or limit freedom.
*Chicago Original $19.00   264 pages

*An original book, bound in the European manner with a sewn binding stronger than ordinary paperback and with attached flaps to strengthen the cover.

REASON AND MORALITY

Alan Gewirth

"A significant contribution to political thinking. If its import is not recognized, the discipline will be the poorer."—*American Political Science Review*

Winner of the 1979 Gordon J. Laing Prize
Cloth $20.00   Paper $9.95 406 pages

TRADITION
Edward Shils.

In this work of sociological analysis, Shils counters a widespread way of thinking about society, defending tradition against those who believe that every generation can and should be self-determining.

Cloth $20.00 344 pages

THE ORIGIN OF FORMALISM IN SOCIAL SCIENCE
Jeffrey T. Bergner

"The central part of the study—its account of the formulation of social science by nineteenth-century neo-Kantian thinkers in Germany—is excellent, and I know of no other source that brings this material together in such a clear and penetrating way for the English reader."—Eugene F. Miller, Department of Political Science, University of Georgia

Cloth $16.00 174 pages

POLITICAL SCIENCE

THE BENEFITS OF OLD AGE
Social-Welfare Policy for the Elderly
Elizabeth Ann Kutza

Kutza argues not for more or fewer policies directed toward older persons, but rather for an increased awareness of our expectations of federal policies. Analyzing both the shortcomings of current programs and the inevitable limitations of public intervention, she proposes some provocative new alternatives.

Cloth $18.00   Paper $5.95   176 pages

LIFE CHANCES
Approaches to Social and Political Theory
Ralf Dahrendorf

"Ralf Dahrendorf's *Life Chances* is brilliant and controversial social theory. Representing a lifetime of research in philosophy, history, political science, sociology, and economics, this book contains seminal discussions on topics ranging from the crisis of legitimacy in social democratic politics to the relationship between social inequality and socio-historical progress."—Richard A. Wright, *The Annals*

Cloth $15.00   Paper $5.95   192 pages

CITY LIMITS
Paul E. Peterson

Peterson argues that local politics are exceptionally limited, and thus take a distinctive and entirely different shape from national politics.

Cloth $27.50   Paper $9.95   280 pages

From MIDWAY REPRINTS

THE AMERICAN VOTER
Angus Campbell, Philip E. Converse, Warren E. Miller, and Donald E. Stokes
Unabridged Edition
Paper $20.00   576 pages

The University of Chicago PRESS

5801 South Ellis Avenue
Chicago, Illinois 60637

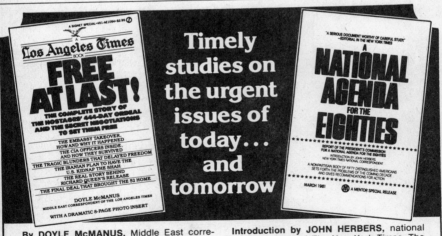

"YES, MY SON, TRANSCENDENTAL MEDITATION WORKS WONDERS...BUT NO MORE THAN GROUP LIFE INSURANCE."

Yes, my son, justly so, thy family's welfare and security are thy heart's utmost concern.

So learn then of Group Life Insurance which can provide much protection at low cost for thy wife and all thine offspring...the insurance that shall go with you wherever thou art employed.

Further, should an employer offer insurance benefits, use thy wits and thy small monies to also purchase supplemental Group Life Insurance.

So haste now and send this coupon and thou shalt learn of wondrous Group Life Insurance... and learn, too, the peace of mind as is found in transcendental meditation.

Or, call today, toll-free
800-424-9883
(In local Wash., DC area,
296-8030)

Origin and Purpose. The Academy was organized December 14, 1889, to promote the progress of political and social science, especially through publications and meetings. The Academy does not take sides in controverted questions, but seeks to gather and present reliable information to assist the public in forming an intelligent and accurate judgment.

Meetings. The Academy holds an annual meeting in the spring extending over two days.

Publications. THE ANNALS is the bimonthly publication of The Academy. Each issue contains articles on some prominent social or political problem, written at the invitation of the editors. Also, monographs are published from time to time, numbers of which are distributed to pertinent professional organizations. These volumes constitute important reference works on the topics with which they deal, and they are extensively cited by authorities throughout the United States and abroad. The papers presented at the meetings of The Academy are included in THE ANNALS.

Membership. Each member of The Academy receives THE ANNALS and may attend the meetings of The Academy. Annual dues: Individual Membership—$20.00 (clothbound, $26.00). Institutional Membership—$35.00 (clothbound, $41.00). Special Membership—contributing, $40.00; sustaining, $60.00; patron, $100. A life membership is $500. Add $2.00 to above rates for membership outside the U.S.A. Dues are payable in U.S. dollars in advance. Special members receive a certificate suitable for framing and may choose either paper or clothbound copies of THE ANNALS.

Single copies of THE ANNALS may be obtained by individual nonmembers of The Academy for $6.00 ($7.50 clothbound) and by members for $5.50 ($7.00 clothbound). Single copies of THE ANNALS may be obtained by *institutional nonmembers* for $7.00 ($9.00 clothbound) and by *institutional members* for $6.50 ($8.50 clothbound). These discounts do not apply when orders are placed through bookstores and dealers. The price to all bookstores and to all dealers is $7.00 per copy ($9.00 clothbound) less 15 percent, with no quantity discount. Orders for 2 books or less must be prepaid (add $1.00 for postage and handling). Orders for 3 books or more must be invoiced.

All correspondence concerning The Academy or THE ANNALS should be addressed to the Academy offices, 3937 Chestnut Street, Philadelphia, Pa. 19104.